ASSASSINATION CLASSROOM

TIME FOR SPORTS DAY

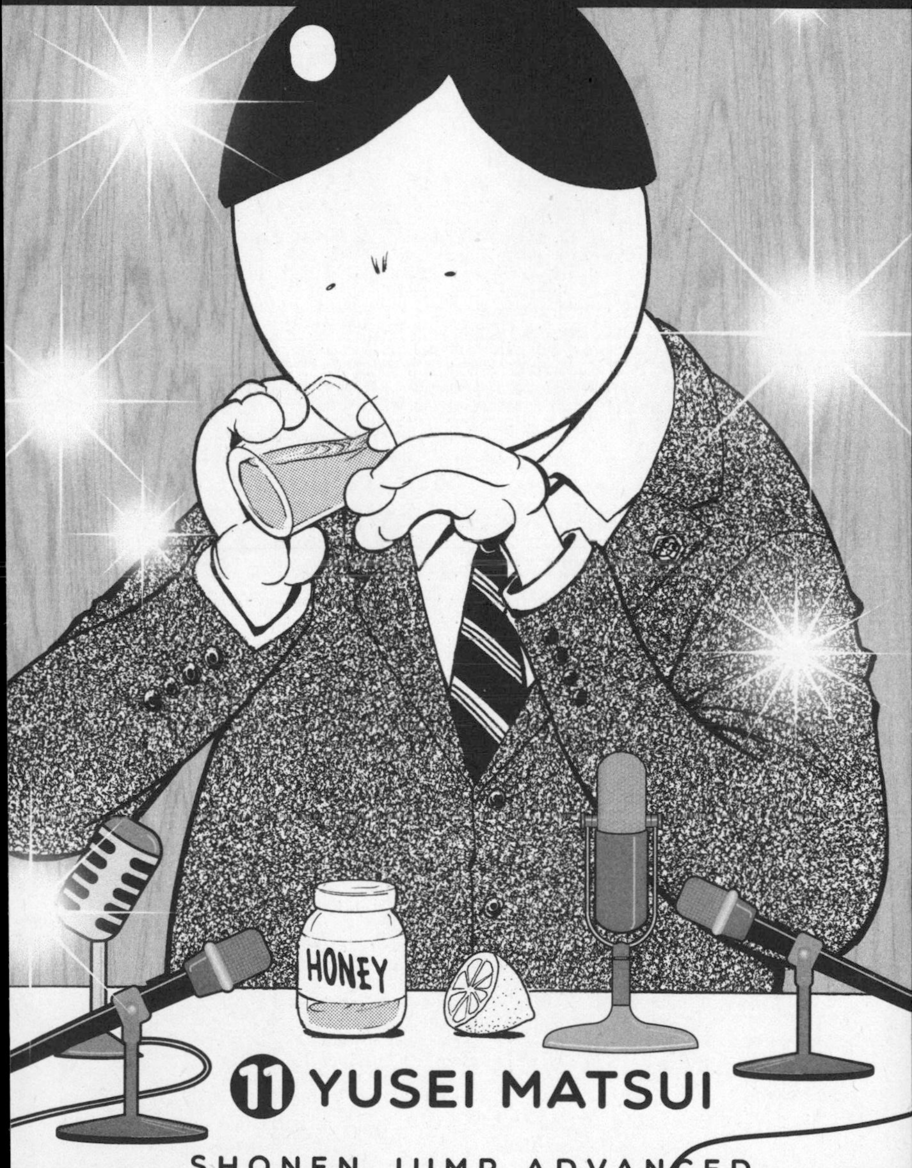
HONEY

11 YUSEI MATSUI

SHONEN JUMP ADVANCED

Koro Tribune

September Issue 2

Published by: Class 3-E Newspaper Staff

Although we have a lot of data on his weaknesses, we are still far from successfully assassinating Koro Sensei...

I EXPECT TO SEE YOU EXECUTE THE BEST ASSASSINATION ATTEMPT YOU ARE CAPABLE OF.
MAKE THE MOST OF YOUR KNOWLEDGE, INGENUITY AND HARD WORK.
THIS IS MY IDEA OF THE MOST FUN EVER.

Story Thus Far

Kunugigaoka Junior High, Class 3-E is led by a monster who has disintegrated the moon and is planning to do the same to the Earth next March.

Even the armies of the world with the latest technology can't kill the super creature Koro Sensei (and collect the thirty million bounty on his tentacles)! So it comes down to his Kunugigaoka Junior High students in 3-E, the so-called "End Class," whom he has promised not to hurt on the condition that he become their teacher. Thanks to Koro Sensei's dedication, his charges are turning into fine students capable of outshining the academically top-ranking students at their school. Likewise, the 3-E students' athleticism and powers of mental concentration are rapidly improving as Mr. Karasuma from the Ministry of Defense molds them into a professional team of assassins. Now the first of three semesters has passed and the clock is ticking... Will the misfit students of 3-E manage to assassinate Koro Sensei before he fulfills his threat to destroy Earth in March?!

YOU'RE LATE.
AND YOU'RE UNDER ARREST.
POLICE

How's it feel to be captured by the world's greatest bounty hunter?

Koro Sensei

A mysterious, man-made, octopus-like creature whose name is a play on the words "koro senai," which means "can't kill." He is capable of flying at Mach 20 and his versatile tentacles protect him from attacks and aid him in everyday activities. Nobody knows who created him or why he wants to teach Class 3-E, but he has proven to be an extremely capable teacher.

FDGT

Kaede Kayano

Class E student. She's the one who named Koro Sensei. She sits at the desk next to Nagisa, and they seem to get along well.

Uh-huh.

Nagisa Shiota

Class E student. Skilled at information gathering, he has been taking notes on Koro Sensei's weaknesses. He has a hidden talent for assassinations and even the Assassin Broker Lovro sees his potential.

Karma Akabane

Class E student. A natural genius who earns top grades. His failure in the final exam of the first semester has forced him to grow up and take things a bit more seriously.

pick up!

Toka Yada

Her big boobs aren't her only attraction. She excels at the piano, tea ceremony, tennis and other activities. On top of that, she is currently perfecting her "womanly charms" under Miss Vitch's tutelage.

Yuma Isogai

The class representative. He comes from a very poor family, so the goldfish he caught at the summer festival became a fine meal. He has always gotten good grades, so how did he fall down to Class E?

Tadaomi Karasuma

Member of the Ministry of Defense and the Class E students' P.E. teacher. Though serious about his duties, he is successfully building good relationships with his students.

It's hard to believe that he's human like us...
JUMP

Irina Jelavich

A sexy assassin hired as an English teacher. She's known for using her "womanly charms" to get close to a target. She often flirts with Karasuma, but hasn't made any progress with him yet.

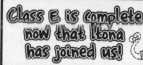

Class E is complete now that Itona has joined us!

Fifteen male students, twelve female students, one machine. The teachers are an octopus, a cougar and a drill sergeant. If we take a graduation photo, we'll definitely need to Photoshop it.

Top Secret

Gakuho Asano

The principal of Kunugigaoka Academy, who built this academically competitive school based on his faith in rationality and hierarchy.

RR
R
R
I
KORO HAIR REJUVENATION TREATMENT!
Unbelievable hair growth! Get thicker, fuller follicles and relive your youth!
IPO

Assassination Class Roster

Always assassinate your target using a method that brings a smile to your face.

I'm available for assassinations anytime. But don't let them get in the way of your studies.

I won't harm students who try to assassinate me. But if your skills are rusty, expect a good scrubbing!

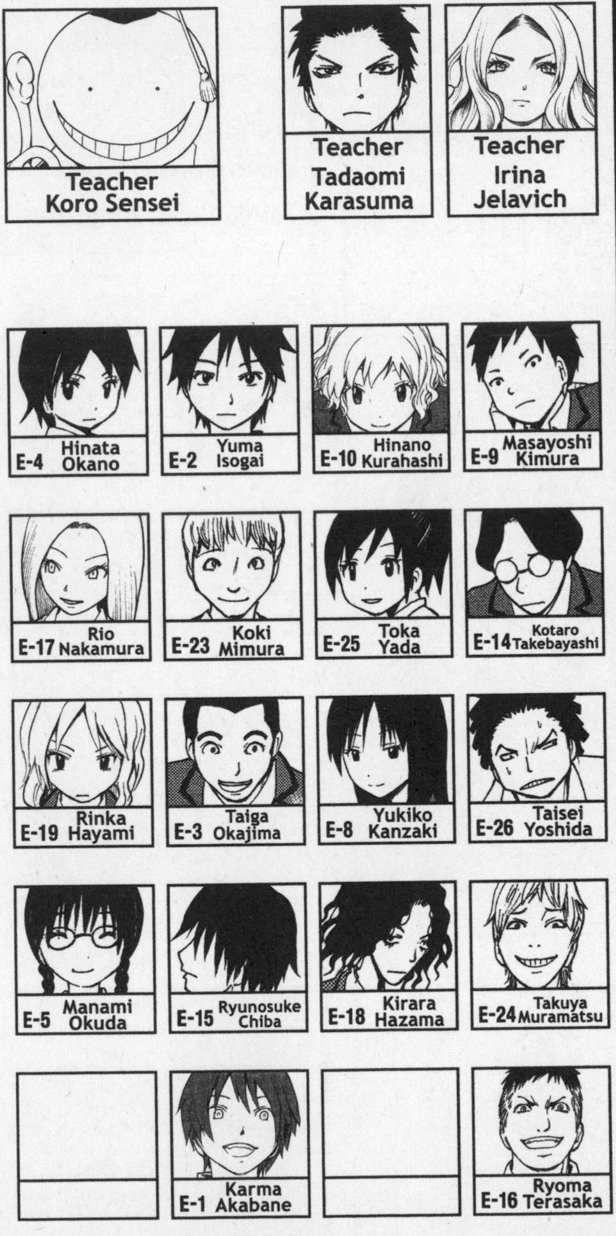
Teacher Irina Jelavich
Teacher Tadaomi Karasuma
Teacher Koro Sensei
E-9 Masayoshi Kimura
E-10 Hinano Kurahashi
E-2 Yuma Isogai
E-4 Hinata Okano
E-14 Kotaro Takebayashi
E-25 Toka Yada
E-23 Koki Mimura
E-17 Rio Nakamura
E-26 Taisei Yoshida
E-8 Yukiko Kanzaki
E-3 Taiga Okajima
E-19 Rinka Hayami
E-24 Takuya Muramatsu
E-18 Kirara Hazama
E-15 Ryunosuke Chiba
E-5 Manami Okuda
E-16 Ryoma Terasaka
E-1 Karma Akabane

Kunugigaoka Junior High

3-E

Koro Sensei Class

Seating Arrangement

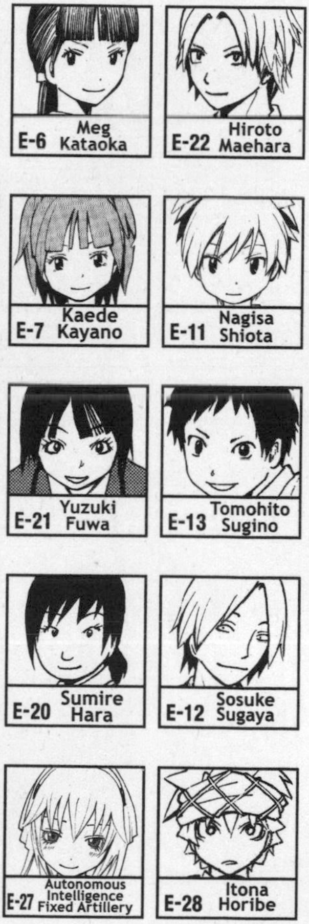
E-22 Hiroto Maehara
E-6 Meg Kataoka
E-11 Nagisa Shiota
E-7 Kaede Kayano
E-13 Tomohito Sugino
E-21 Yuzuki Fuwa
E-12 Sosuke Sugaya
E-20 Sumire Hara
E-28 Itona Horibe
E-27 Autonomous Intelligence Fixed Artillery

Individual Statistics

E-7 Kaede Kayano

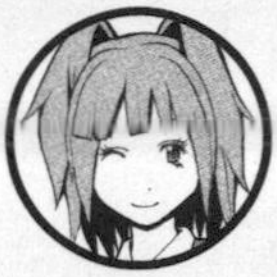

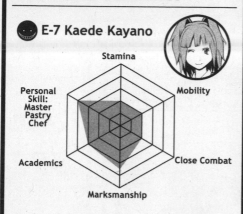

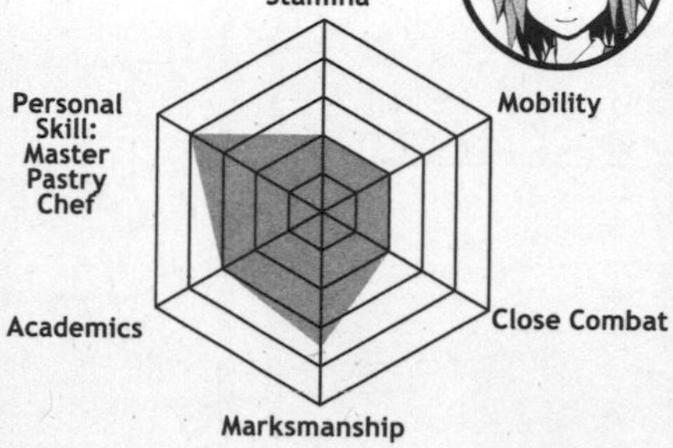
Stamina
Mobility
Close Combat
Marksmanship
Academics
Personal Skill: Master Pastry Chef

E-8 Yukiko Kanzaki

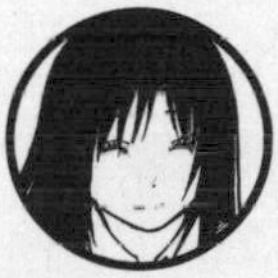

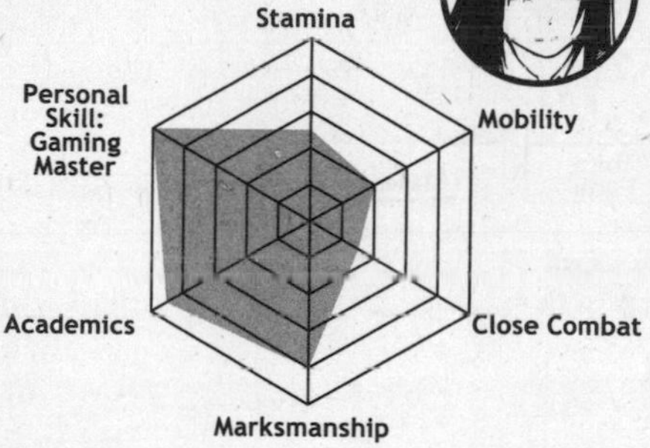
Stamina
Mobility
Close Combat
Marksmanship
Academics
Personal Skill: Gaming Master

E-9 Masayoshi Kimura

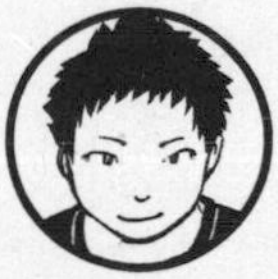

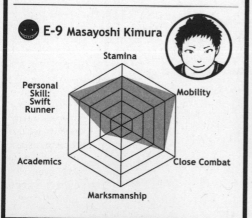

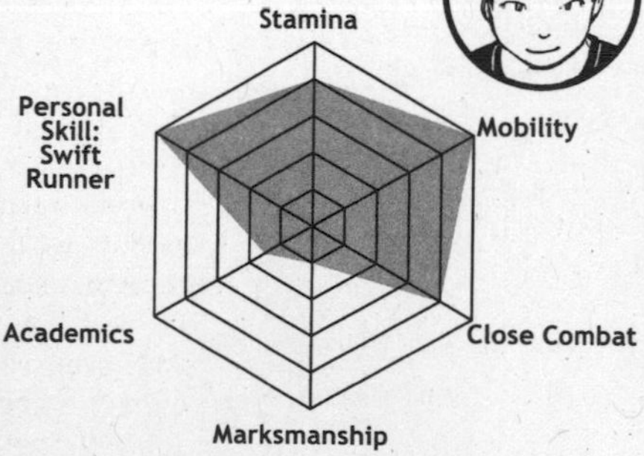
Stamina
Mobility
Close Combat
Marksmanship
Academics
Personal Skill: Swift Runner

ASSASSINATION CLASSROOM 11 CONTENTS

(ANSWER SHEET)

Grade	3	Class	E	Name	CONTENTS	Score	

(Q 1): The nex

(1) $y=2x^2$

(2) $y=-3x^2$

(3) $y=4x^2+1$

(4) $y=-5x^2-1$

(Q 2): The figur
Use several

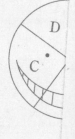

D
C

). 3): The two circl
each of the two circ
nd write down you
roof.

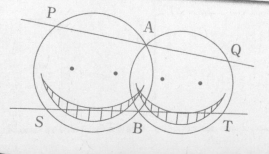

P
A
Q
S
B
T

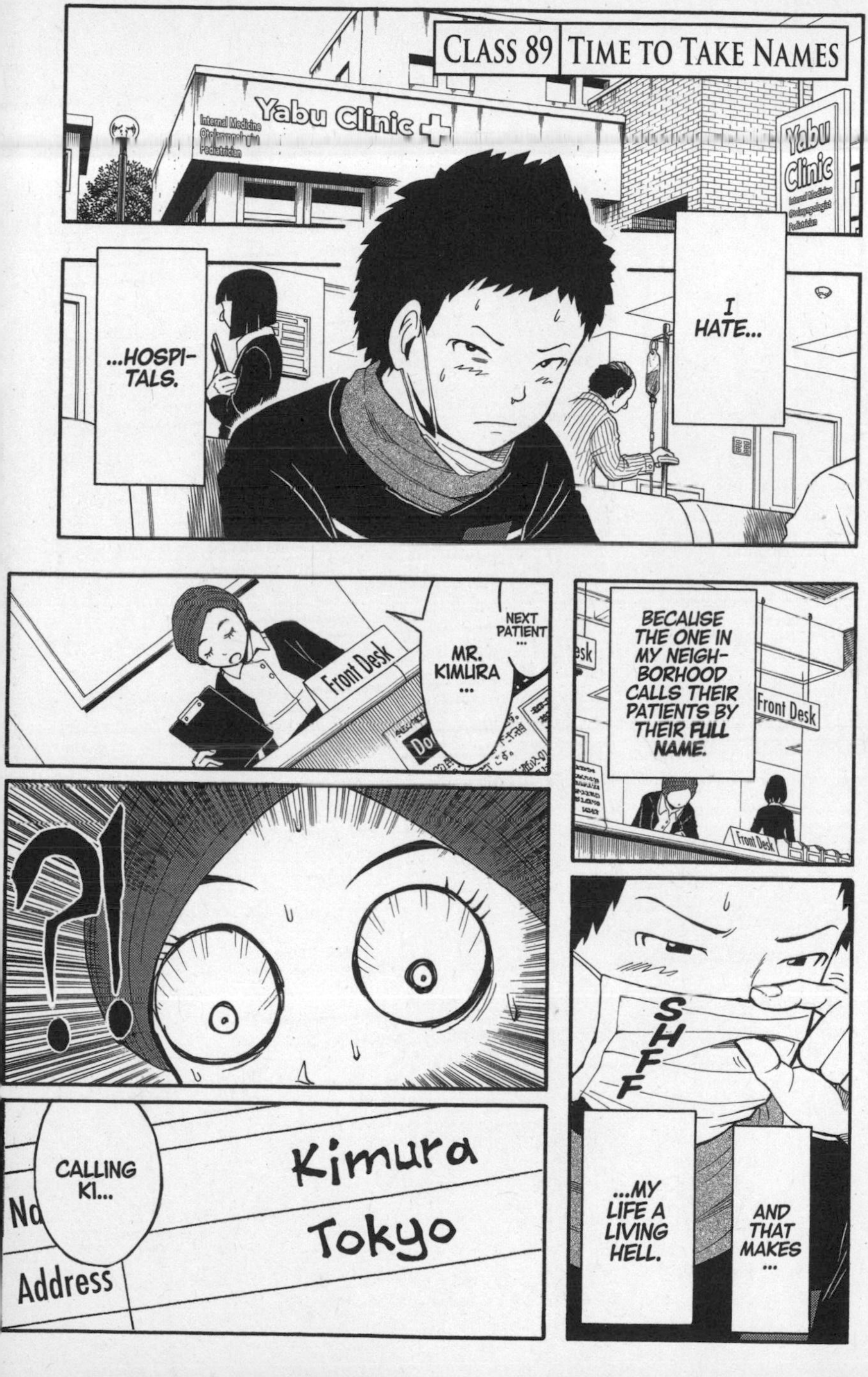

Class 89 Time to Take Names
Yabu Clinic
Internal Medicine
Pediatrician
Yabu Clinic
I HATE...
...HOSPITALS.
BECAUSE THE ONE IN MY NEIGHBORHOOD CALLS THEIR PATIENTS BY THEIR FULL NAME.
Front Desk
Front Desk
NEXT PATIENT...
MR. KIMURA...
Front Desk
?!
CALLING KI...
Kimura
Tokyo
Address
SHFF
AND THAT MAKES...
...MY LIFE A LIVING HELL.

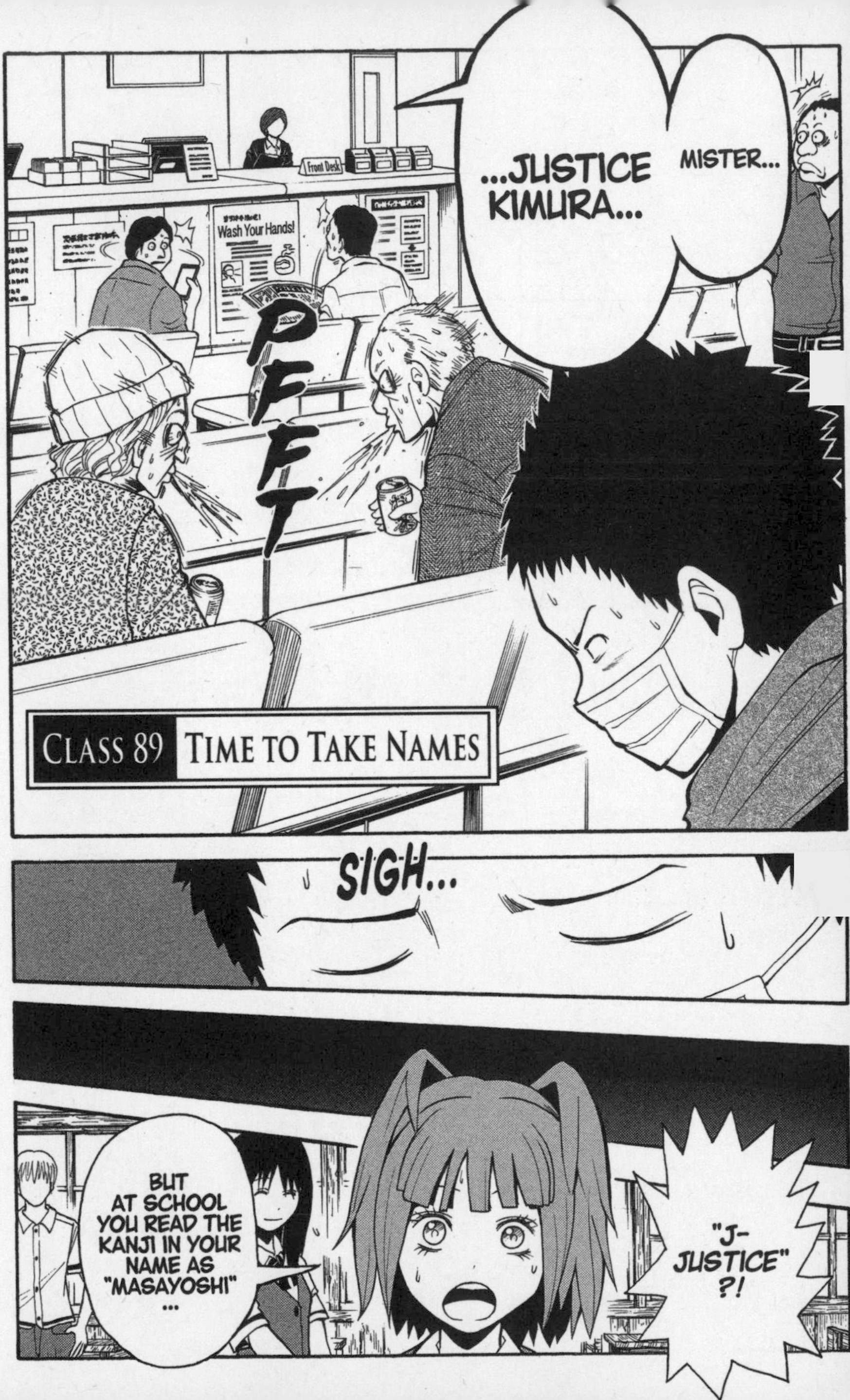
MISTER...
...JUSTICE KIMURA...
Front Desk
Wash Your Hands!
PFFT
CLASS 89 TIME TO TAKE NAMES
SIGH...
"J-JUSTICE"?!
BUT AT SCHOOL YOU READ THE KANJI IN YOUR NAME AS "MASAYOSHI"...

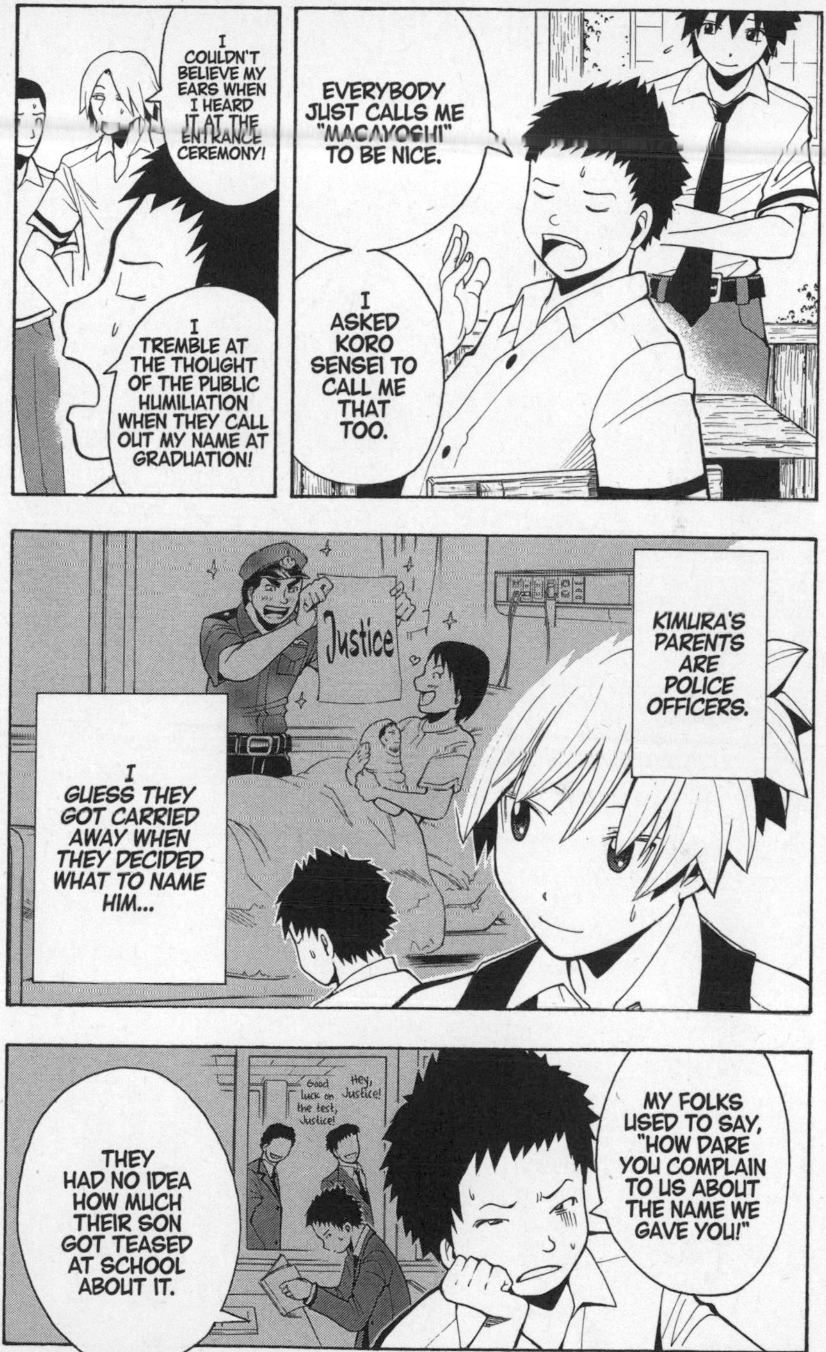
EVERYBODY JUST CALLS ME "MACAYOSHI" TO BE NICE.
I ASKED KORO SENSEI TO CALL ME THAT TOO.
I COULDN'T BELIEVE MY EARS WHEN I HEARD IT AT THE ENTRANCE CEREMONY!
I TREMBLE AT THE THOUGHT OF THE PUBLIC HUMILIATION WHEN THEY CALL OUT MY NAME AT GRADUATION!
KIMURA'S PARENTS ARE POLICE OFFICERS.
Justice
I GUESS THEY GOT CARRIED AWAY WHEN THEY DECIDED WHAT TO NAME HIM...
MY FOLKS USED TO SAY, "HOW DARE YOU COMPLAIN TO US ABOUT THE NAME WE GAVE YOU!"
Hey, Justice!
Good luck on the test, Justice!
THEY HAD NO IDEA HOW MUCH THEIR SON GOT TEASED AT SCHOOL ABOUT IT.

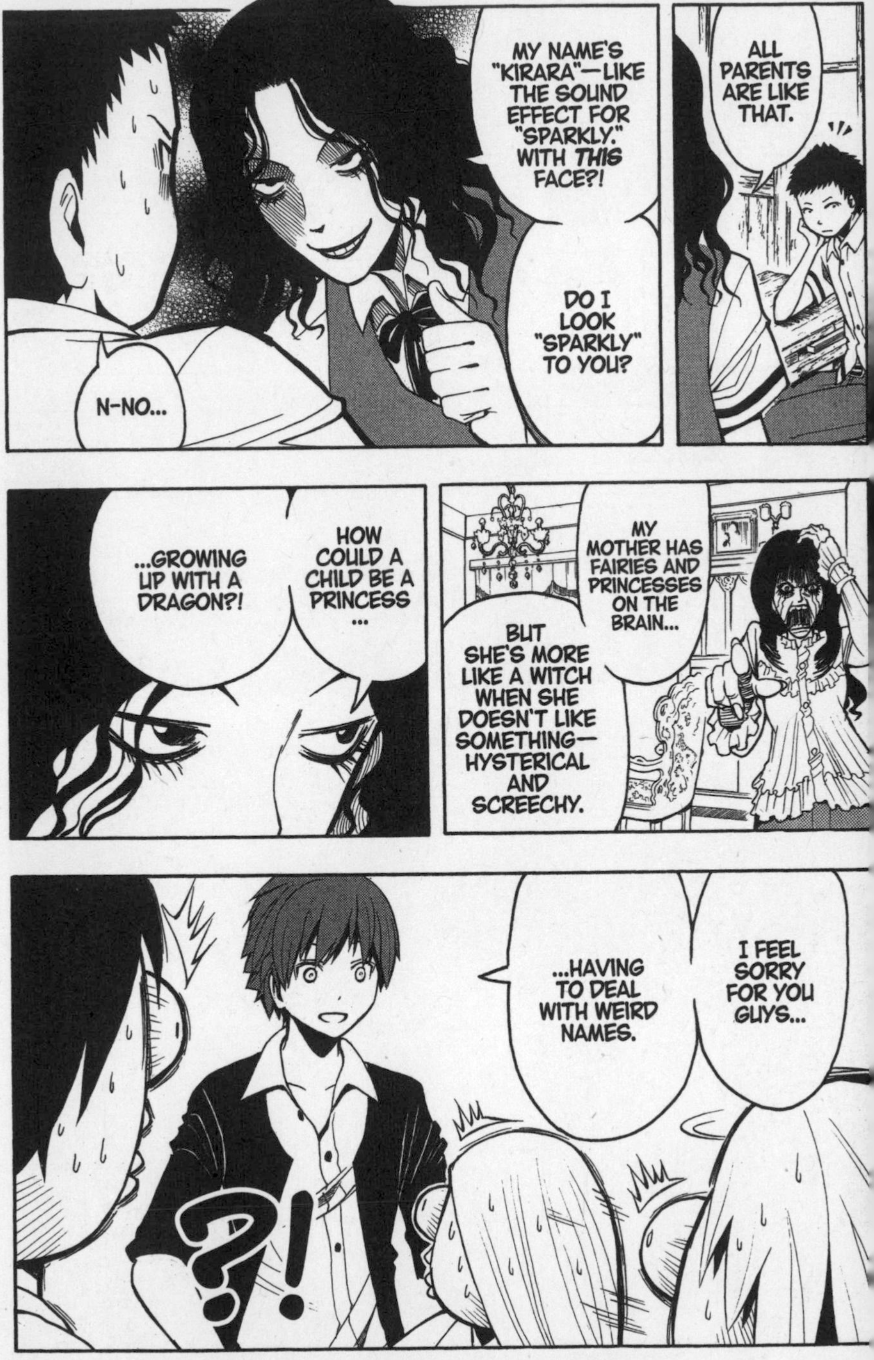
ALL PARENTS ARE LIKE THAT.
MY NAME'S "KIRARA"—LIKE THE SOUND EFFECT FOR "SPARKLY." WITH *THIS* FACE?!
DO I LOOK "SPARKLY" TO YOU?
N-NO...
MY MOTHER HAS FAIRIES AND PRINCESSES ON THE BRAIN...
BUT SHE'S MORE LIKE A WITCH WHEN SHE DOESN'T LIKE SOMETHING—HYSTERICAL AND SCREECHY.
HOW COULD A CHILD BE A PRINCESS ...
...GROWING UP WITH A DRAGON?!
I FEEL SORRY FOR YOU GUYS...
...HAVING TO DEAL WITH WEIRD NAMES.
?!

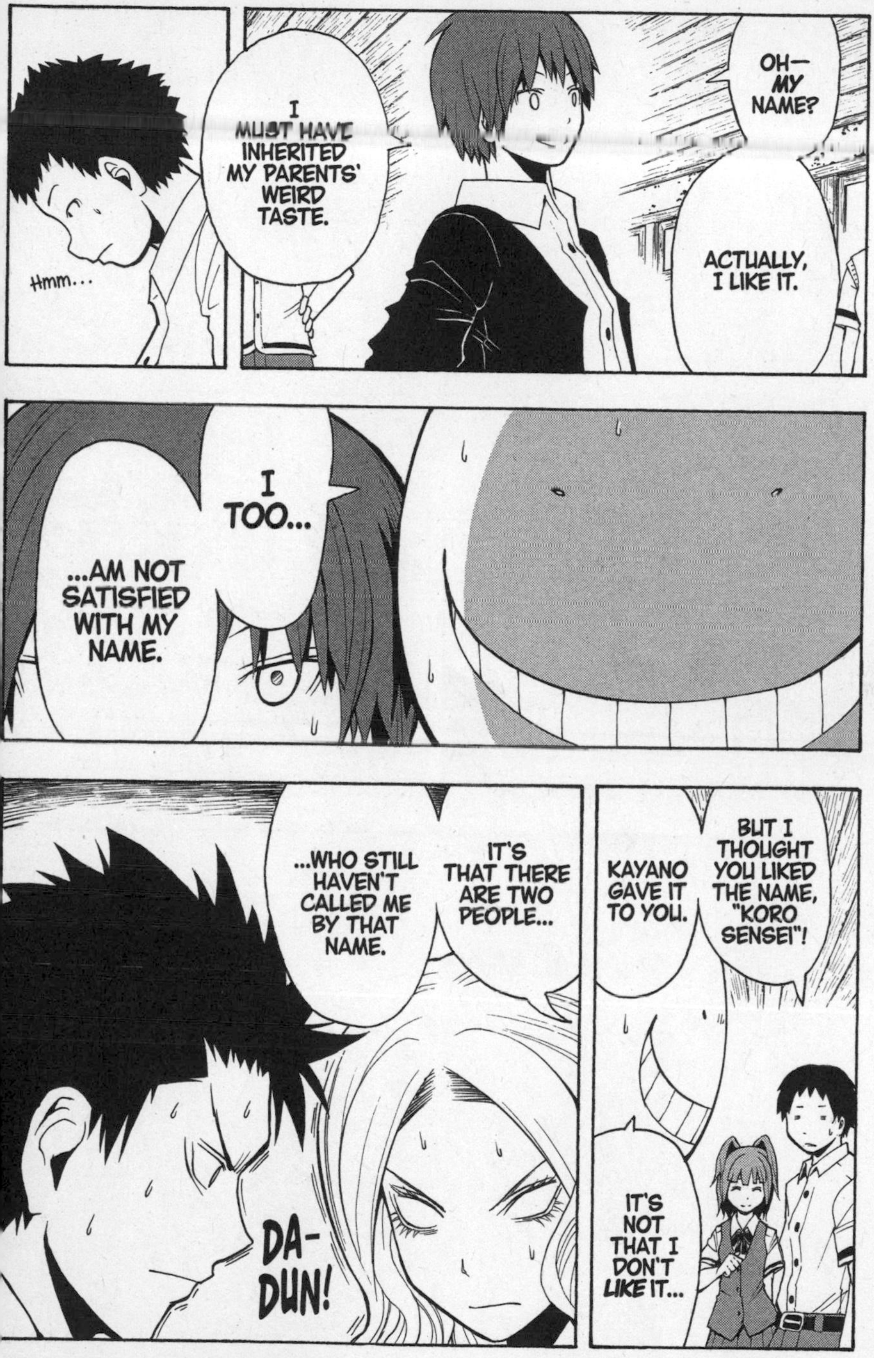
OH— MY NAME?
ACTUALLY, I LIKE IT.
I MUST HAVE INHERITED MY PARENTS' WEIRD TASTE.
Hmm...
I TOO...
...AM NOT SATISFIED WITH MY NAME.
BUT I THOUGHT YOU LIKED THE NAME, "KORO SENSEI"!
KAYANO GAVE IT TO YOU.
IT'S NOT THAT I DON'T LIKE IT...
IT'S THAT THERE ARE TWO PEOPLE...
...WHO STILL HAVEN'T CALLED ME BY THAT NAME.
DA-DUN!

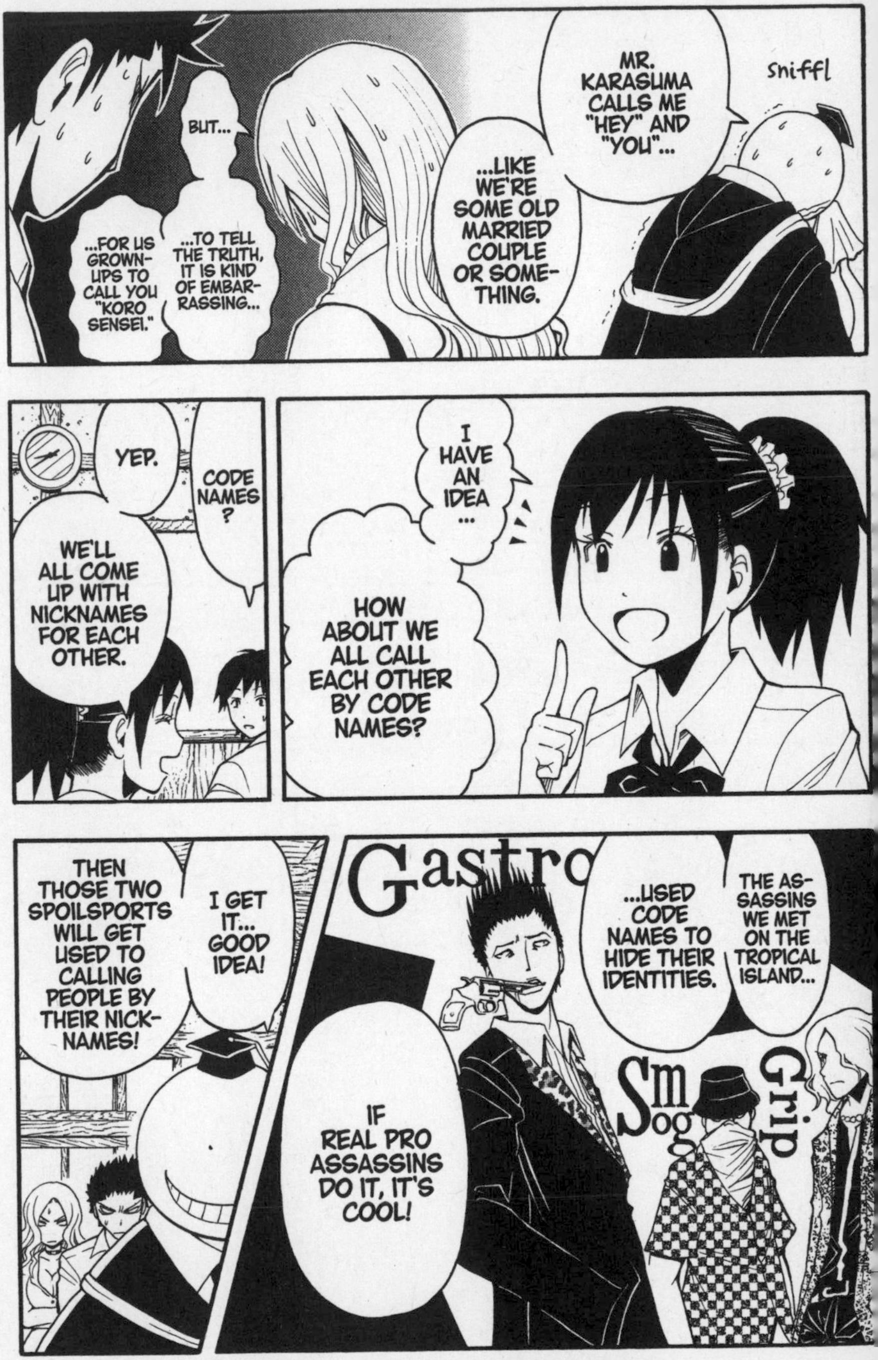
Sniffl
MR. KARASUMA CALLS ME "HEY" AND "YOU"...
...LIKE WE'RE SOME OLD MARRIED COUPLE OR SOME-THING.
BUT...
...TO TELL THE TRUTH, IT IS KIND OF EMBAR-RASSING...
...FOR US GROWN-UPS TO CALL YOU "KORO SENSEI."
I HAVE AN IDEA...
HOW ABOUT WE ALL CALL EACH OTHER BY CODE NAMES?
CODE NAMES?
YEP.
WE'LL ALL COME UP WITH NICKNAMES FOR EACH OTHER.
THE AS-SASSINS WE MET ON THE TROPICAL ISLAND...
...USED CODE NAMES TO HIDE THEIR IDENTITIES.
Gastro
Grip
Smog
IF REAL PRO ASSASSINS DO IT, IT'S COOL!
I GET IT... GOOD IDEA!
THEN THOSE TWO SPOILSPORTS WILL GET USED TO CALLING PEOPLE BY THEIR NICK-NAMES!

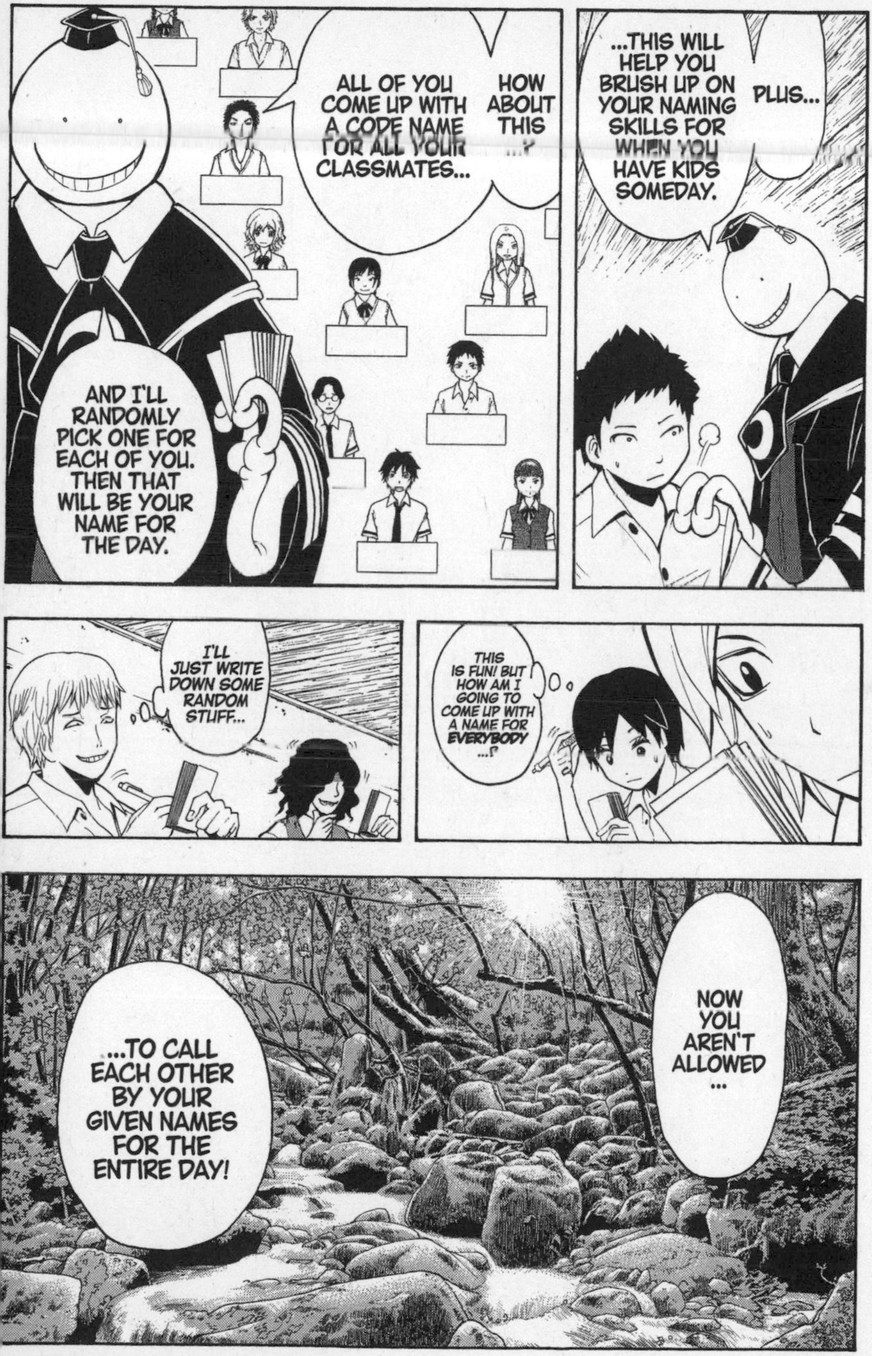
PLUS...
...THIS WILL HELP YOU BRUSH UP ON YOUR NAMING SKILLS FOR WHEN YOU HAVE KIDS SOMEDAY.
HOW ABOUT THIS ...?
ALL OF YOU COME UP WITH A CODE NAME FOR ALL YOUR CLASSMATES...
AND I'LL RANDOMLY PICK ONE FOR EACH OF YOU. THEN THAT WILL BE YOUR NAME FOR THE DAY.
THIS IS FUN! BUT HOW AM I GOING TO COME UP WITH A NAME FOR EVERYBODY ...!?
I'LL JUST WRITE DOWN SOME RANDOM STUFF...
NOW YOU AREN'T ALLOWED ...
...TO CALL EACH OTHER BY YOUR GIVEN NAMES FOR THE ENTIRE DAY!

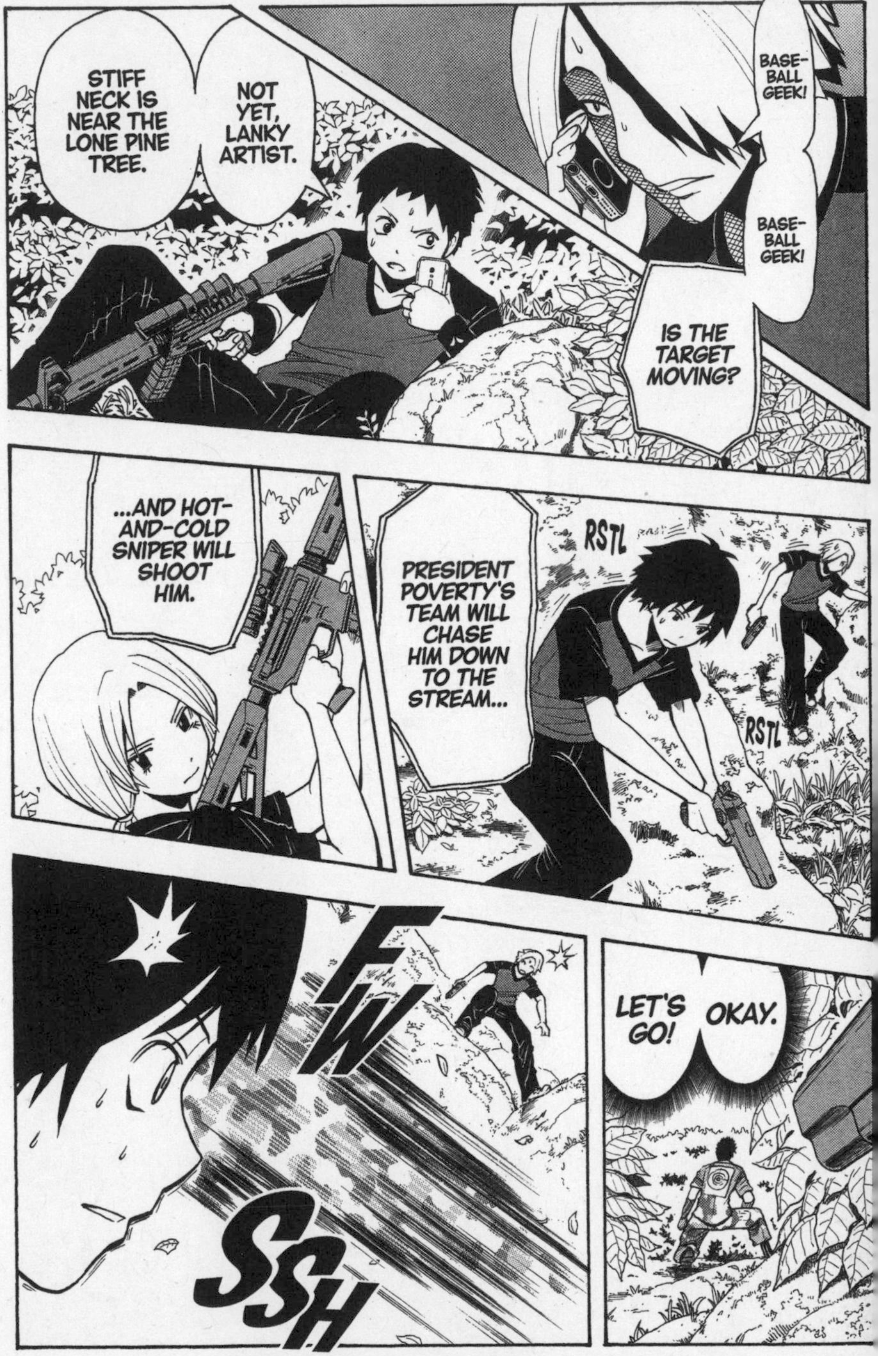
BASE-BALL GEEK!
BASE-BALL GEEK!
IS THE TARGET MOVING?
NOT YET, LANKY ARTIST.
STIFF NECK IS NEAR THE LONE PINE TREE.
RSTL
RSTL
PRESIDENT POVERTY'S TEAM WILL CHASE HIM DOWN TO THE STREAM...
...AND HOT-AND-COLD SNIPER WILL SHOOT HIM.
OKAY.
LET'S GO!
FW
SSH

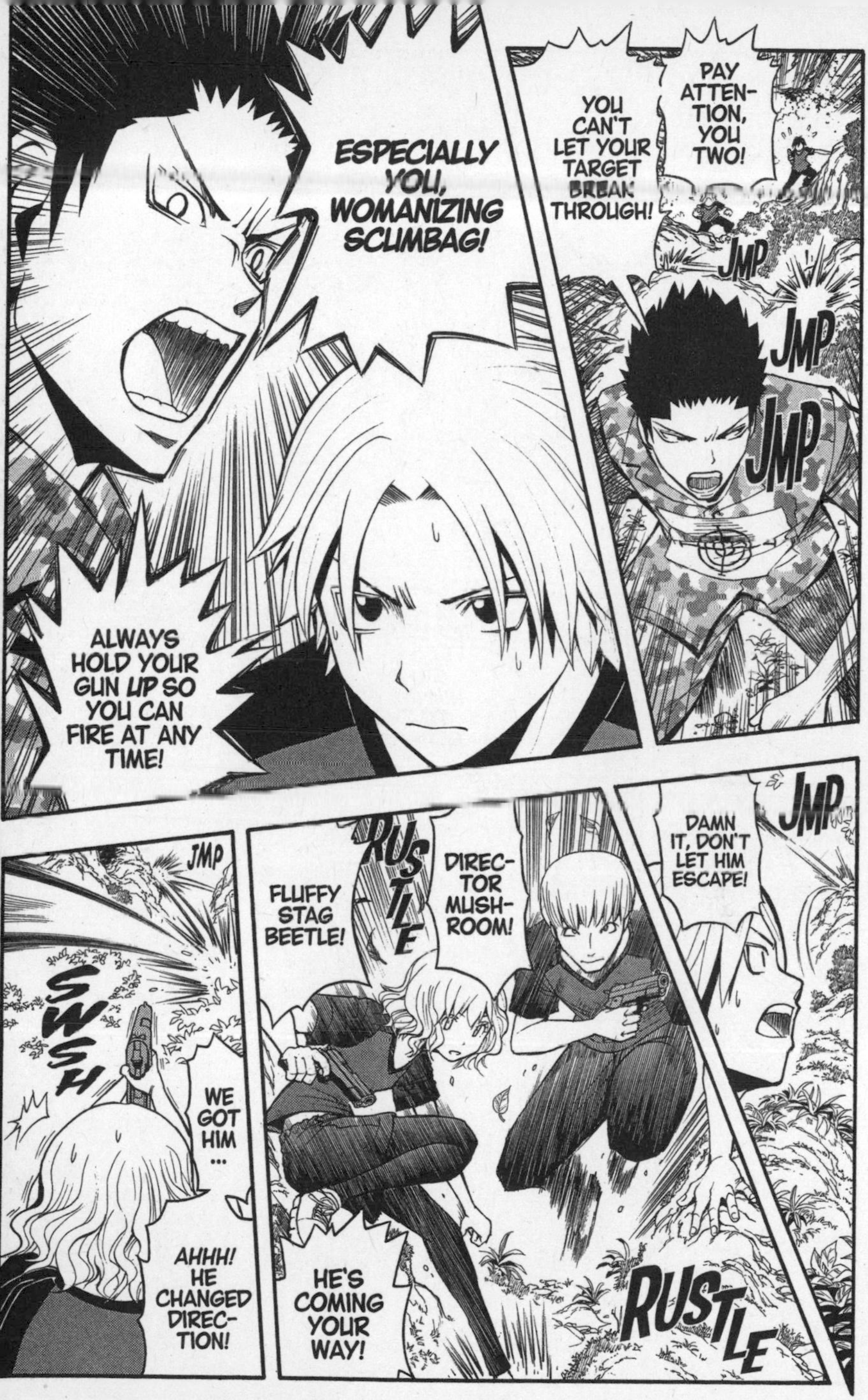
PAY ATTENTION, YOU TWO!
YOU CAN'T LET YOUR TARGET BREAK THROUGH!
JMP
JMP
JMP
ESPECIALLY YOU, WOMANIZING SCUMBAG!
ALWAYS HOLD YOUR GUN UP SO YOU CAN FIRE AT ANY TIME!
JMP
DAMN IT, DON'T LET HIM ESCAPE!
RUSTLE
DIRECTOR MUSHROOM!
RUSTLE
FLUFFY STAG BEETLE!
HE'S COMING YOUR WAY!
JMP
SWSH
WE GOT HIM...
AHHH! HE CHANGED DIRECTION!

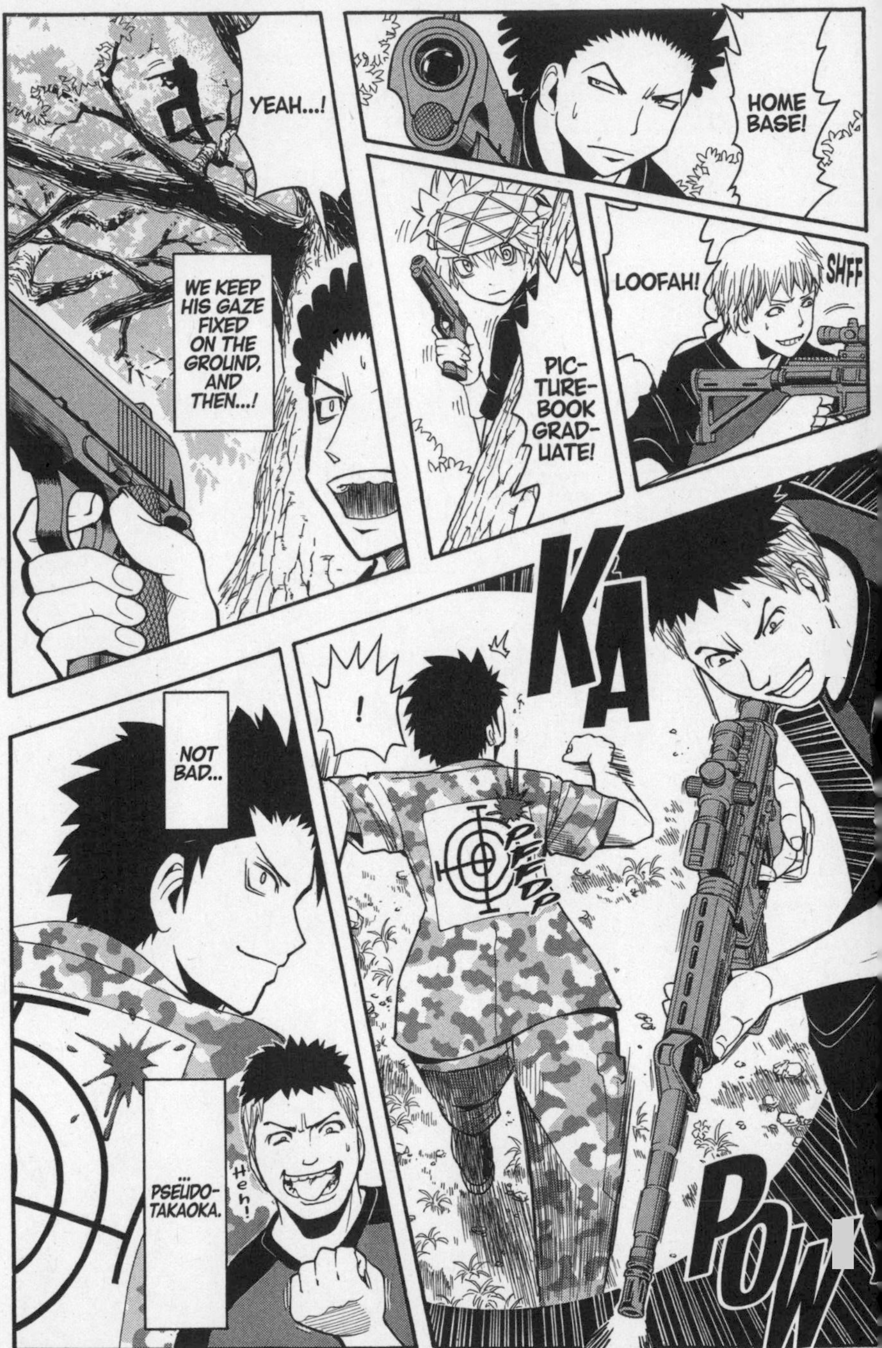
HOME BASE!
SHFF
LOOFAH!
PICTURE-BOOK GRADUATE!
YEAH...!
WE KEEP HIS GAZE FIXED ON THE GROUND, AND THEN...!
KA
POW
!
NOT BAD...
Heh!
...PSEUDO-TAKAOKA.

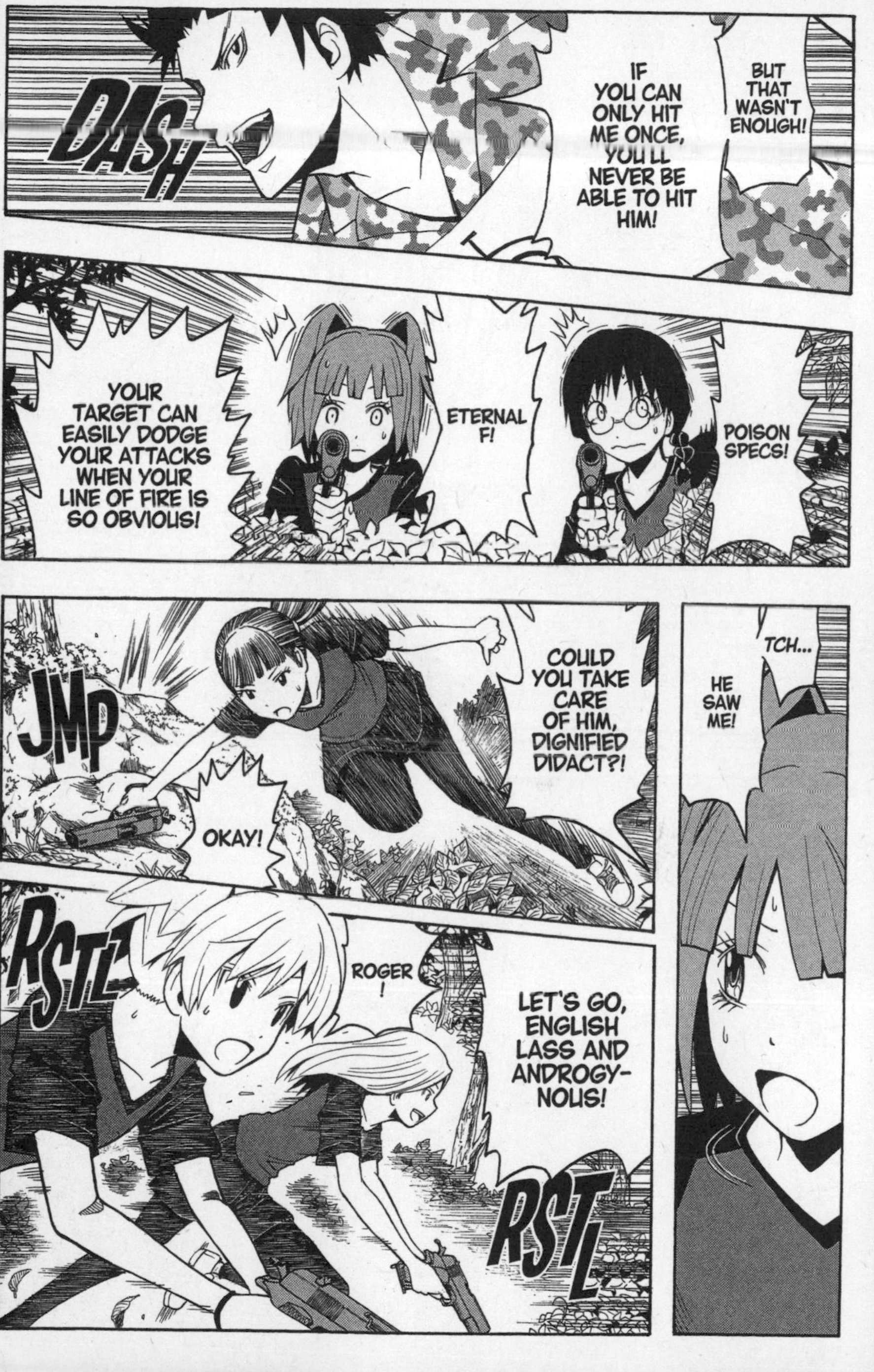
BUT THAT WASN'T ENOUGH!
IF YOU CAN ONLY HIT ME ONCE, YOU'LL NEVER BE ABLE TO HIT HIM!
DASH
POISON SPECS!
ETERNAL F!
YOUR TARGET CAN EASILY DODGE YOUR ATTACKS WHEN YOUR LINE OF FIRE IS SO OBVIOUS!
TCH...
HE SAW ME!
COULD YOU TAKE CARE OF HIM, DIGNIFIED DIDACT?!
OKAY!
JMP
LET'S GO, ENGLISH LASS AND ANDROGY-NOUS!
ROGER!
RSTL
RSTL

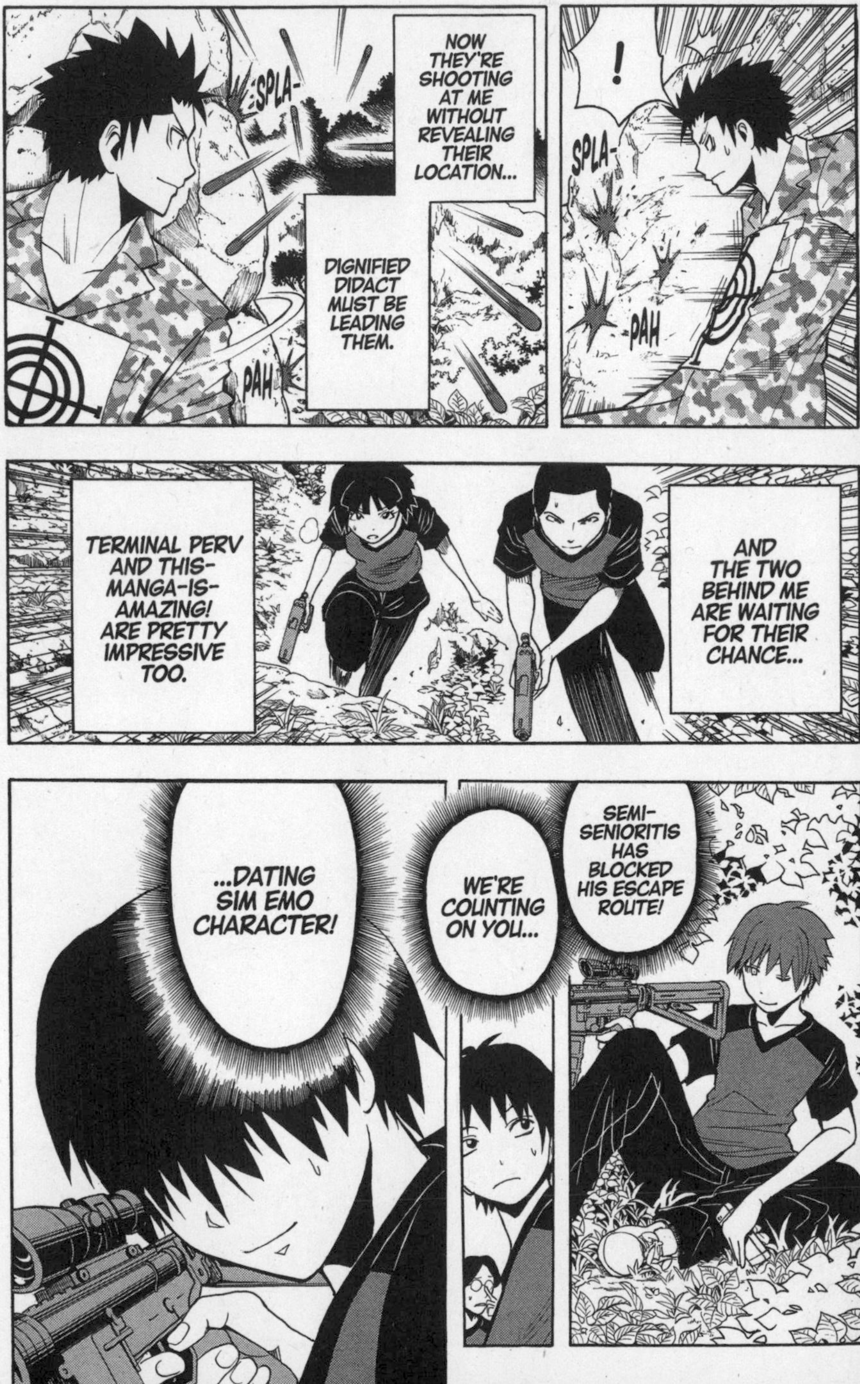
!
SPLA-
PAH
NOW THEY'RE SHOOTING AT ME WITHOUT REVEALING THEIR LOCATION...
DIGNIFIED DIDACT MUST BE LEADING THEM.
SPLA-
PAH
AND THE TWO BEHIND ME ARE WAITING FOR THEIR CHANCE...
TERMINAL PERV AND THIS-MANGA-IS-AMAZING! ARE PRETTY IMPRESSIVE TOO.
SEMI-SENIORITIS HAS BLOCKED HIS ESCAPE ROUTE!
WE'RE COUNTING ON YOU...
...DATING SIM EMO CHARACTER!

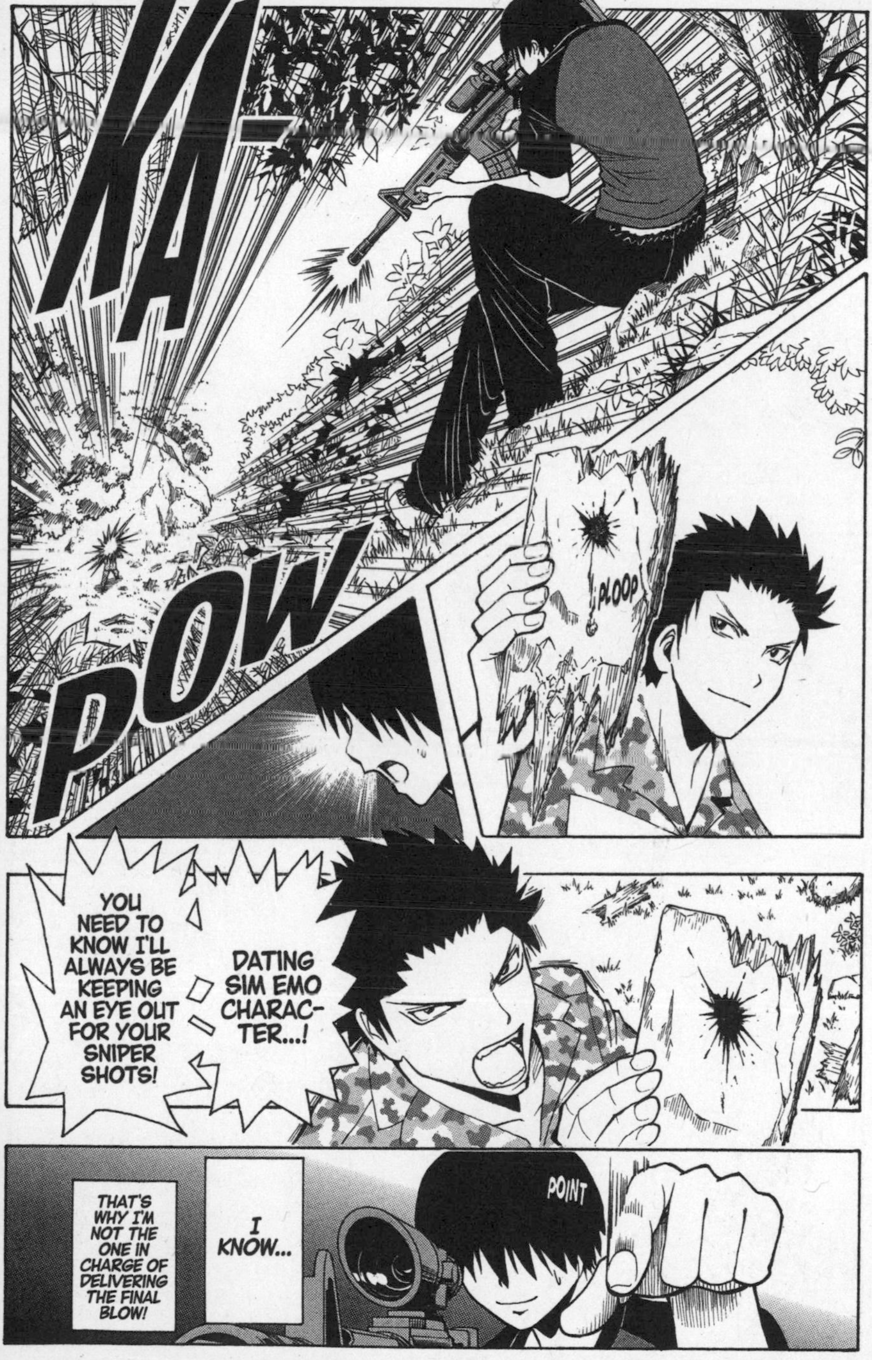
KA-
POW
PLOOP
DATING SIM EMO CHARACTER...!
YOU NEED TO KNOW I'LL ALWAYS BE KEEPING AN EYE OUT FOR YOUR SNIPER SHOTS!
POINT
I KNOW...
THAT'S WHY I'M NOT THE ONE IN CHARGE OF DELIVERING THE FINAL BLOW!

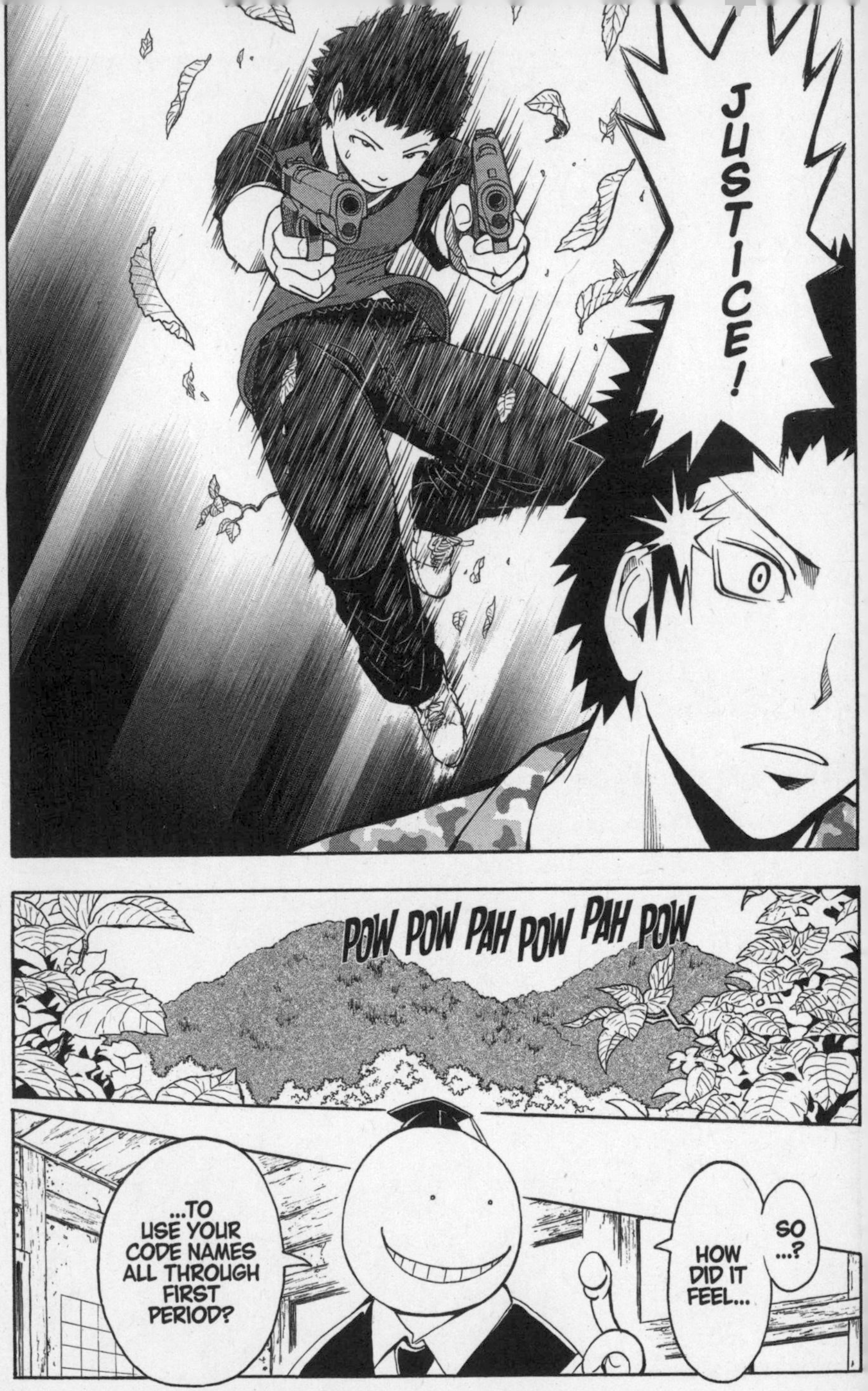
JUSTICE!
POW POW PAH POW PAH POW
SO ...?
HOW DID IT FEEL...
...TO USE YOUR CODE NAMES ALL THROUGH FIRST PERIOD?

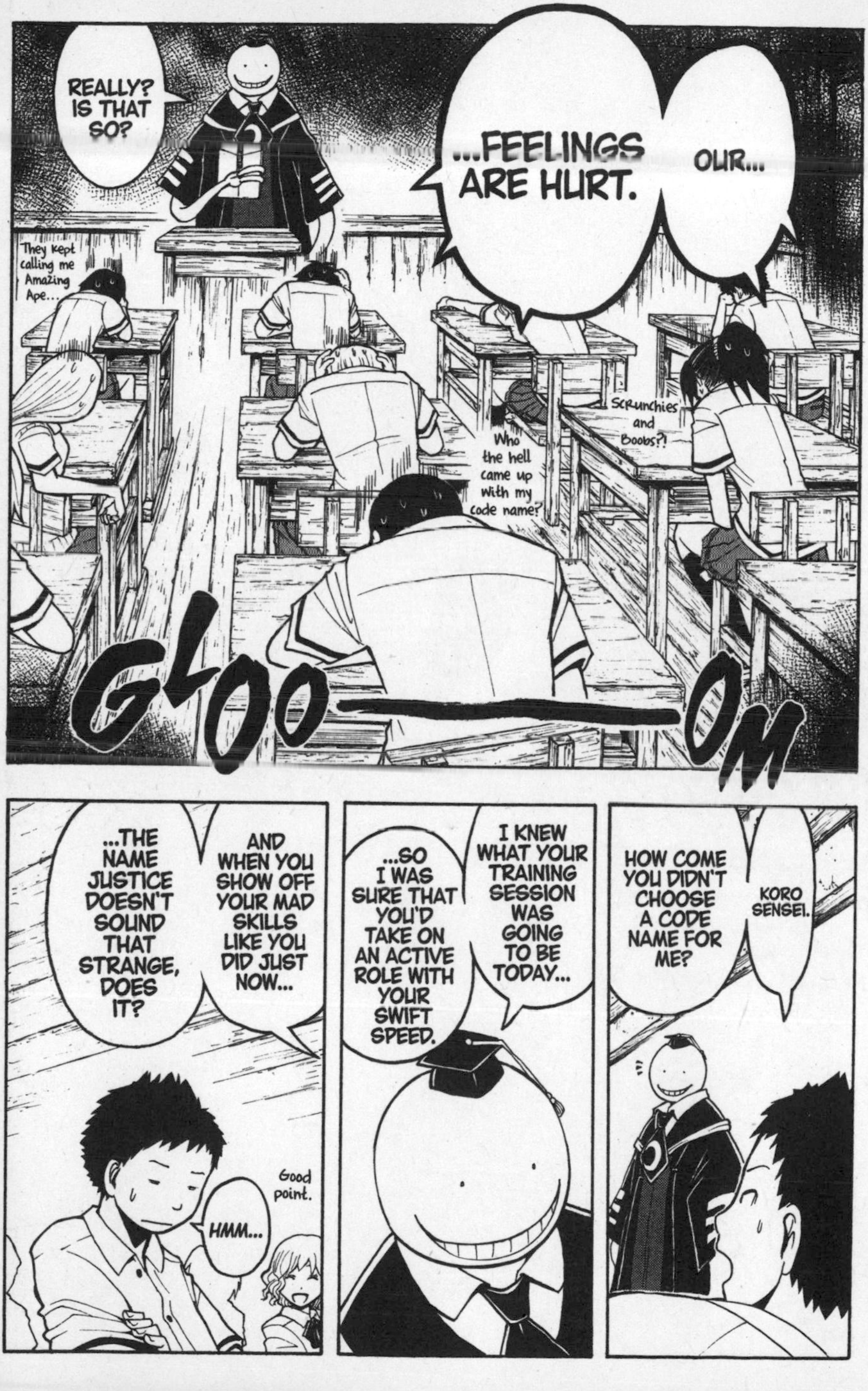
OUR...
...FEELINGS ARE HURT.
REALLY? IS THAT SO?
Scrunchies and Boobs?!
Who the hell came up with my code name?
They kept calling me Amazing Ape...
GLOO——OM
KORO SENSEI.
HOW COME YOU DIDN'T CHOOSE A CODE NAME FOR ME?
I KNEW WHAT YOUR TRAINING SESSION WAS GOING TO BE TODAY...
...SO I WAS SURE THAT YOU'D TAKE ON AN ACTIVE ROLE WITH YOUR SWIFT SPEED.
AND WHEN YOU SHOW OFF YOUR MAD SKILLS LIKE YOU DID JUST NOW...
...THE NAME JUSTICE DOESN'T SOUND THAT STRANGE, DOES IT?
Good point.
HMM...

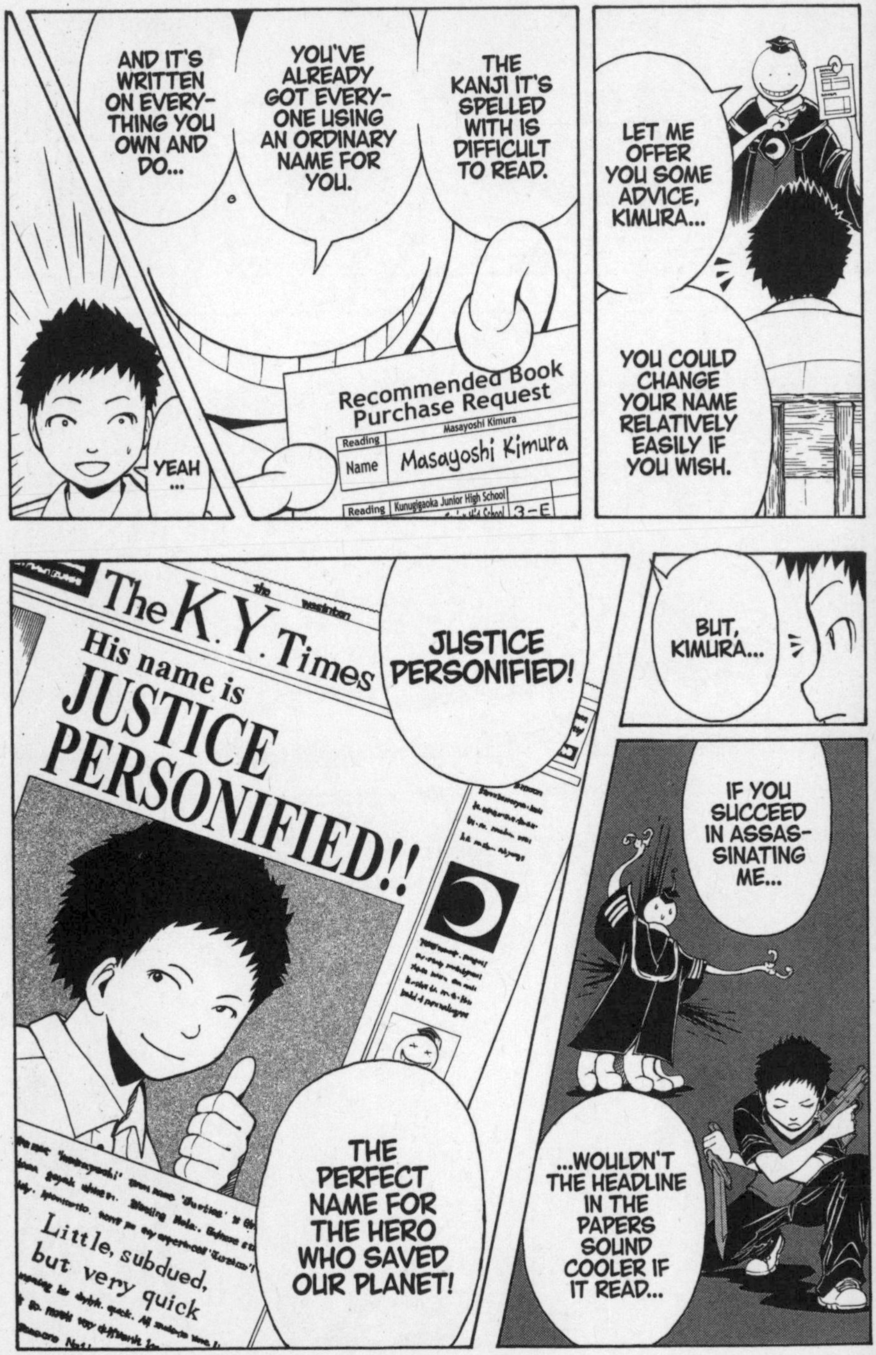
LET ME OFFER YOU SOME ADVICE, KIMURA...
YOU COULD CHANGE YOUR NAME RELATIVELY EASILY IF YOU WISH.
THE KANJI IT'S SPELLED WITH IS DIFFICULT TO READ.
YOU'VE ALREADY GOT EVERYONE USING AN ORDINARY NAME FOR YOU.
AND IT'S WRITTEN ON EVERYTHING YOU OWN AND DO...
Recommended Book Purchase Request
Reading Masayoshi Kimura
Name Masayoshi Kimura
Reading Kunugigaoka Junior High School 3-E
YEAH...
BUT, KIMURA...
IF YOU SUCCEED IN ASSASSINATING ME...
...WOULDN'T THE HEADLINE IN THE PAPERS SOUND COOLER IF IT READ...
JUSTICE PERSONIFIED!
The K.Y. Times
His name is JUSTICE PERSONIFIED!!
Little, subdued, but very quick
THE PERFECT NAME FOR THE HERO WHO SAVED OUR PLANET!

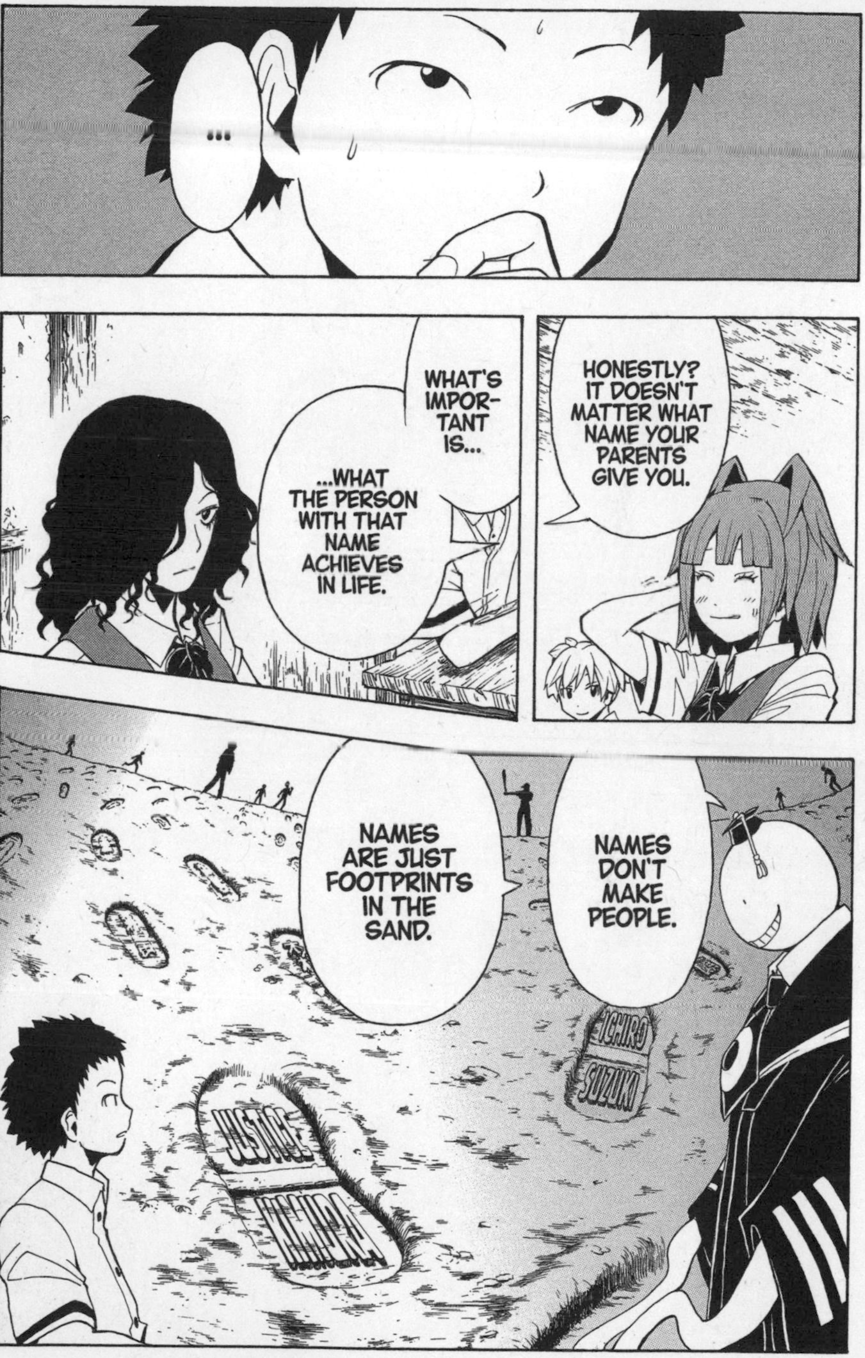
...
HONESTLY? IT DOESN'T MATTER WHAT NAME YOUR PARENTS GIVE YOU.
WHAT'S IMPOR-TANT IS...
...WHAT THE PERSON WITH THAT NAME ACHIEVES IN LIFE.
NAMES DON'T MAKE PEOPLE.
NAMES ARE JUST FOOTPRINTS IN THE SAND.
ICHIRO
SUZUKI

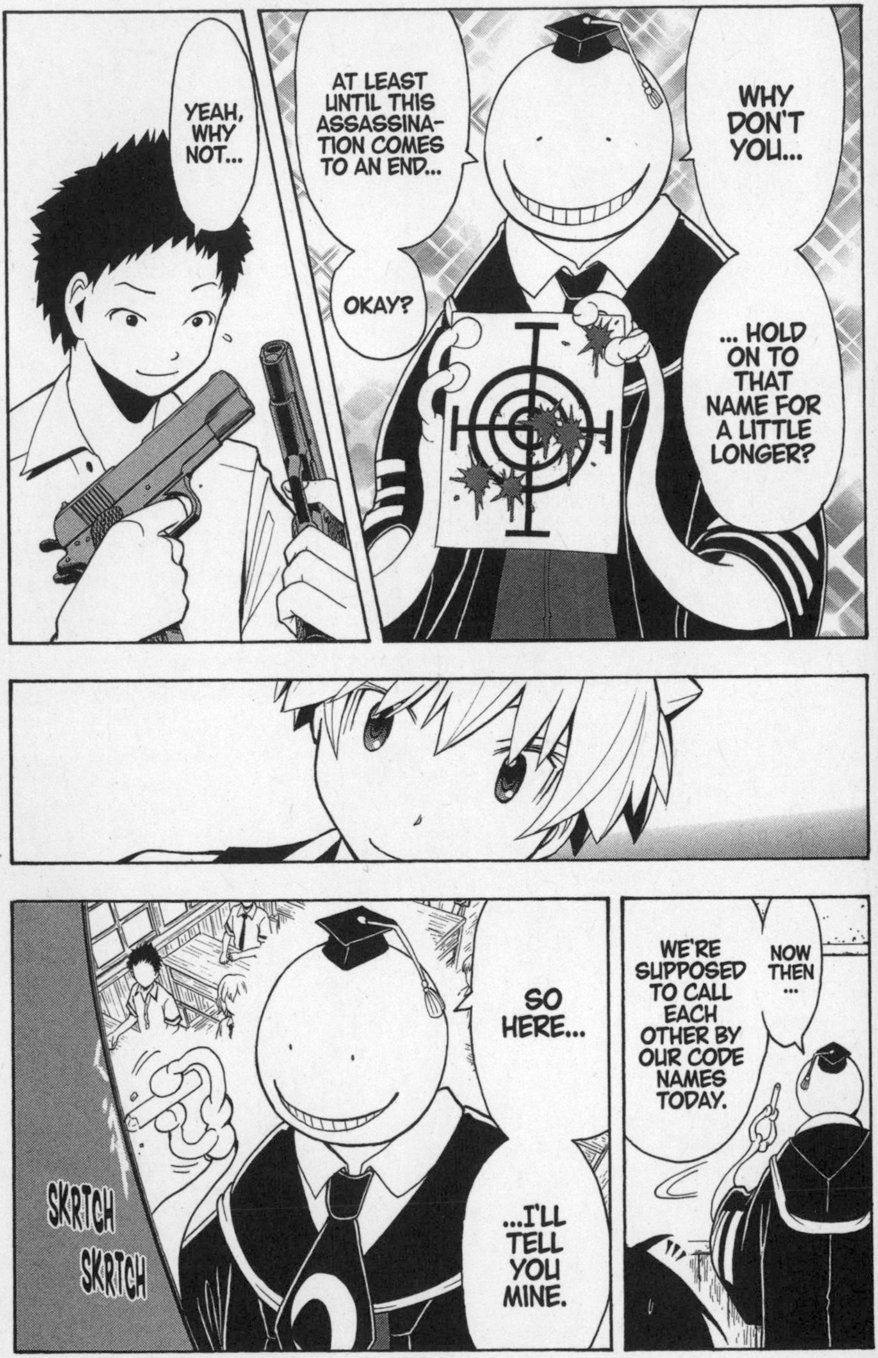
WHY DON'T YOU...
... HOLD ON TO THAT NAME FOR A LITTLE LONGER?
AT LEAST UNTIL THIS ASSASSINA-TION COMES TO AN END...
OKAY?
YEAH, WHY NOT...
NOW THEN ...
WE'RE SUPPOSED TO CALL EACH OTHER BY OUR CODE NAMES TODAY.
SO HERE...
...I'LL TELL YOU MINE.
SKRTCH
SKRTCH

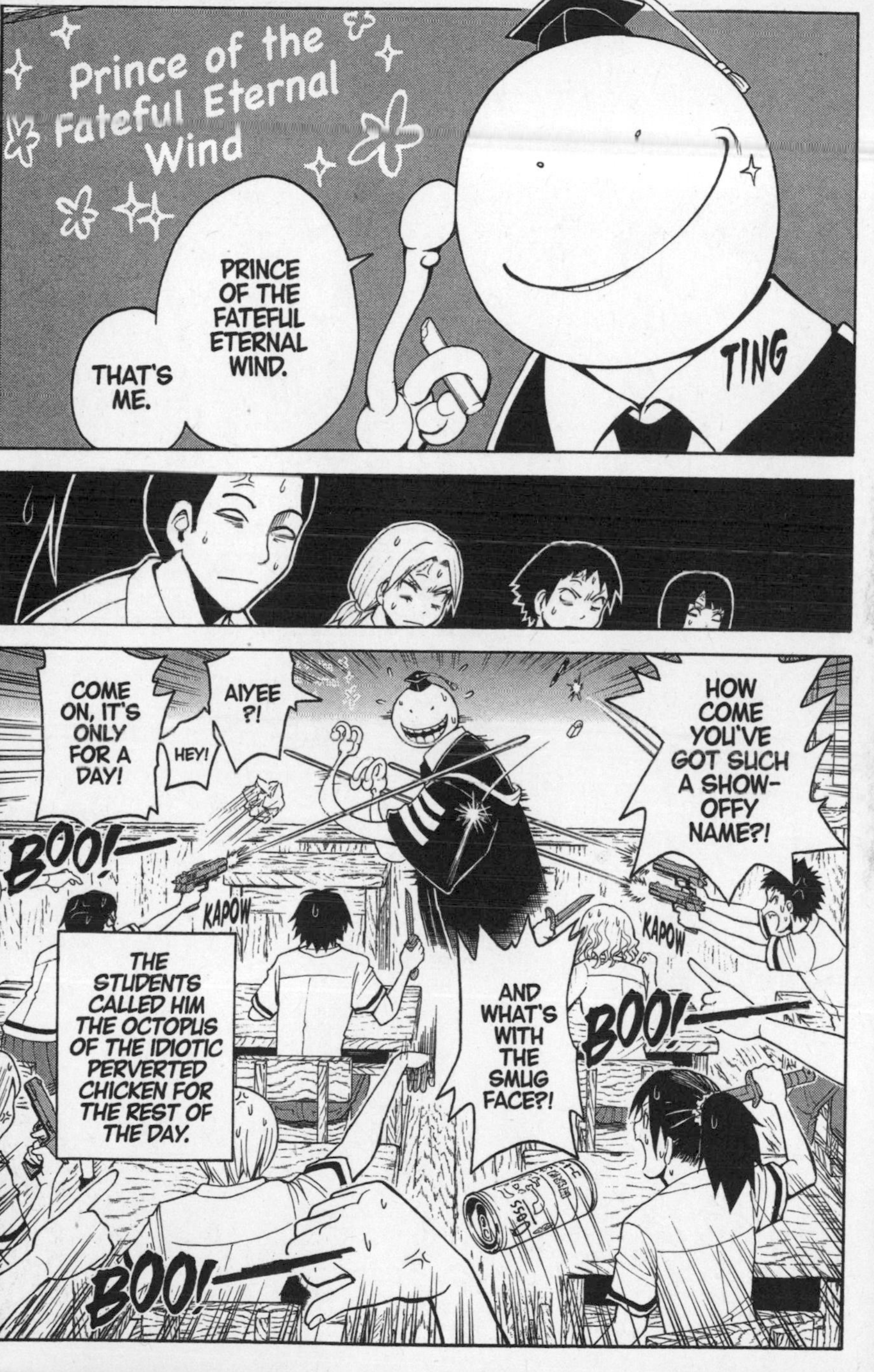
Prince of the Fateful Eternal Wind
PRINCE OF THE FATEFUL ETERNAL WIND.
THAT'S ME.
TING
HOW COME YOU'VE GOT SUCH A SHOW-OFFY NAME?!
AIYEE ?!
HEY!
COME ON, IT'S ONLY FOR A DAY!
BOO!
KAPOW
KAPOW
BOO!
AND WHAT'S WITH THE SMUG FACE?!
THE STUDENTS CALLED HIM THE OCTOPUS OF THE IDIOTIC PERVERTED CHICKEN FOR THE REST OF THE DAY.
BOO!

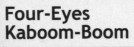

Class E Codenames

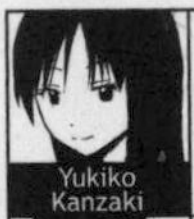 Yukiko Kanzaki	**Mistress Kanzaki**
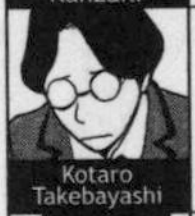 Kotaro Takebayashi	**Four-Eyes Kaboom-Boom**
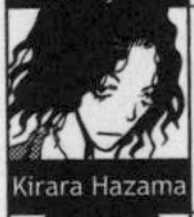 Kirara Hazama	**The Darkness of Class E**
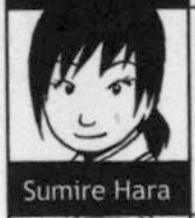 Sumire Hara	**Kunugigaoka Mom**
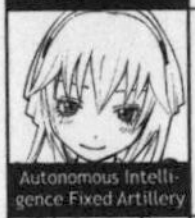 Autonomous Intelligence Fixed Artillery	**Box o' Moe**
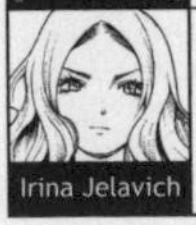 Irina Jelavich	**Bitchy Vitchy**

Assassins Wanted!

BEST IDEA ANNOUNCED!

Many excellent ideas were submitted for this project! Matsui Sensei has chosen to draw the best assassin out of the 936 pieces of artwork that were sent to us!*

*A call for fan submissions was announced in Weekly Shonen Jump 2014, Issue 15.

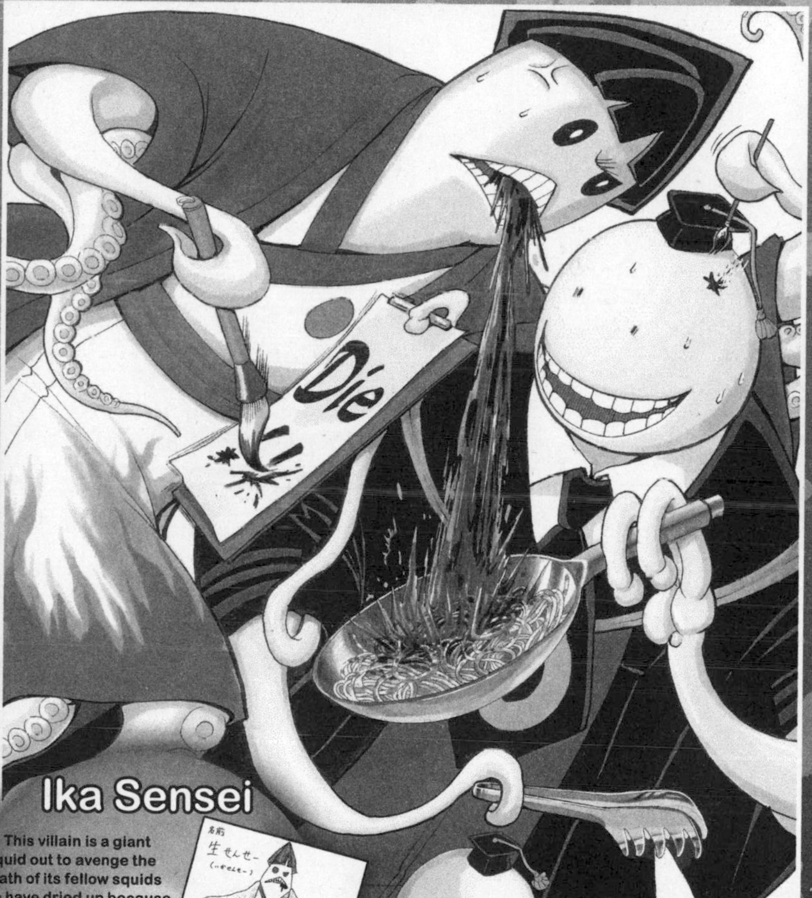
Die

Ika Sensei

This villain is a giant squid out to avenge the death of its fellow squids who have dried up because of the changes in the ocean tides due to Koro Sensei having destroyed most of the moon. It sneaks into Kunugigaoka Junior High. The squid ink it spits out of its mouth can melt Koro Sensei!

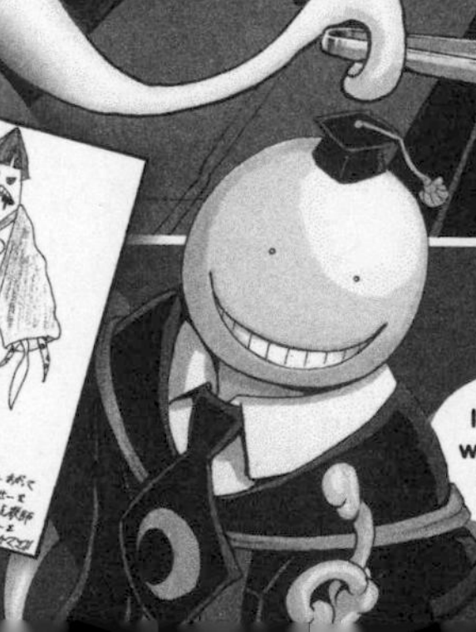

Koro Sensei's Counterplan

I'll block the large brush with the writing paper and block the ink it's spitting out with a pan of pasta. But I can't find a way to block the small brush...

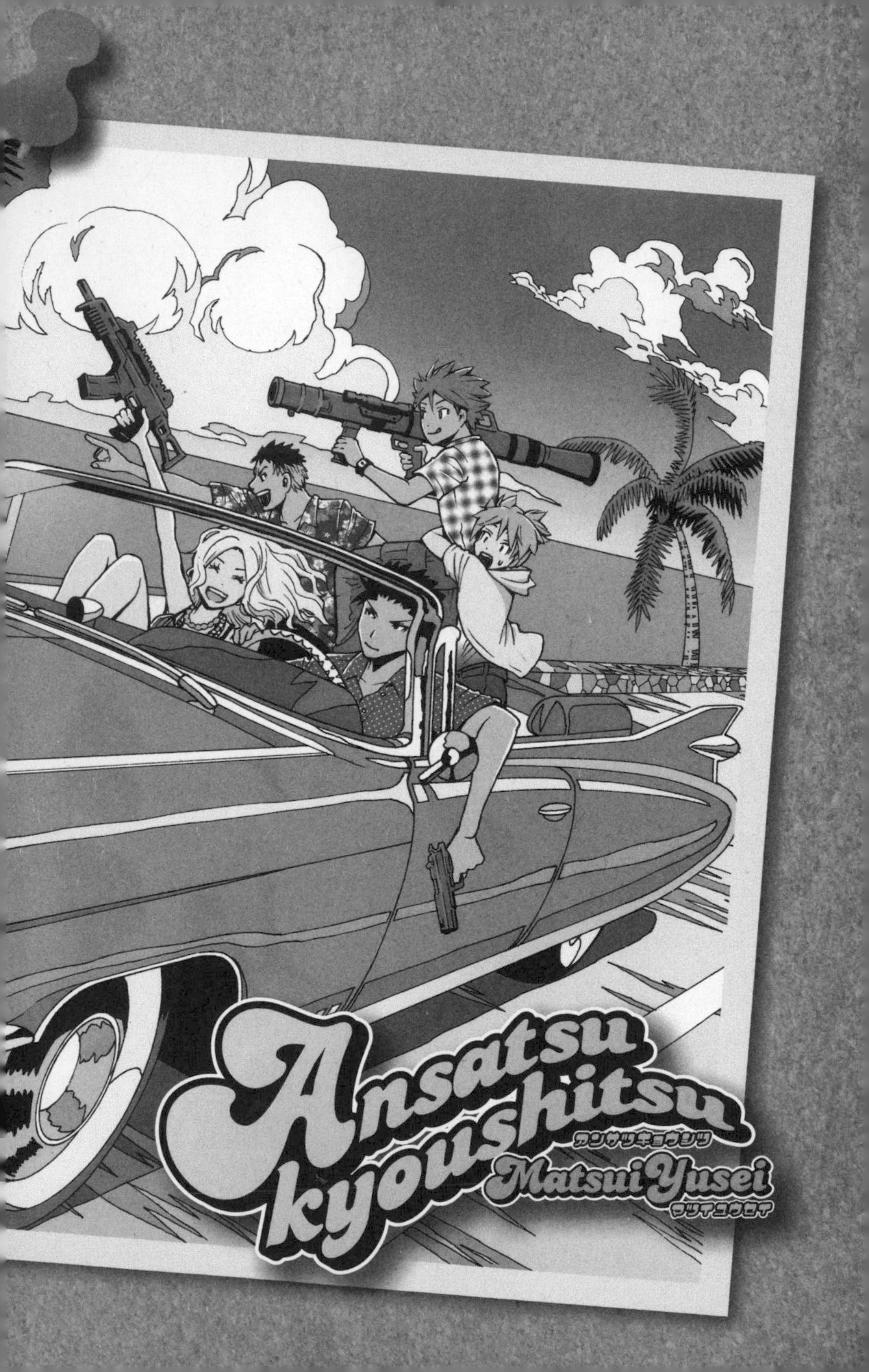
Ansatsu kyoushitsu
アンサツキョウシツ
Matsui Yusei
マツイユウセイ

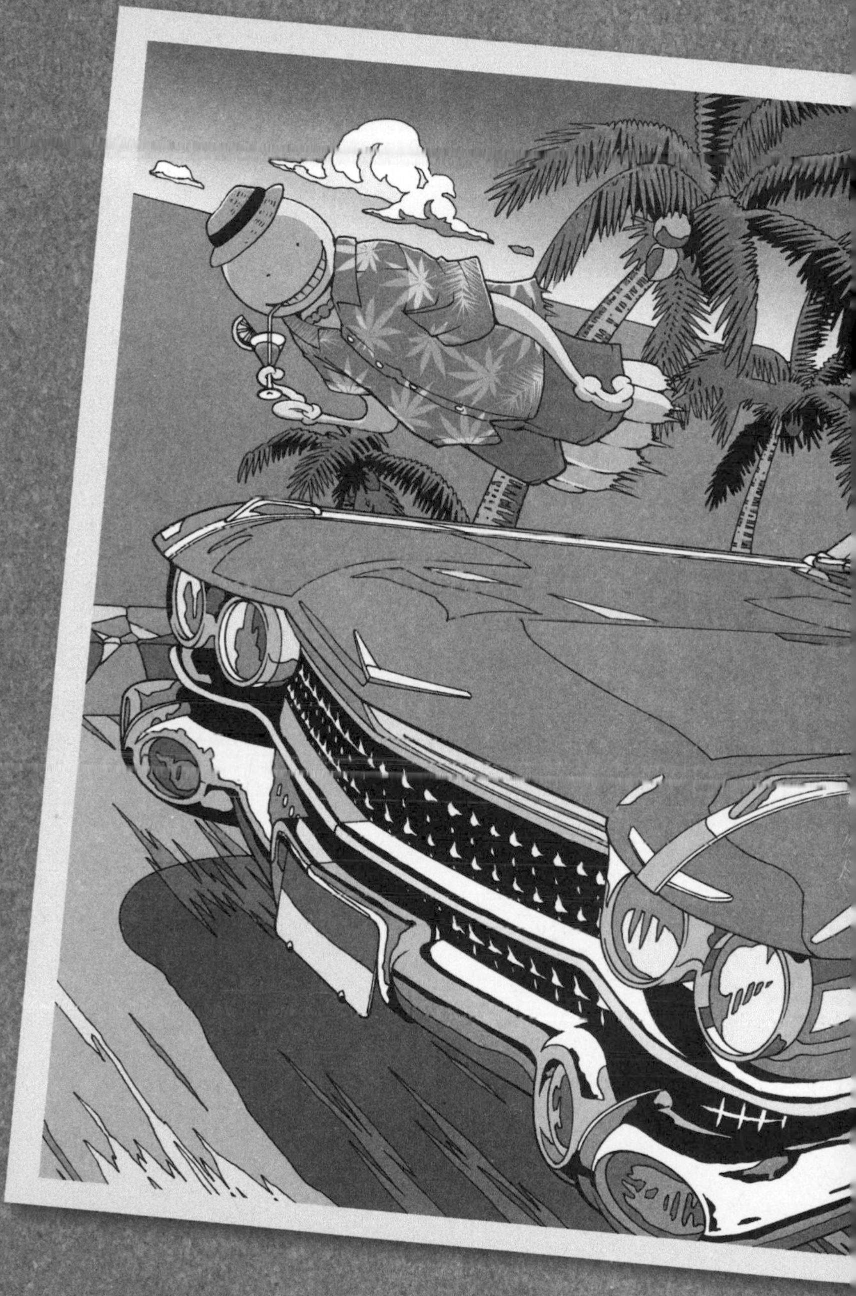

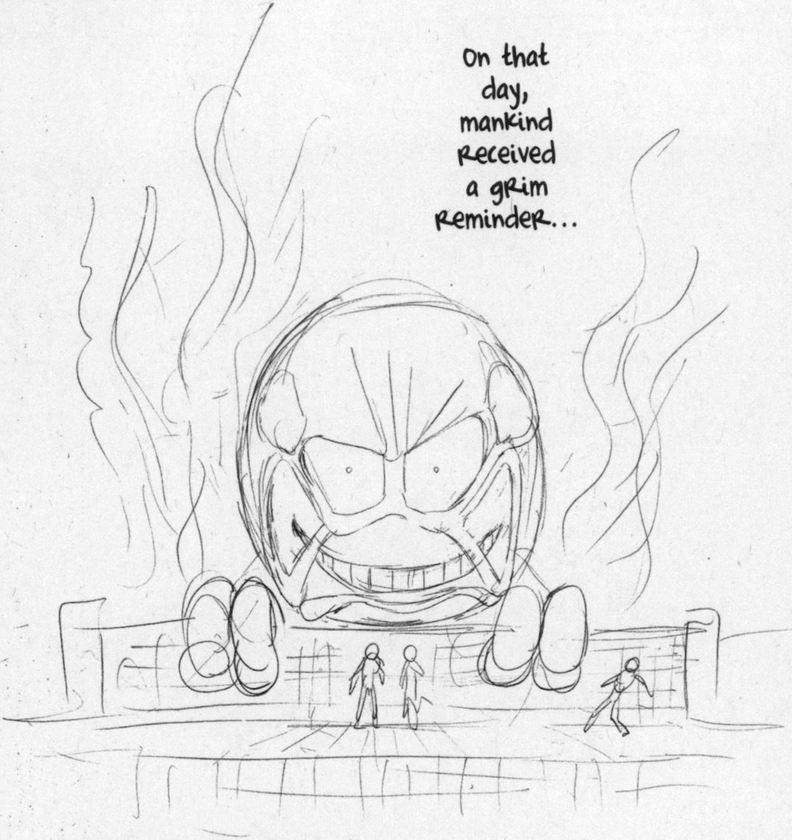
On that day, mankind received a grim reminder...

This is an illustration I was thinking about drawing for the first page of this graphic novel. It was rejected.

Reason: I just couldn't make it look enough like that other manga.

CLASS 90 MAKING TIME FOR MR. HANDSOME

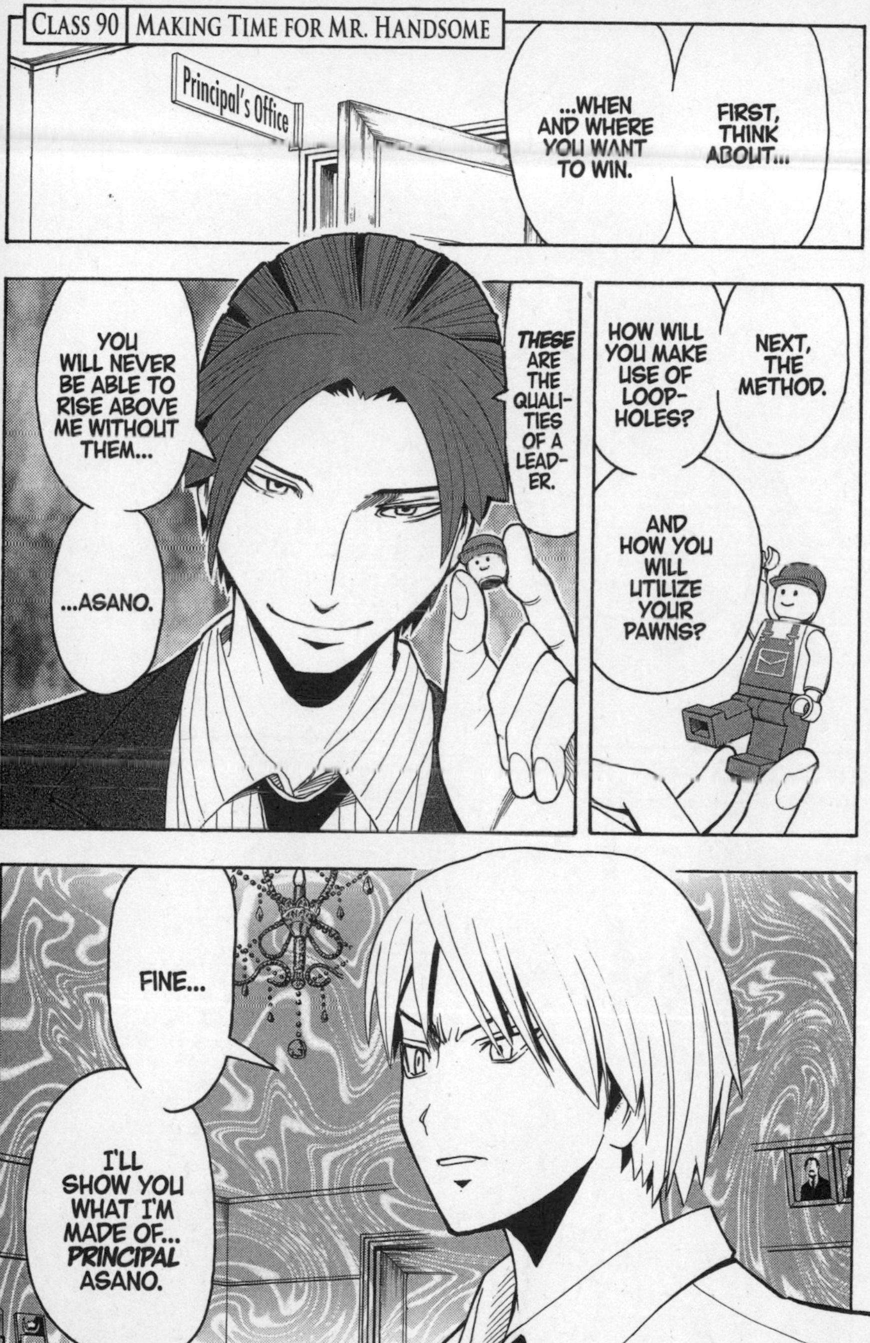
FIRST, THINK ABOUT...
...WHEN AND WHERE YOU WANT TO WIN.
Principal's Office
NEXT, THE METHOD.
HOW WILL YOU MAKE USE OF LOOP-HOLES?
AND HOW YOU WILL UTILIZE YOUR PAWNS?
THESE ARE THE QUALI-TIES OF A LEAD-ER.
YOU WILL NEVER BE ABLE TO RISE ABOVE ME WITHOUT THEM...
...ASANO.
FINE...
I'LL SHOW YOU WHAT I'M MADE OF... PRINCIPAL ASANO.

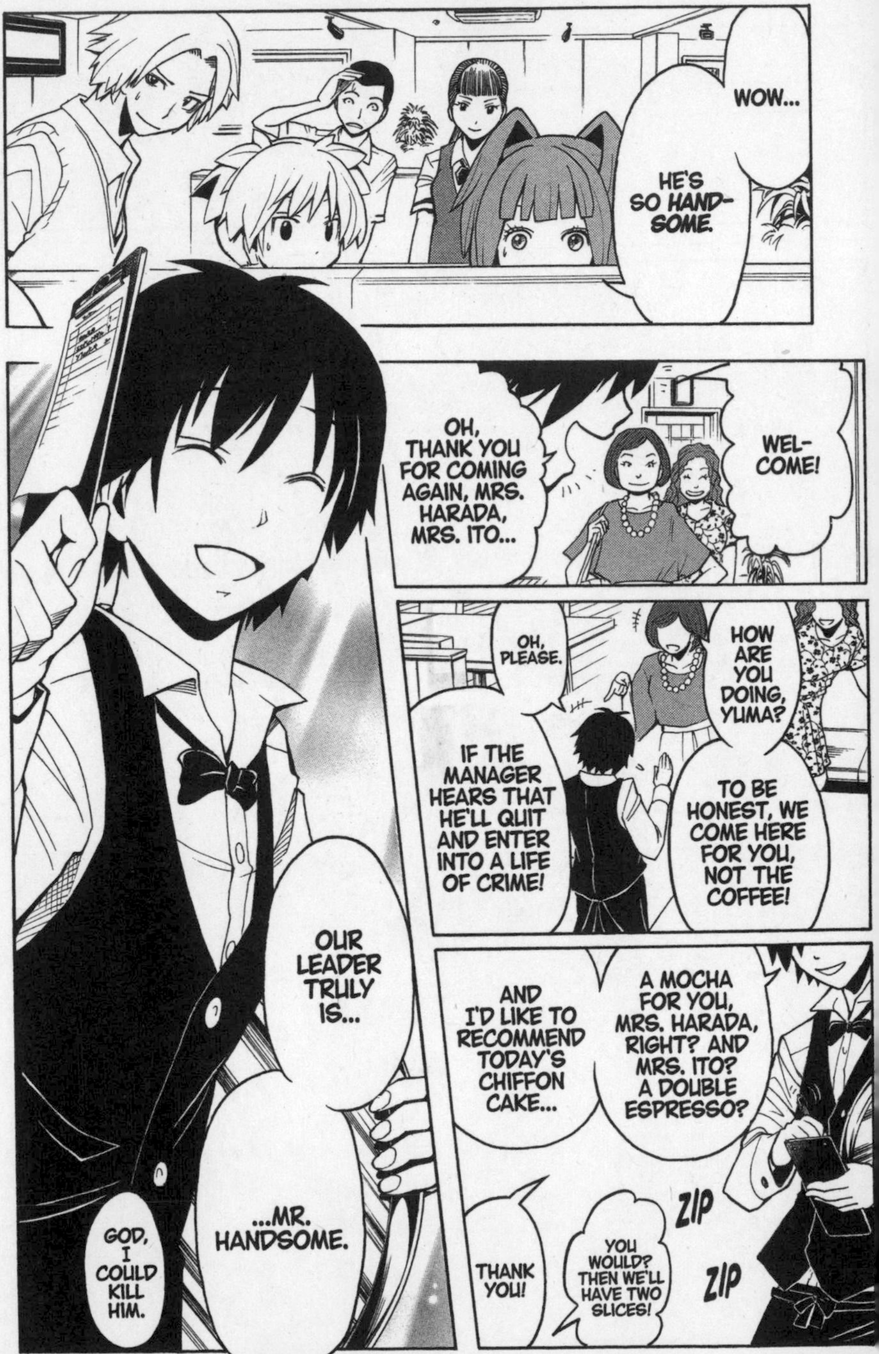
WOW...
HE'S SO HANDSOME.
WELCOME!
OH, THANK YOU FOR COMING AGAIN, MRS. HARADA, MRS. ITO...
HOW ARE YOU DOING, YUMA?
TO BE HONEST, WE COME HERE FOR YOU, NOT THE COFFEE!
OH, PLEASE.
IF THE MANAGER HEARS THAT HE'LL QUIT AND ENTER INTO A LIFE OF CRIME!
A MOCHA FOR YOU, MRS. HARADA, RIGHT? AND MRS. ITO? A DOUBLE ESPRESSO?
AND I'D LIKE TO RECOMMEND TODAY'S CHIFFON CAKE...
ZIP
ZIP
YOU WOULD? THEN WE'LL HAVE TWO SLICES!
THANK YOU!
OUR LEADER TRULY IS...
...MR. HANDSOME.
GOD, I COULD KILL HIM.

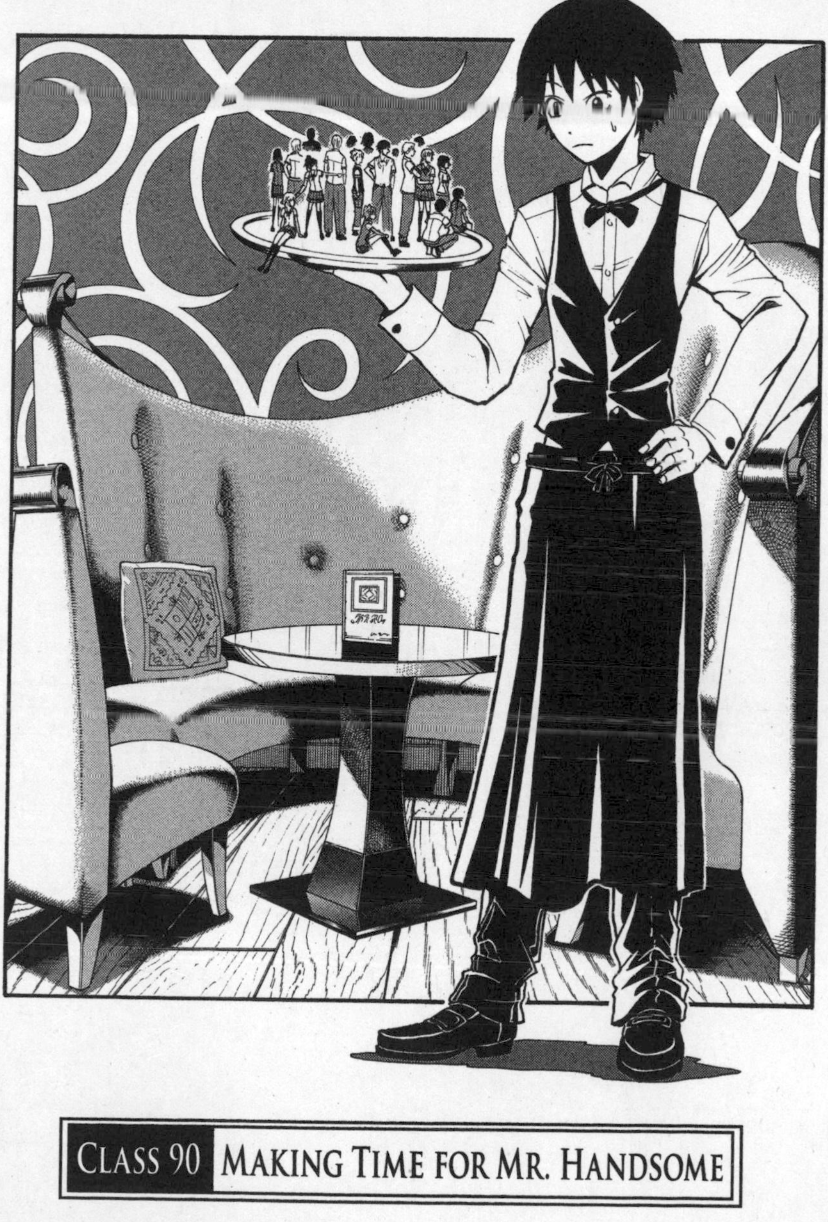

Class 90 Making Time for Mr. Handsome

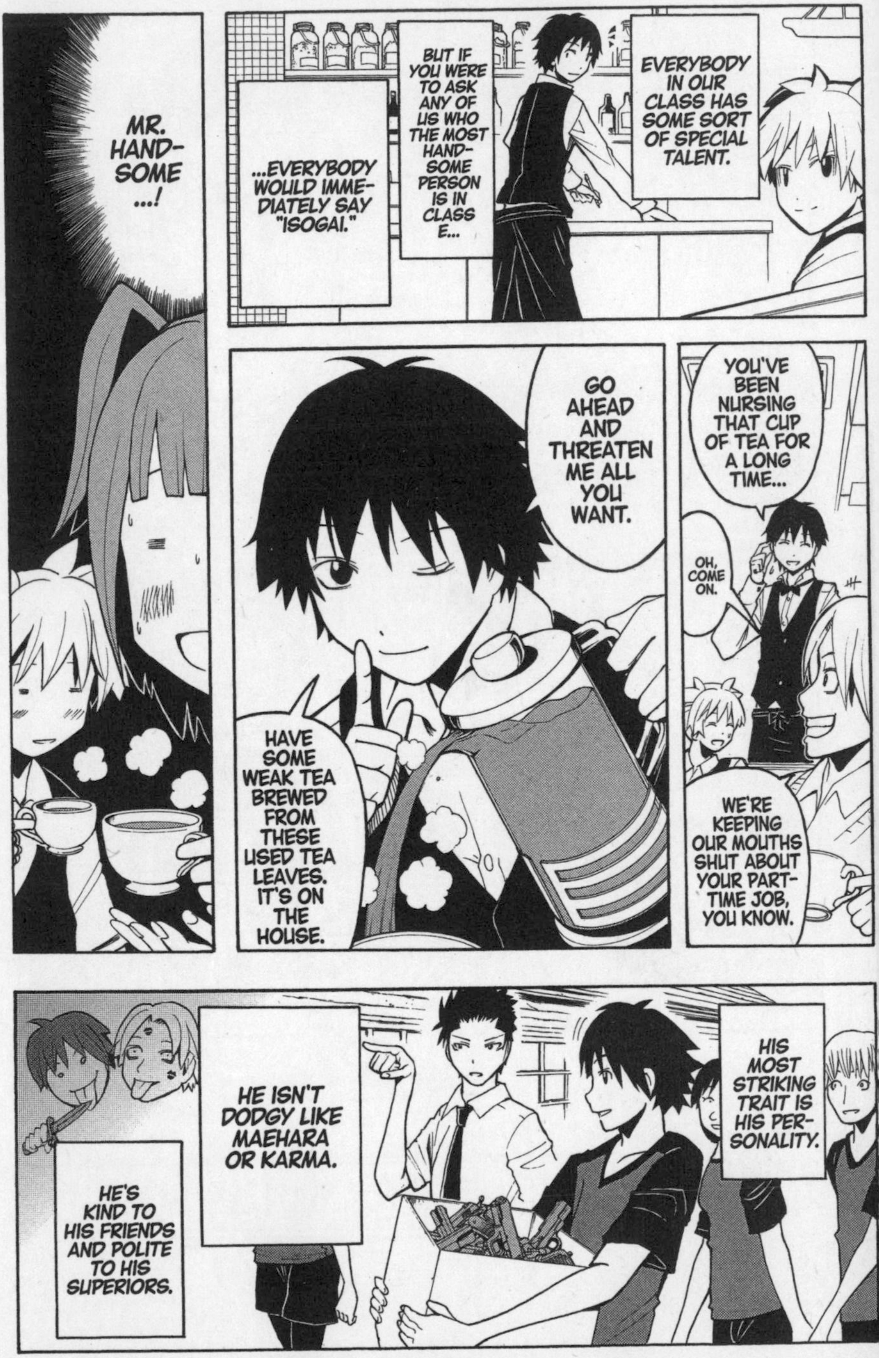
EVERYBODY IN OUR CLASS HAS SOME SORT OF SPECIAL TALENT.
BUT IF YOU WERE TO ASK ANY OF US WHO THE MOST HAND-SOME PERSON IS IN CLASS E...
...EVERYBODY WOULD IMME-DIATELY SAY "ISOGAI."
YOU'VE BEEN NURSING THAT CUP OF TEA FOR A LONG TIME...
OH, COME ON.
WE'RE KEEPING OUR MOUTHS SHUT ABOUT YOUR PART-TIME JOB, YOU KNOW.
GO AHEAD AND THREATEN ME ALL YOU WANT.
HAVE SOME WEAK TEA BREWED FROM THESE USED TEA LEAVES. IT'S ON THE HOUSE.
MR. HAND-SOME ...!
HIS MOST STRIKING TRAIT IS HIS PER-SONALITY.
HE ISN'T DODGY LIKE MAEHARA OR KARMA.
HE'S KIND TO HIS FRIENDS AND POLITE TO HIS SUPERIORS.

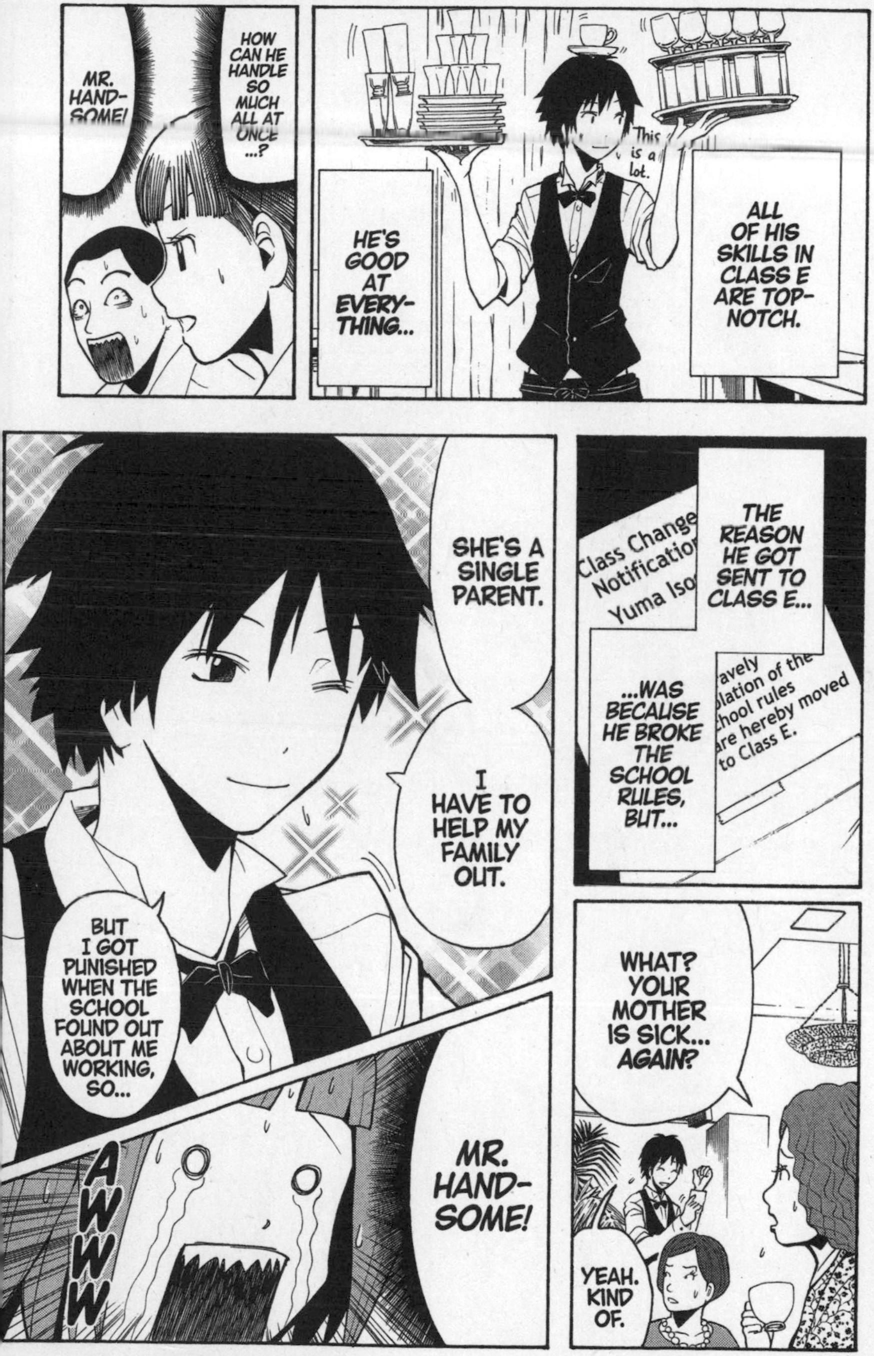
This is a lot.
ALL OF HIS SKILLS IN CLASS E ARE TOP-NOTCH.
HE'S GOOD AT EVERYTHING...
HOW CAN HE HANDLE SO MUCH ALL AT ONCE ...?
MR. HANDSOME!
THE REASON HE GOT SENT TO CLASS E...
Class Change Notification
Yuma Iso
...WAS BECAUSE HE BROKE THE SCHOOL RULES, BUT...
ravely
olation of the
chool rules
are hereby moved
to Class E.
WHAT? YOUR MOTHER IS SICK... AGAIN?
YEAH. KIND OF.
SHE'S A SINGLE PARENT.
I HAVE TO HELP MY FAMILY OUT.
BUT I GOT PUNISHED WHEN THE SCHOOL FOUND OUT ABOUT ME WORKING, SO...
MR. HANDSOME!
AWWW

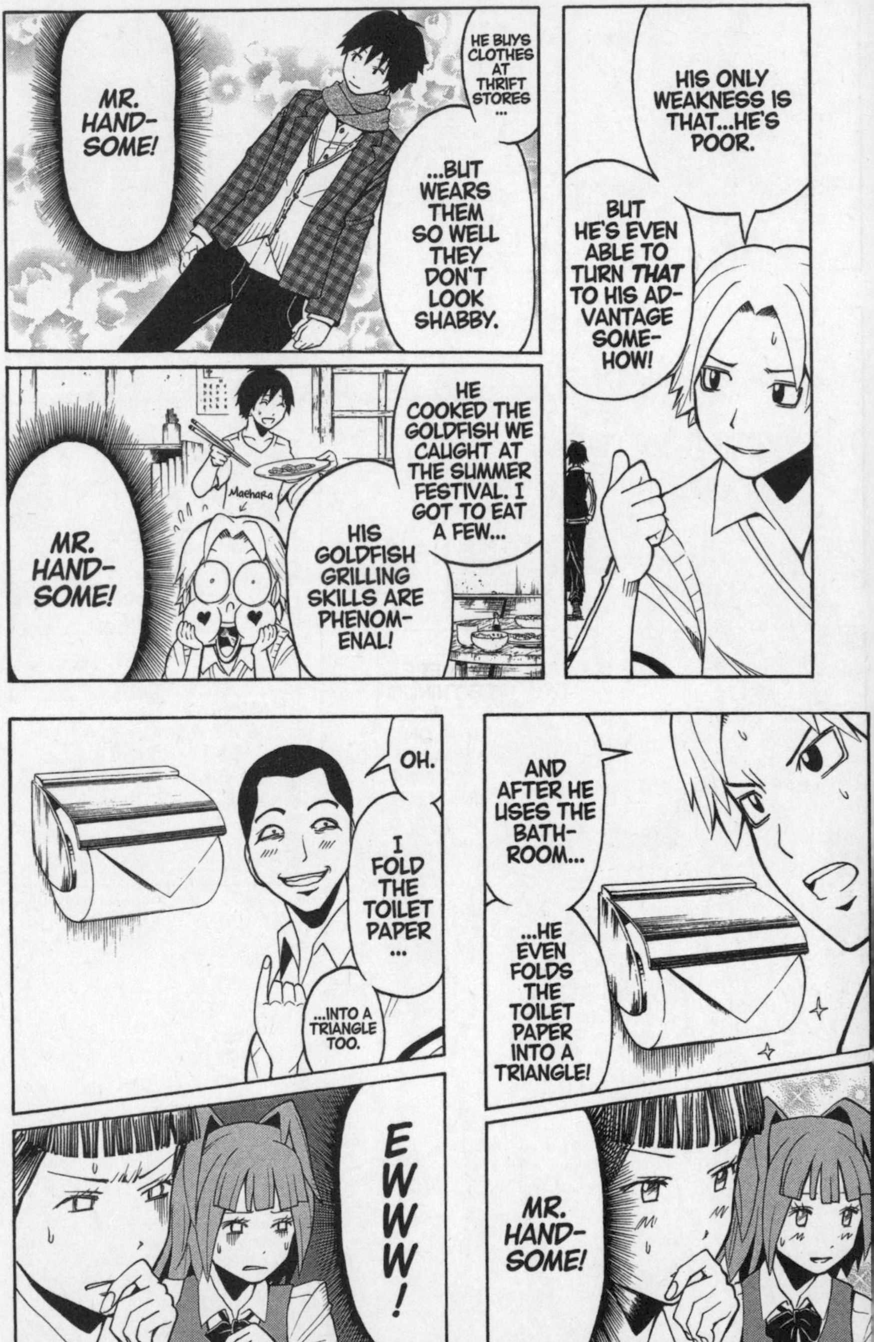
HIS ONLY WEAKNESS IS THAT...HE'S POOR.
BUT HE'S EVEN ABLE TO TURN *THAT* TO HIS ADVANTAGE SOMEHOW!
HE BUYS CLOTHES AT THRIFT STORES...
...BUT WEARS THEM SO WELL THEY DON'T LOOK SHABBY.
MR. HANDSOME!
HE COOKED THE GOLDFISH WE CAUGHT AT THE SUMMER FESTIVAL. I GOT TO EAT A FEW...
HIS GOLDFISH GRILLING SKILLS ARE PHENOMENAL!
Maehara
MR. HANDSOME!
AND AFTER HE USES THE BATHROOM...
...HE EVEN FOLDS THE TOILET PAPER INTO A TRIANGLE!
OH.
I FOLD THE TOILET PAPER...
...INTO A TRIANGLE TOO.
MR. HANDSOME!
EWWW!

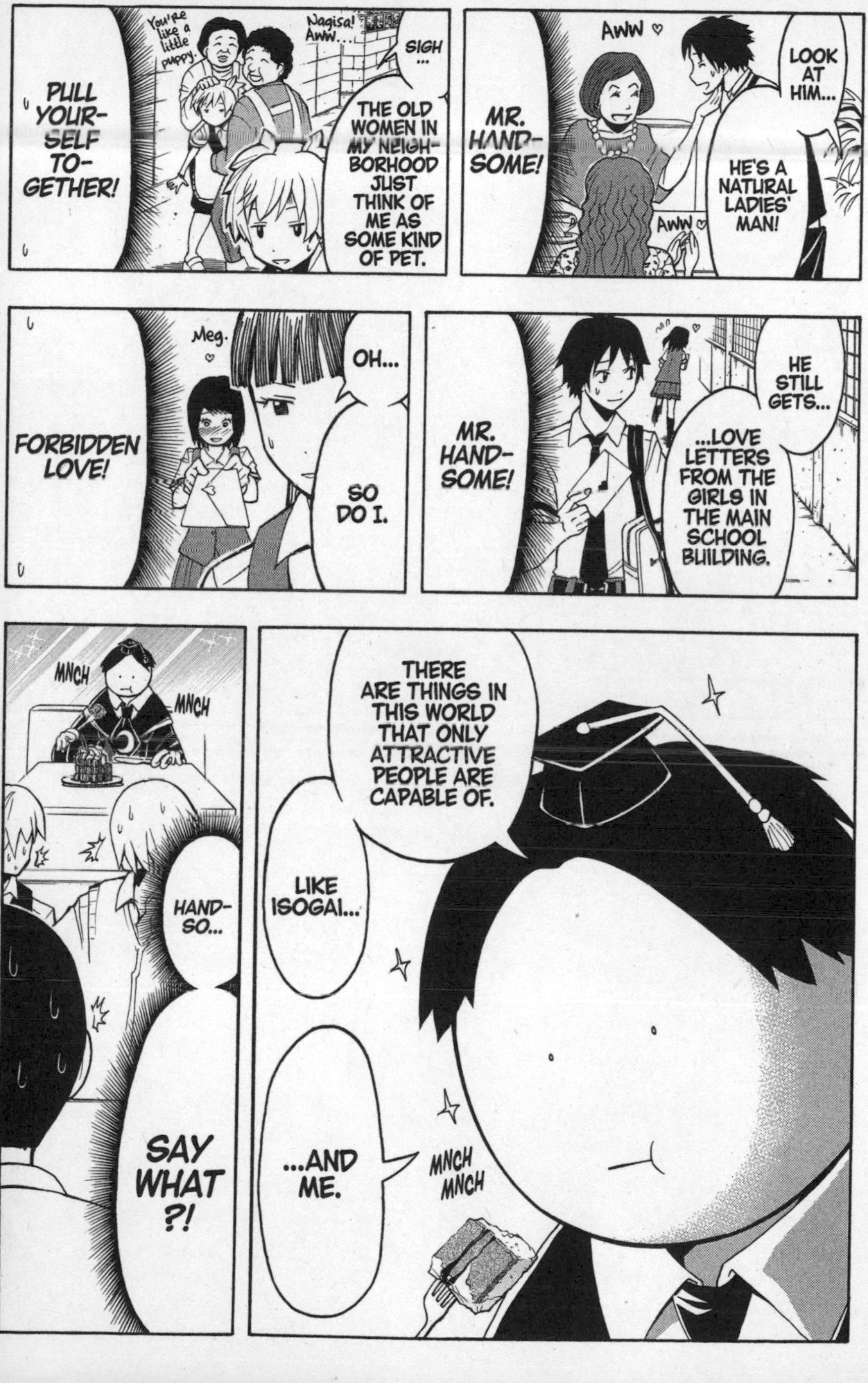
LOOK AT HIM...
AWW
HE'S A NATURAL LADIES' MAN!
AWW
MR. HANDSOME!
Nagisa! Aww...
You're like a little puppy.
SIGH...
THE OLD WOMEN IN MY NEIGHBORHOOD JUST THINK OF ME AS SOME KIND OF PET.
PULL YOURSELF TOGETHER!
HE STILL GETS...
...LOVE LETTERS FROM THE GIRLS IN THE MAIN SCHOOL BUILDING.
MR. HANDSOME!
OH...
SO DO I.
Meg.
FORBIDDEN LOVE!
THERE ARE THINGS IN THIS WORLD THAT ONLY ATTRACTIVE PEOPLE ARE CAPABLE OF.
LIKE ISOGAI...
...AND ME.
MNCH MNCH
MNCH
MNCH
HANDSO...
SAY WHAT?!

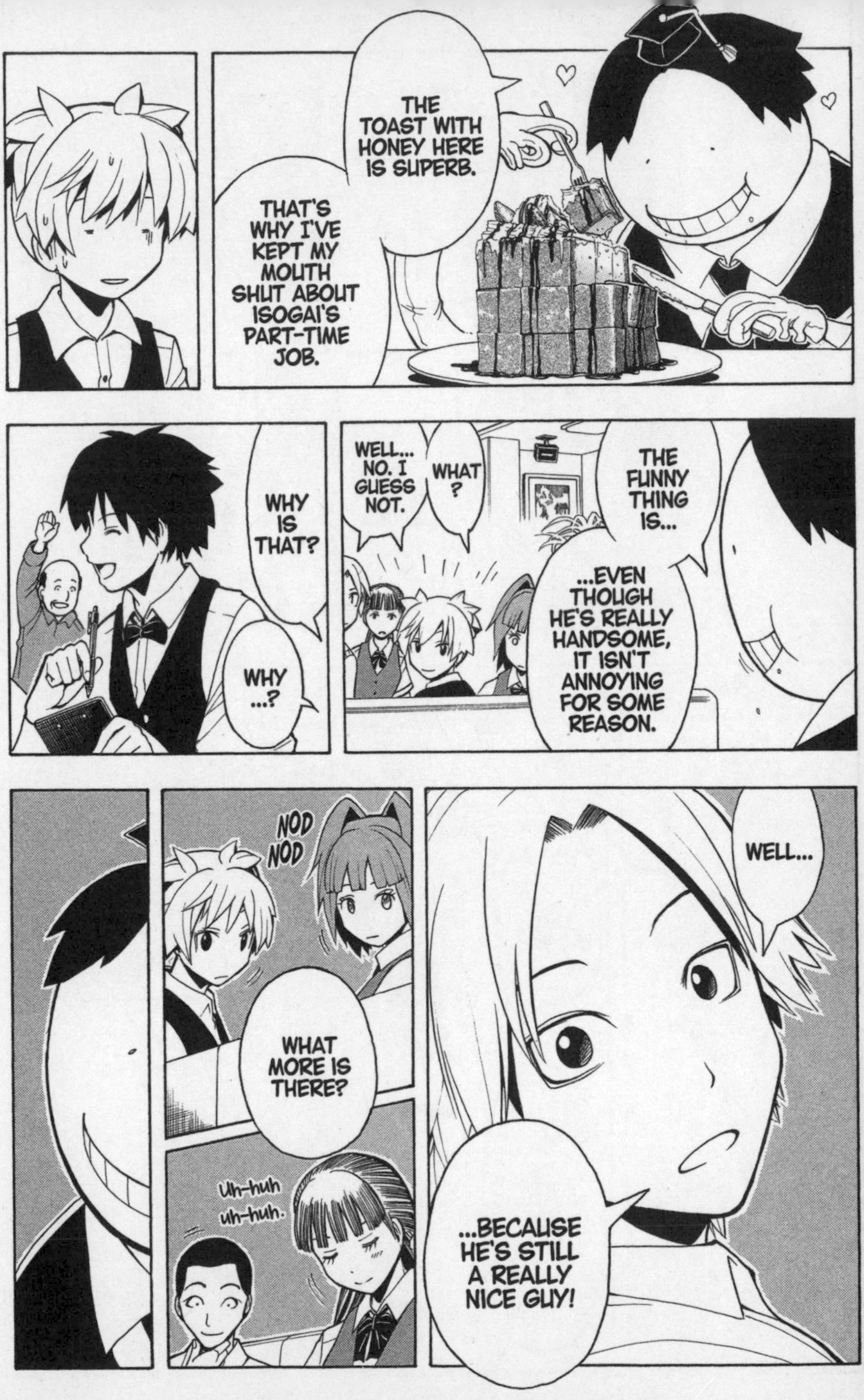
THE TOAST WITH HONEY HERE IS SUPERB.
THAT'S WHY I'VE KEPT MY MOUTH SHUT ABOUT ISOGAI'S PART-TIME JOB.
THE FUNNY THING IS...
...EVEN THOUGH HE'S REALLY HANDSOME, IT ISN'T ANNOYING FOR SOME REASON.
WHAT?
WELL... NO. I GUESS NOT.
WHY IS THAT?
WHY...?
WELL...
...BECAUSE HE'S STILL A REALLY NICE GUY!
NOD NOD
WHAT MORE IS THERE?
Uh-huh uh-huh.

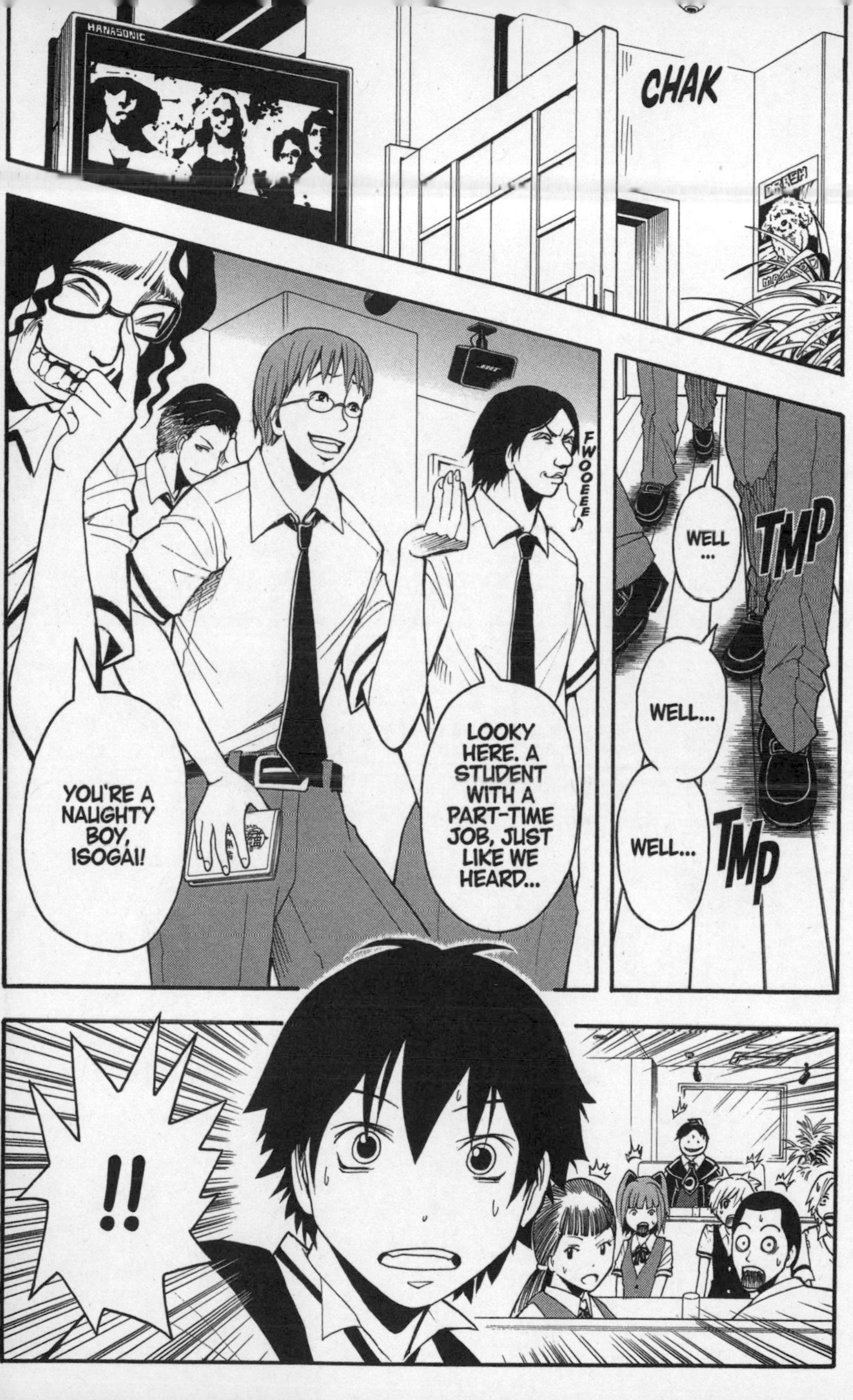
CHAK
WELL ...
TMP
WELL...
WELL...
TMP
FWOOEEE
LOOKY HERE. A STUDENT WITH A PART-TIME JOB, JUST LIKE WE HEARD...
YOU'RE A NAUGHTY BOY, ISOGAI!
!!

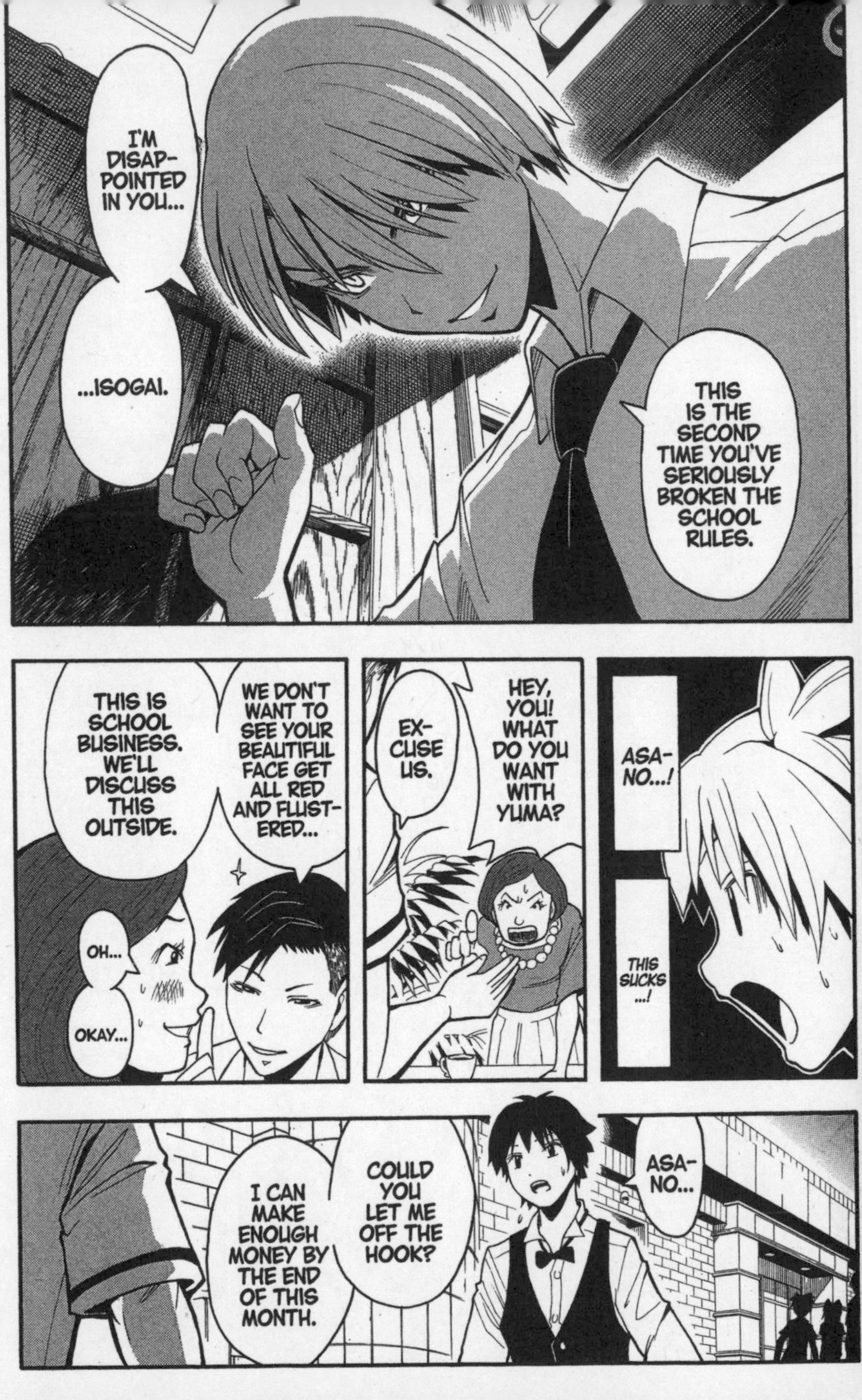
I'M DISAPPOINTED IN YOU...
...ISOGAI.
THIS IS THE SECOND TIME YOU'VE SERIOUSLY BROKEN THE SCHOOL RULES.
ASA-NO...!
THIS SUCKS...!
HEY, YOU! WHAT DO YOU WANT WITH YUMA?
EX-CUSE US.
WE DON'T WANT TO SEE YOUR BEAUTIFUL FACE GET ALL RED AND FLUSTERED...
THIS IS SCHOOL BUSINESS. WE'LL DISCUSS THIS OUTSIDE.
OH...
OKAY...
ASA-NO...
COULD YOU LET ME OFF THE HOOK?
I CAN MAKE ENOUGH MONEY BY THE END OF THIS MONTH.

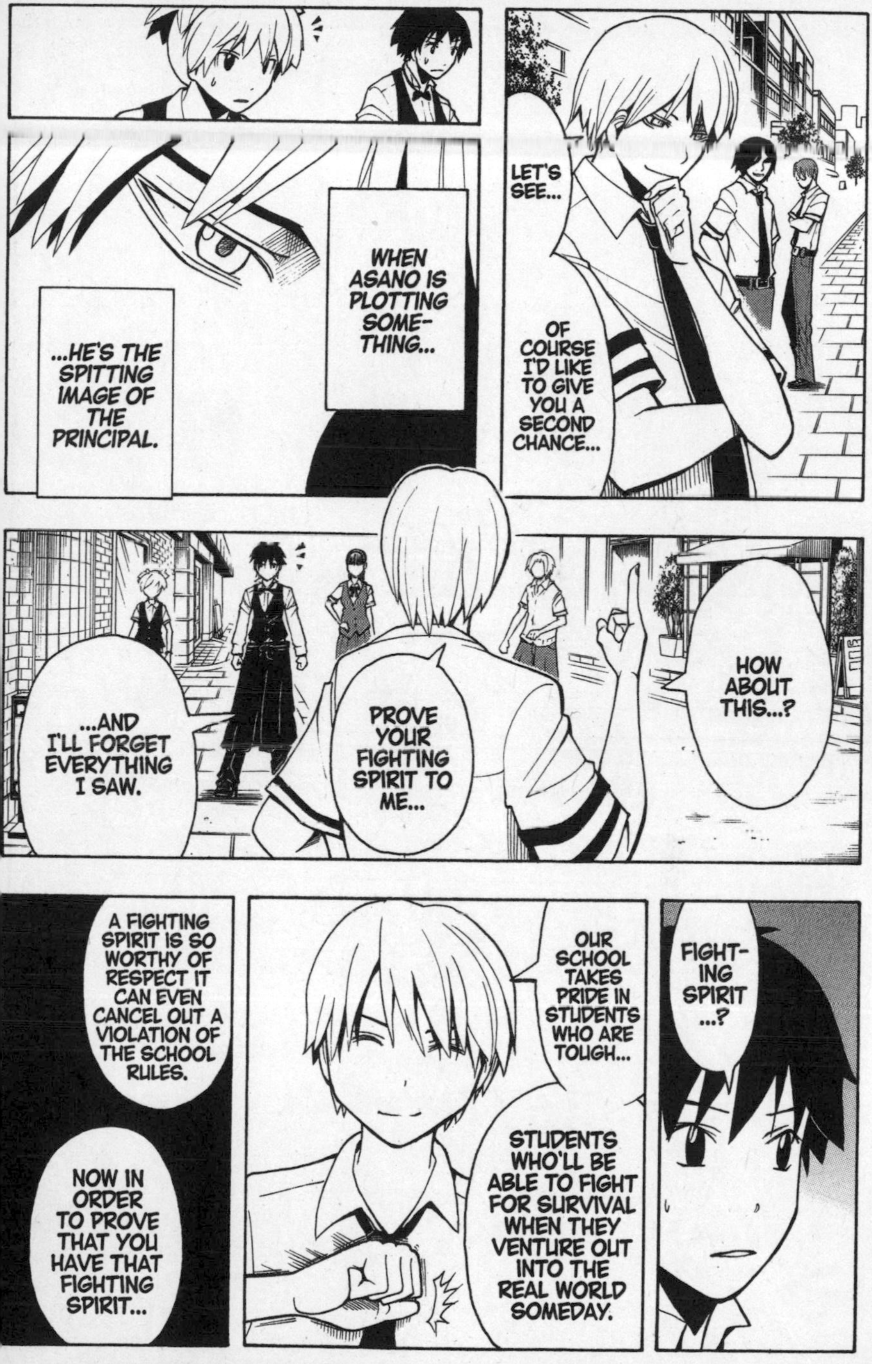
LET'S SEE...
OF COURSE I'D LIKE TO GIVE YOU A SECOND CHANCE...
WHEN ASANO IS PLOTTING SOME-THING...
...HE'S THE SPITTING IMAGE OF THE PRINCIPAL.
HOW ABOUT THIS...?
PROVE YOUR FIGHTING SPIRIT TO ME...
...AND I'LL FORGET EVERYTHING I SAW.
FIGHT-ING SPIRIT ...?
OUR SCHOOL TAKES PRIDE IN STUDENTS WHO ARE TOUGH...
STUDENTS WHO'LL BE ABLE TO FIGHT FOR SURVIVAL WHEN THEY VENTURE OUT INTO THE REAL WORLD SOMEDAY.
A FIGHTING SPIRIT IS SO WORTHY OF RESPECT IT CAN EVEN CANCEL OUT A VIOLATION OF THE SCHOOL RULES.
NOW IN ORDER TO PROVE THAT YOU HAVE THAT FIGHTING SPIRIT...

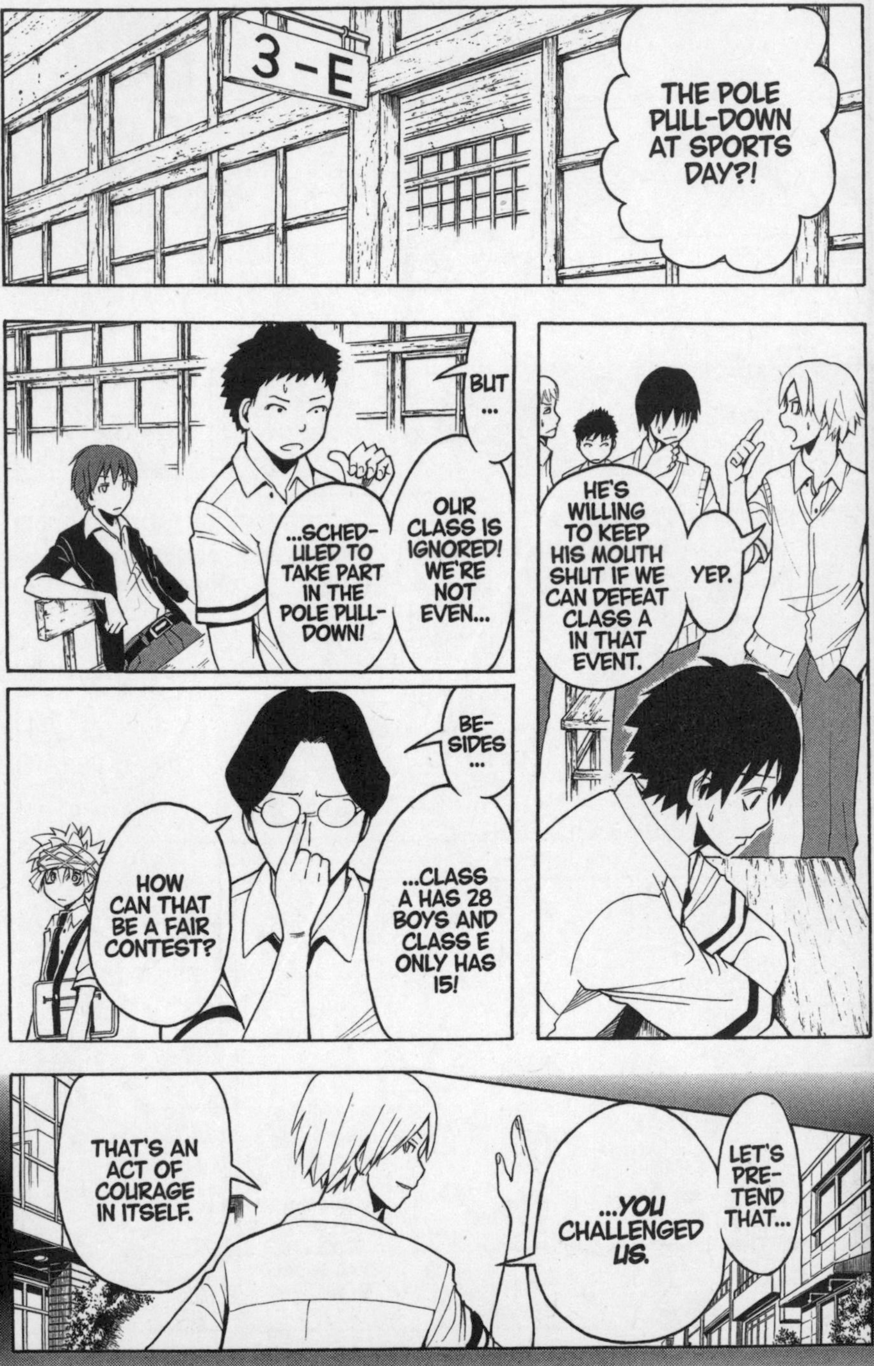
THE POLE PULL-DOWN AT SPORTS DAY?!
YEP.
HE'S WILLING TO KEEP HIS MOUTH SHUT IF WE CAN DEFEAT CLASS A IN THAT EVENT.
BUT...
OUR CLASS IS IGNORED! WE'RE NOT EVEN...
...SCHED-ULED TO TAKE PART IN THE POLE PULL-DOWN!
BE-SIDES...
...CLASS A HAS 28 BOYS AND CLASS E ONLY HAS 15!
HOW CAN THAT BE A FAIR CONTEST?
LET'S PRE-TEND THAT...
...*YOU* CHALLENGED US.
THAT'S AN ACT OF COURAGE IN ITSELF.

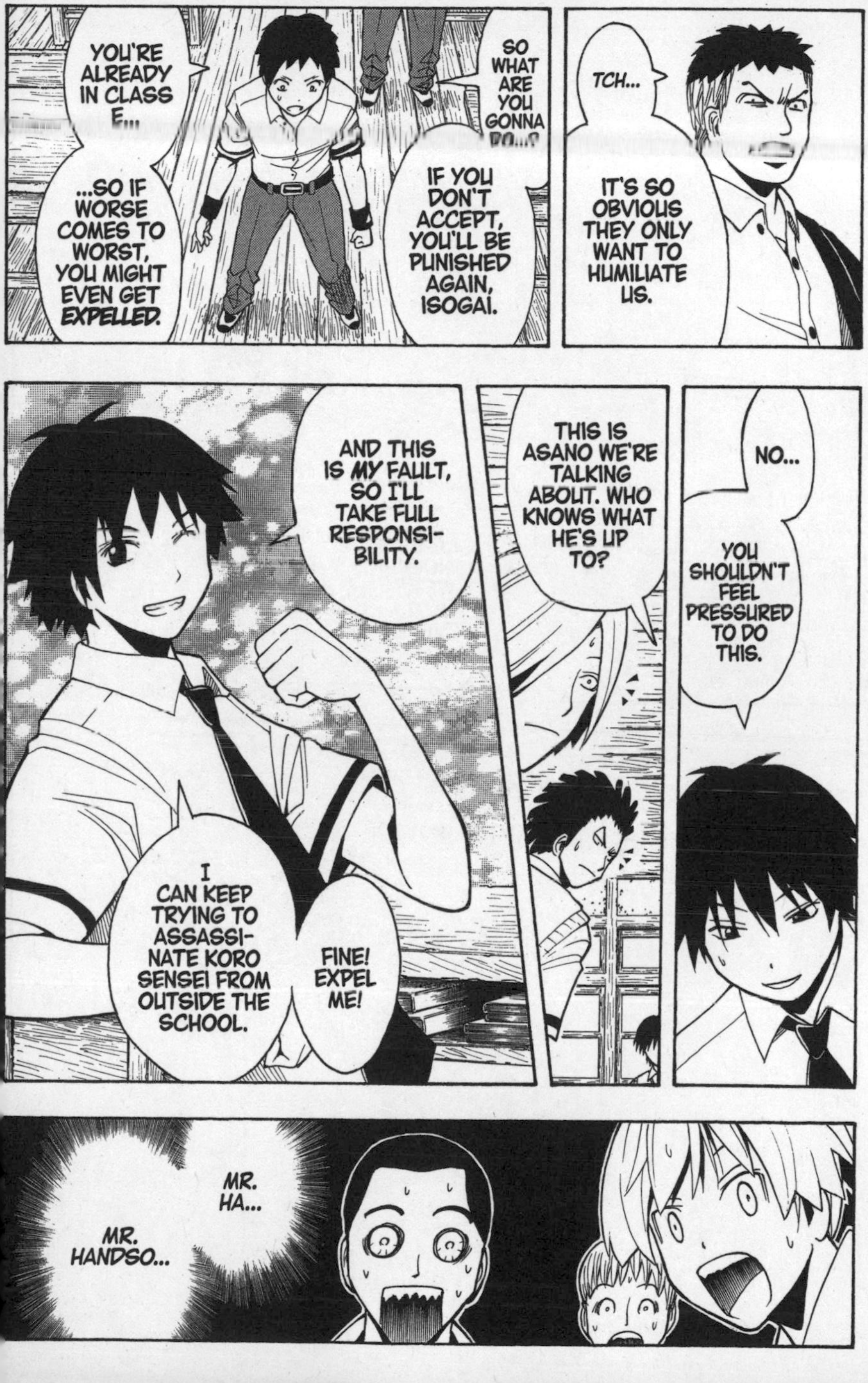
TCH...
IT'S SO OBVIOUS THEY ONLY WANT TO HUMILIATE US.
SO WHAT ARE YOU GONNA DO...?
IF YOU DON'T ACCEPT, YOU'LL BE PUNISHED AGAIN, ISOGAI.
YOU'RE ALREADY IN CLASS E...
...SO IF WORSE COMES TO WORST, YOU MIGHT EVEN GET *EXPELLED*.
NO...
YOU SHOULDN'T FEEL PRESSURED TO DO THIS.
THIS IS ASANO WE'RE TALKING ABOUT. WHO KNOWS WHAT HE'S UP TO?
AND THIS IS *MY* FAULT, SO I'LL TAKE FULL RESPONSI-BILITY.
FINE! EXPEL ME!
I CAN KEEP TRYING TO ASSASSI-NATE KORO SENSEI FROM OUTSIDE THE SCHOOL.
MR. HA...
MR. HANDSO...

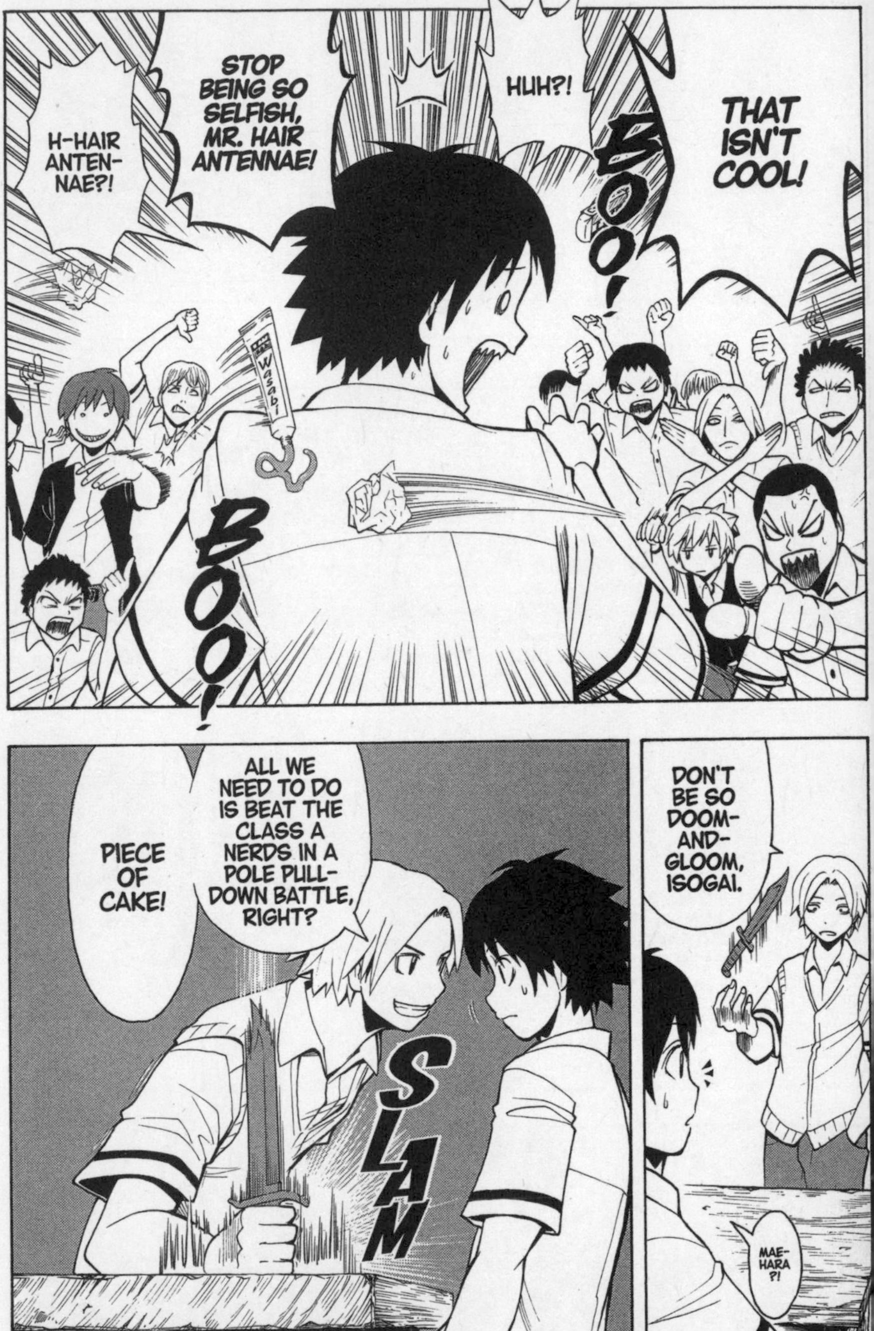
THAT ISN'T COOL!
BOOO!
HUH?!
STOP BEING SO SELFISH, MR. HAIR ANTENNAE!
H-HAIR ANTEN-NAE?!
BOOO!
DON'T BE SO DOOM-AND-GLOOM, ISOGAI.
MAE-HARA?!
ALL WE NEED TO DO IS BEAT THE CLASS A NERDS IN A POLE PULL-DOWN BATTLE, RIGHT?
PIECE OF CAKE!
SLAM

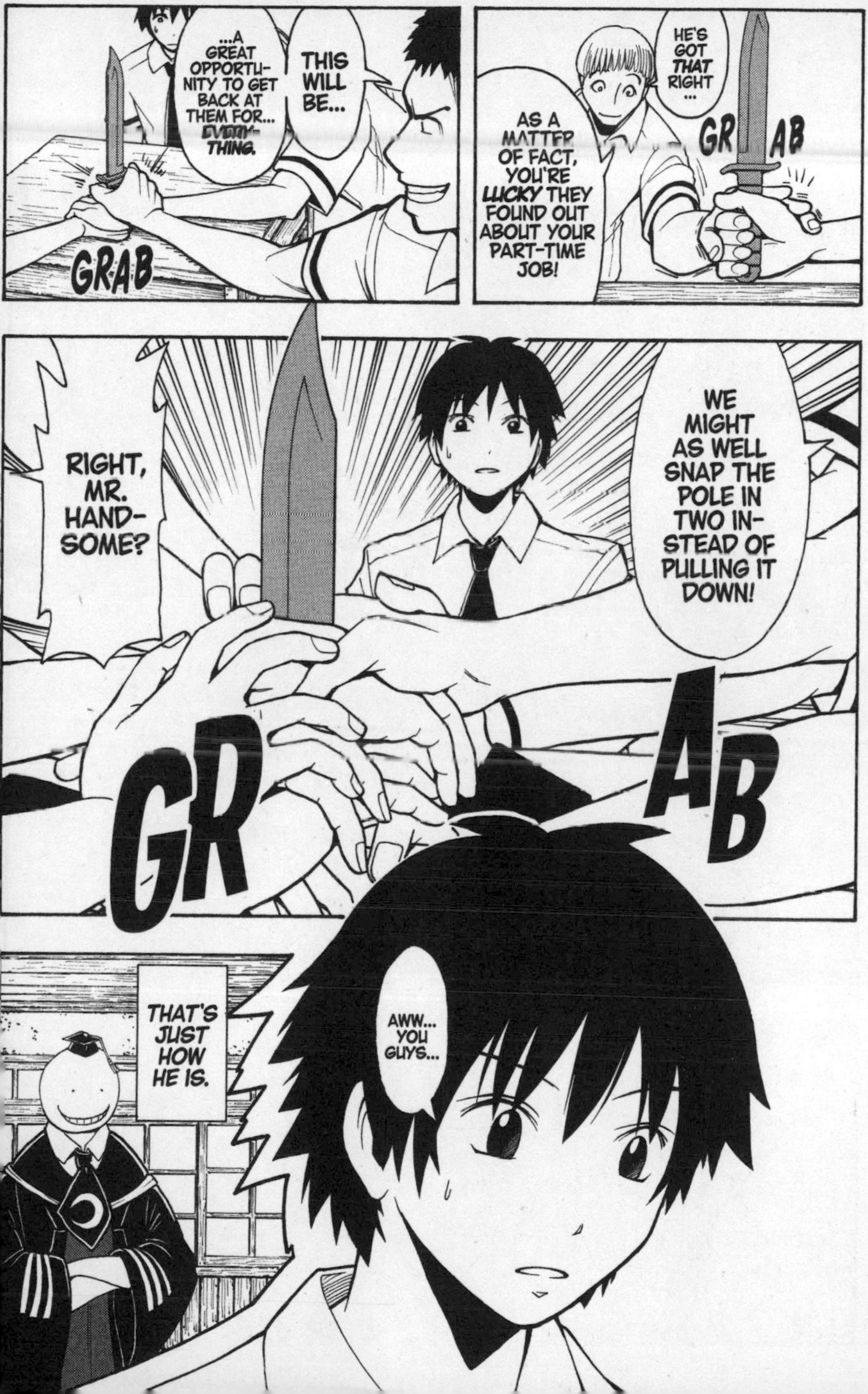
HE'S GOT THAT RIGHT...
AS A MATTER OF FACT, YOU'RE LUCKY THEY FOUND OUT ABOUT YOUR PART-TIME JOB!
GRAB
THIS WILL BE...
...A GREAT OPPORTUNITY TO GET BACK AT THEM FOR... EVERYTHING.
GRAB
WE MIGHT AS WELL SNAP THE POLE IN TWO INSTEAD OF PULLING IT DOWN!
RIGHT, MR. HANDSOME?
GRAB
AWW... YOU GUYS...
THAT'S JUST HOW HE IS.

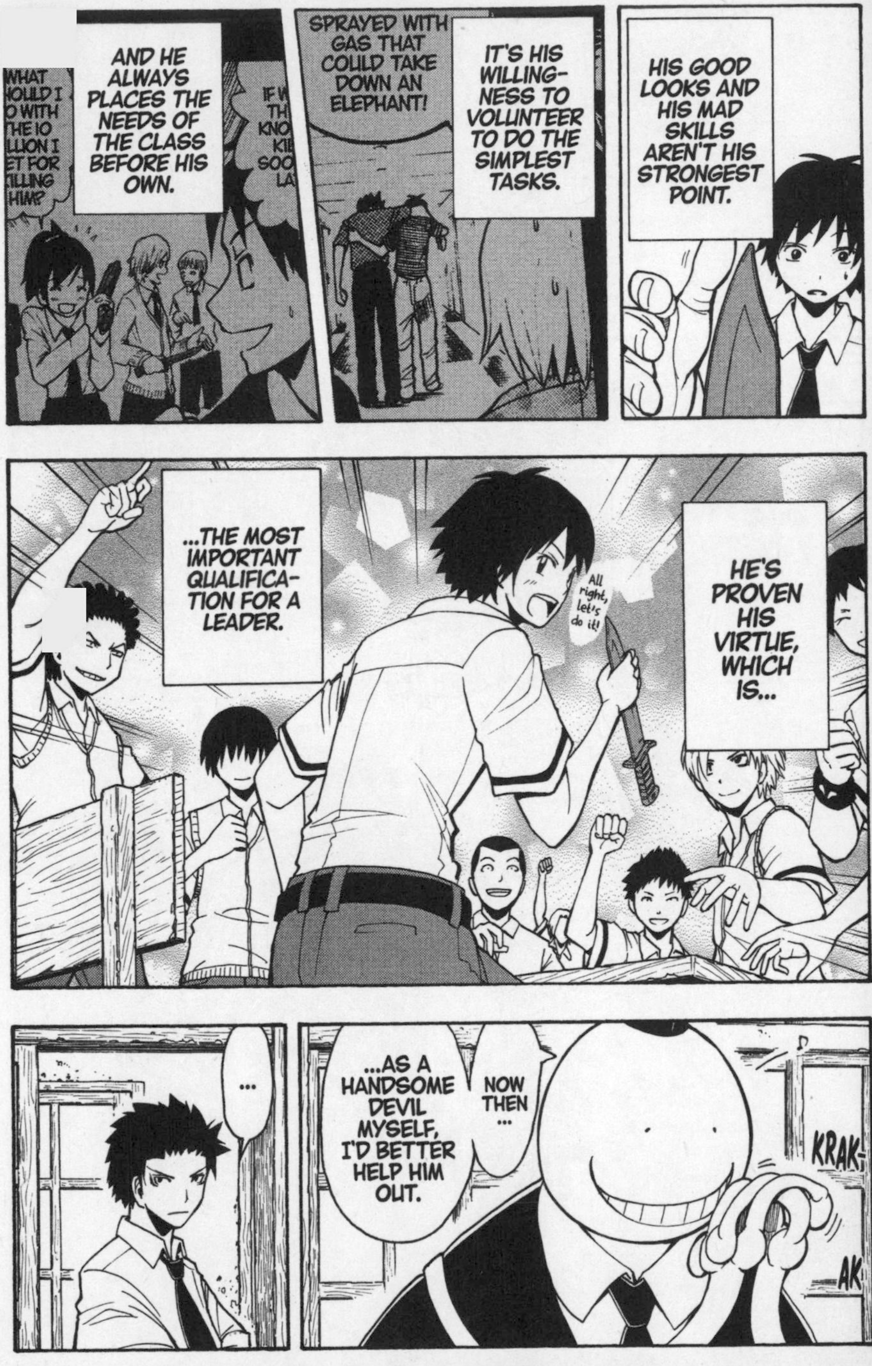
HIS GOOD LOOKS AND HIS MAD SKILLS AREN'T HIS STRONGEST POINT.
IT'S HIS WILLINGNESS TO VOLUNTEER TO DO THE SIMPLEST TASKS.
SPRAYED WITH GAS THAT COULD TAKE DOWN AN ELEPHANT!
AND HE ALWAYS PLACES THE NEEDS OF THE CLASS BEFORE HIS OWN.
HE'S PROVEN HIS VIRTUE, WHICH IS...
All right, let's do it!
...THE MOST IMPORTANT QUALIFICATION FOR A LEADER.
NOW THEN ...
...AS A HANDSOME DEVIL MYSELF, I'D BETTER HELP HIM OUT.
KRAK-
AK
...

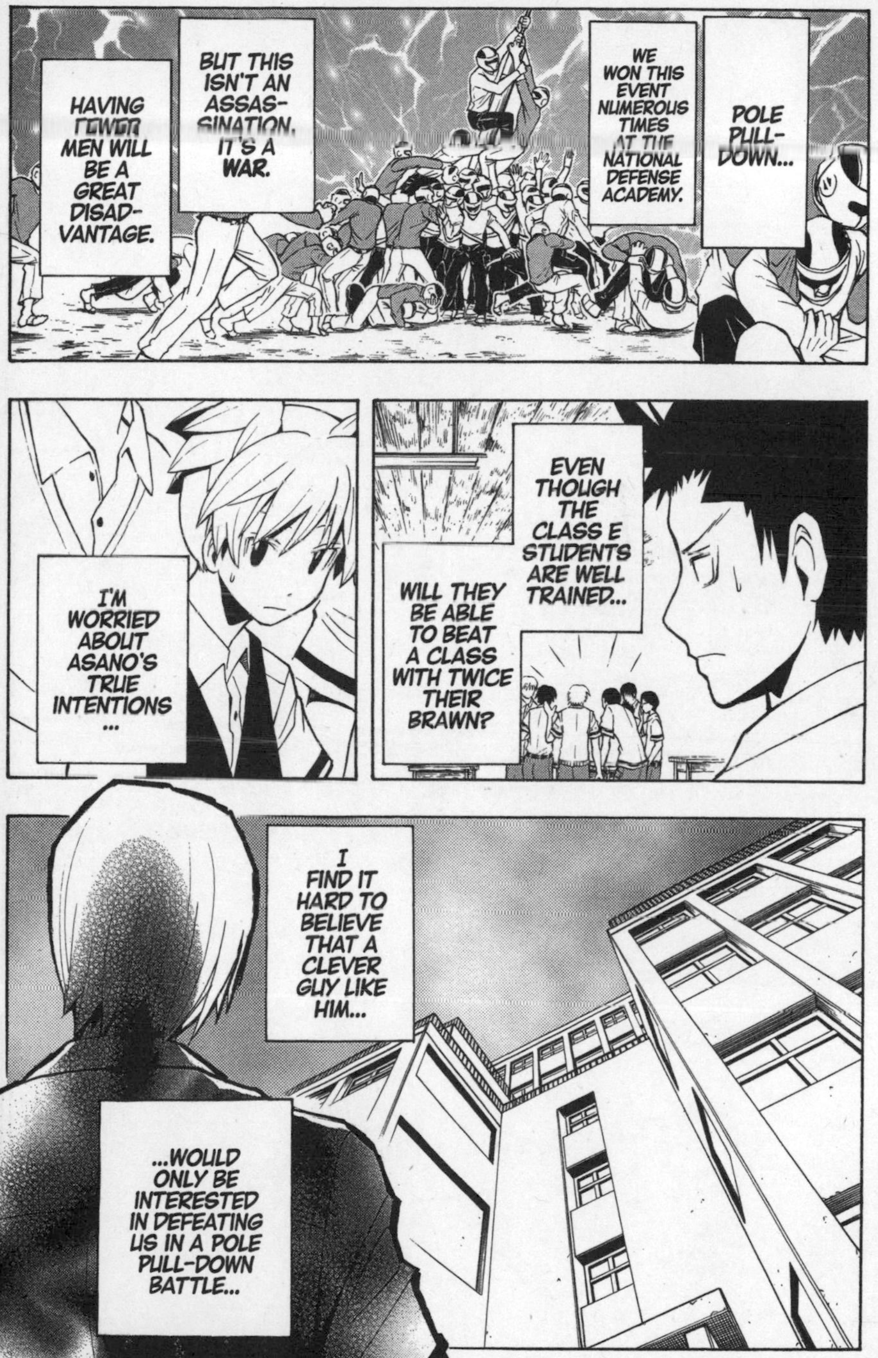
POLE PULL-DOWN...
WE WON THIS EVENT NUMEROUS TIMES AT THE NATIONAL DEFENSE ACADEMY.
BUT THIS ISN'T AN ASSASSINATION, IT'S A WAR.
HAVING FEWER MEN WILL BE A GREAT DISADVANTAGE.
EVEN THOUGH THE CLASS E STUDENTS ARE WELL TRAINED...
WILL THEY BE ABLE TO BEAT A CLASS WITH TWICE THEIR BRAWN?
I'M WORRIED ABOUT ASANO'S TRUE INTENTIONS...
I FIND IT HARD TO BELIEVE THAT A CLEVER GUY LIKE HIM...
...WOULD ONLY BE INTERESTED IN DEFEATING US IN A POLE PULL-DOWN BATTLE...

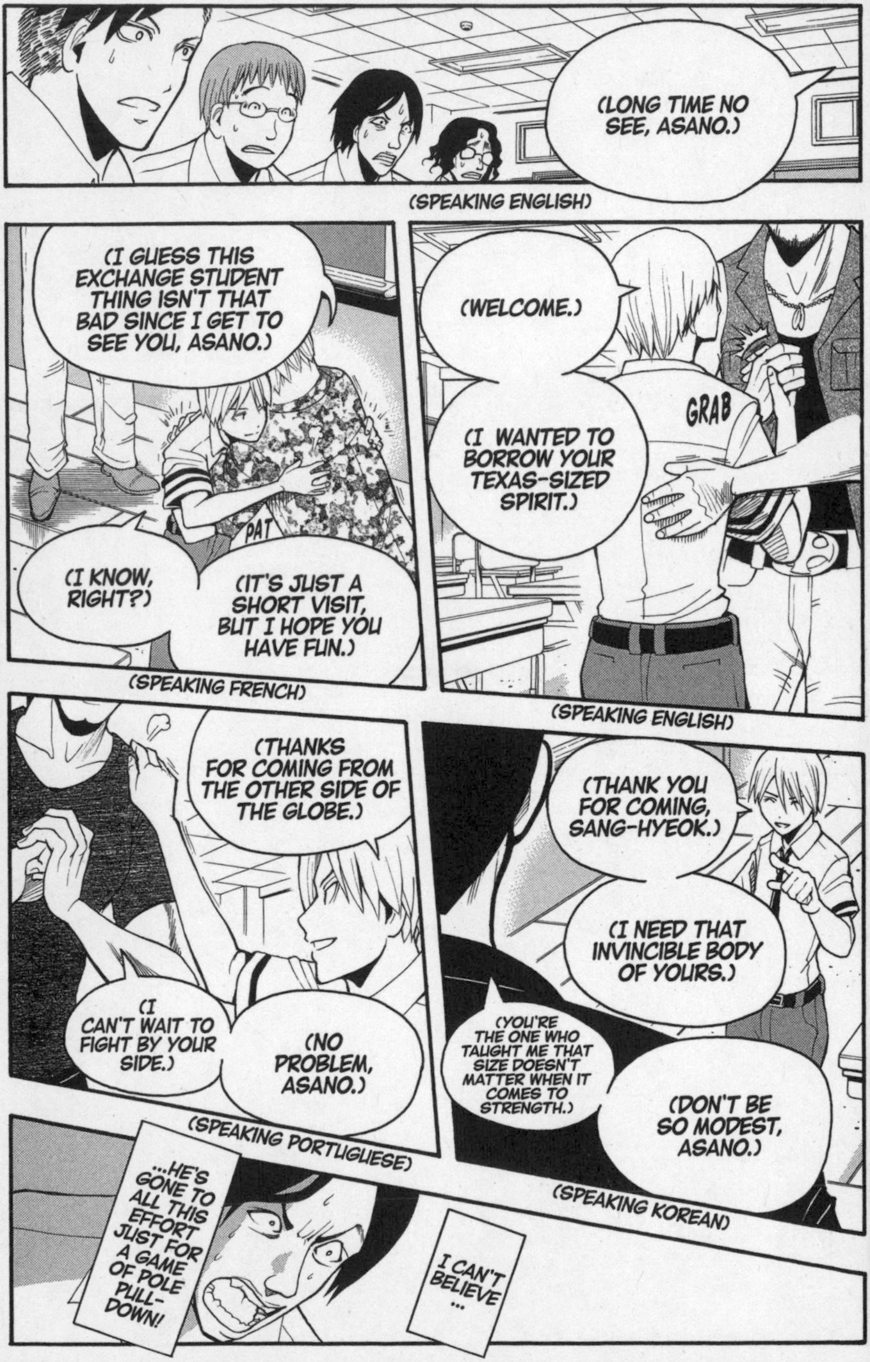
(LONG TIME NO SEE, ASANO.)
(SPEAKING ENGLISH)
(WELCOME.)
GRAB
(I WANTED TO BORROW YOUR TEXAS-SIZED SPIRIT.)
(SPEAKING ENGLISH)
(I GUESS THIS EXCHANGE STUDENT THING ISN'T THAT BAD SINCE I GET TO SEE YOU, ASANO.)
PAT
(IT'S JUST A SHORT VISIT, BUT I HOPE YOU HAVE FUN.)
(I KNOW, RIGHT?)
(SPEAKING FRENCH)
(THANK YOU FOR COMING, SANG-HYEOK.)
(I NEED THAT INVINCIBLE BODY OF YOURS.)
(DON'T BE SO MODEST, ASANO.)
(YOU'RE THE ONE WHO TAUGHT ME THAT SIZE DOESN'T MATTER WHEN IT COMES TO STRENGTH.)
(SPEAKING KOREAN)
(THANKS FOR COMING FROM THE OTHER SIDE OF THE GLOBE.)
(NO PROBLEM, ASANO.)
(I CAN'T WAIT TO FIGHT BY YOUR SIDE.)
(SPEAKING PORTUGUESE)
I CAN'T BELIEVE...
...HE'S GONE TO ALL THIS EFFORT JUST FOR A GAME OF POLE PULL-DOWN!

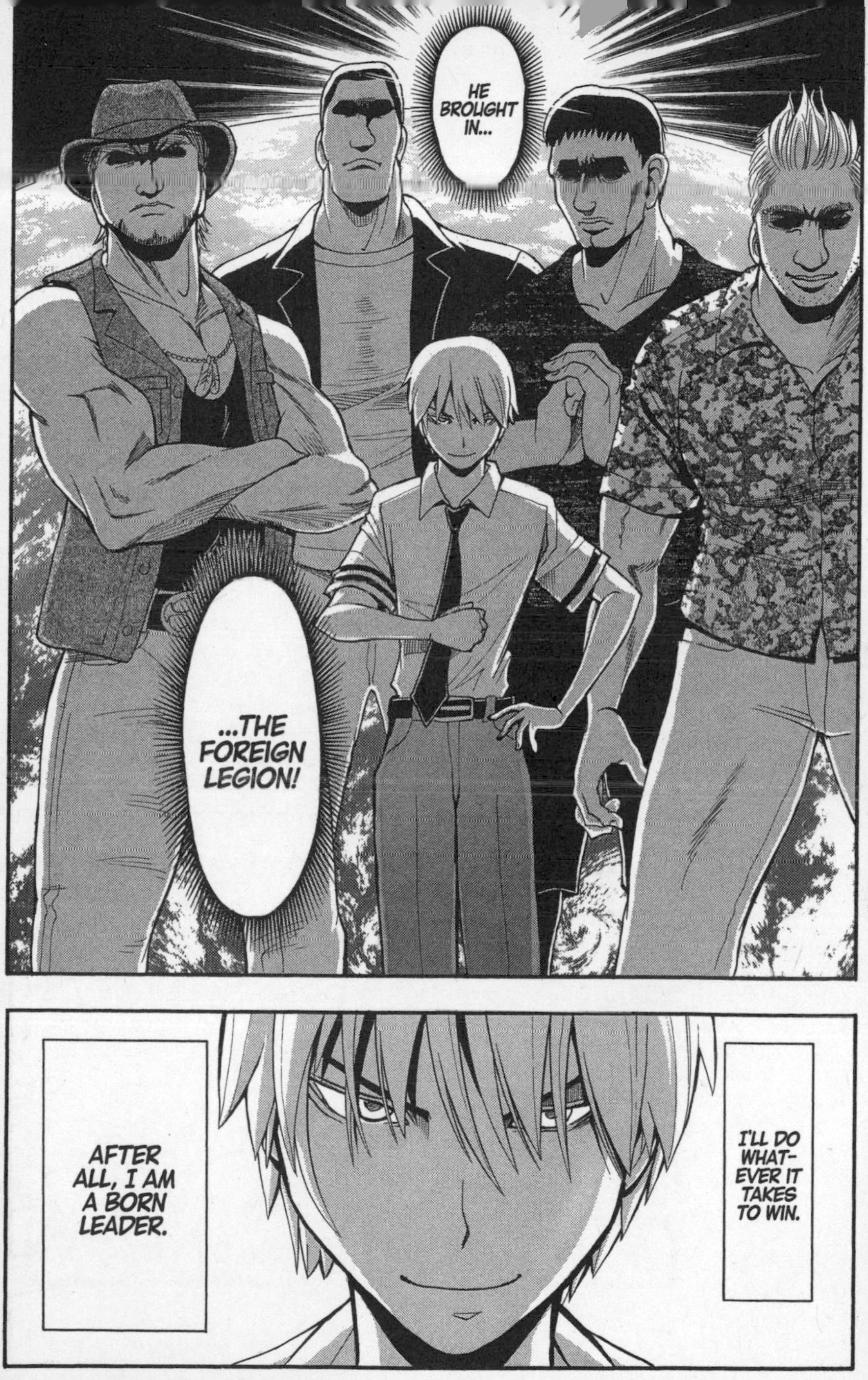
HE BROUGHT IN...
...THE FOREIGN LEGION!
I'LL DO WHAT-EVER IT TAKES TO WIN.
AFTER ALL, I AM A BORN LEADER.

(NEED MY HELP?)
(JUST ONE ZAAAP WITH THIS AND THE WHOLE CLASS WILL VAPORIZE.)
(DON'T...)
(NO ZAAAP-ING...)

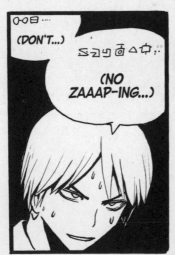

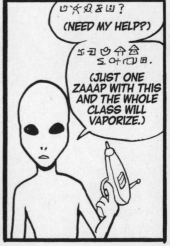

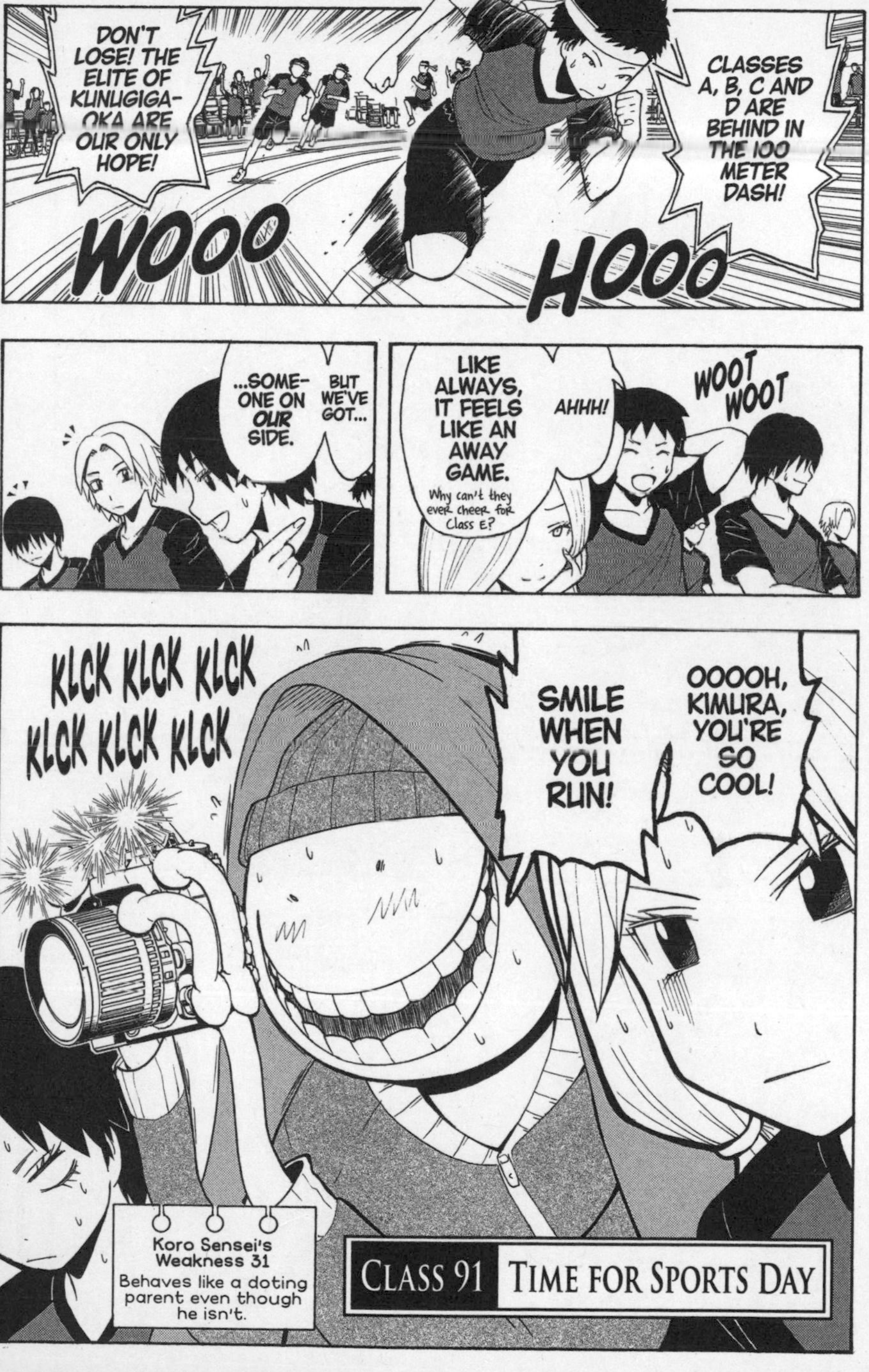
CLASSES A, B, C AND D ARE BEHIND IN THE 100 METER DASH!
HOOO
WOOO
DON'T LOSE! THE ELITE OF KUNUGIGAOKA ARE OUR ONLY HOPE!
WOOT WOOT
AHHH!
LIKE ALWAYS, IT FEELS LIKE AN AWAY GAME.
Why can't they ever cheer for Class E?
BUT WE'VE GOT...
...SOMEONE ON OUR SIDE.
OOOOH, KIMURA, YOU'RE SO COOL!
SMILE WHEN YOU RUN!
KLCK KLCK KLCK KLCK KLCK KLCK
CLASS 91 TIME FOR SPORTS DAY
Koro Sensei's Weakness 31
Behaves like a doting parent even though he isn't.

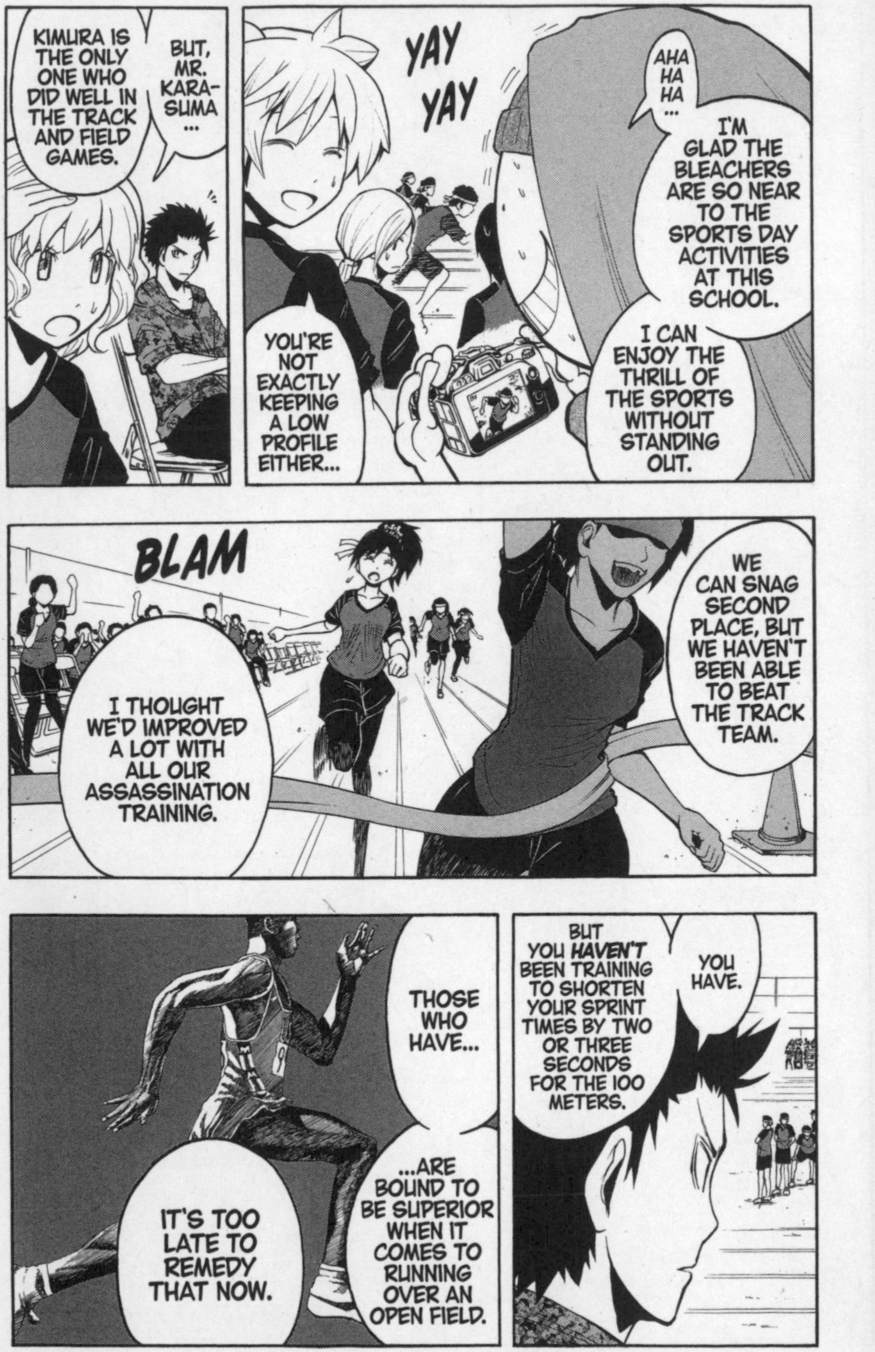
AHA HA HA ...
I'M GLAD THE BLEACHERS ARE SO NEAR TO THE SPORTS DAY ACTIVITIES AT THIS SCHOOL.
I CAN ENJOY THE THRILL OF THE SPORTS WITHOUT STANDING OUT.
YAY YAY
YOU'RE NOT EXACTLY KEEPING A LOW PROFILE EITHER...
BUT, MR. KARASUMA ...
KIMURA IS THE ONLY ONE WHO DID WELL IN THE TRACK AND FIELD GAMES.
WE CAN SNAG SECOND PLACE, BUT WE HAVEN'T BEEN ABLE TO BEAT THE TRACK TEAM.
BLAM
I THOUGHT WE'D IMPROVED A LOT WITH ALL OUR ASSASSINATION TRAINING.
YOU HAVE.
BUT YOU **HAVEN'T** BEEN TRAINING TO SHORTEN YOUR SPRINT TIMES BY TWO OR THREE SECONDS FOR THE 100 METERS.
THOSE WHO HAVE...
...ARE BOUND TO BE SUPERIOR WHEN IT COMES TO RUNNING OVER AN OPEN FIELD.
IT'S TOO LATE TO REMEDY THAT NOW.

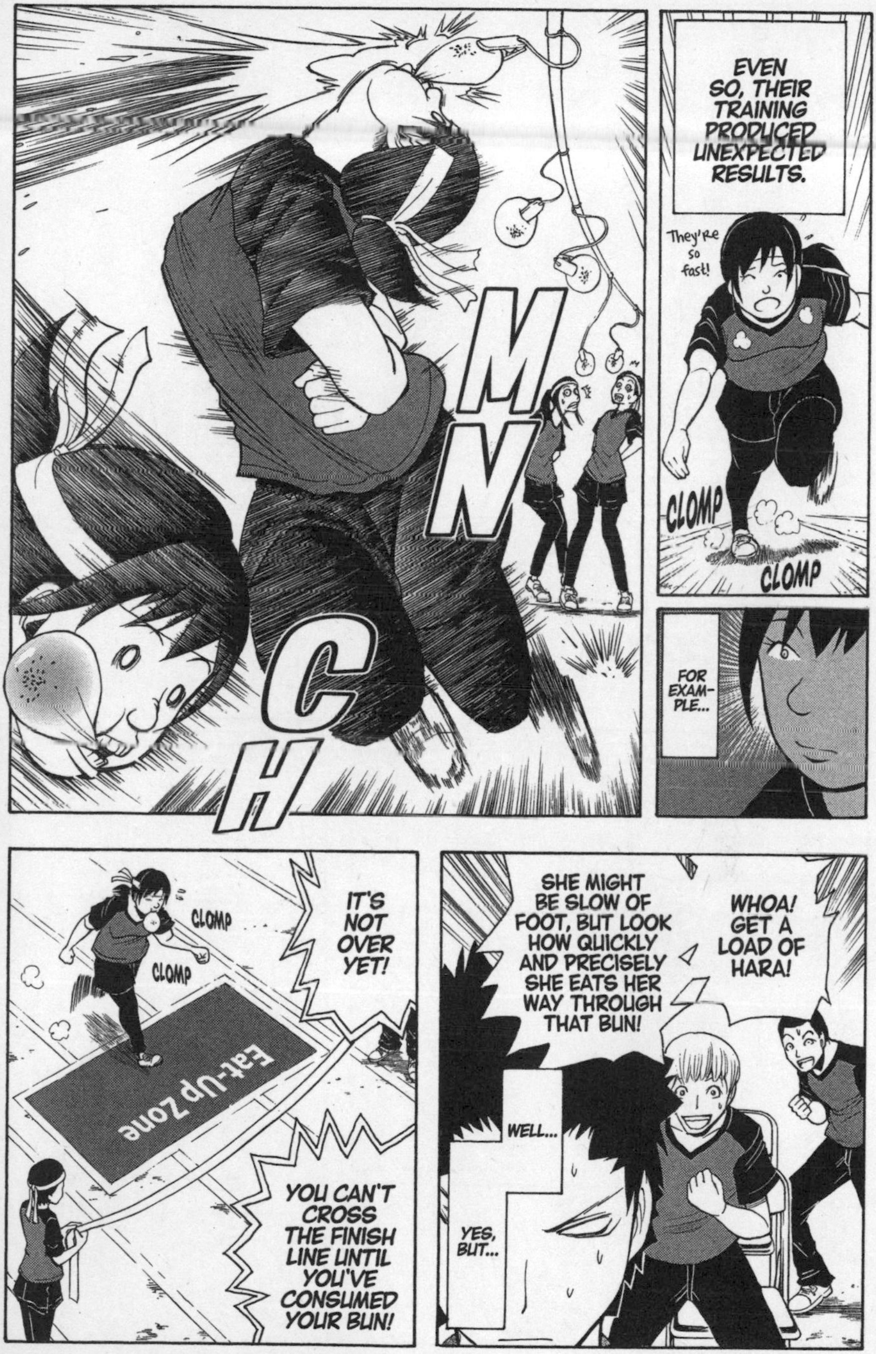
EVEN SO, THEIR TRAINING PRODUCED UNEXPECTED RESULTS.
They're so fast!
CLOMP
CLOMP
FOR EXAMPLE...
MNCH
WHOA! GET A LOAD OF HARA!
SHE MIGHT BE SLOW OF FOOT, BUT LOOK HOW QUICKLY AND PRECISELY SHE EATS HER WAY THROUGH THAT BUN!
WELL...
YES, BUT...
IT'S NOT OVER YET!
CLOMP
CLOMP
Eat-Up Zone
YOU CAN'T CROSS THE FINISH LINE UNTIL YOU'VE CONSUMED YOUR BUN!

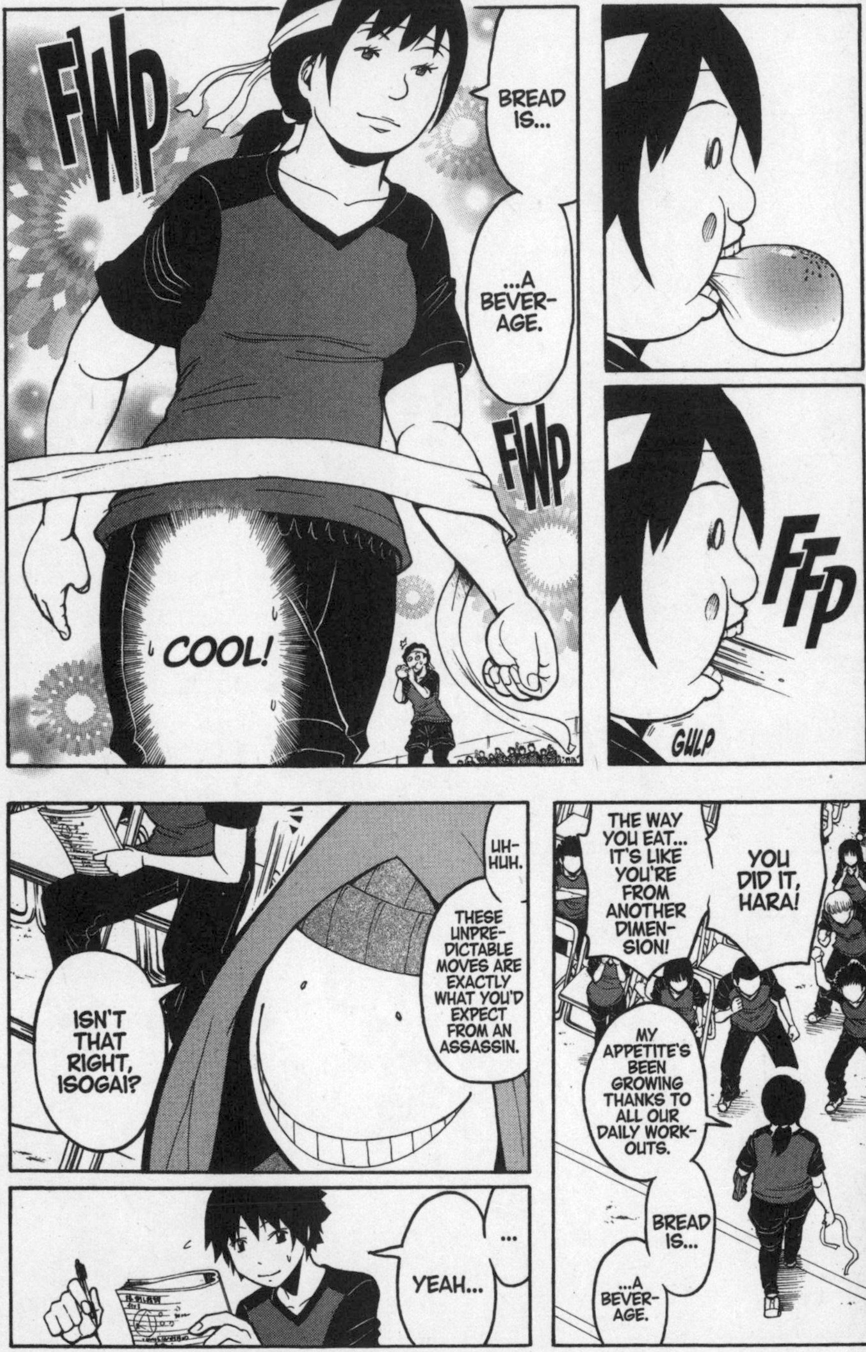
FFP
GULP
BREAD IS...
FWP
...A BEVERAGE.
FWP
COOL!
YOU DID IT, HARA!
THE WAY YOU EAT... IT'S LIKE YOU'RE FROM ANOTHER DIMENSION!
MY APPETITE'S BEEN GROWING THANKS TO ALL OUR DAILY WORKOUTS.
BREAD IS...
...A BEVERAGE.
UH-HUH.
THESE UNPREDICTABLE MOVES ARE EXACTLY WHAT YOU'D EXPECT FROM AN ASSASSIN.
ISN'T THAT RIGHT, ISOGAI?
...
YEAH...

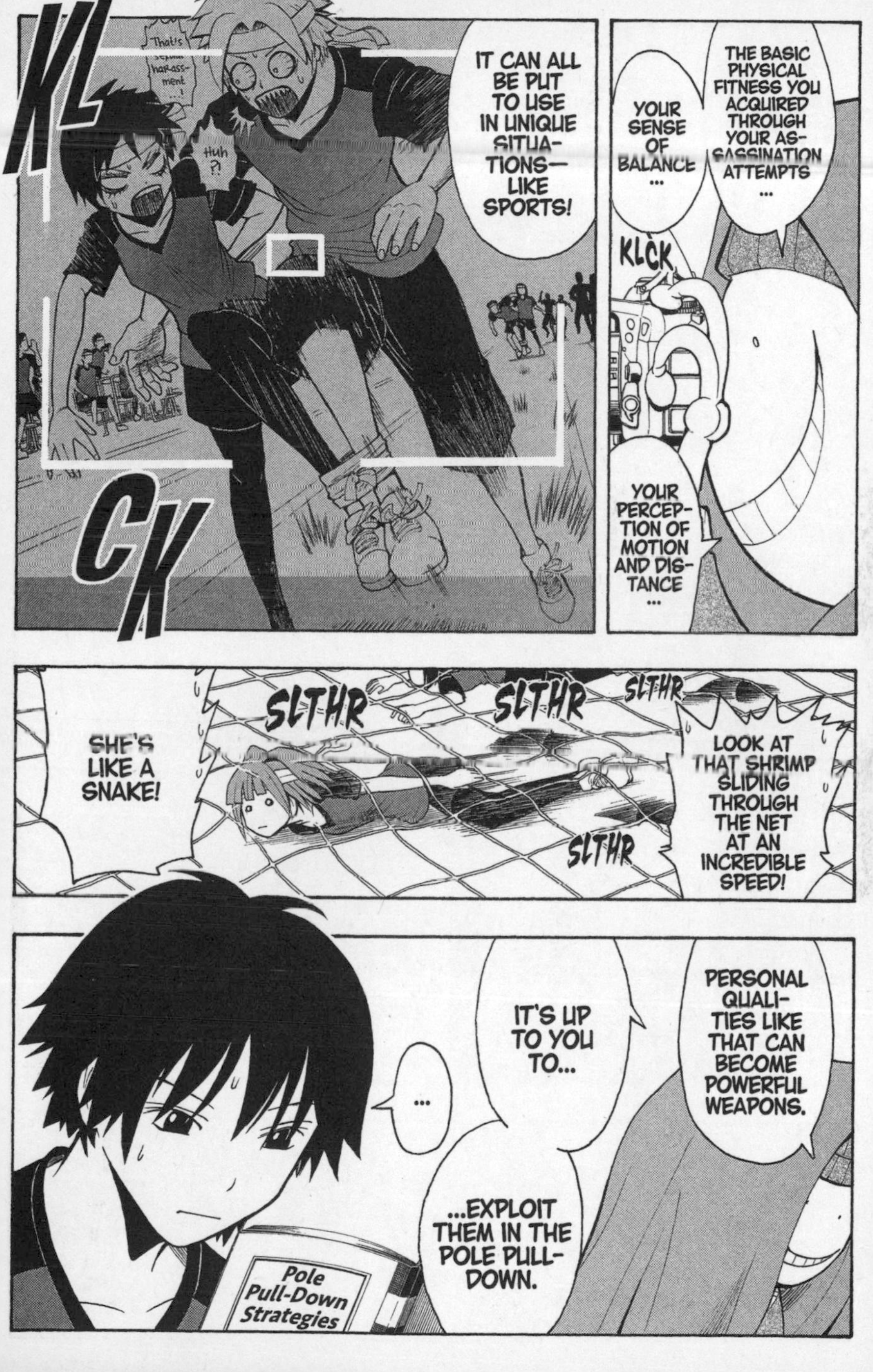
THE BASIC PHYSICAL FITNESS YOU ACQUIRED THROUGH YOUR ASSASSINATION ATTEMPTS...
YOUR SENSE OF BALANCE...
KLCK
YOUR PERCEPTION OF MOTION AND DISTANCE...
IT CAN ALL BE PUT TO USE IN UNIQUE SITUATIONS—LIKE SPORTS!
That's sexual harassment...!
Huh?!
KL
CK
LOOK AT THAT SHRIMP SLIDING THROUGH THE NET AT AN INCREDIBLE SPEED!
SLTHR
SLTHR
SLTHR
SLTHR
SHE'S LIKE A SNAKE!
PERSONAL QUALITIES LIKE THAT CAN BECOME POWERFUL WEAPONS.
IT'S UP TO YOU TO...
...EXPLOIT THEM IN THE POLE PULL-DOWN.
...
Pole Pull-Down Strategies

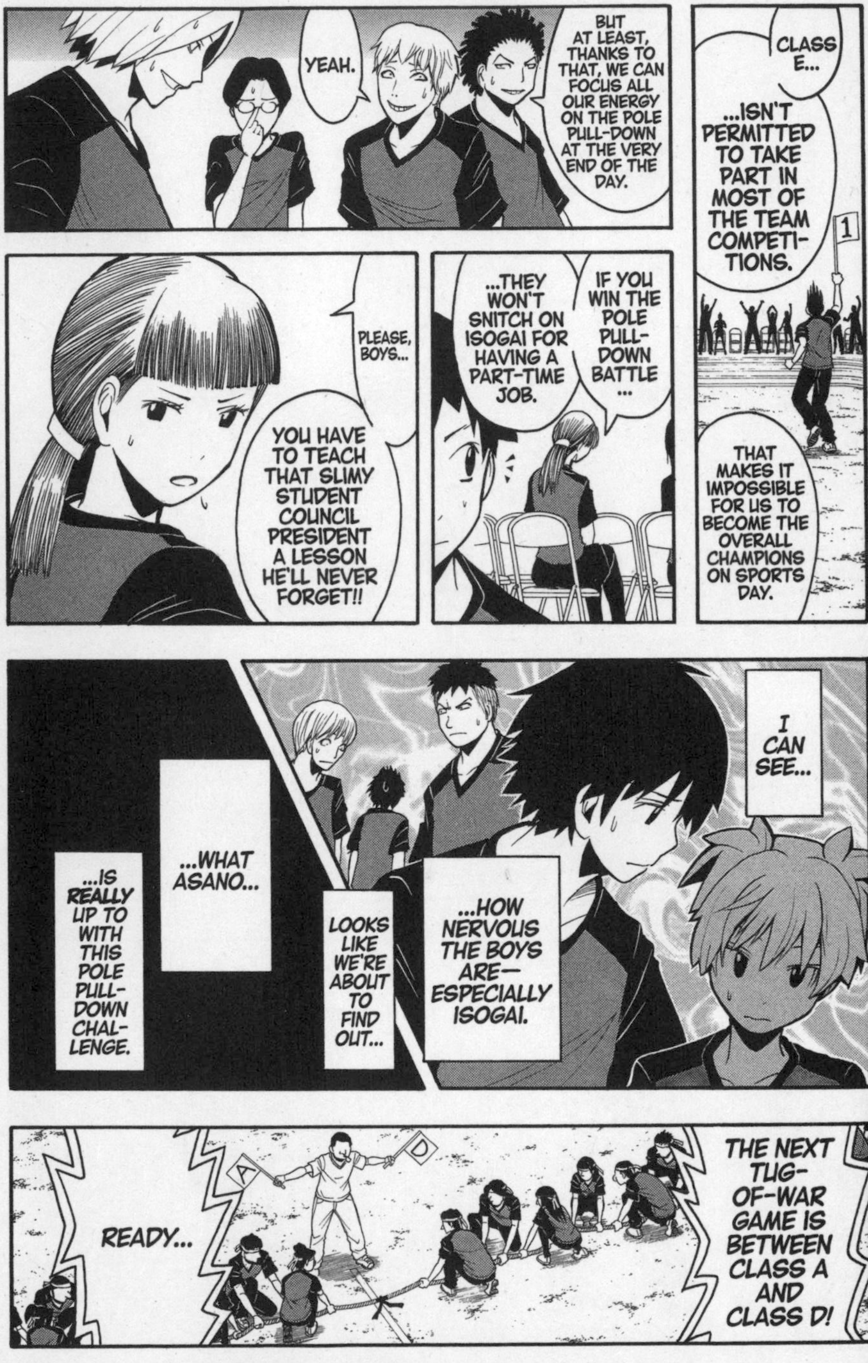
CLASS E...
...ISN'T PERMITTED TO TAKE PART IN MOST OF THE TEAM COMPETITI-TIONS.
THAT MAKES IT IMPOSSIBLE FOR US TO BECOME THE OVERALL CHAMPIONS ON SPORTS DAY.
BUT AT LEAST, THANKS TO THAT, WE CAN FOCUS ALL OUR ENERGY ON THE POLE PULL-DOWN AT THE VERY END OF THE DAY.
YEAH.
IF YOU WIN THE POLE PULL-DOWN BATTLE...
...THEY WON'T SNITCH ON ISOGAI FOR HAVING A PART-TIME JOB.
PLEASE, BOYS...
YOU HAVE TO TEACH THAT SLIMY STUDENT COUNCIL PRESIDENT A LESSON HE'LL NEVER FORGET!!
I CAN SEE...
...HOW NERVOUS THE BOYS ARE—ESPECIALLY ISOGAI.
LOOKS LIKE WE'RE ABOUT TO FIND OUT...
...WHAT ASANO...
...IS REALLY UP TO WITH THIS POLE PULL-DOWN CHAL-LENGE.
THE NEXT TUG-OF-WAR GAME IS BETWEEN CLASS A AND CLASS D!
READY...

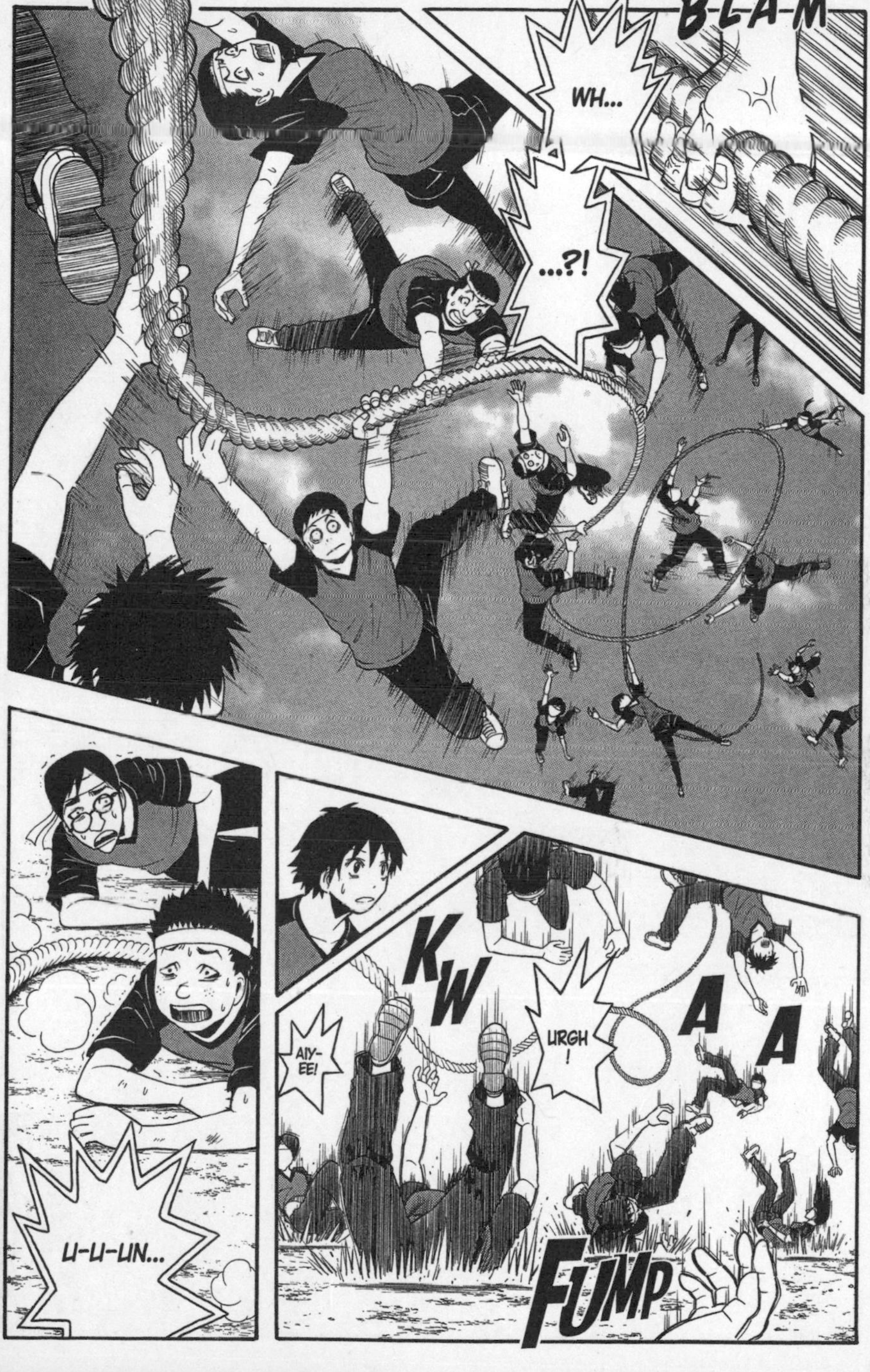
B-L-A-M
WH...
...?!
KWAAA
URGH!
AIY-EE!
FUMP
U-U-UN...

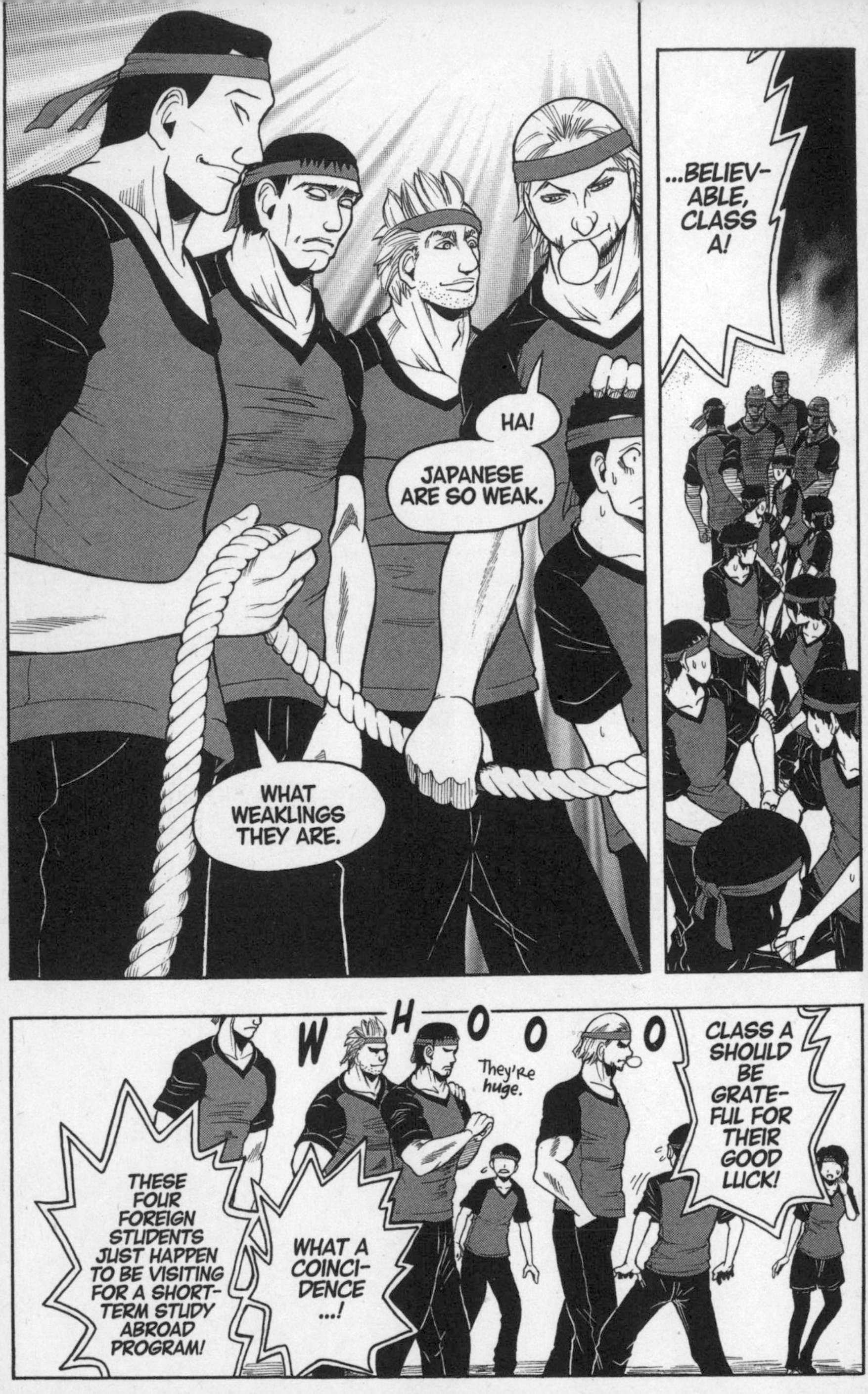
...BELIEVABLE, CLASS A!
HA!
JAPANESE ARE SO WEAK.
WHAT WEAKLINGS THEY ARE.
CLASS A SHOULD BE GRATEFUL FOR THEIR GOOD LUCK!
WHOOO
They're huge.
WHAT A COINCIDENCE ...!
THESE FOUR FOREIGN STUDENTS JUST HAPPEN TO BE VISITING FOR A SHORT-TERM STUDY ABROAD PROGRAM!

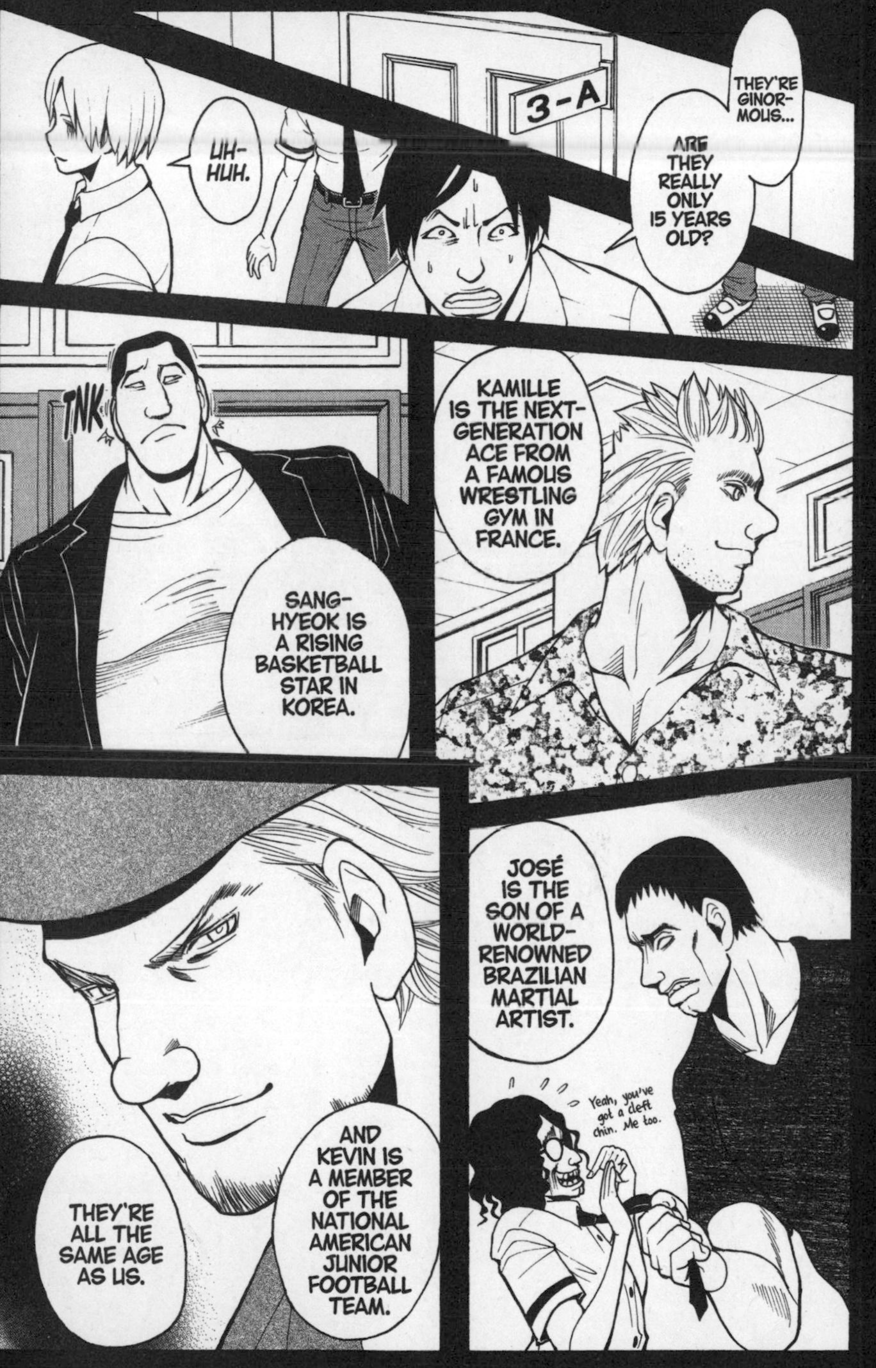
THEY'RE GINORMOUS...
ARE THEY REALLY ONLY 15 YEARS OLD?
UH-HUH.
KAMILLE IS THE NEXT-GENERATION ACE FROM A FAMOUS WRESTLING GYM IN FRANCE.
TNK
SANG-HYEOK IS A RISING BASKETBALL STAR IN KOREA.
JOSÉ IS THE SON OF A WORLD-RENOWNED BRAZILIAN MARTIAL ARTIST.
Yeah, you've got a cleft chin. Me too.
AND KEVIN IS A MEMBER OF THE NATIONAL AMERICAN JUNIOR FOOTBALL TEAM.
THEY'RE ALL THE SAME AGE AS US.

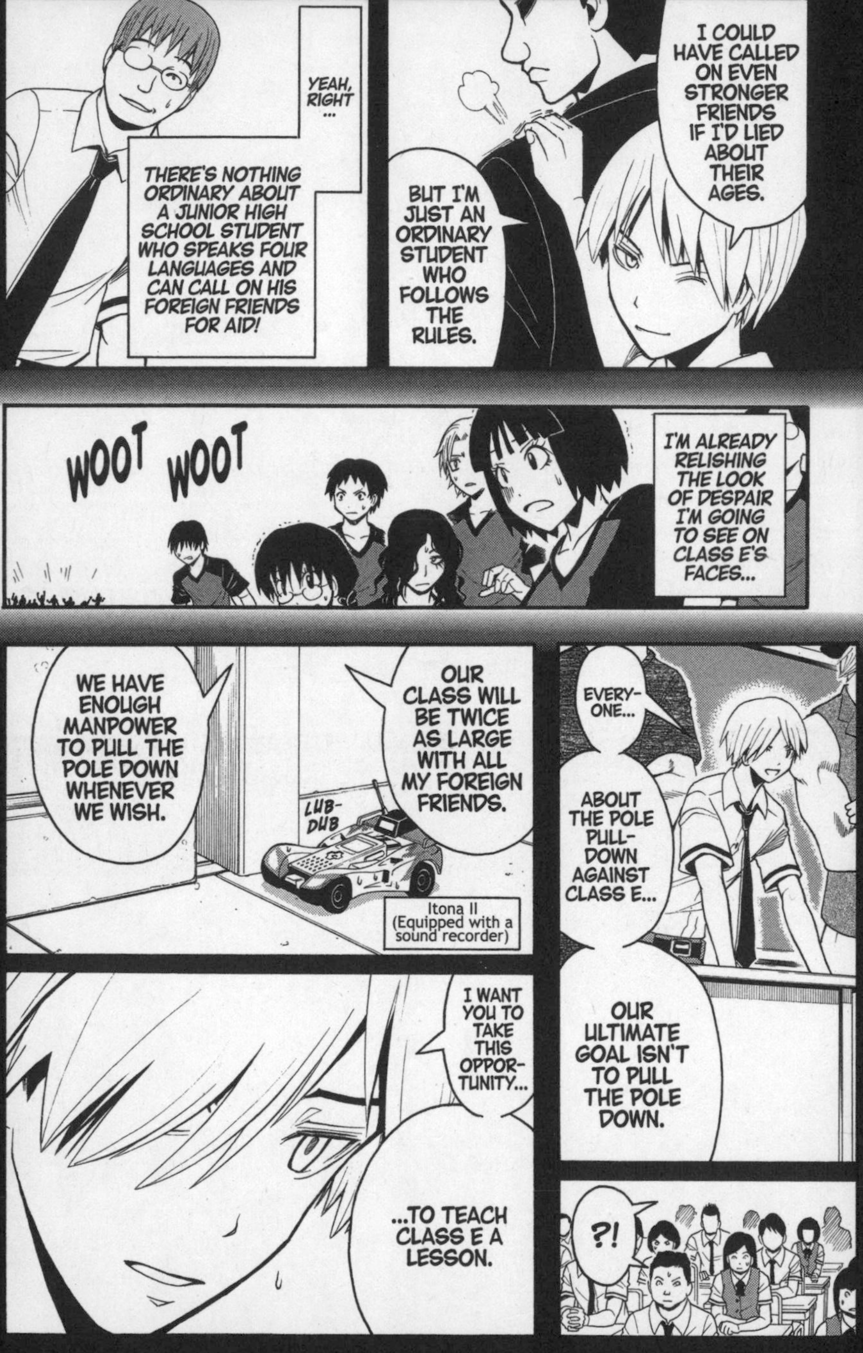
I COULD HAVE CALLED ON EVEN STRONGER FRIENDS IF I'D LIED ABOUT THEIR AGES.
BUT I'M JUST AN ORDINARY STUDENT WHO FOLLOWS THE RULES.
YEAH, RIGHT...
THERE'S NOTHING ORDINARY ABOUT A JUNIOR HIGH SCHOOL STUDENT WHO SPEAKS FOUR LANGUAGES AND CAN CALL ON HIS FOREIGN FRIENDS FOR AID!
I'M ALREADY RELISHING THE LOOK OF DESPAIR I'M GOING TO SEE ON CLASS E'S FACES...
WOOT WOOT
EVERY-ONE...
ABOUT THE POLE PULL-DOWN AGAINST CLASS E...
OUR ULTIMATE GOAL ISN'T TO PULL THE POLE DOWN.
OUR CLASS WILL BE TWICE AS LARGE WITH ALL MY FOREIGN FRIENDS.
WE HAVE ENOUGH MANPOWER TO PULL THE POLE DOWN WHENEVER WE WISH.
LUB-DUB
Itona II (Equipped with a sound recorder)
I WANT YOU TO TAKE THIS OPPOR-TUNITY...
...TO TEACH CLASS E A LESSON.
?!

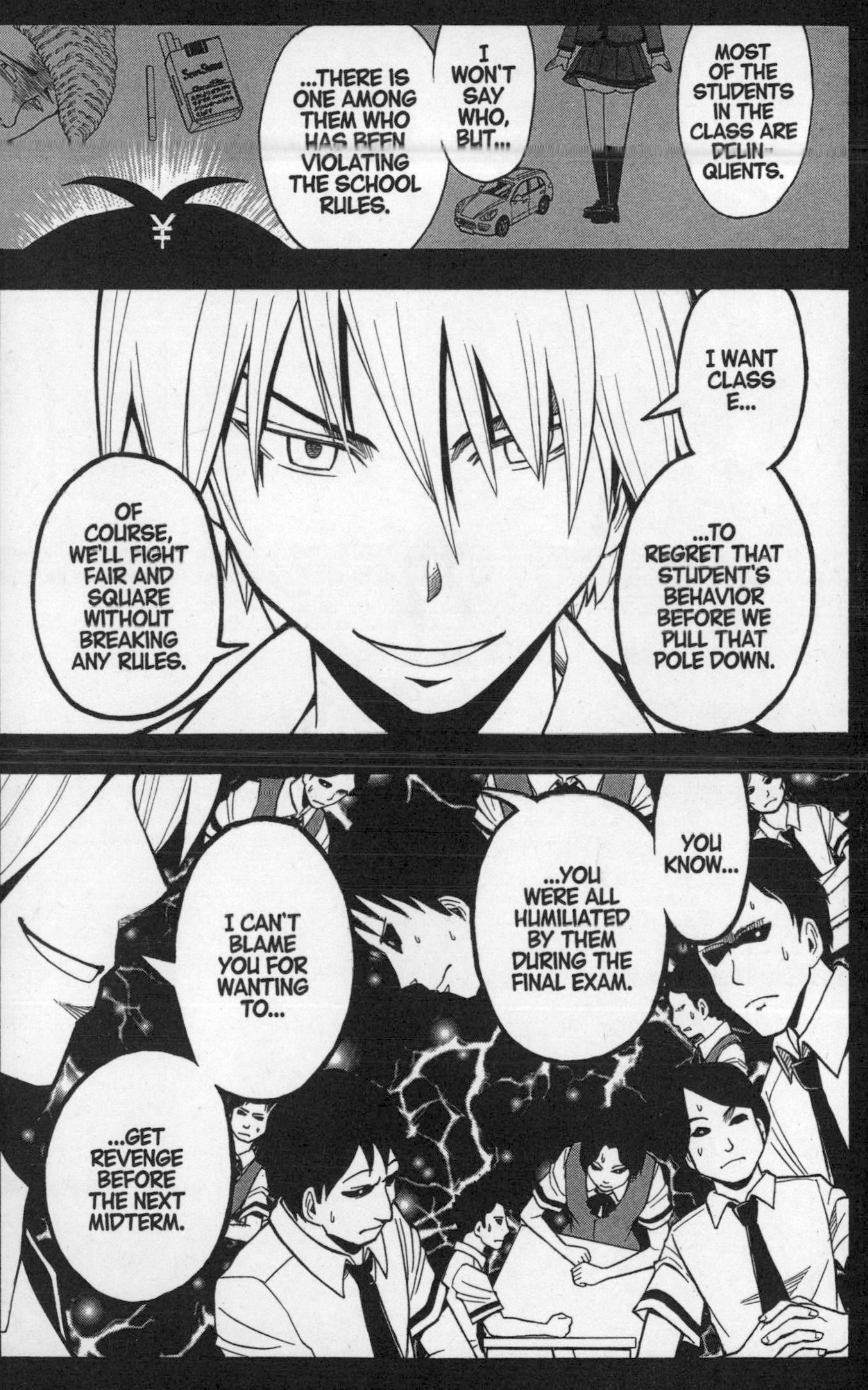
MOST OF THE STUDENTS IN THE CLASS ARE DELIN-QUENTS.
I WON'T SAY WHO, BUT...
...THERE IS ONE AMONG THEM WHO HAS BEEN VIOLATING THE SCHOOL RULES.
I WANT CLASS E...
...TO REGRET THAT STUDENT'S BEHAVIOR BEFORE WE PULL THAT POLE DOWN.
OF COURSE, WE'LL FIGHT FAIR AND SQUARE WITHOUT BREAKING ANY RULES.
YOU KNOW...
...YOU WERE ALL HUMILIATED BY THEM DURING THE FINAL EXAM.
I CAN'T BLAME YOU FOR WANTING TO...
...GET REVENGE BEFORE THE NEXT MIDTERM.

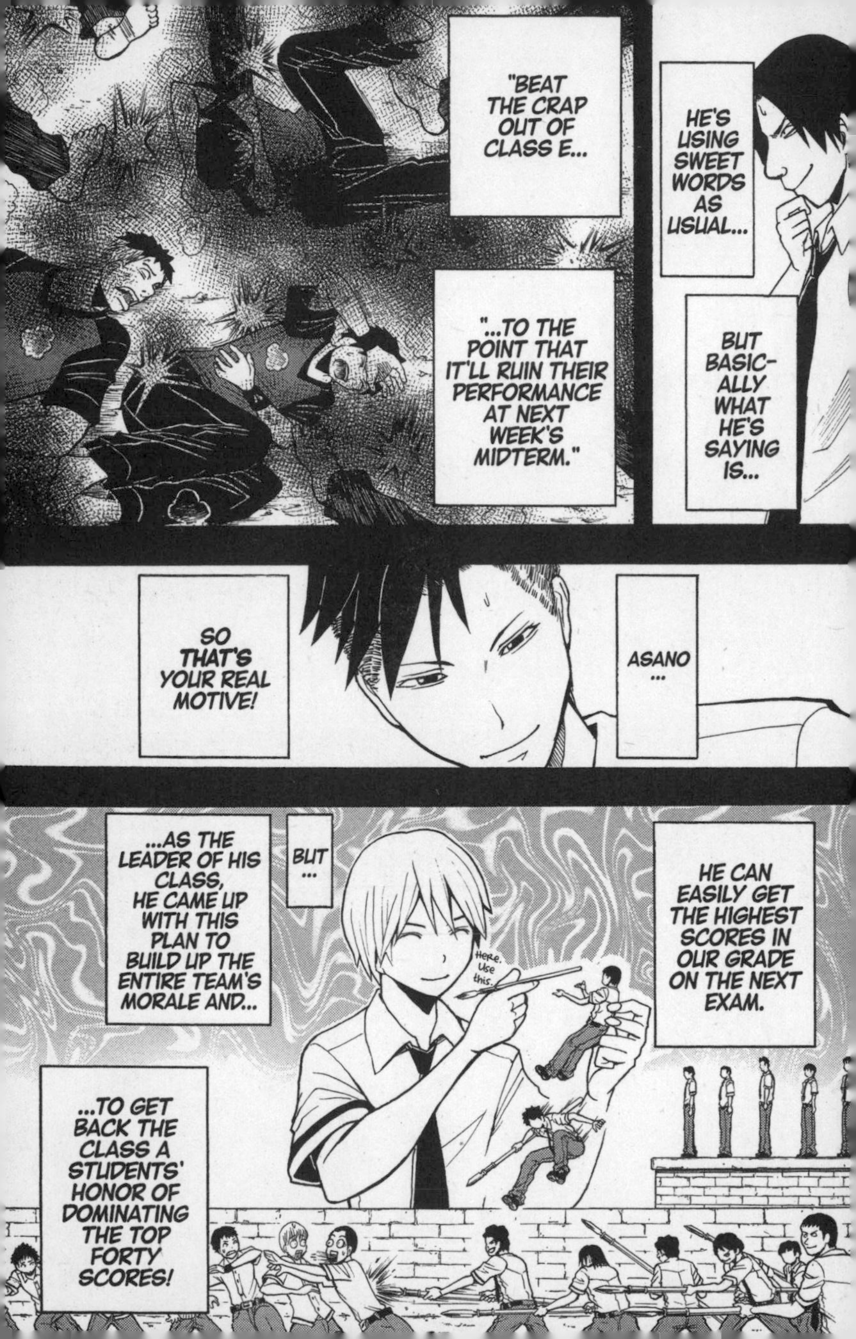
HE'S USING SWEET WORDS AS USUAL...
BUT BASIC-ALLY WHAT HE'S SAYING IS...
"BEAT THE CRAP OUT OF CLASS E...
"...TO THE POINT THAT IT'LL RUIN THEIR PERFORMANCE AT NEXT WEEK'S MIDTERM."
ASANO ...
SO THAT'S YOUR REAL MOTIVE!
HE CAN EASILY GET THE HIGHEST SCORES IN OUR GRADE ON THE NEXT EXAM.
BUT ...
...AS THE LEADER OF HIS CLASS, HE CAME UP WITH THIS PLAN TO BUILD UP THE ENTIRE TEAM'S MORALE AND...
Here. Use this.
...TO GET BACK THE CLASS A STUDENTS' HONOR OF DOMINATING THE TOP FORTY SCORES!

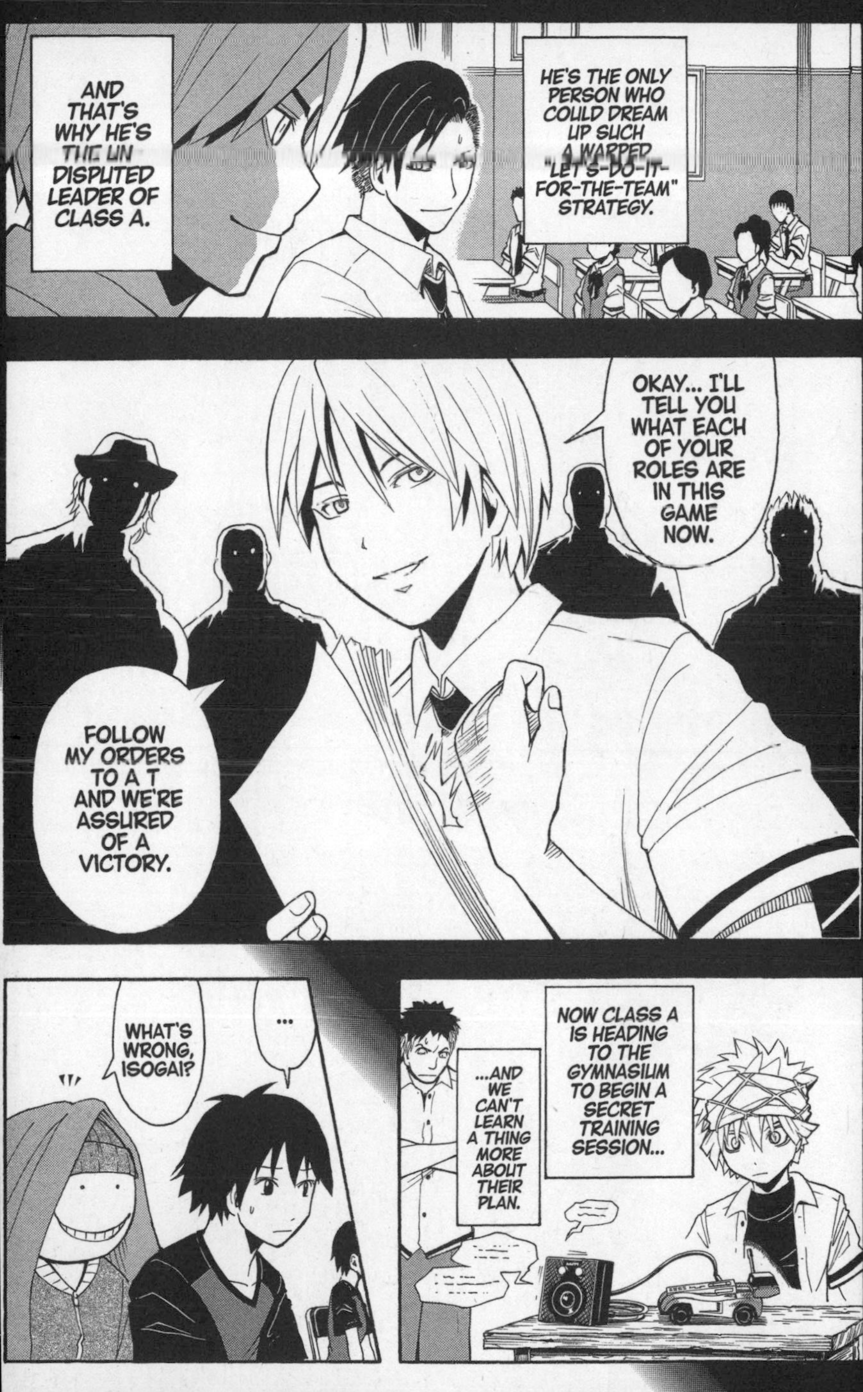
HE'S THE ONLY PERSON WHO COULD DREAM UP SUCH A WARPED "LET'S-DO-IT-FOR-THE-TEAM" STRATEGY.
AND THAT'S WHY HE'S THE UN-DISPUTED LEADER OF CLASS A.
OKAY... I'LL TELL YOU WHAT EACH OF YOUR ROLES ARE IN THIS GAME NOW.
FOLLOW MY ORDERS TO A T AND WE'RE ASSURED OF A VICTORY.
NOW CLASS A IS HEADING TO THE GYMNASIUM TO BEGIN A SECRET TRAINING SESSION...
...AND WE CAN'T LEARN A THING MORE ABOUT THEIR PLAN.
...
WHAT'S WRONG, ISOGAI?

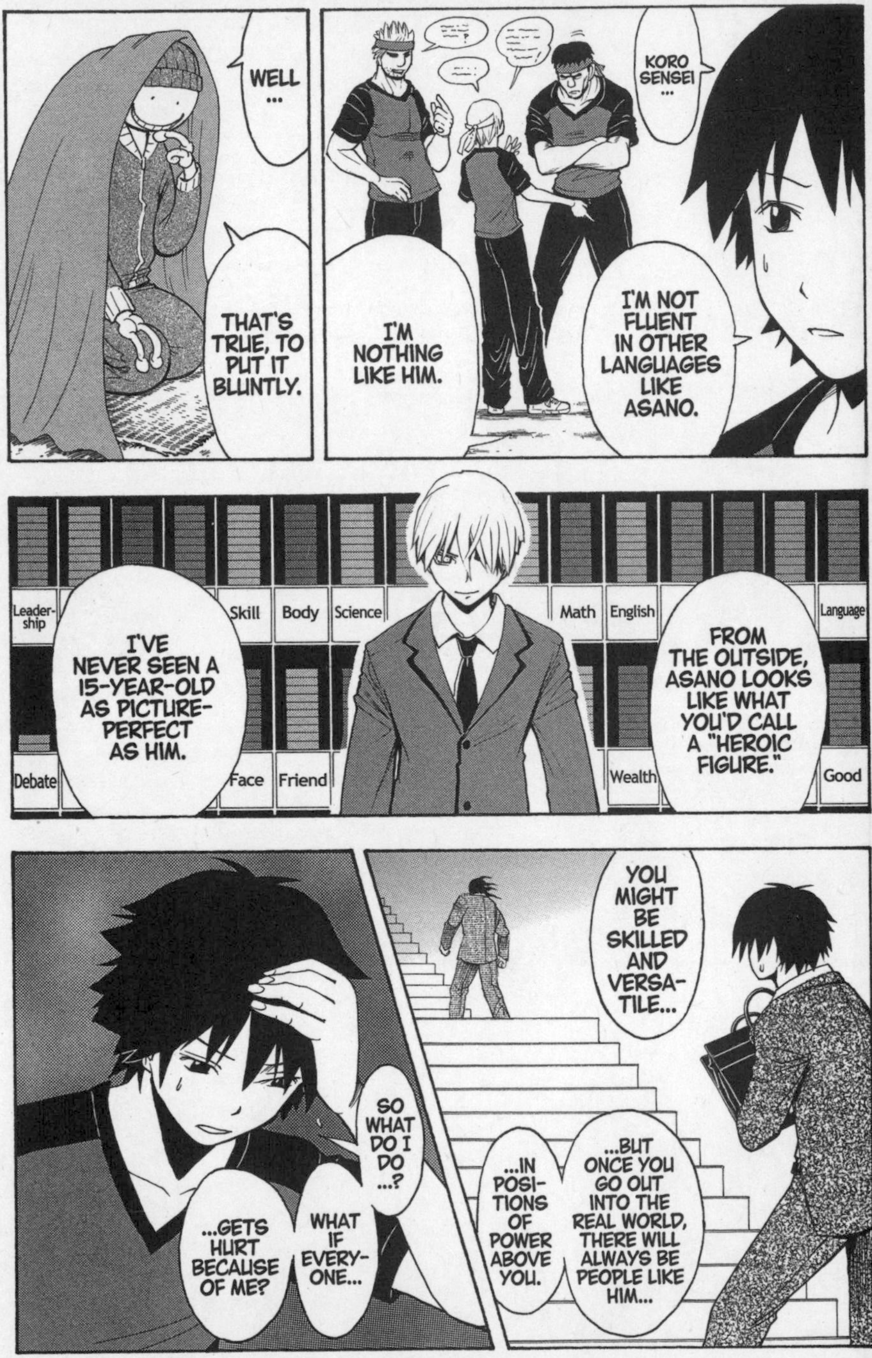
KORO SENSEI ...
I'M NOT FLUENT IN OTHER LANGUAGES LIKE ASANO.
I'M NOTHING LIKE HIM.
WELL ...
THAT'S TRUE, TO PUT IT BLUNTLY.
Language
English
Math
Science
Body
Skill
Leader-ship
Good
Wealth
Friend
Face
Debate
FROM THE OUTSIDE, ASANO LOOKS LIKE WHAT YOU'D CALL A "HEROIC FIGURE."
I'VE NEVER SEEN A 15-YEAR-OLD AS PICTURE-PERFECT AS HIM.
YOU MIGHT BE SKILLED AND VERSATILE...
...BUT ONCE YOU GO OUT INTO THE REAL WORLD, THERE WILL ALWAYS BE PEOPLE LIKE HIM...
...IN POSITIONS OF POWER ABOVE YOU.
SO WHAT DO I DO ...?
WHAT IF EVERYONE...
...GETS HURT BECAUSE OF ME?

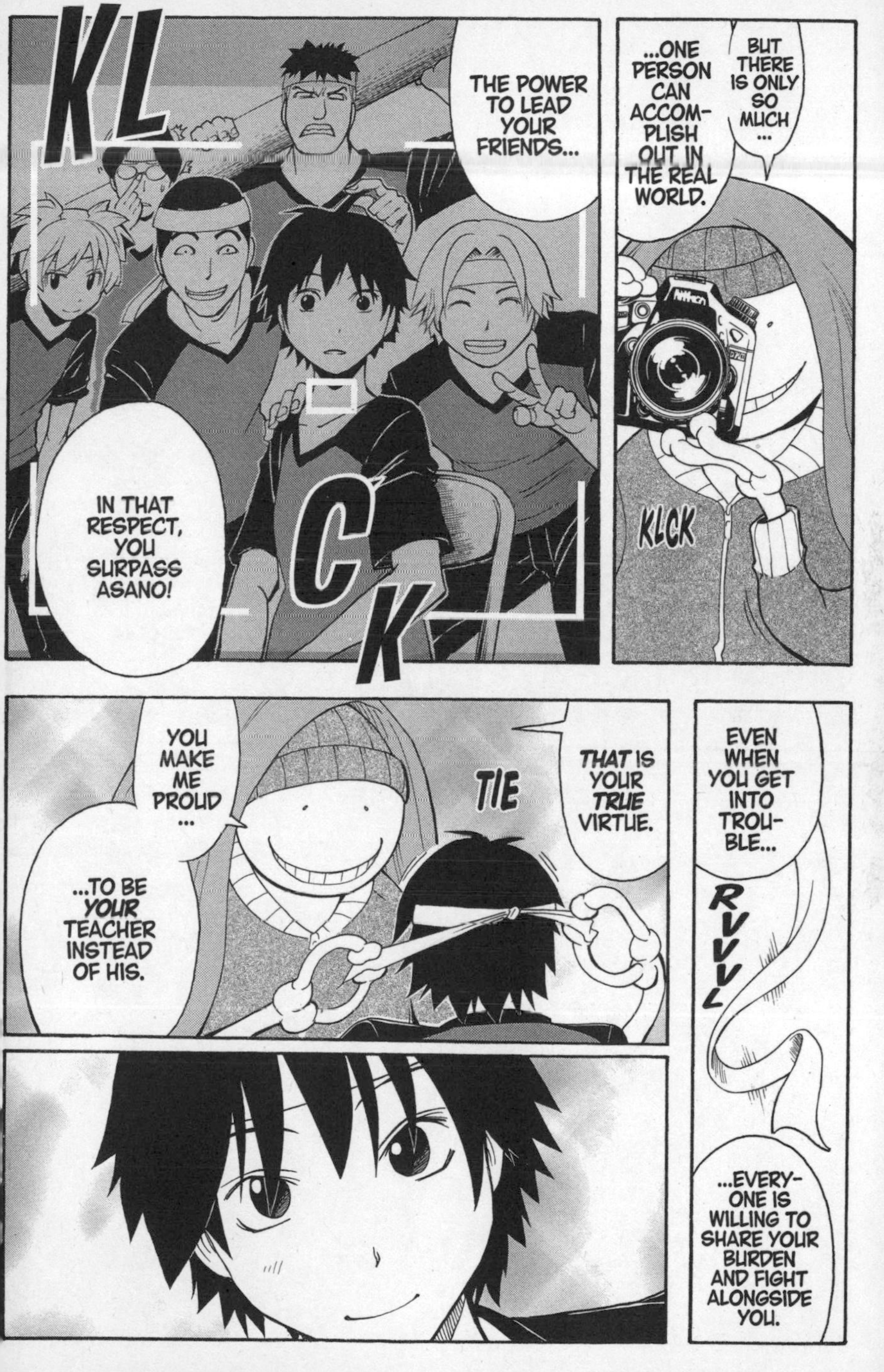
BUT THERE IS ONLY SO MUCH...
...ONE PERSON CAN ACCOMPLISH OUT IN THE REAL WORLD.
KLCK
KL
THE POWER TO LEAD YOUR FRIENDS...
IN THAT RESPECT, YOU SURPASS ASANO!
CK
EVEN WHEN YOU GET INTO TROUBLE...
RVVVL
...EVERYONE IS WILLING TO SHARE YOUR BURDEN AND FIGHT ALONGSIDE YOU.
THAT IS YOUR *TRUE* VIRTUE.
TIE
YOU MAKE ME PROUD...
...TO BE *YOUR* TEACHER INSTEAD OF HIS.

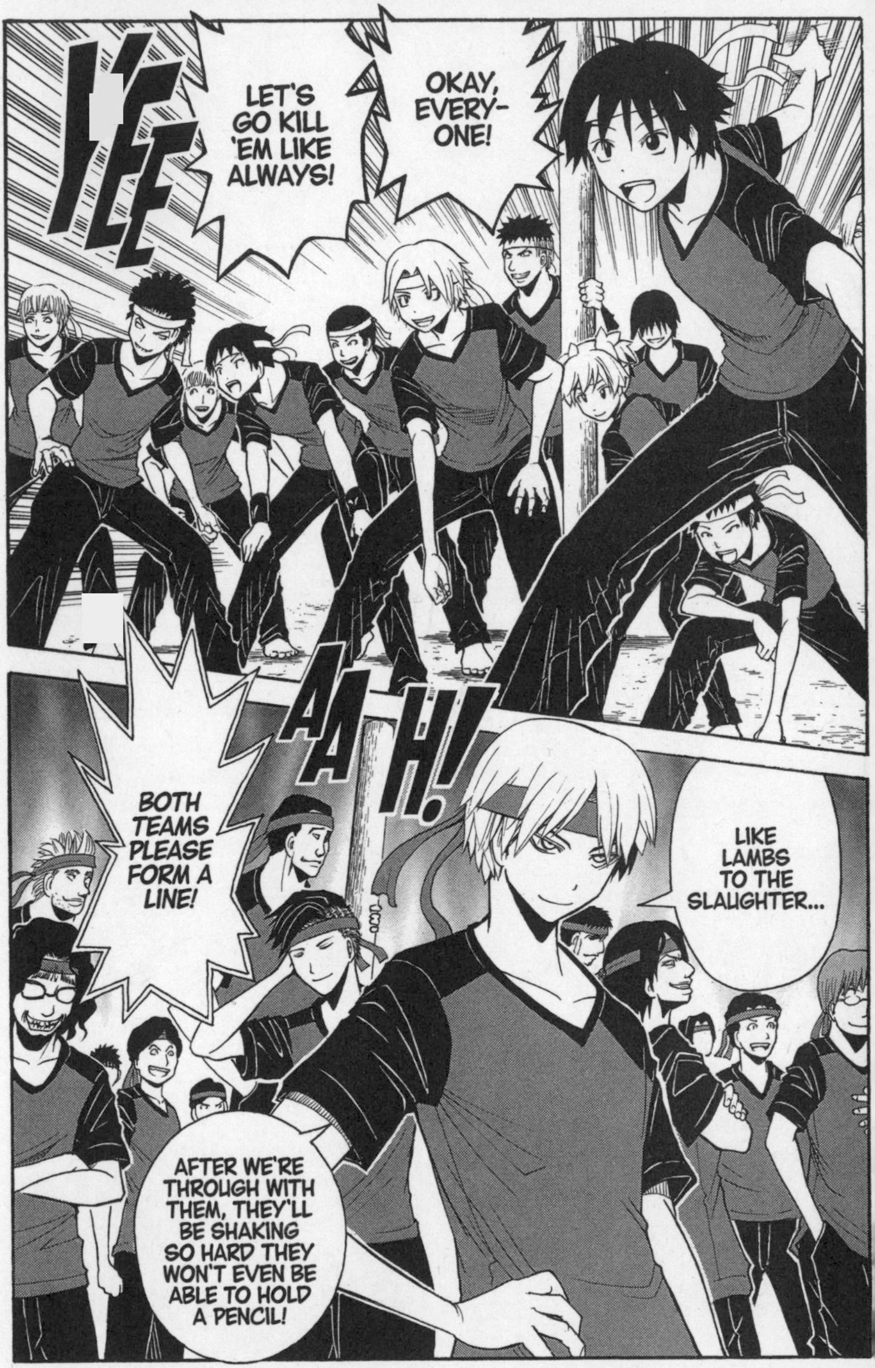
OKAY, EVERY-ONE!
LET'S GO KILL 'EM LIKE ALWAYS!
YEE
AAH!
LIKE LAMBS TO THE SLAUGHTER...
BOTH TEAMS PLEASE FORM A LINE!
AFTER WE'RE THROUGH WITH THEM, THEY'LL BE SHAKING SO HARD THEY WON'T EVEN BE ABLE TO HOLD A PENCIL!

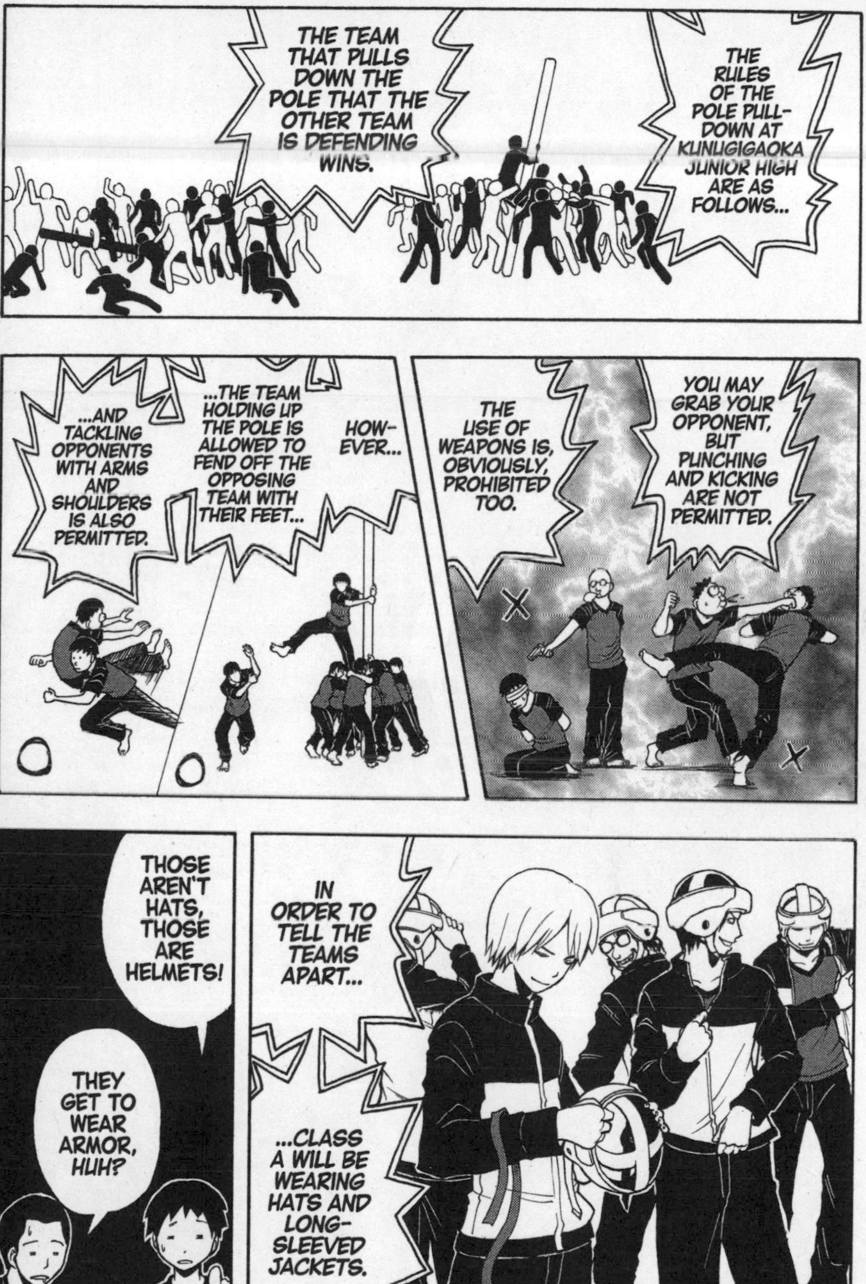
THE RULES OF THE POLE PULL-DOWN AT KUNUGIGAOKA JUNIOR HIGH ARE AS FOLLOWS...
THE TEAM THAT PULLS DOWN THE POLE THAT THE OTHER TEAM IS DEFENDING WINS.
YOU MAY GRAB YOUR OPPONENT, BUT PUNCHING AND KICKING ARE NOT PERMITTED.
THE USE OF WEAPONS IS, OBVIOUSLY, PROHIBITED TOO.
HOW-EVER...
...THE TEAM HOLDING UP THE POLE IS ALLOWED TO FEND OFF THE OPPOSING TEAM WITH THEIR FEET...
...AND TACKLING OPPONENTS WITH ARMS AND SHOULDERS IS ALSO PERMITTED.
IN ORDER TO TELL THE TEAMS APART...
...CLASS A WILL BE WEARING HATS AND LONG-SLEEVED JACKETS.
THOSE AREN'T HATS, THOSE ARE HELMETS!
THEY GET TO WEAR ARMOR, HUH?

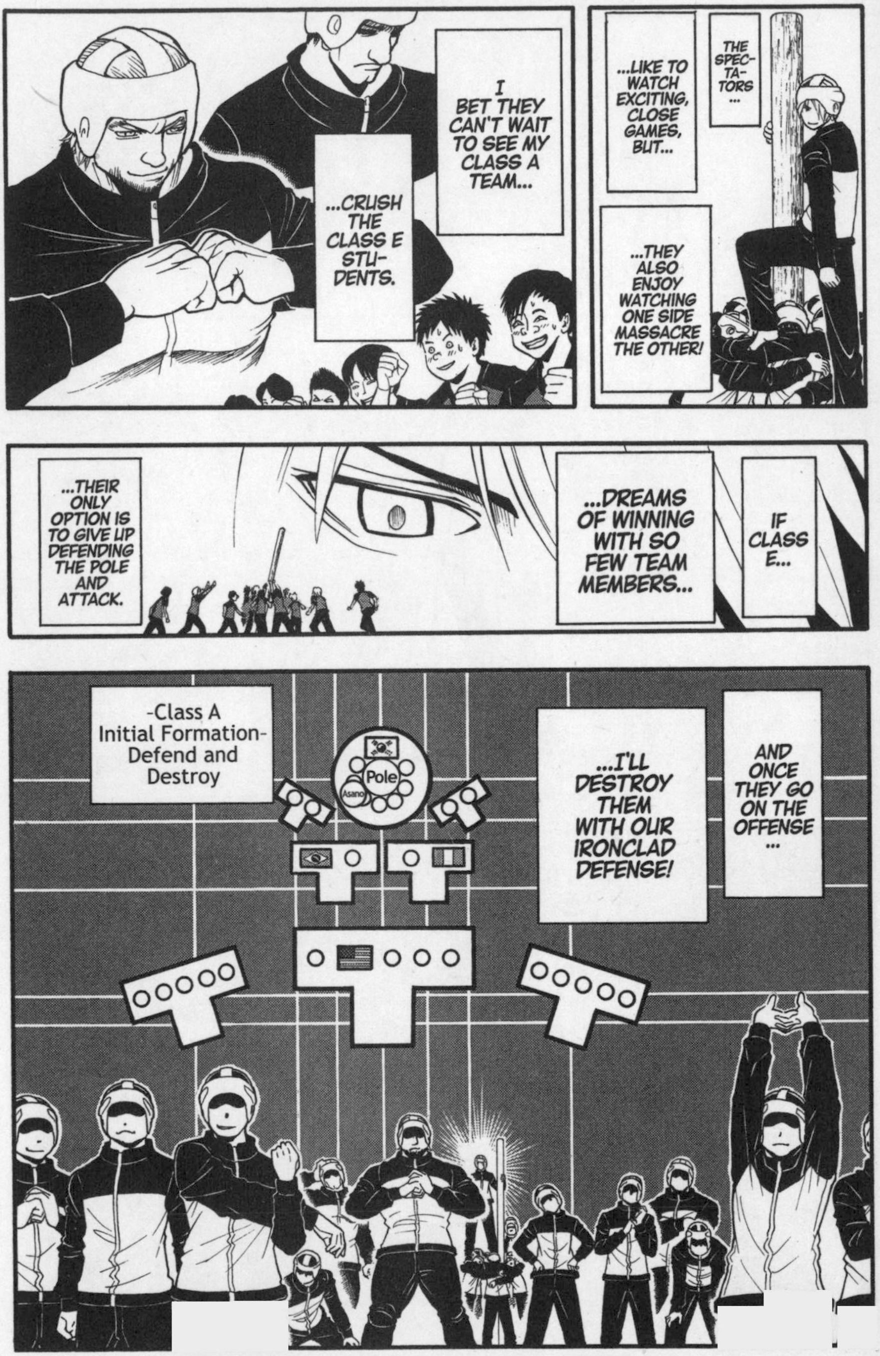
THE SPECTATORS...
...LIKE TO WATCH EXCITING, CLOSE GAMES, BUT...
...THEY ALSO ENJOY WATCHING ONE SIDE MASSACRE THE OTHER!
I BET THEY CAN'T WAIT TO SEE MY CLASS A TEAM...
...CRUSH THE CLASS E STUDENTS.
IF CLASS E...
...DREAMS OF WINNING WITH SO FEW TEAM MEMBERS...
...THEIR ONLY OPTION IS TO GIVE UP DEFENDING THE POLE AND ATTACK.
AND ONCE THEY GO ON THE OFFENSE...
...I'LL DESTROY THEM WITH OUR IRONCLAD DEFENSE!
-Class A Initial Formation- Defend and Destroy
Pole
Asano

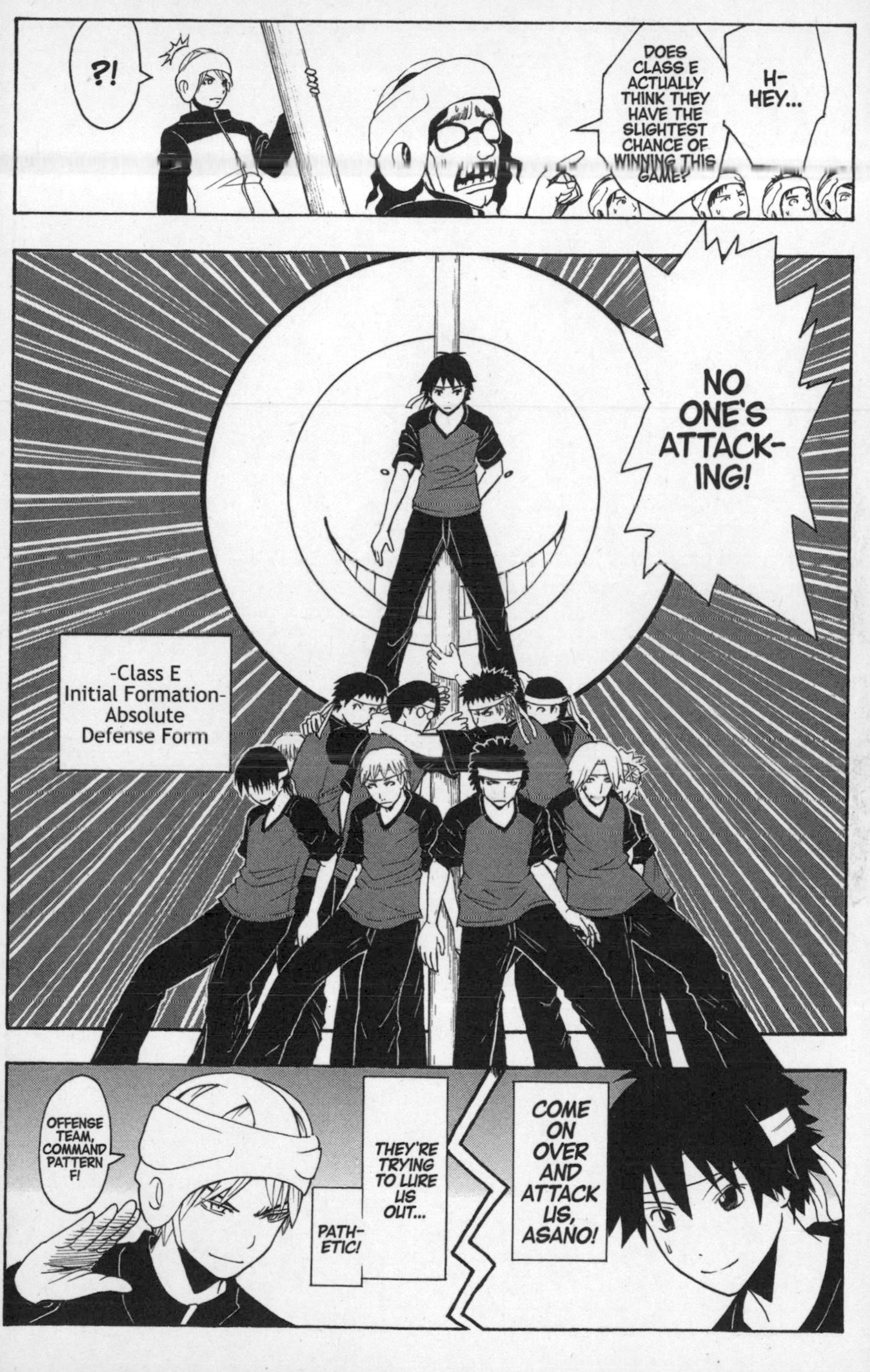
H-HEY...
DOES CLASS E ACTUALLY THINK THEY HAVE THE SLIGHTEST CHANCE OF WINNING THIS GAME?
?!
NO ONE'S ATTACK-ING!
-Class E Initial Formation- Absolute Defense Form
COME ON OVER AND ATTACK US, ASANO!
THEY'RE TRYING TO LURE US OUT...
PATH-ETIC!
OFFENSE TEAM, COMMAND PATTERN F!

E-20 SUMIRE HARA

- ☺ BIRTHDAY: MAY 8
- ☺ HEIGHT: 5' 1"
- ☺ WEIGHT: 132 LBS.
- ☺ FAVORITE SUBJECT: HOME ECONOMICS
- ☺ LEAST FAVORITE SUBJECT: MATHEMATICS
- ☺ HOBBY/SKILL: HOME COOKING
- ☺ FUTURE GOAL: PROFESSIONAL HOMEMAKER
- ☺ FAVORITE DISH: SWISS ROLLS
- ☺ FAVORITE MOVE: CROCODILE DEATH ROLL

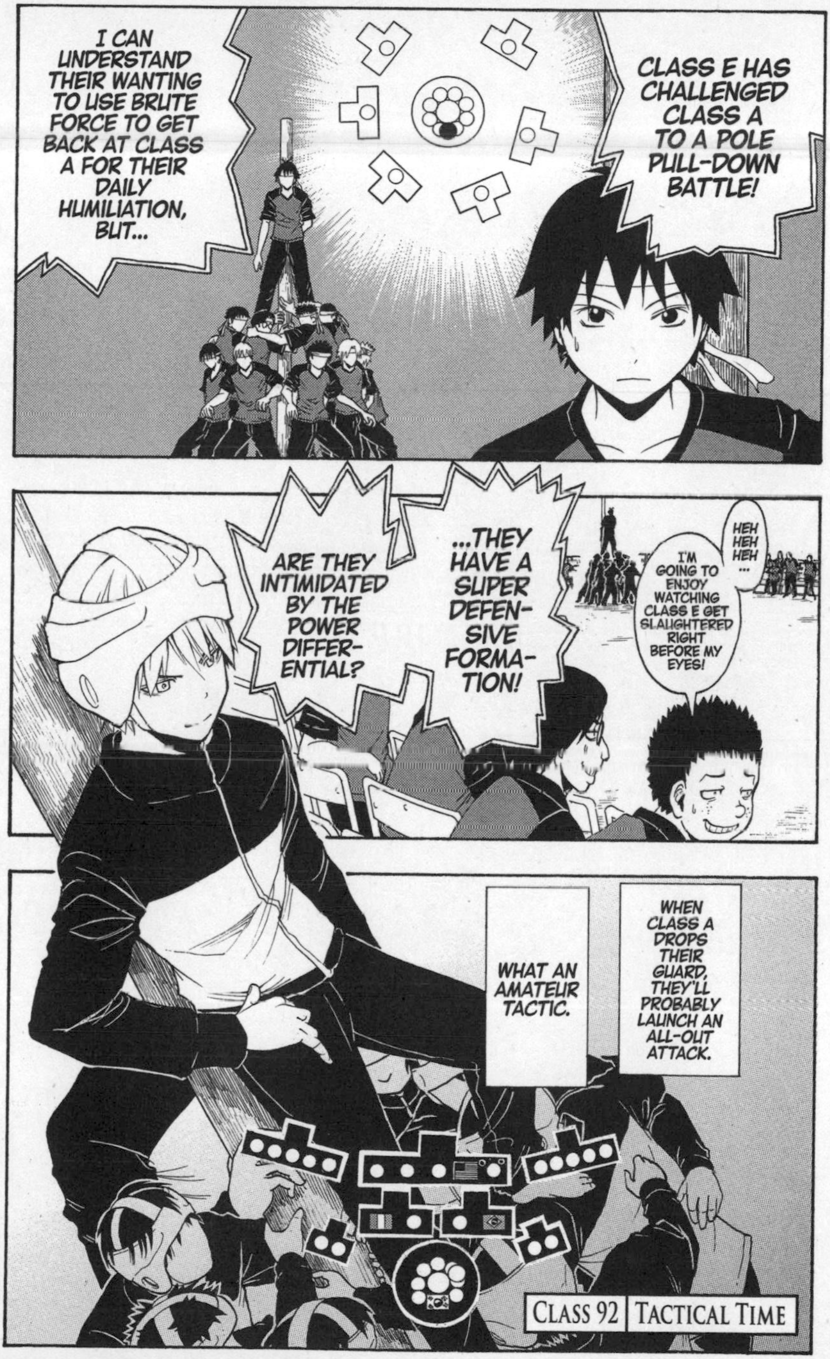
CLASS E HAS CHALLENGED CLASS A TO A POLE PULL-DOWN BATTLE!
I CAN UNDERSTAND THEIR WANTING TO USE BRUTE FORCE TO GET BACK AT CLASS A FOR THEIR DAILY HUMILIATION, BUT...
HEH HEH HEH...
I'M GOING TO ENJOY WATCHING CLASS E GET SLAUGHTERED RIGHT BEFORE MY EYES!
...THEY HAVE A SUPER DEFEN-SIVE FORMA-TION!
ARE THEY INTIMIDATED BY THE POWER DIFFER-ENTIAL?
WHEN CLASS A DROPS THEIR GUARD, THEY'LL PROBABLY LAUNCH AN ALL-OUT ATTACK.
WHAT AN AMATEUR TACTIC.
CLASS 92 TACTICAL TIME

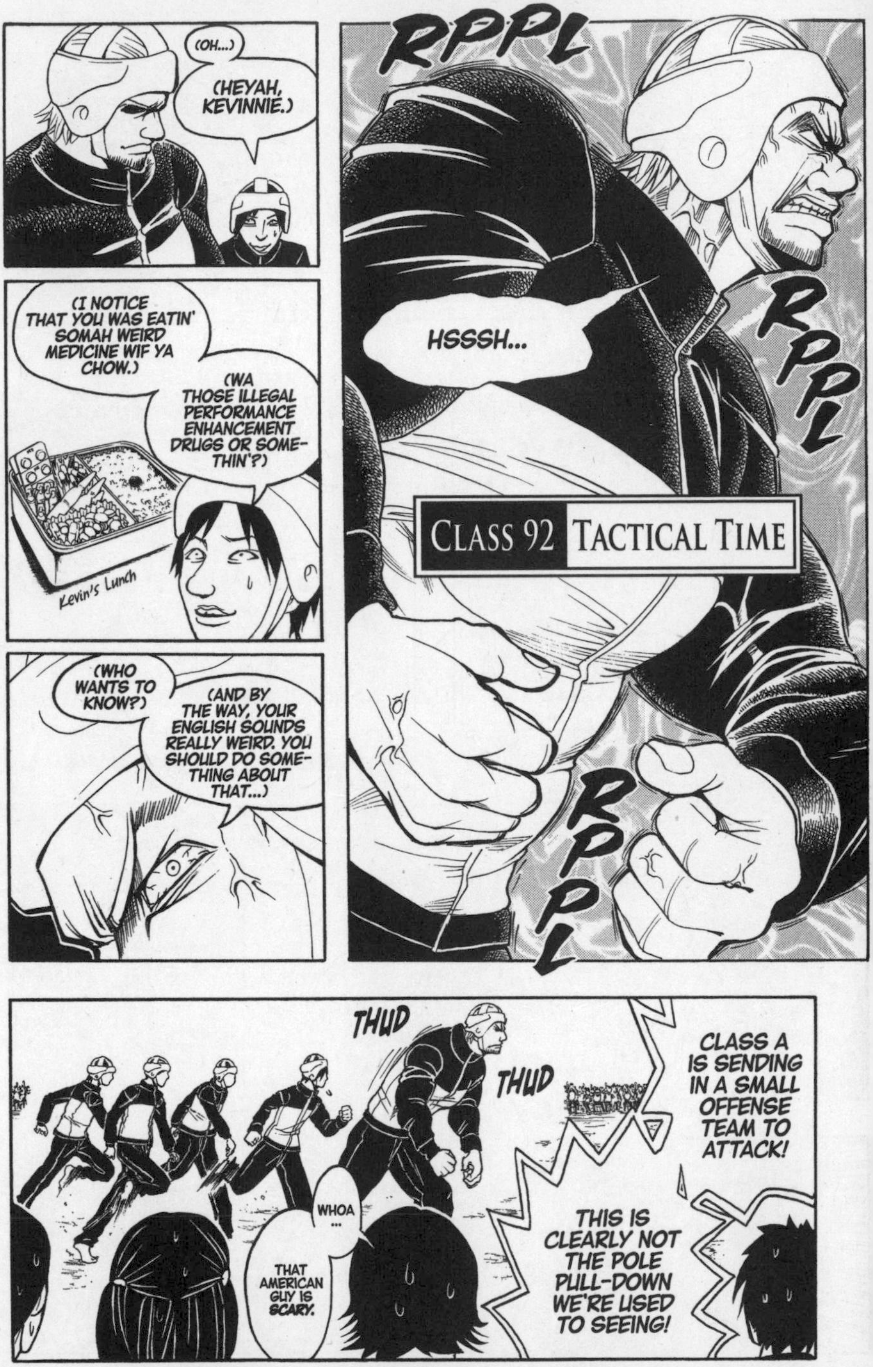
RPPL
HSSSH...
CLASS 92 TACTICAL TIME
RPPL
RPPL
(OH...)
(HEYAH, KEVINNIE.)
(I NOTICE THAT YOU WAS EATIN' SOMAH WEIRD MEDICINE WIF YA CHOW.)
(WA THOSE ILLEGAL PERFORMANCE ENHANCEMENT DRUGS OR SOME-THIN'?)
Kevin's Lunch
(WHO WANTS TO KNOW?)
(AND BY THE WAY, YOUR ENGLISH SOUNDS REALLY WEIRD. YOU SHOULD DO SOME-THING ABOUT THAT...)
CLASS A IS SENDING IN A SMALL OFFENSE TEAM TO ATTACK!
THIS IS CLEARLY NOT THE POLE PULL-DOWN WE'RE USED TO SEEING!
THUD
THUD
WHOA ...
THAT AMERICAN GUY IS SCARY.

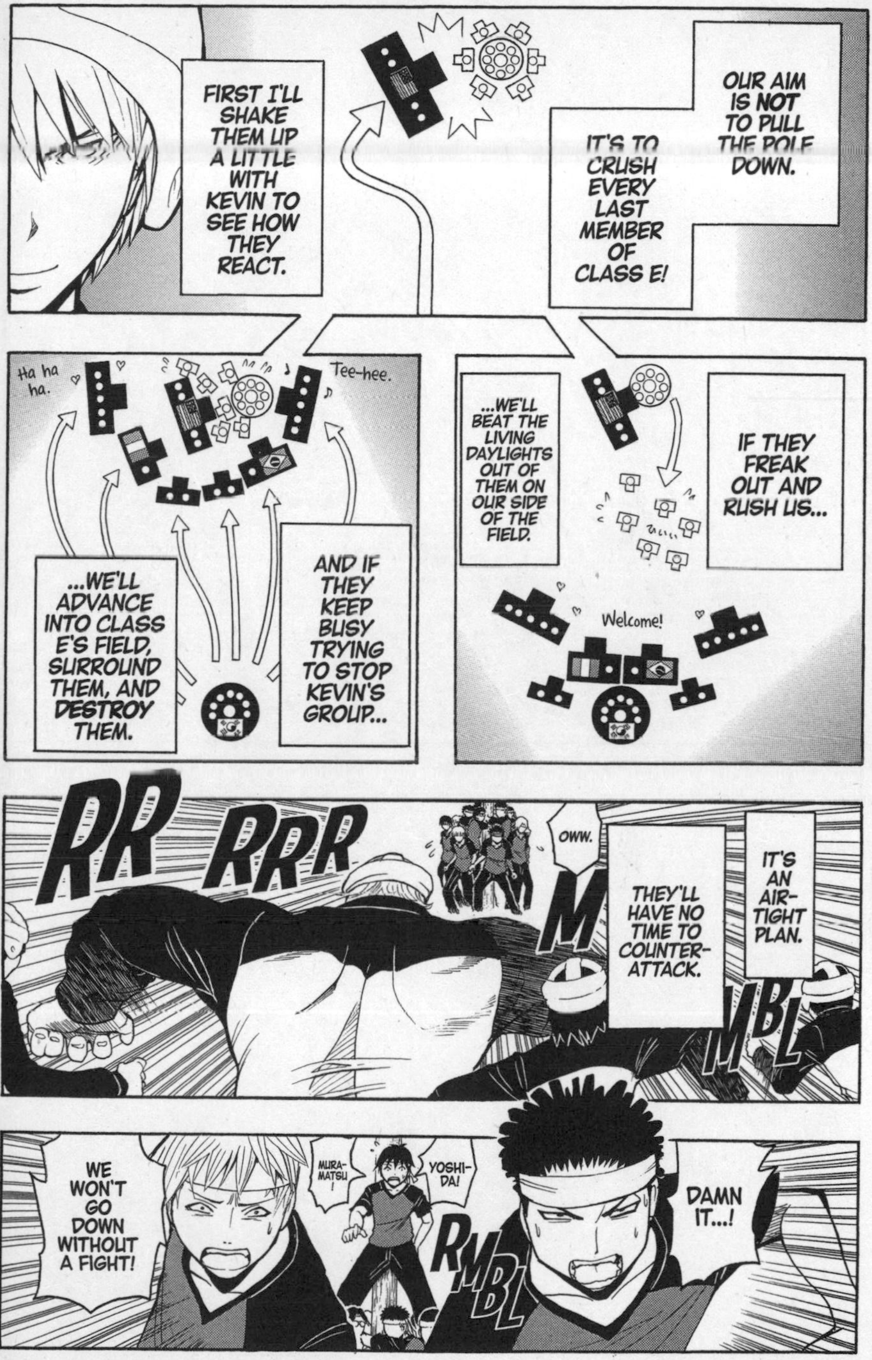
OUR AIM IS NOT TO PULL THE POLE DOWN.
IT'S TO CRUSH EVERY LAST MEMBER OF CLASS E!
FIRST I'LL SHAKE THEM UP A LITTLE WITH KEVIN TO SEE HOW THEY REACT.
IF THEY FREAK OUT AND RUSH US...
...WE'LL BEAT THE LIVING DAYLIGHTS OUT OF THEM ON OUR SIDE OF THE FIELD.
Welcome!
Tee-hee.
AND IF THEY KEEP BUSY TRYING TO STOP KEVIN'S GROUP...
Ha ha ha.
...WE'LL ADVANCE INTO CLASS E'S FIELD, SURROUND THEM, AND DESTROY THEM.
IT'S AN AIR-TIGHT PLAN.
THEY'LL HAVE NO TIME TO COUNTER-ATTACK.
OWW.
M
MBL
RRR
RR
DAMN IT...!
RMBL
YOSHI-DA!
MURA-MATSU!
WE WON'T GO DOWN WITHOUT A FIGHT!

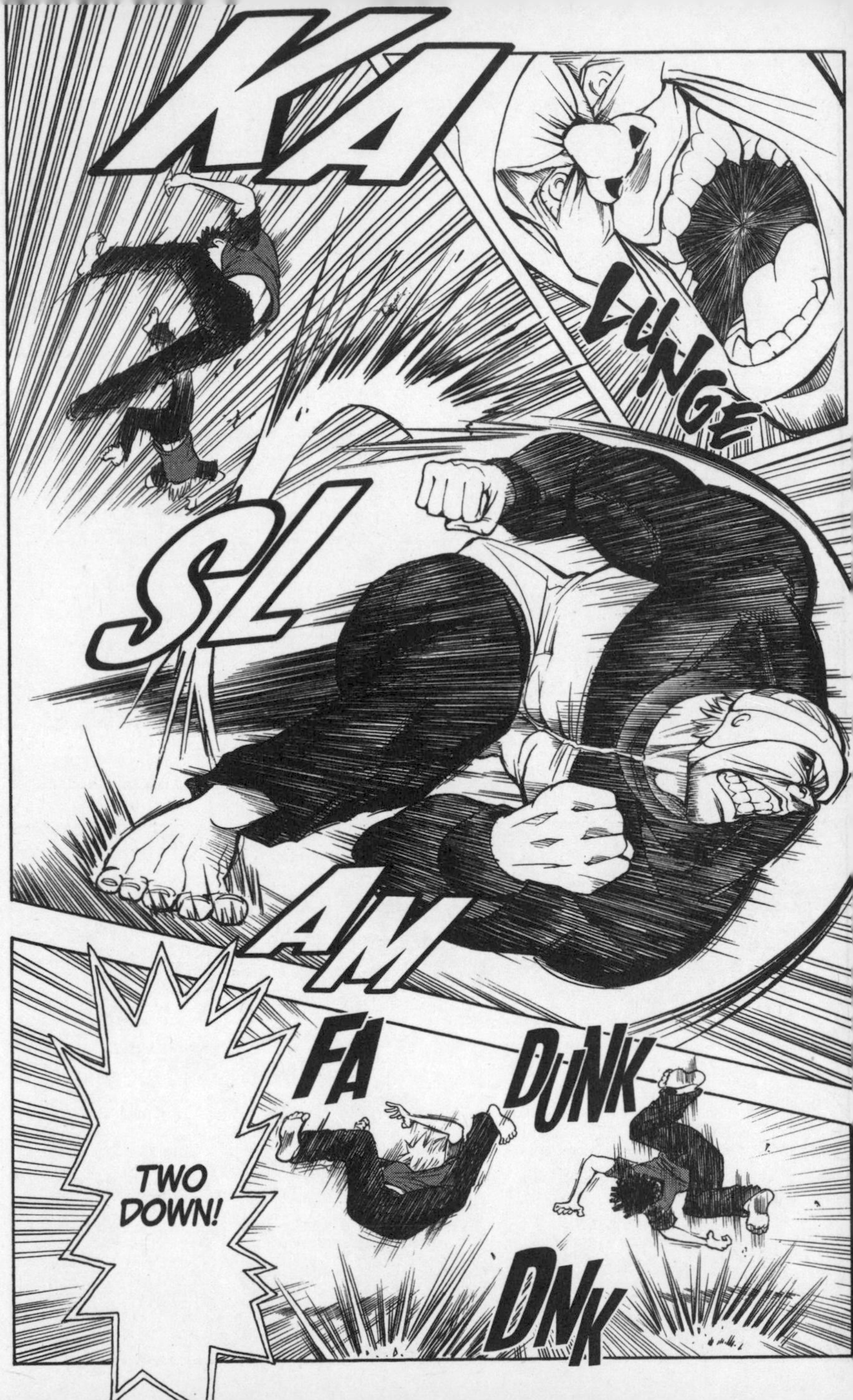
KA
LUNGE
SL
AM
DUNK
FA
TWO DOWN!
DNK

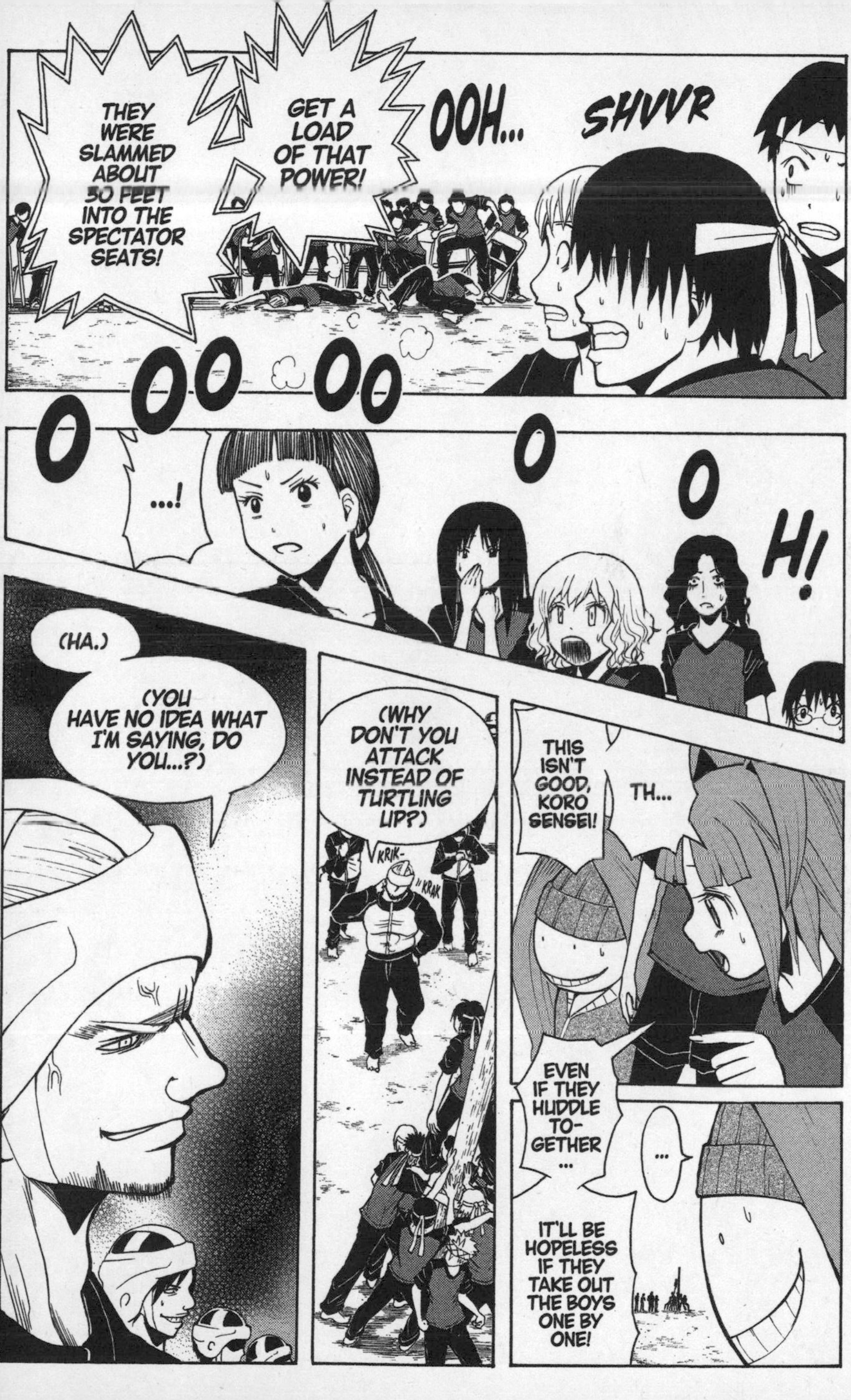
SHVVR
OOH...
GET A LOAD OF THAT POWER!
THEY WERE SLAMMED ABOUT 50 FEET INTO THE SPECTATOR SEATS!
OOOOOOOOOH!
...!
TH...
THIS ISN'T GOOD, KORO SENSEI!
...
EVEN IF THEY HUDDLE TO-GETHER...
IT'LL BE HOPELESS IF THEY TAKE OUT THE BOYS ONE BY ONE!
(WHY DON'T YOU ATTACK INSTEAD OF TURTLING UP?)
KRIK-
KRAK
(HA.)
(YOU HAVE NO IDEA WHAT I'M SAYING, DO YOU...?)

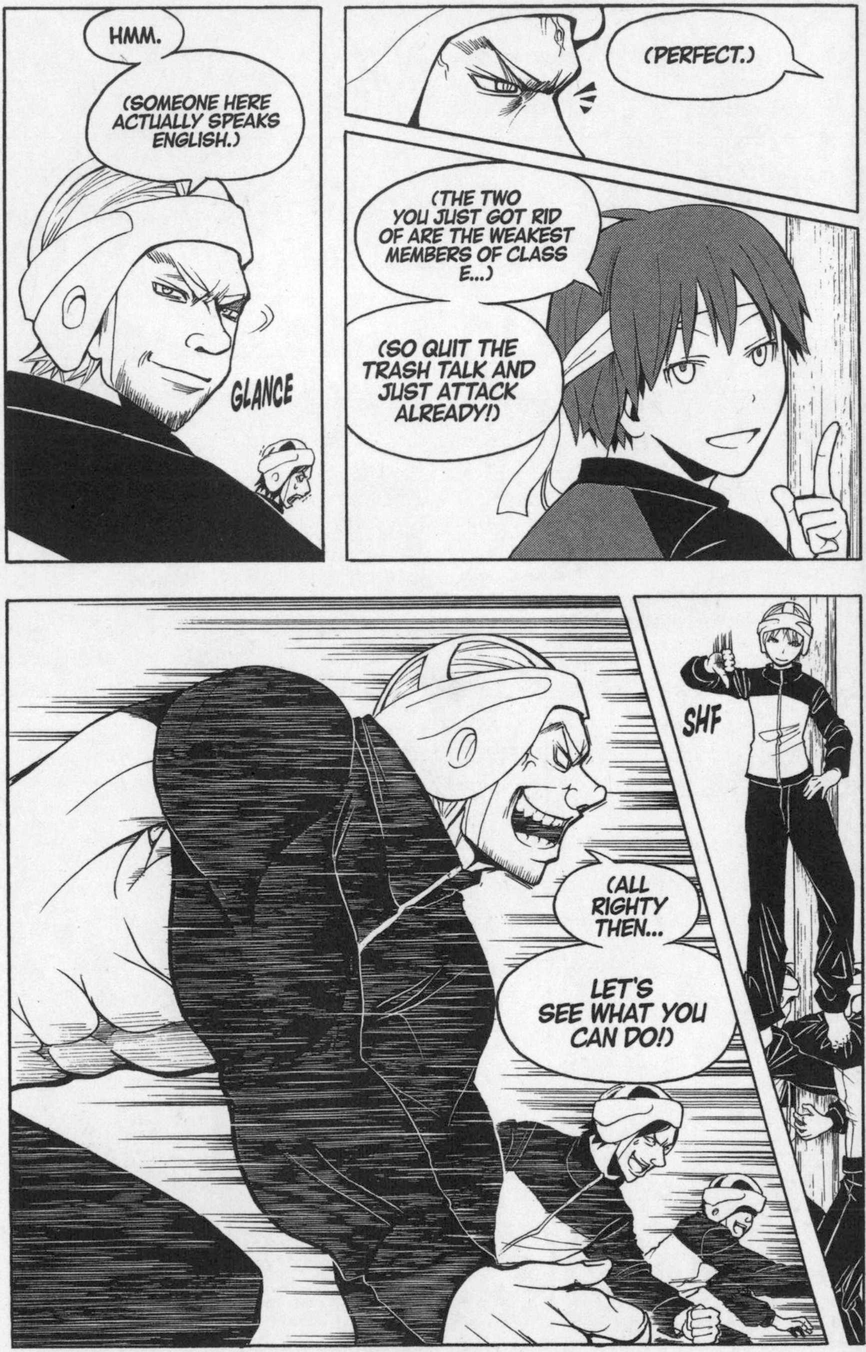
(PERFECT.)
(THE TWO YOU JUST GOT RID OF ARE THE WEAKEST MEMBERS OF CLASS E...)
(SO QUIT THE TRASH TALK AND JUST ATTACK ALREADY!)
HMM.
(SOMEONE HERE ACTUALLY SPEAKS ENGLISH.)
GLANCE
SHF
(ALL RIGHTY THEN...
LET'S SEE WHAT YOU CAN DO!)

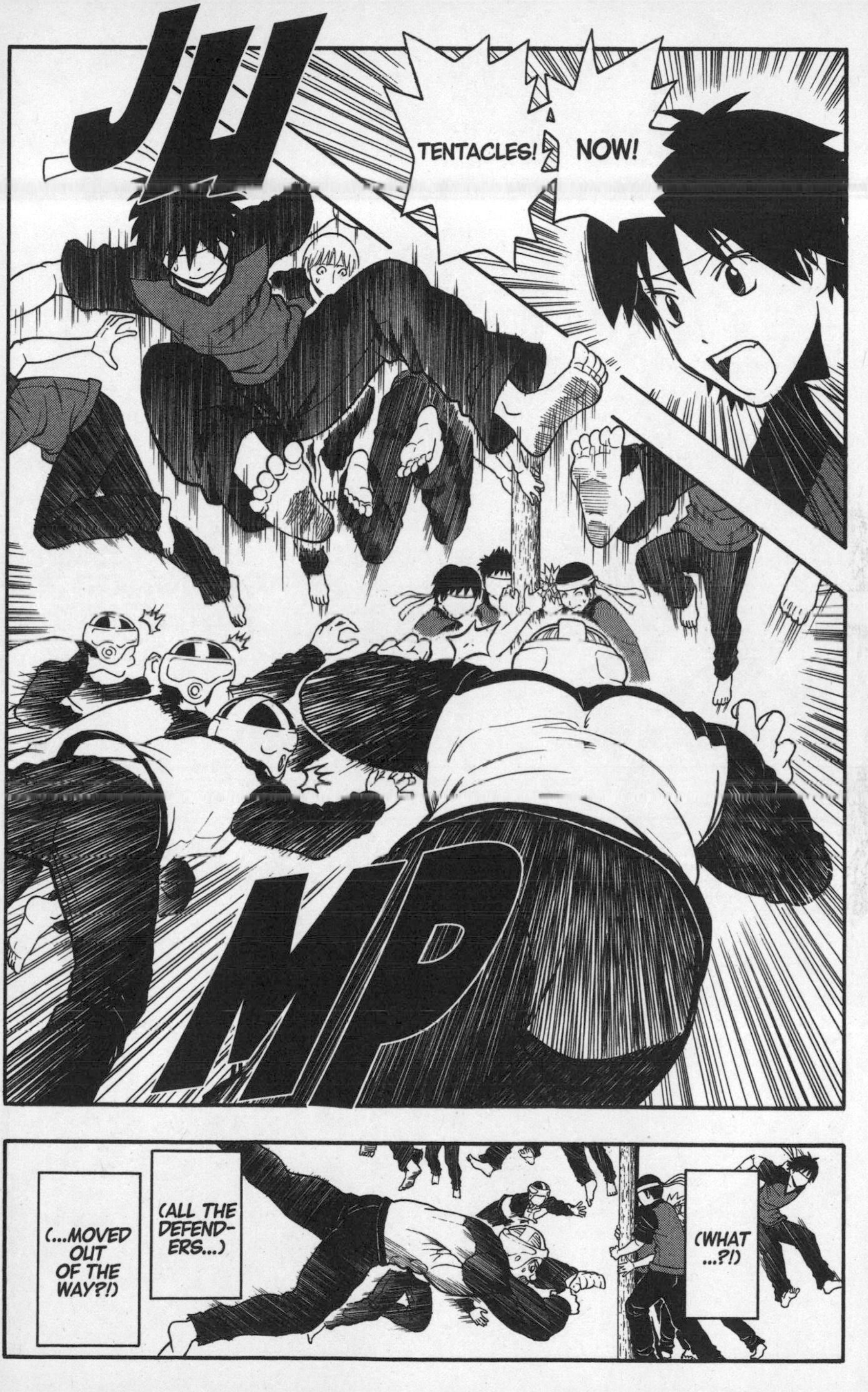
TENTACLES! NOW!
JU
MP
(WHAT ...?!)
(ALL THE DEFEND-ERS...)
(...MOVED OUT OF THE WAY?!)

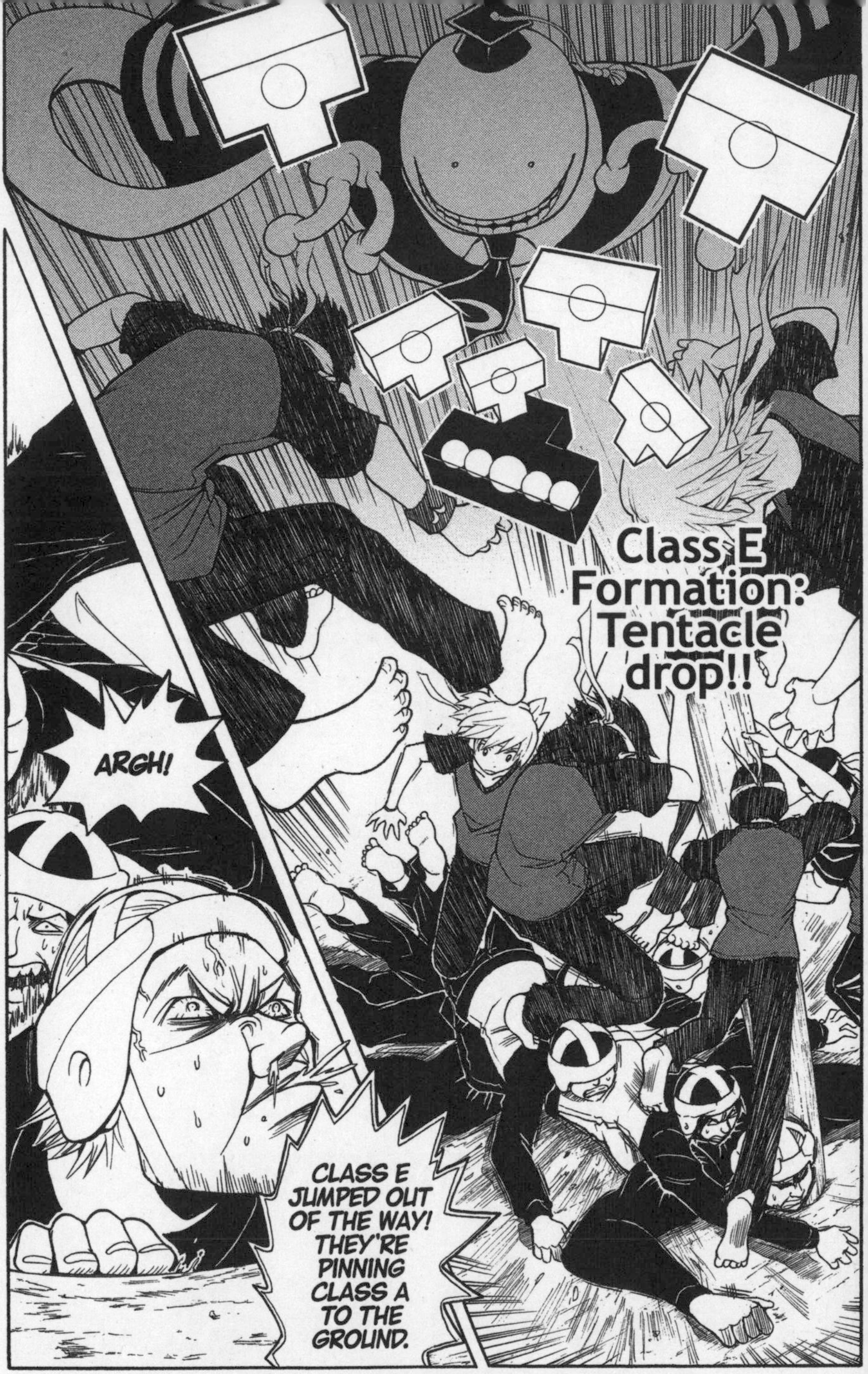
Class E Formation: Tentacle drop!!
ARGH!
CLASS E JUMPED OUT OF THE WAY! THEY'RE PINNING CLASS A TO THE GROUND.

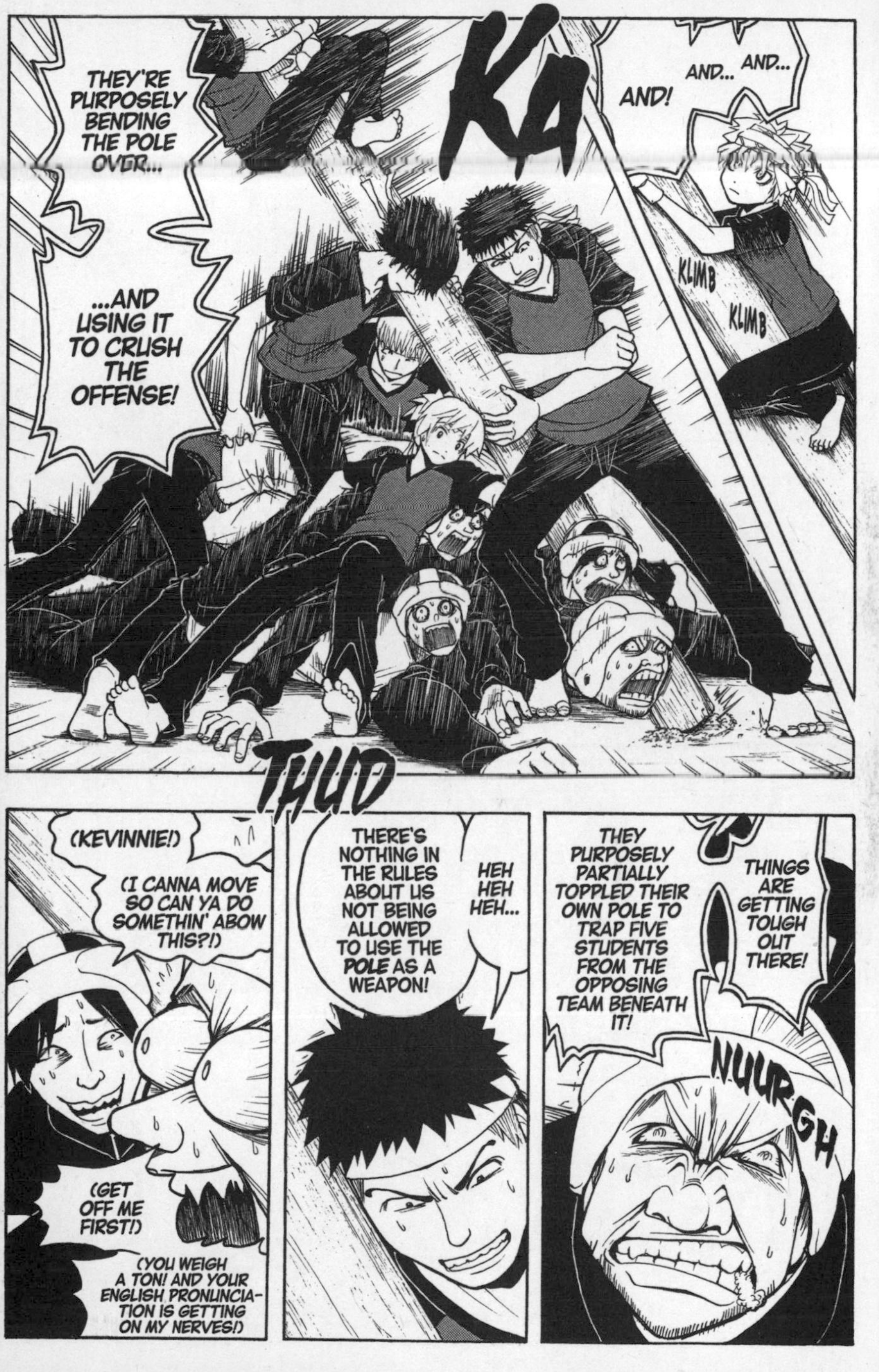
AND... AND...
AND!
KA
THEY'RE PURPOSELY BENDING THE POLE OVER...
...AND USING IT TO CRUSH THE OFFENSE!
KLIMB
KLIMB
THUD
THINGS ARE GETTING TOUGH OUT THERE!
THEY PURPOSELY PARTIALLY TOPPLED THEIR OWN POLE TO TRAP FIVE STUDENTS FROM THE OPPOSING TEAM BENEATH IT!
NUURGH
HEH HEH HEH...
THERE'S NOTHING IN THE RULES ABOUT US NOT BEING ALLOWED TO USE THE POLE AS A WEAPON!
(KEVINNIE!)
(I CANNA MOVE SO CAN YA DO SOMETHIN' ABOW THIS?!)
(GET OFF ME FIRST!)
(YOU WEIGH A TON! AND YOUR ENGLISH PRONUNCIATION IS GETTING ON MY NERVES!)

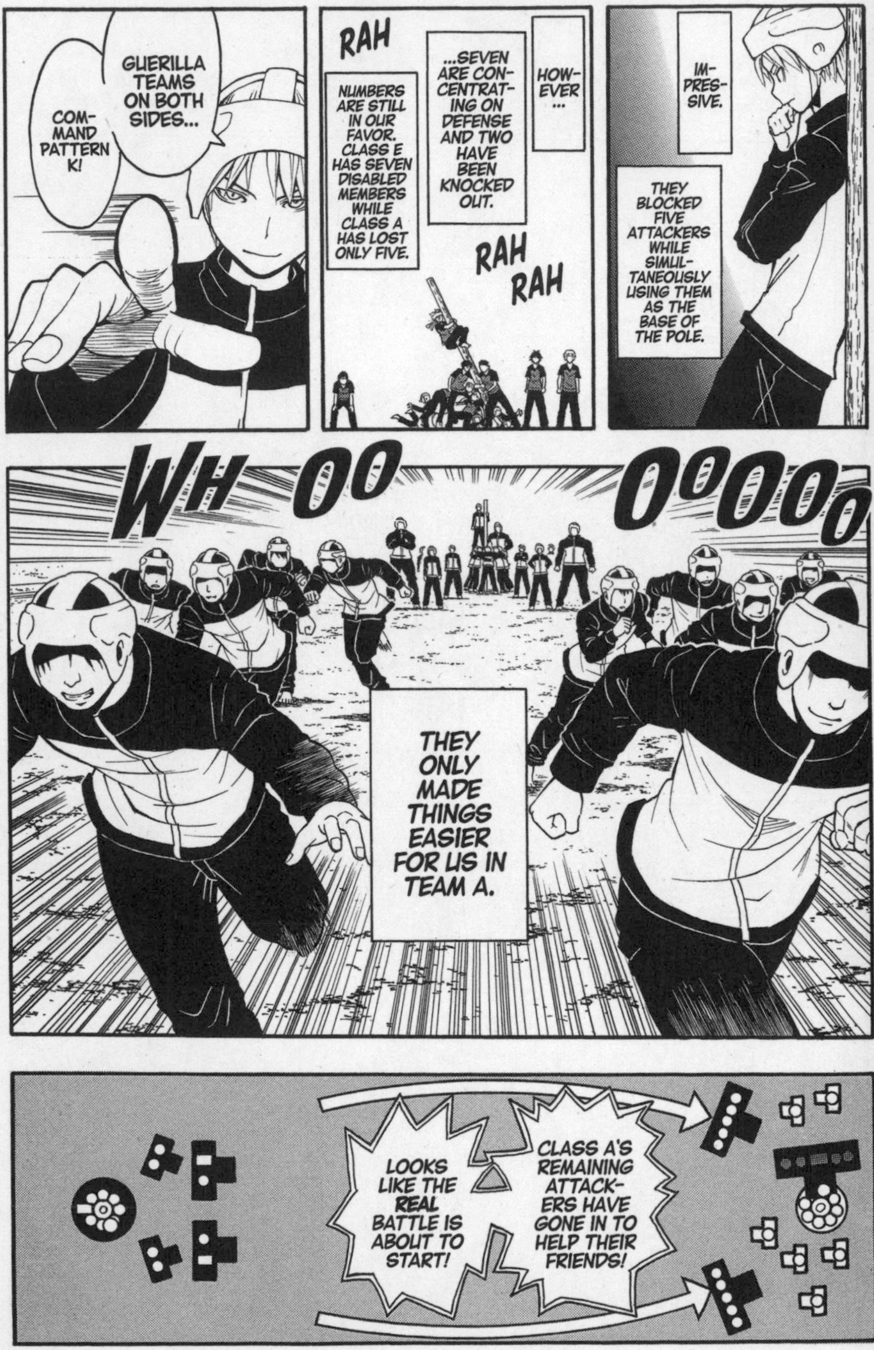
IM-PRES-SIVE.
THEY BLOCKED FIVE ATTACKERS WHILE SIMUL-TANEOUSLY USING THEM AS THE BASE OF THE POLE.
HOW-EVER ...
...SEVEN ARE CON-CENTRAT-ING ON DEFENSE AND TWO HAVE BEEN KNOCKED OUT.
NUMBERS ARE STILL IN OUR FAVOR. CLASS E HAS SEVEN DISABLED MEMBERS WHILE CLASS A HAS LOST ONLY FIVE.
RAH
RAH RAH
GUERILLA TEAMS ON BOTH SIDES...
COM-MAND PATTERN K!
WH OO OOOOO
THEY ONLY MADE THINGS EASIER FOR US IN TEAM A.
CLASS A'S REMAINING ATTACK-ERS HAVE GONE IN TO HELP THEIR FRIENDS!
LOOKS LIKE THE REAL BATTLE IS ABOUT TO START!

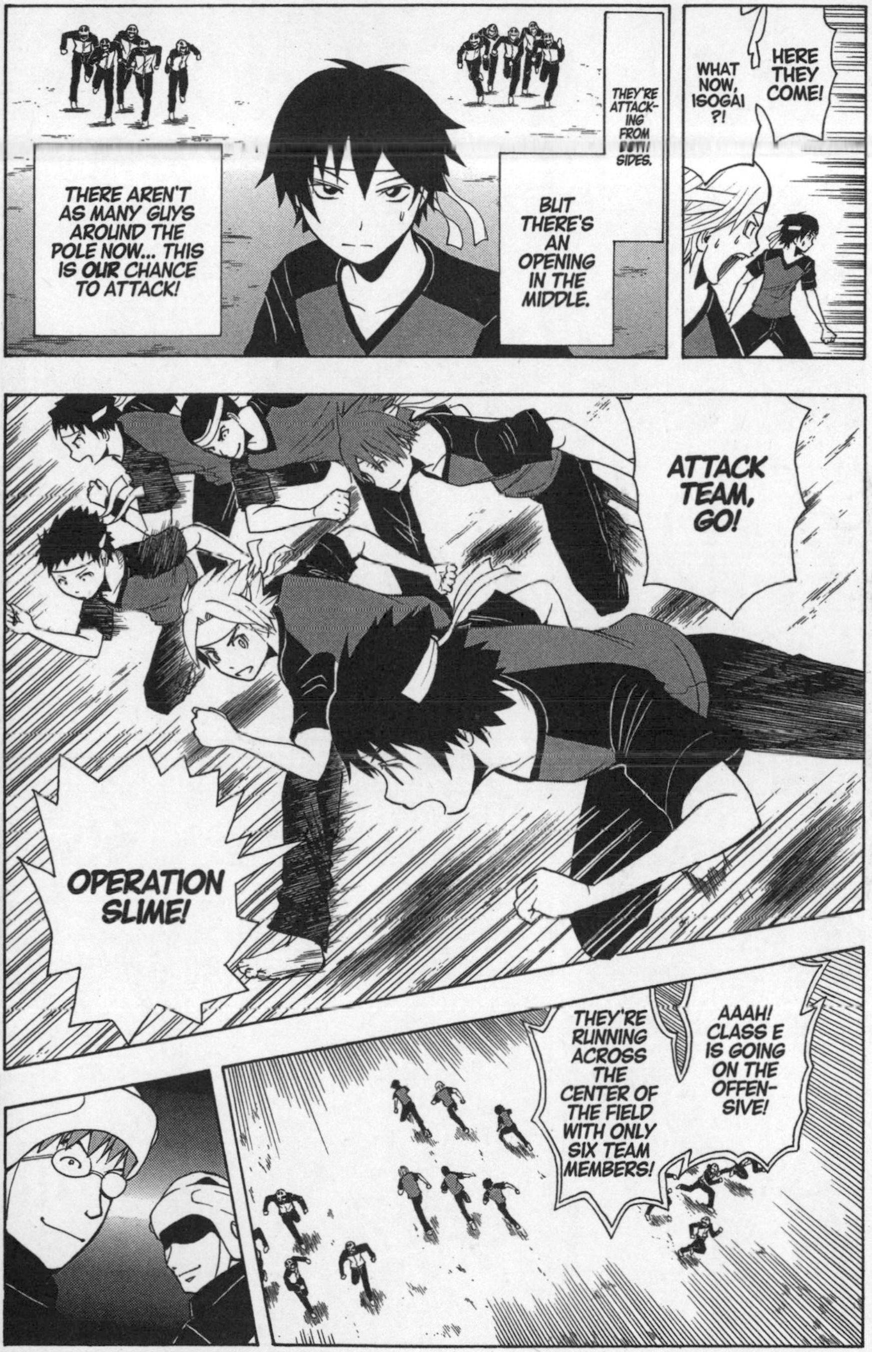
HERE THEY COME!
WHAT NOW, ISOGAI ?!
THEY'RE ATTACKING FROM BOTH SIDES.
BUT THERE'S AN OPENING IN THE MIDDLE.
THERE AREN'T AS MANY GUYS AROUND THE POLE NOW... THIS IS OUR CHANCE TO ATTACK!
ATTACK TEAM, GO!
OPERATION SLIME!
AAAH! CLASS E IS GOING ON THE OFFENSIVE!
THEY'RE RUNNING ACROSS THE CENTER OF THE FIELD WITH ONLY SIX TEAM MEMBERS!

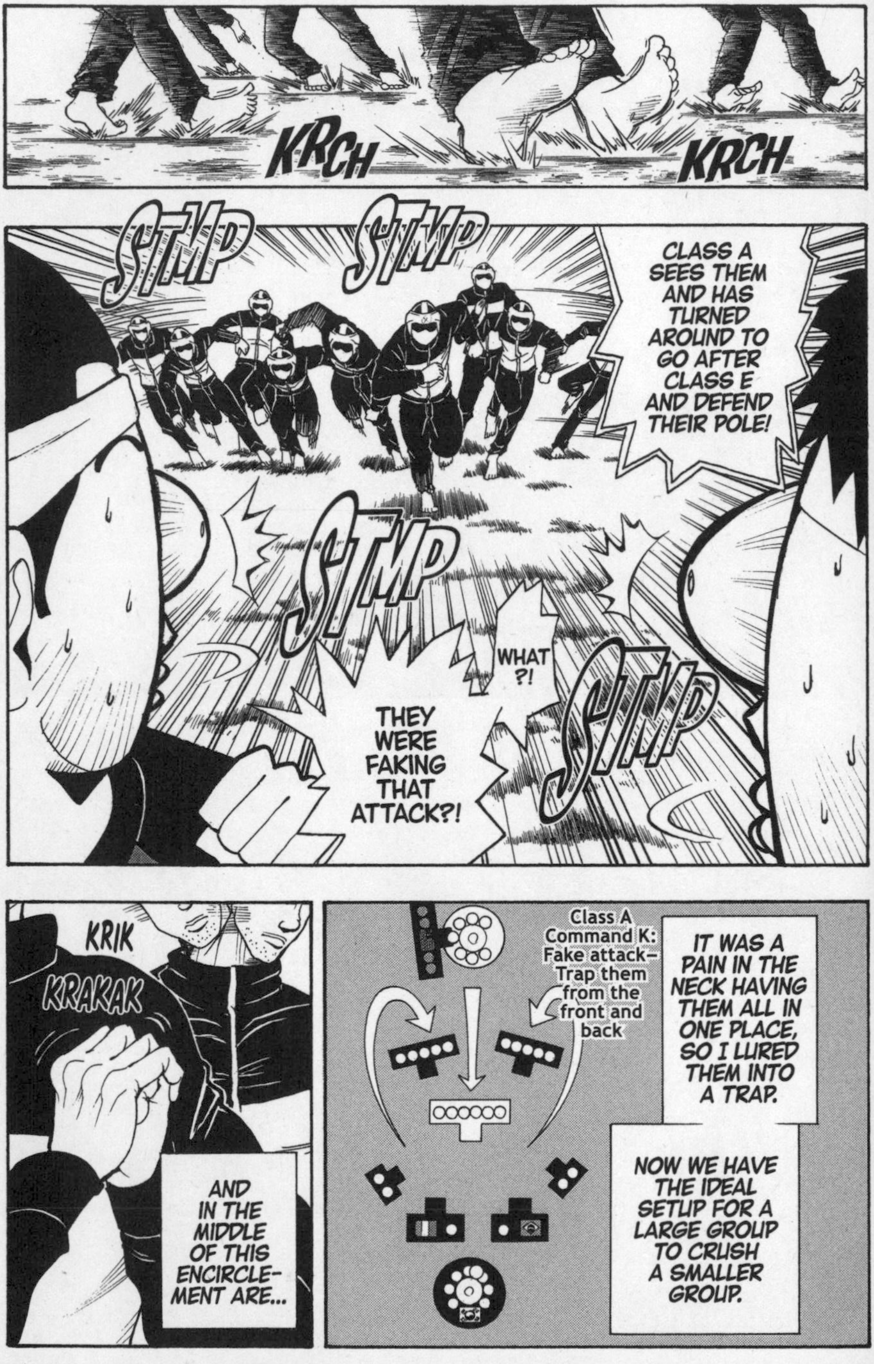
KRCH
KRCH
CLASS A SEES THEM AND HAS TURNED AROUND TO GO AFTER CLASS E AND DEFEND THEIR POLE!
STMP
STMP
STMP
STMP
WHAT?!
THEY WERE FAKING THAT ATTACK?!
Class A Command K: Fake attack—Trap them from the front and back
IT WAS A PAIN IN THE NECK HAVING THEM ALL IN ONE PLACE, SO I LURED THEM INTO A TRAP.
NOW WE HAVE THE IDEAL SETUP FOR A LARGE GROUP TO CRUSH A SMALLER GROUP.
KRIK
KRAKAK
AND IN THE MIDDLE OF THIS ENCIRCLEMENT ARE...

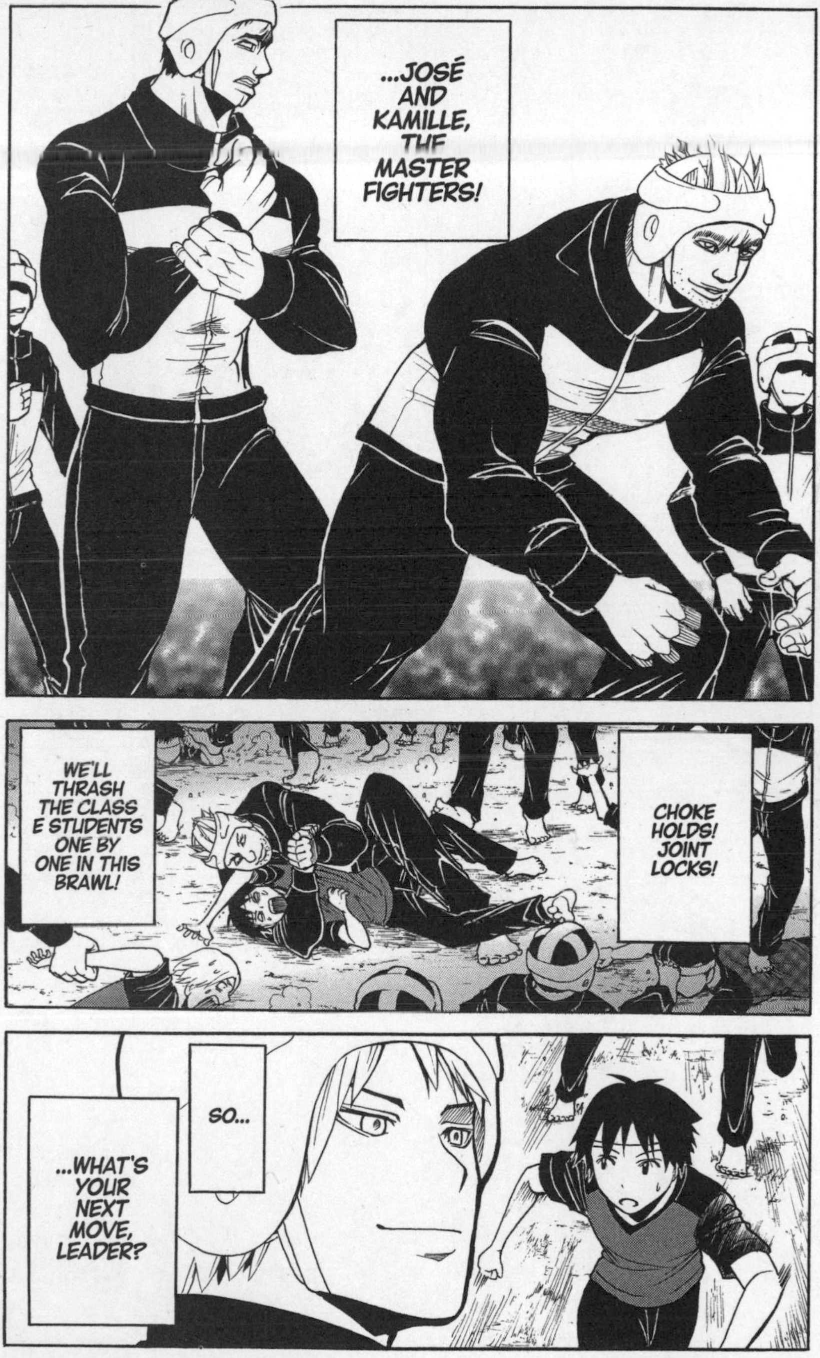
...JOSÉ AND KAMILLE, THE MASTER FIGHTERS!
CHOKE HOLDS! JOINT LOCKS!
WE'LL THRASH THE CLASS E STUDENTS ONE BY ONE IN THIS BRAWL!
SO...
...WHAT'S YOUR NEXT MOVE, LEADER?

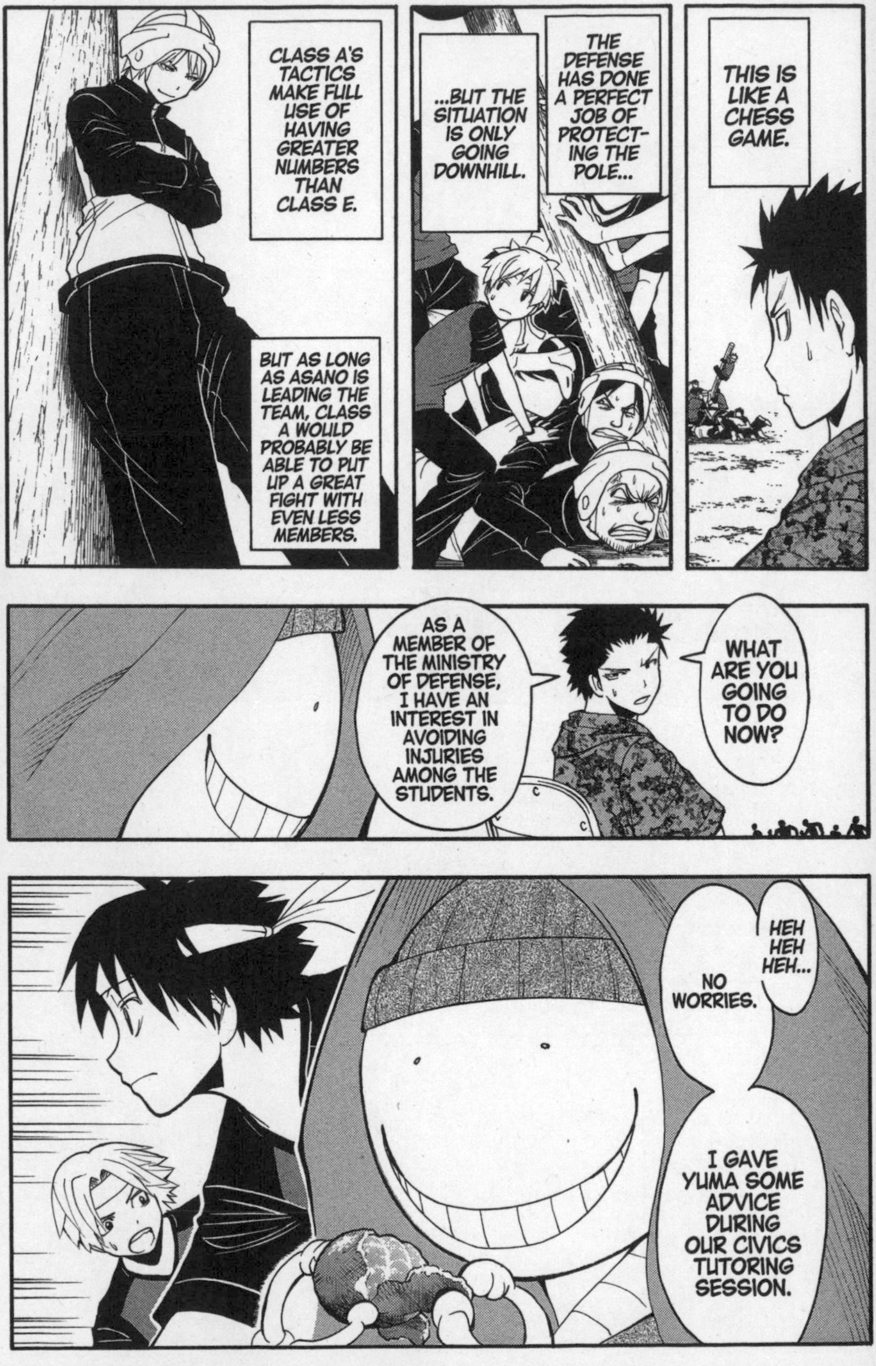
THIS IS LIKE A CHESS GAME.
THE DEFENSE HAS DONE A PERFECT JOB OF PROTECT-ING THE POLE...
...BUT THE SITUATION IS ONLY GOING DOWNHILL.
CLASS A'S TACTICS MAKE FULL USE OF HAVING GREATER NUMBERS THAN CLASS E.
BUT AS LONG AS ASANO IS LEADING THE TEAM, CLASS A WOULD PROBABLY BE ABLE TO PUT UP A GREAT FIGHT WITH EVEN LESS MEMBERS.
WHAT ARE YOU GOING TO DO NOW?
AS A MEMBER OF THE MINISTRY OF DEFENSE, I HAVE AN INTEREST IN AVOIDING INJURIES AMONG THE STUDENTS.
HEH HEH HEH...
NO WORRIES.
I GAVE YUMA SOME ADVICE DURING OUR CIVICS TUTORING SESSION.

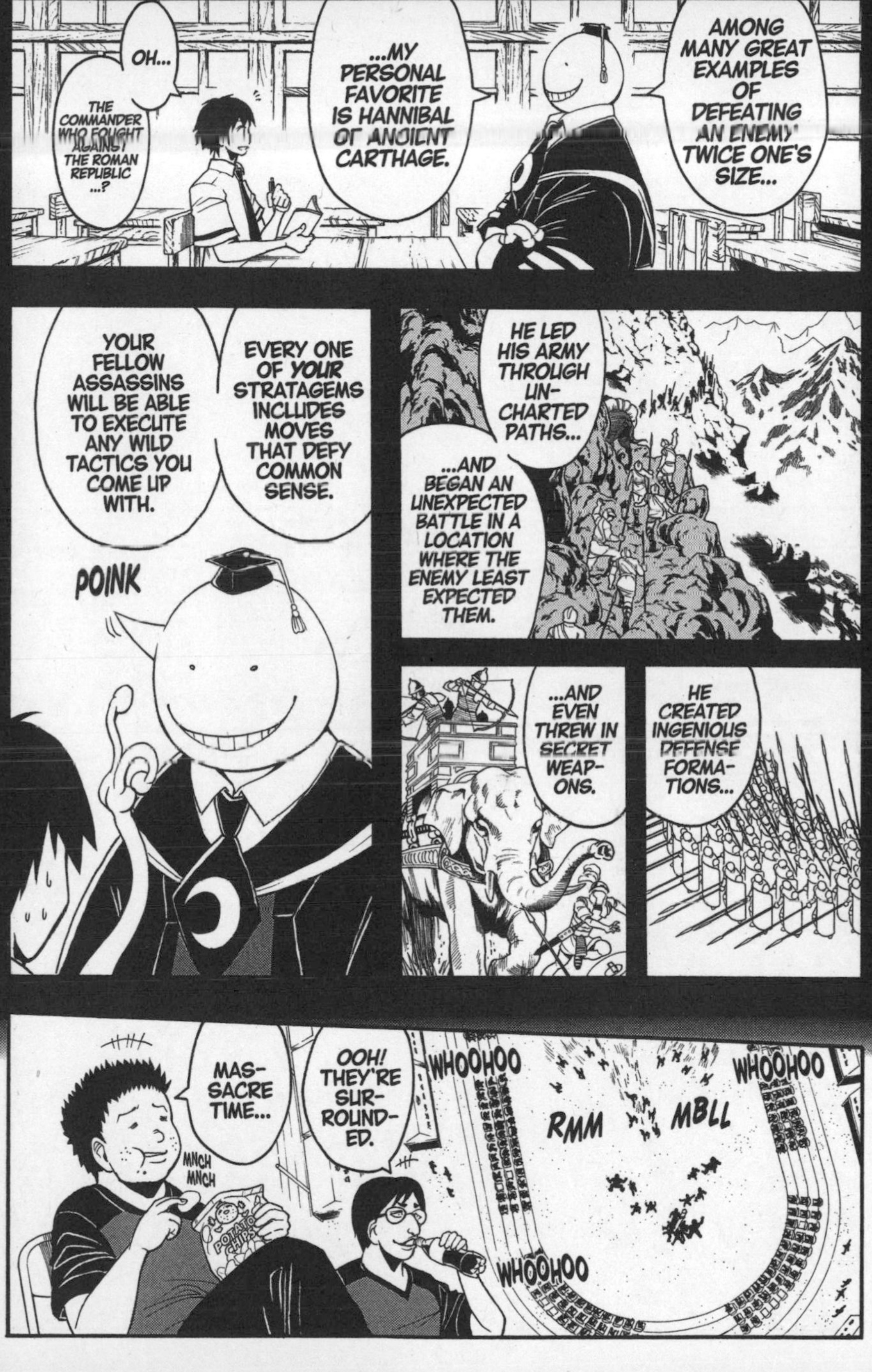
AMONG MANY GREAT EXAMPLES OF DEFEATING AN ENEMY TWICE ONE'S SIZE...
...MY PERSONAL FAVORITE IS HANNIBAL OF ANCIENT CARTHAGE.
OH...
THE COMMANDER WHO FOUGHT AGAINST THE ROMAN REPUBLIC ...?
HE LED HIS ARMY THROUGH UN-CHARTED PATHS...
...AND BEGAN AN UNEXPECTED BATTLE IN A LOCATION WHERE THE ENEMY LEAST EXPECTED THEM.
HE CREATED INGENIOUS DEFENSE FORMA-TIONS...
...AND EVEN THREW IN SECRET WEAP-ONS.
EVERY ONE OF YOUR STRATAGEMS INCLUDES MOVES THAT DEFY COMMON SENSE.
YOUR FELLOW ASSASSINS WILL BE ABLE TO EXECUTE ANY WILD TACTICS YOU COME UP WITH.
POINK
WHOOHOO
MBLL
RMM
WHOOHOO
WHOOHOO
OOH! THEY'RE SUR-ROUND-ED.
MAS-SACRE TIME...
MNCH MNCH
POTATO CHIPS

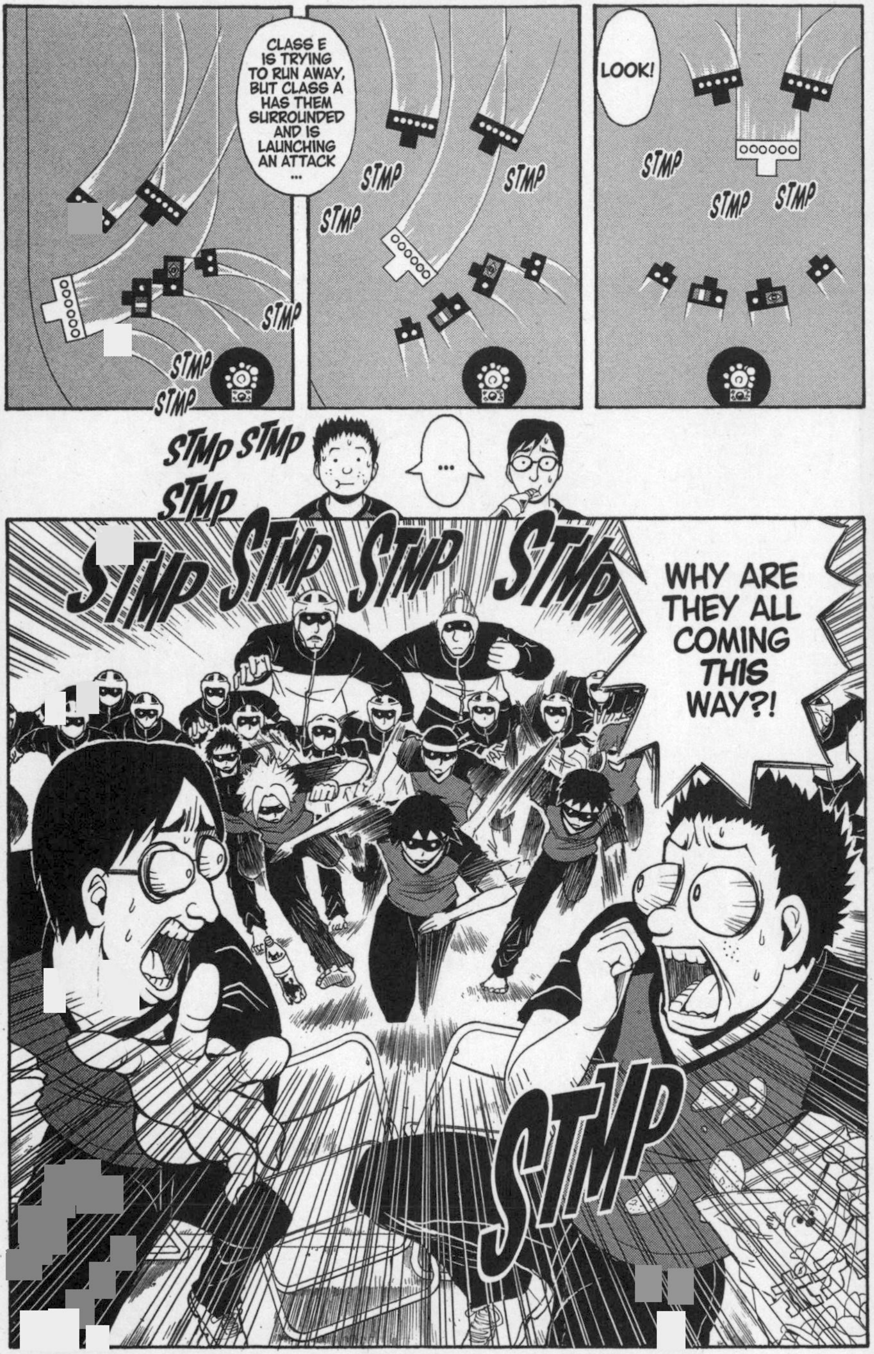
LOOK!
STMP
STMP STMP
CLASS E IS TRYING TO RUN AWAY, BUT CLASS A HAS THEM SURROUNDED AND IS LAUNCHING AN ATTACK ...
STMP
STMP
STMP
STMP
STMP
...
STMP STMP
STMP
WHY ARE THEY ALL COMING THIS WAY?!
STMP STMP STMP STMP
STMP

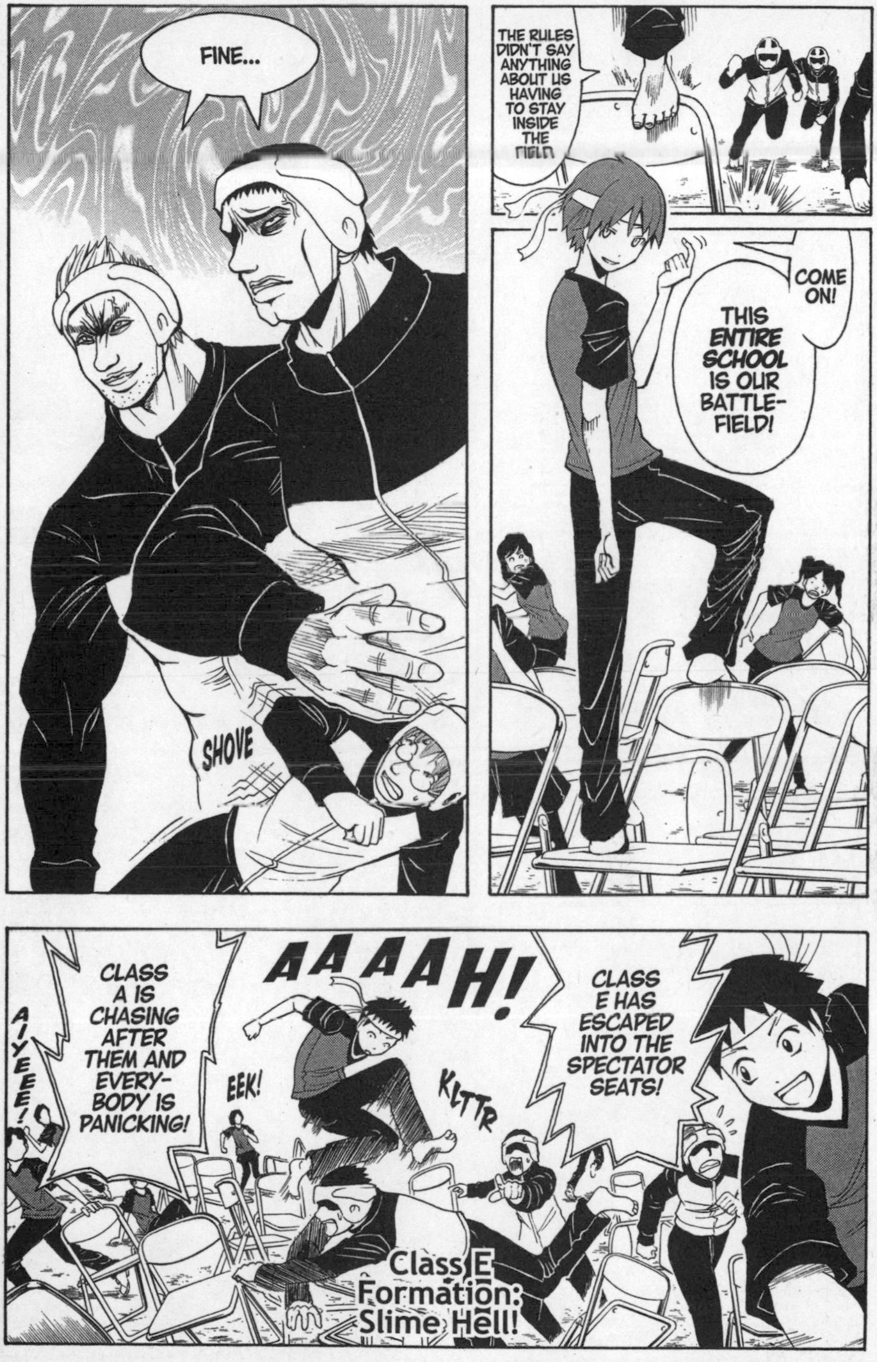
THE RULES DIDN'T SAY ANYTHING ABOUT US HAVING TO STAY INSIDE THE FIELD
COME ON!
THIS ENTIRE SCHOOL IS OUR BATTLE-FIELD!
FINE...
SHOVE
CLASS E HAS ESCAPED INTO THE SPECTATOR SEATS!
AAAAH!
KLTTR
CLASS A IS CHASING AFTER THEM AND EVERY-BODY IS PANICKING!
EEK!
AIYEEE!
Class E Formation: Slime Hell!

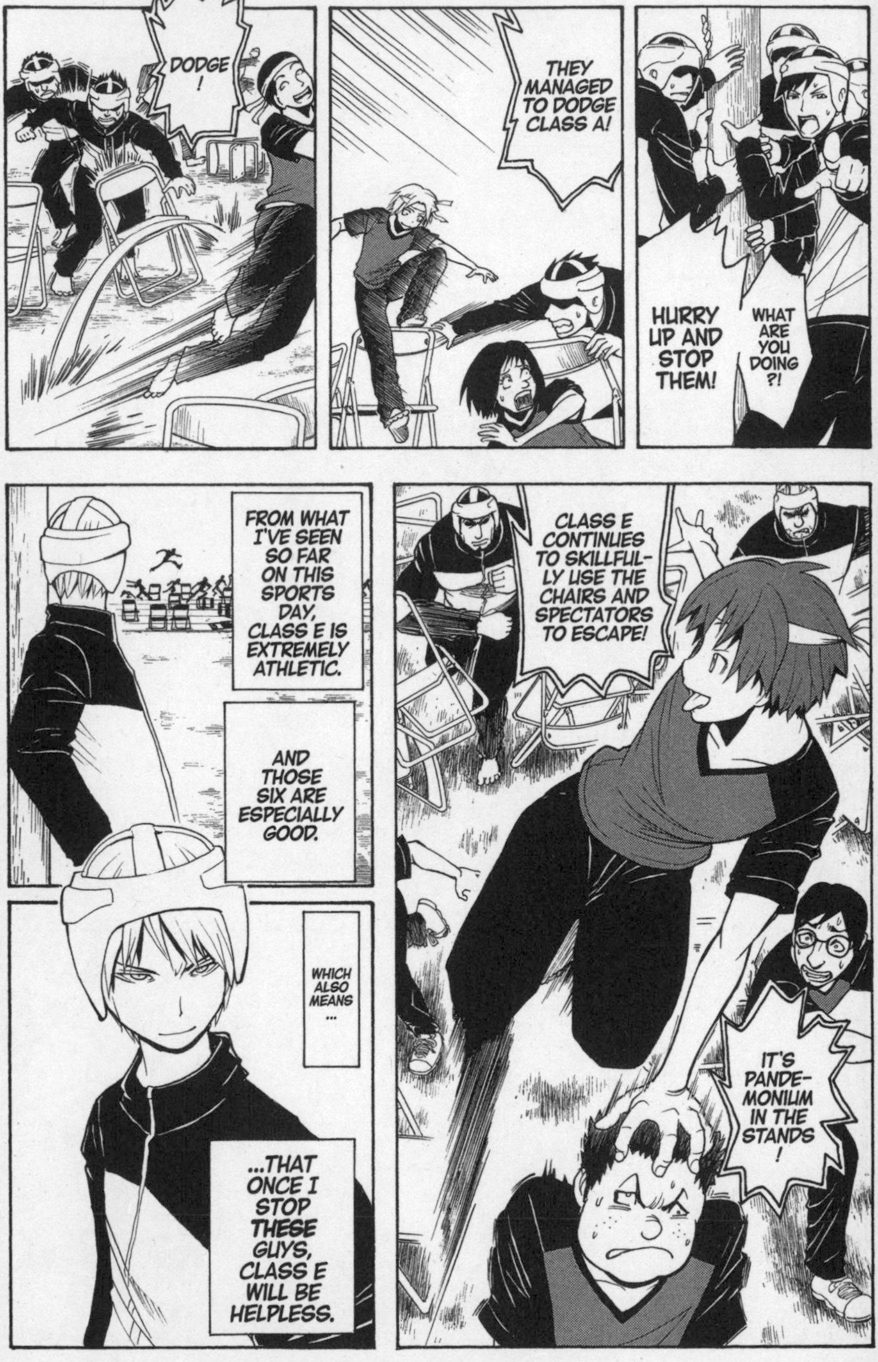
WHAT ARE YOU DOING ?!
HURRY UP AND STOP THEM!
THEY MANAGED TO DODGE CLASS A!
DODGE !
CLASS E CONTINUES TO SKILLFULLY USE THE CHAIRS AND SPECTATORS TO ESCAPE!
IT'S PANDEMONIUM IN THE STANDS !
FROM WHAT I'VE SEEN SO FAR ON THIS SPORTS DAY, CLASS E IS EXTREMELY ATHLETIC.
AND THOSE SIX ARE ESPECIALLY GOOD.
WHICH ALSO MEANS ...
...THAT ONCE I STOP THESE GUYS, CLASS E WILL BE HELPLESS.

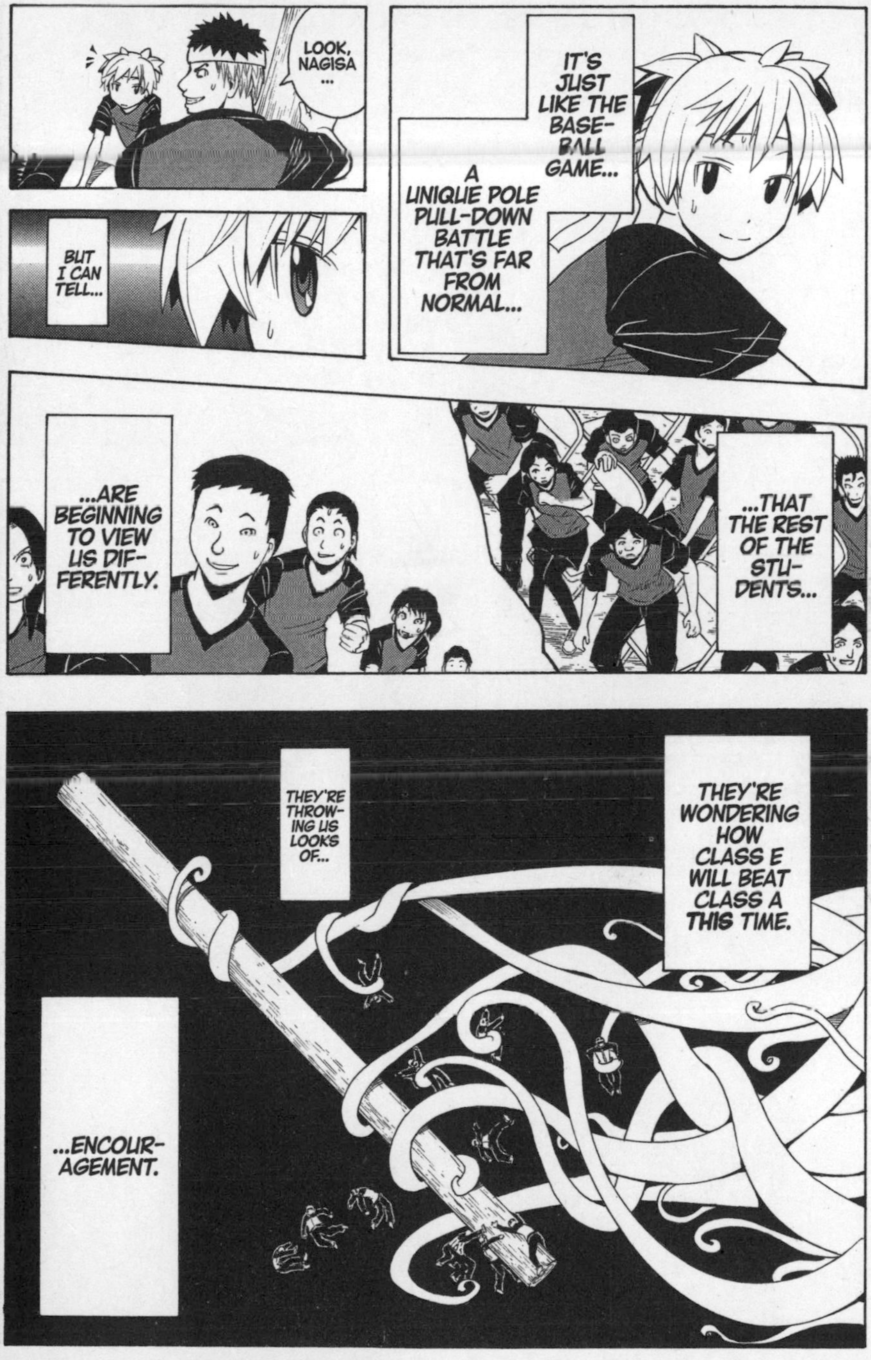
IT'S JUST LIKE THE BASE-BALL GAME...
A UNIQUE POLE PULL-DOWN BATTLE THAT'S FAR FROM NORMAL...
LOOK, NAGISA...
BUT I CAN TELL...
...THAT THE REST OF THE STU-DENTS...
...ARE BEGINNING TO VIEW US DIF-FERENTLY.
THEY'RE WONDERING HOW CLASS E WILL BEAT CLASS A THIS TIME.
THEY'RE THROW-ING US LOOKS OF...
...ENCOUR-AGEMENT.

Koro Sensei's Secrets, Encyclopedia Entry ①

How He Changes His Outfit So Super Fast

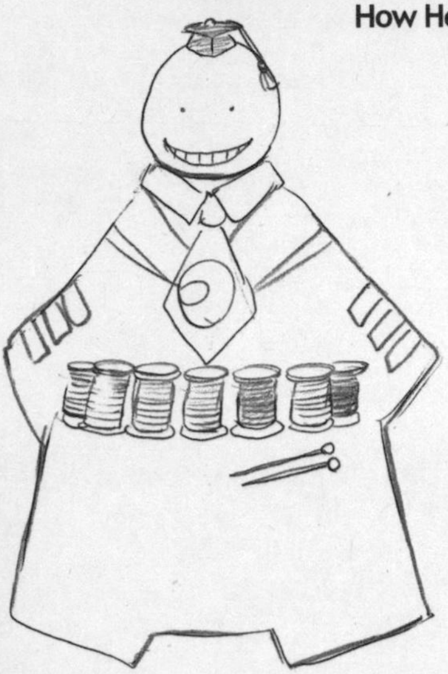

① Koro Sensei has various spools of colored thread and knitting needles squirreled away inside his baggy robe.

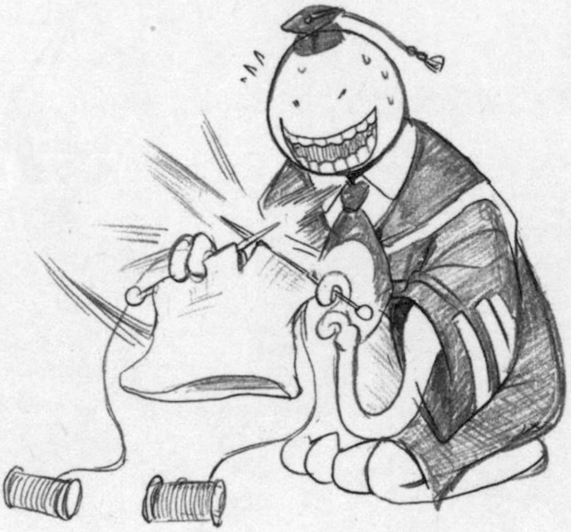

② He knits at Mach 20! Because he creates his clothes from scratch, he can make them any color, shape or design!

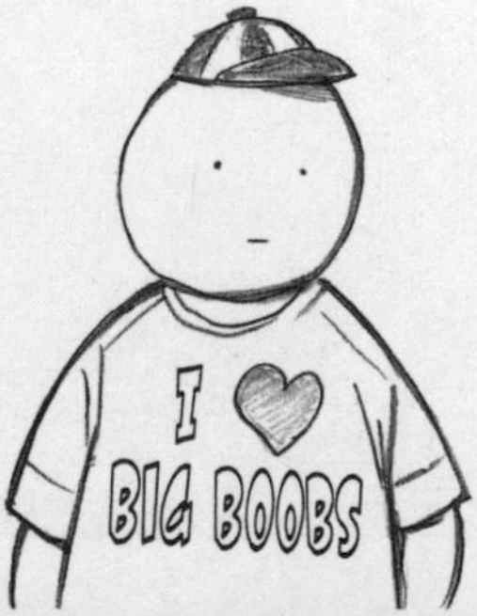
I
BIG BOOBS

③ Finished! Once he's done enjoying a new outfit, he unravels it into thread again. This process is both budget-friendly and efficient!

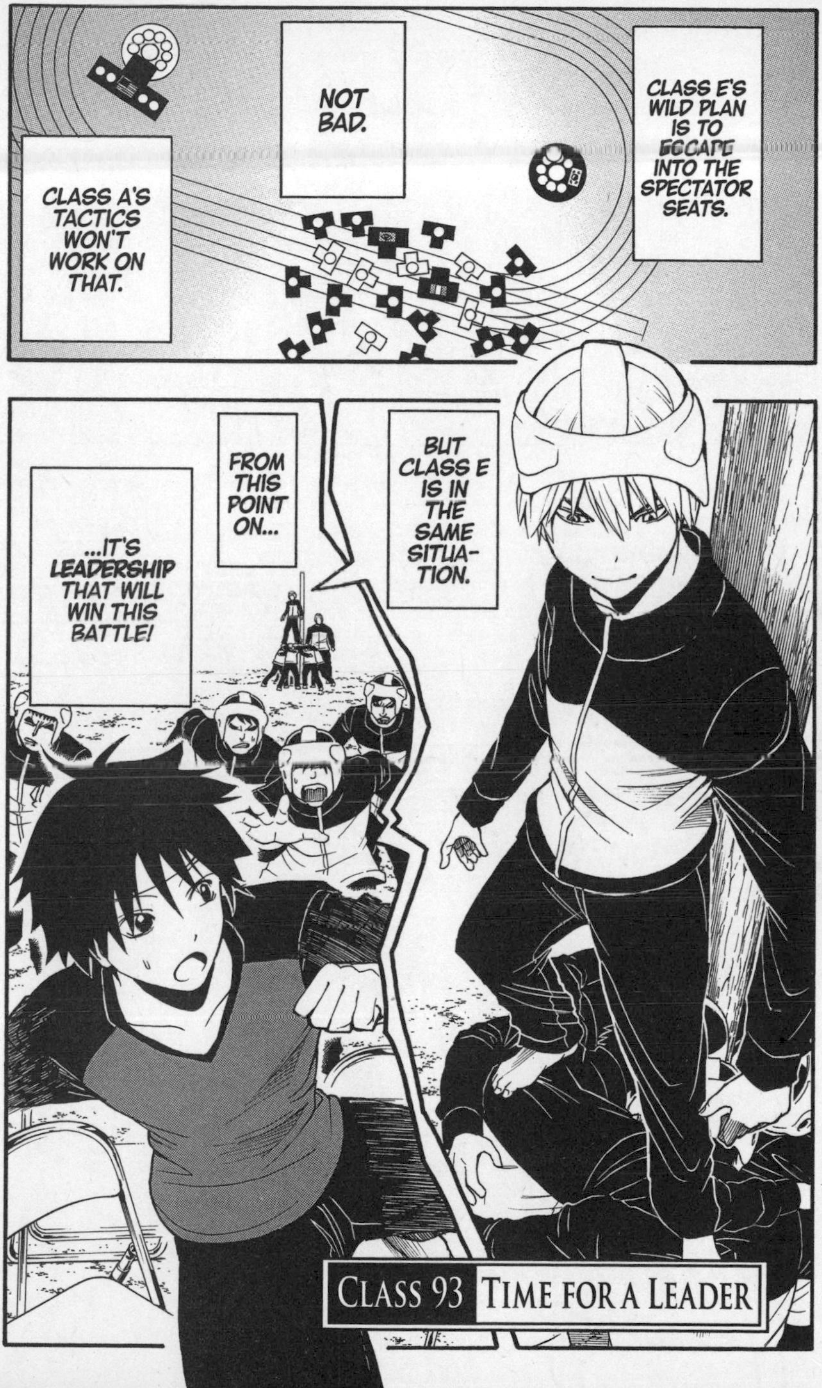
CLASS E'S WILD PLAN IS TO ESCAPE INTO THE SPECTATOR SEATS.
NOT BAD.
CLASS A'S TACTICS WON'T WORK ON THAT.
BUT CLASS E IS IN THE SAME SITUATION.
FROM THIS POINT ON...
...IT'S LEADERSHIP THAT WILL WIN THIS BATTLE!
CLASS 93 TIME FOR A LEADER

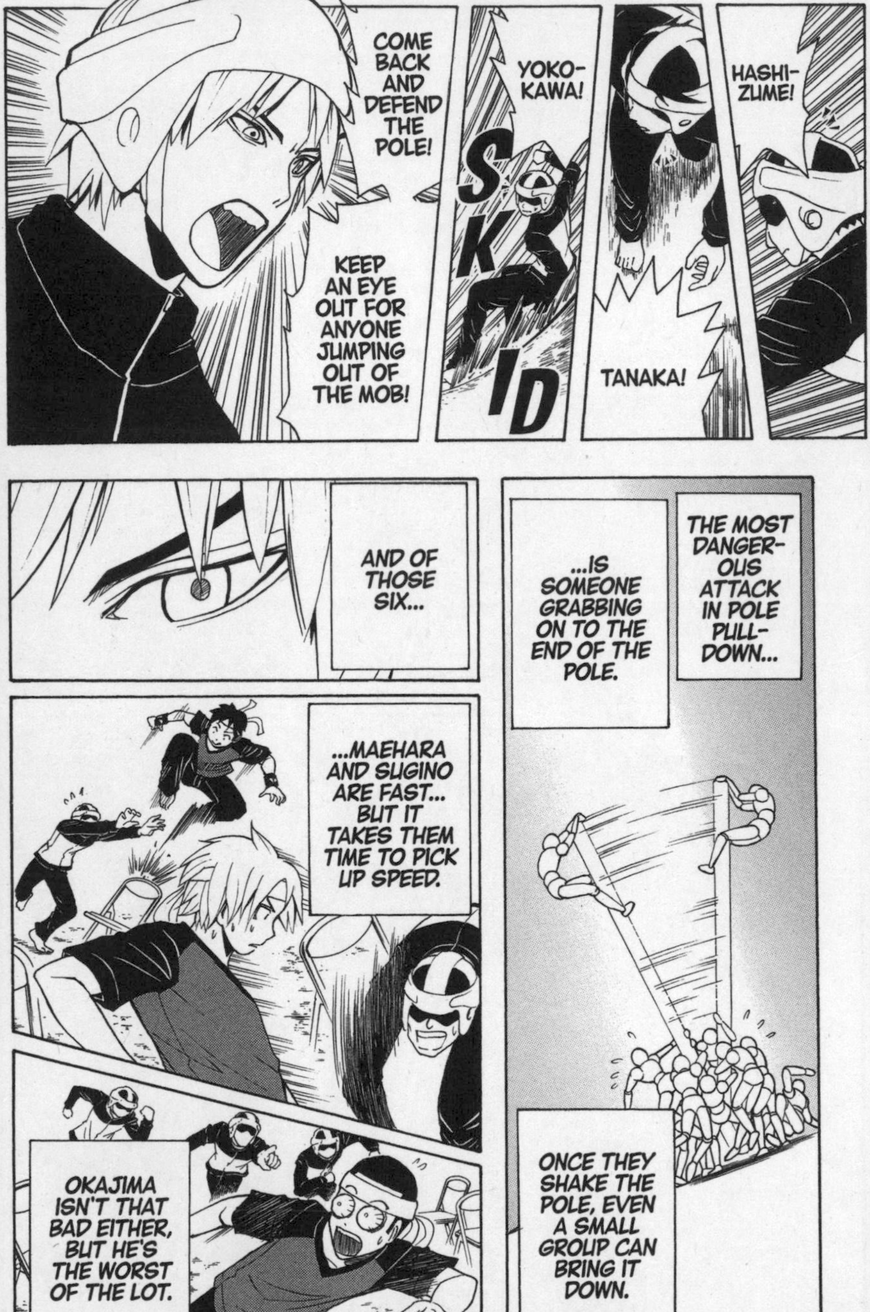
HASHI-ZUME!
TANAKA!
YOKO-KAWA!
SKID
COME BACK AND DEFEND THE POLE!
KEEP AN EYE OUT FOR ANYONE JUMPING OUT OF THE MOB!
THE MOST DANGER-OUS ATTACK IN POLE PULL-DOWN...
...IS SOMEONE GRABBING ON TO THE END OF THE POLE.
ONCE THEY SHAKE THE POLE, EVEN A SMALL GROUP CAN BRING IT DOWN.
AND OF THOSE SIX...
...MAEHARA AND SUGINO ARE FAST... BUT IT TAKES THEM TIME TO PICK UP SPEED.
OKAJIMA ISN'T THAT BAD EITHER, BUT HE'S THE WORST OF THE LOT.

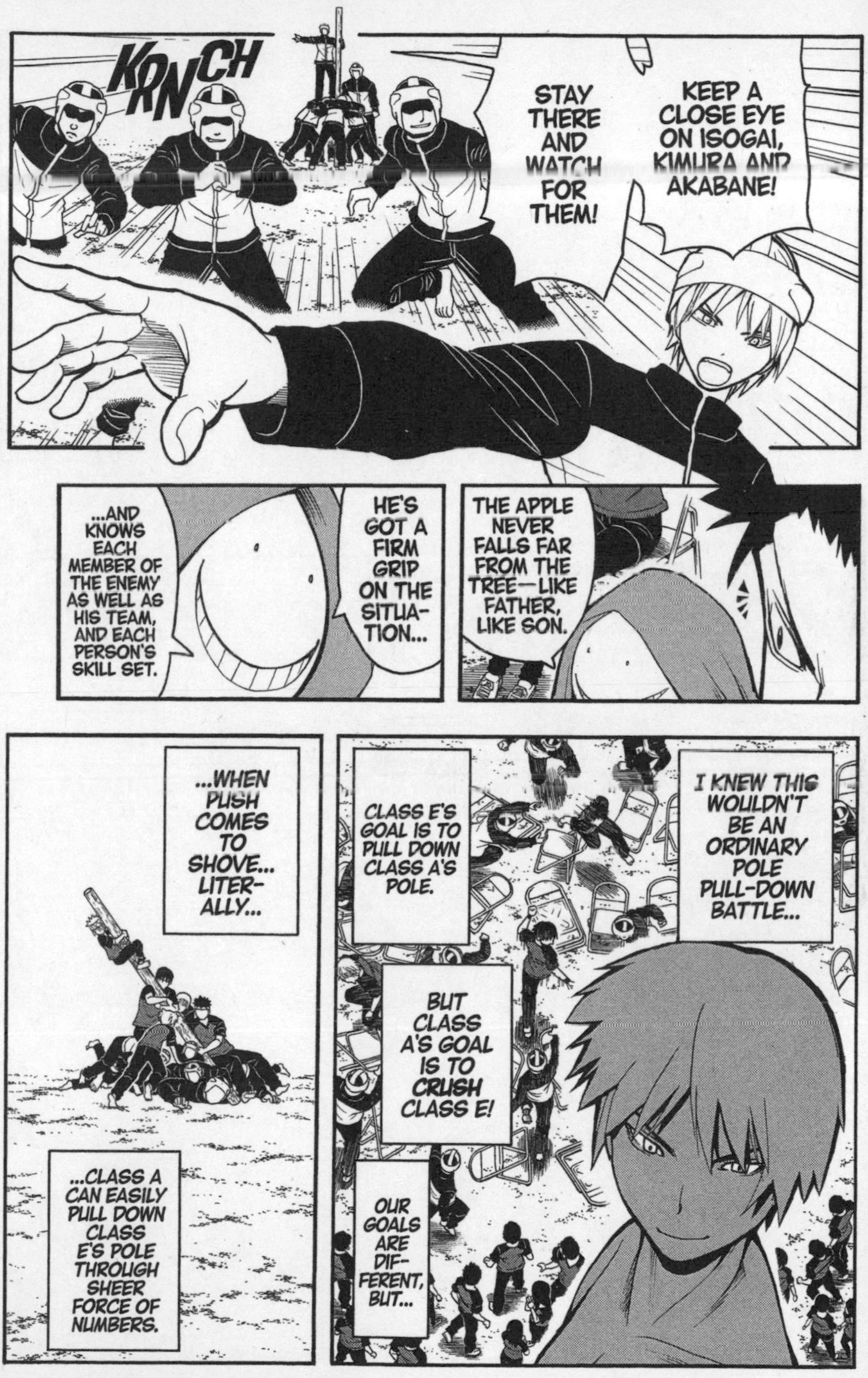
KRNCH
KEEP A CLOSE EYE ON ISOGAI, KIMURA AND AKABANE!
STAY THERE AND WATCH FOR THEM!
THE APPLE NEVER FALLS FAR FROM THE TREE—LIKE FATHER, LIKE SON.
HE'S GOT A FIRM GRIP ON THE SITUATION...
...AND KNOWS EACH MEMBER OF THE ENEMY AS WELL AS HIS TEAM, AND EACH PERSON'S SKILL SET.
I KNEW THIS WOULDN'T BE AN ORDINARY POLE PULL-DOWN BATTLE...
CLASS E'S GOAL IS TO PULL DOWN CLASS A'S POLE.
BUT CLASS A'S GOAL IS TO CRUSH CLASS E!
OUR GOALS ARE DIFFERENT, BUT...
...WHEN PUSH COMES TO SHOVE... LITERALLY...
...CLASS A CAN EASILY PULL DOWN CLASS E'S POLE THROUGH SHEER FORCE OF NUMBERS.

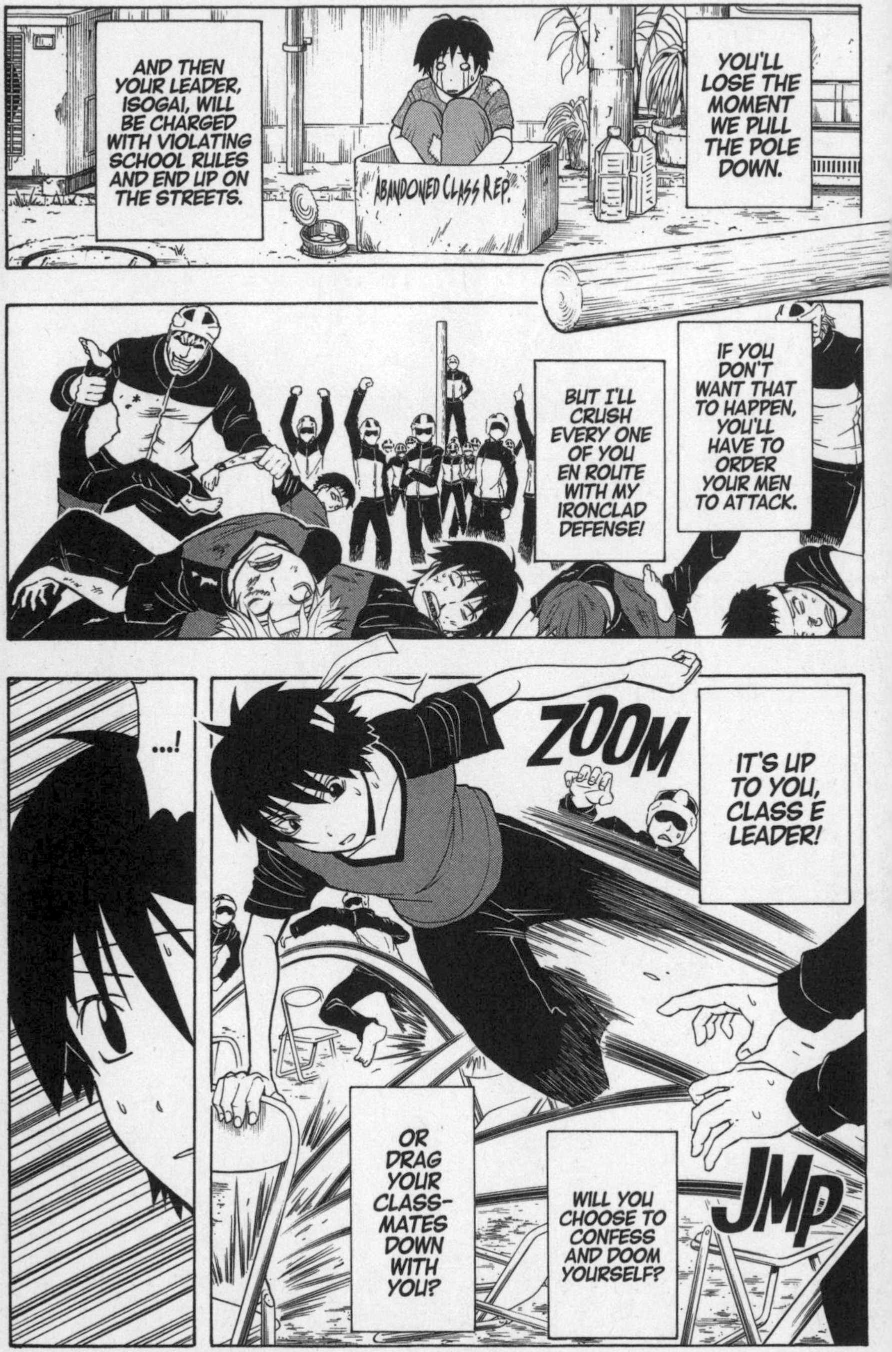
YOU'LL LOSE THE MOMENT WE PULL THE POLE DOWN.
ABANDONED CLASS REP.
AND THEN YOUR LEADER, ISOGAI, WILL BE CHARGED WITH VIOLATING SCHOOL RULES AND END UP ON THE STREETS.
IF YOU DON'T WANT THAT TO HAPPEN, YOU'LL HAVE TO ORDER YOUR MEN TO ATTACK.
BUT I'LL CRUSH EVERY ONE OF YOU EN ROUTE WITH MY IRONCLAD DEFENSE!
ZOOM
IT'S UP TO YOU, CLASS E LEADER!
JMP
WILL YOU CHOOSE TO CONFESS AND DOOM YOURSELF?
OR DRAG YOUR CLASS-MATES DOWN WITH YOU?
...!

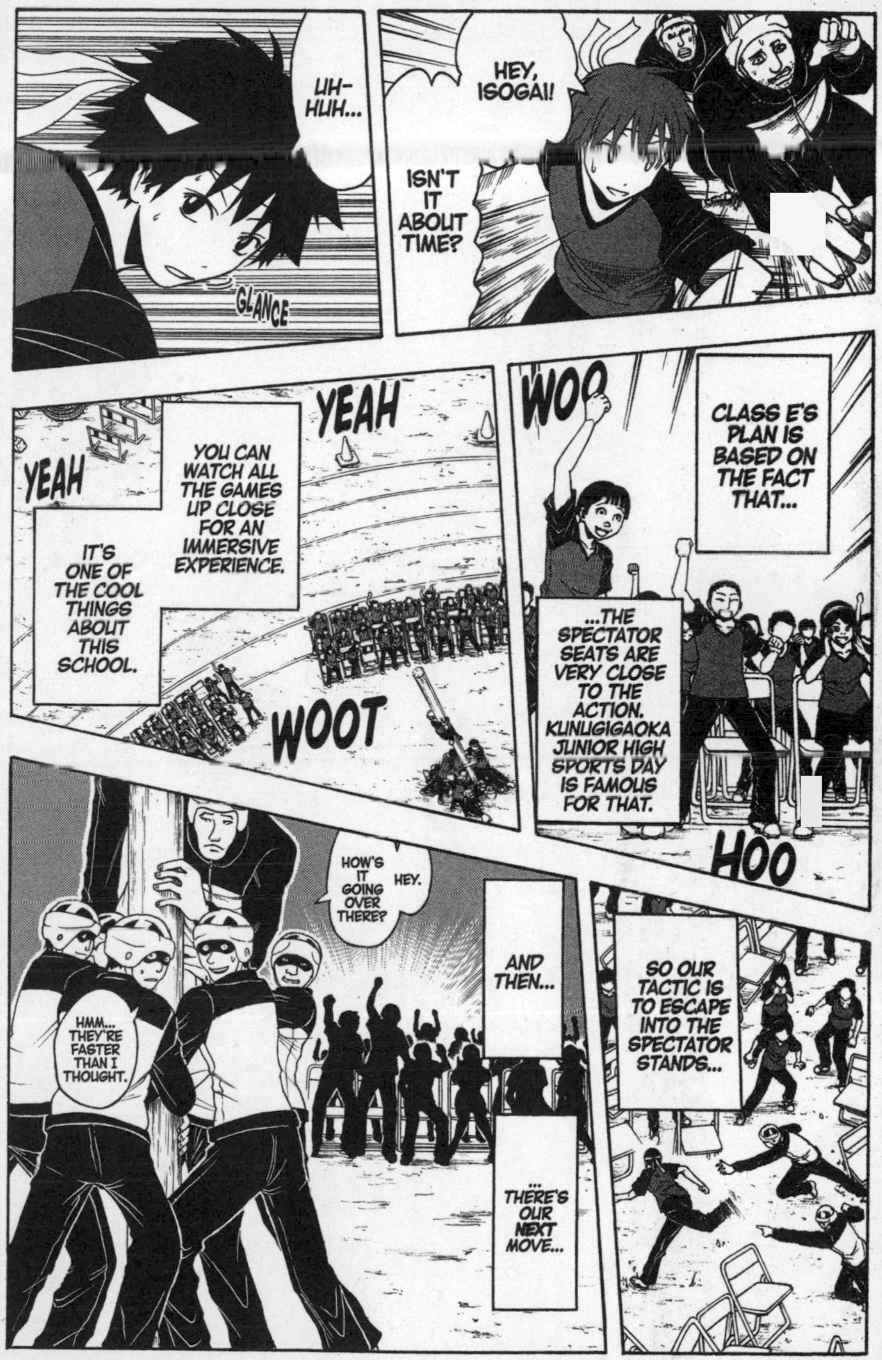
HEY, ISOGAI!
ISN'T IT ABOUT TIME?
UH-HUH...
GLANCE
CLASS E'S PLAN IS BASED ON THE FACT THAT...
WOO
...THE SPECTATOR SEATS ARE VERY CLOSE TO THE ACTION. KUNUGIGAOKA JUNIOR HIGH SPORTS DAY IS FAMOUS FOR THAT.
HOO
YEAH
YOU CAN WATCH ALL THE GAMES UP CLOSE FOR AN IMMERSIVE EXPERIENCE.
IT'S ONE OF THE COOL THINGS ABOUT THIS SCHOOL.
YEAH
WOOT
SO OUR TACTIC IS TO ESCAPE INTO THE SPECTATOR STANDS...
AND THEN...
...THERE'S OUR NEXT MOVE...
HEY.
HOW'S IT GOING OVER THERE?
HMM... THEY'RE FASTER THAN I THOUGHT.

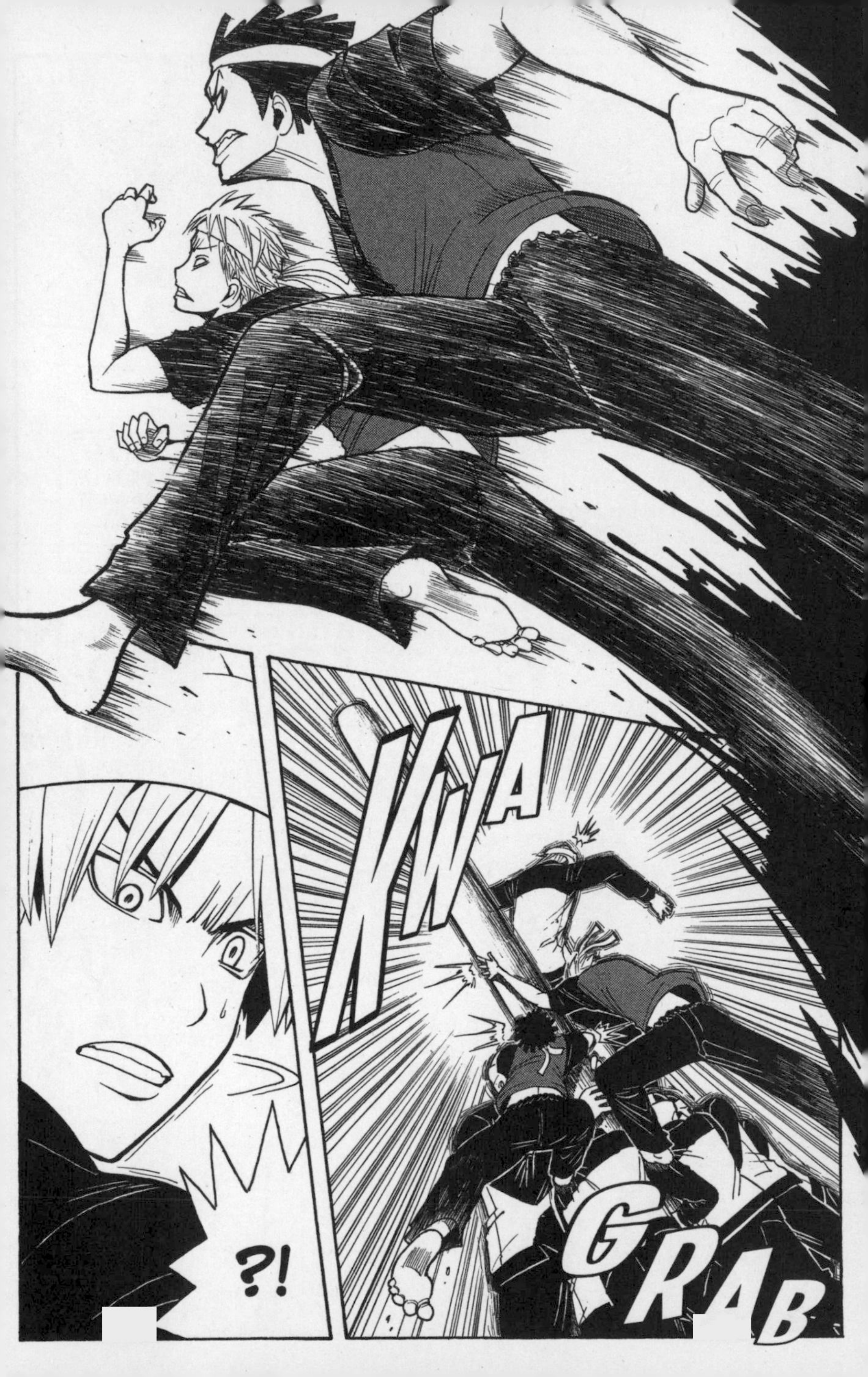
XWA
GRAB
?!

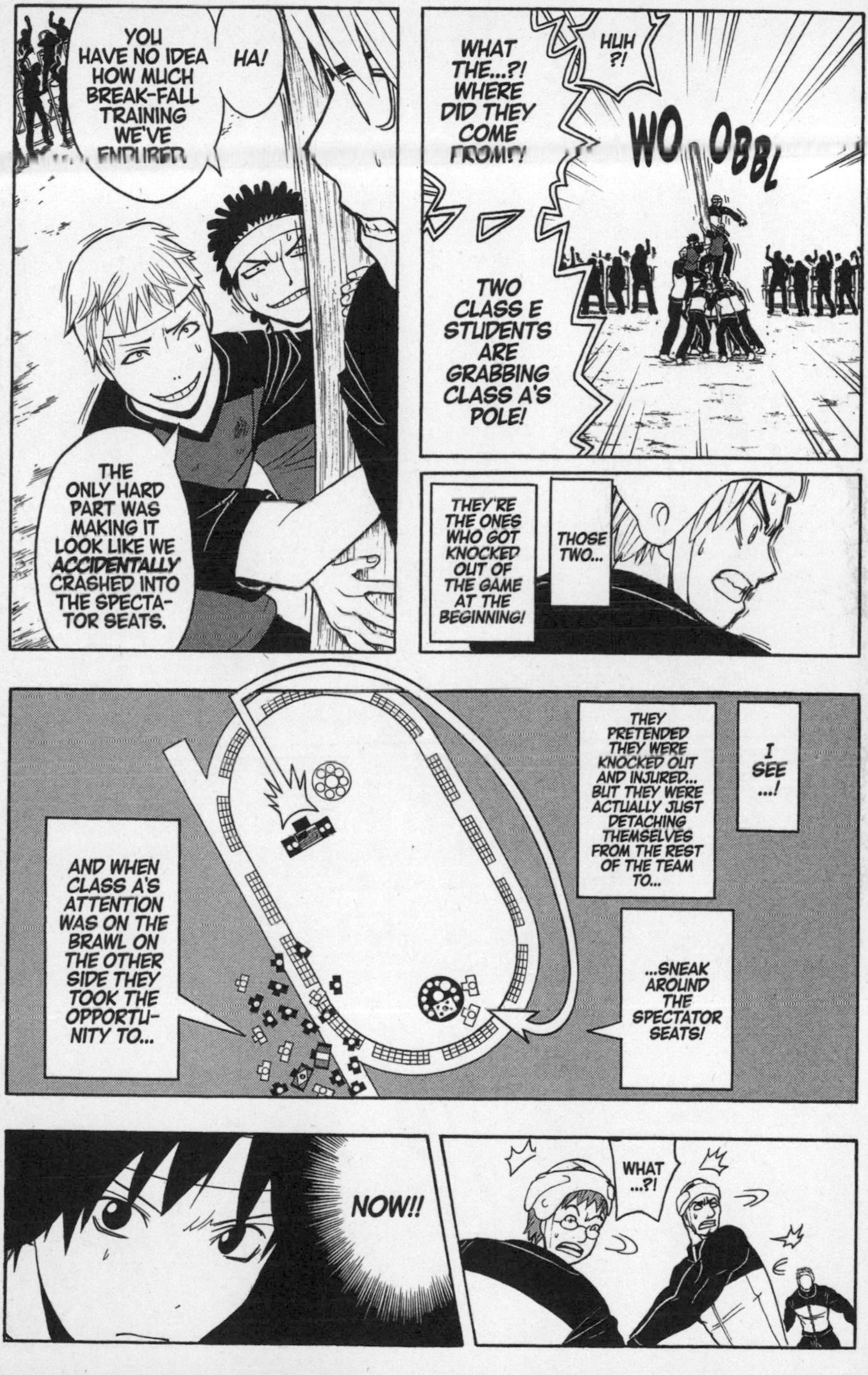
HUH?!
WHAT THE...?! WHERE DID THEY COME FROM!?
WO OBBL
TWO CLASS E STUDENTS ARE GRABBING CLASS A'S POLE!
THOSE TWO...
THEY'RE THE ONES WHO GOT KNOCKED OUT OF THE GAME AT THE BEGINNING!
HA!
YOU HAVE NO IDEA HOW MUCH BREAK-FALL TRAINING WE'VE ENDURED.
THE ONLY HARD PART WAS MAKING IT LOOK LIKE WE ACCIDENTALLY CRASHED INTO THE SPECTATOR SEATS.
I SEE...!
THEY PRETENDED THEY WERE KNOCKED OUT AND INJURED... BUT THEY WERE ACTUALLY JUST DETACHING THEMSELVES FROM THE REST OF THE TEAM TO...
...SNEAK AROUND THE SPECTATOR SEATS!
AND WHEN CLASS A'S ATTENTION WAS ON THE BRAWL ON THE OTHER SIDE THEY TOOK THE OPPORTUNITY TO...
WHAT...?!
NOW!!

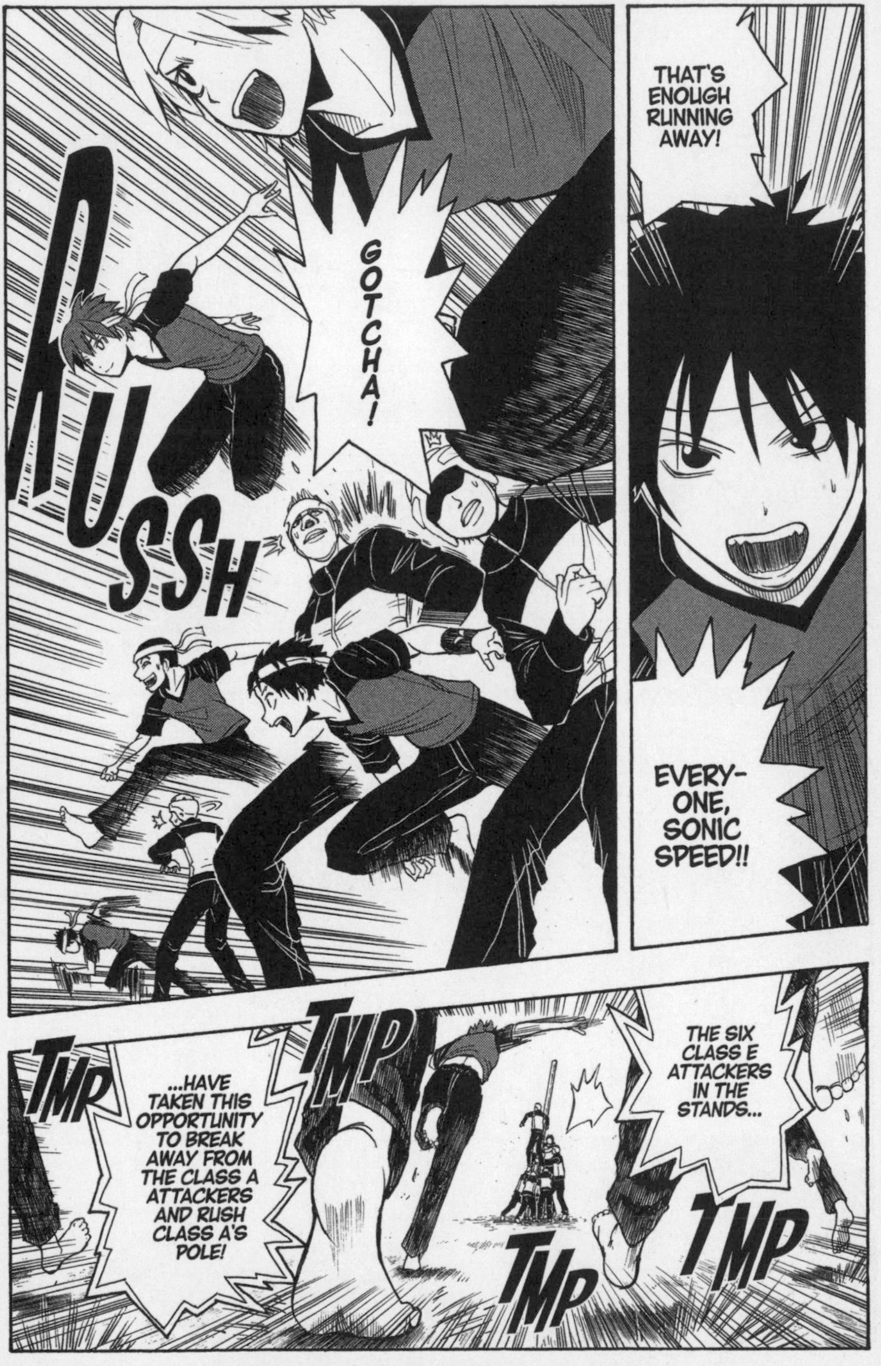
THAT'S ENOUGH RUNNING AWAY!
EVERY-ONE, SONIC SPEED!!
GOTCHA!
RUSSH
THE SIX CLASS E ATTACKERS IN THE STANDS...
TMP
TMP
TMP
...HAVE TAKEN THIS OPPORTUNITY TO BREAK AWAY FROM THE CLASS A ATTACKERS AND RUSH CLASS A'S POLE!
TMP

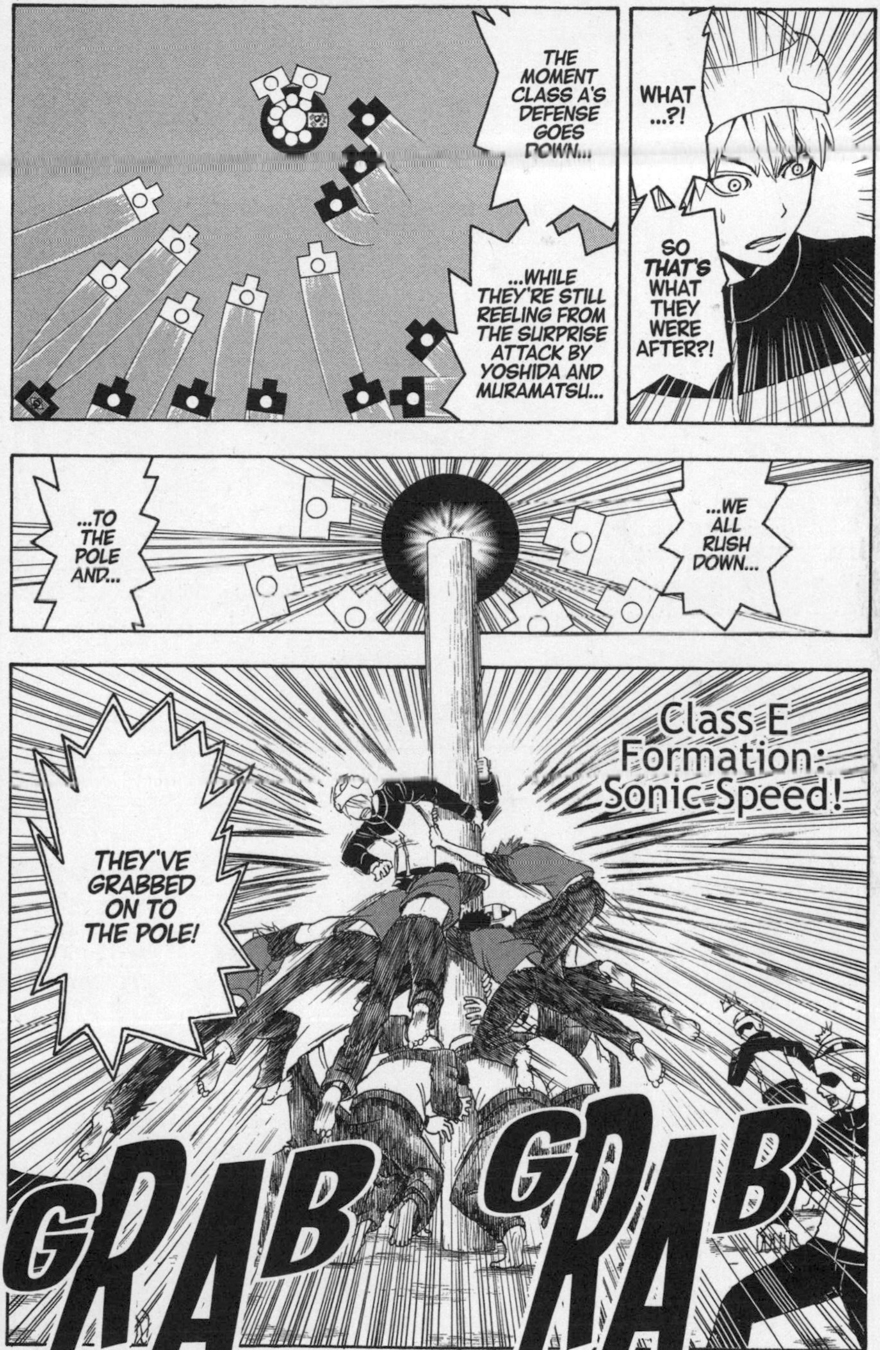
WHAT ...?!
SO THAT'S WHAT THEY WERE AFTER?!
THE MOMENT CLASS A'S DEFENSE GOES DOWN...
...WHILE THEY'RE STILL REELING FROM THE SURPRISE ATTACK BY YOSHIDA AND MURAMATSU...
...WE ALL RUSH DOWN...
...TO THE POLE AND...
Class E Formation: Sonic Speed!
THEY'VE GRABBED ON TO THE POLE!
GRAB
GRAB

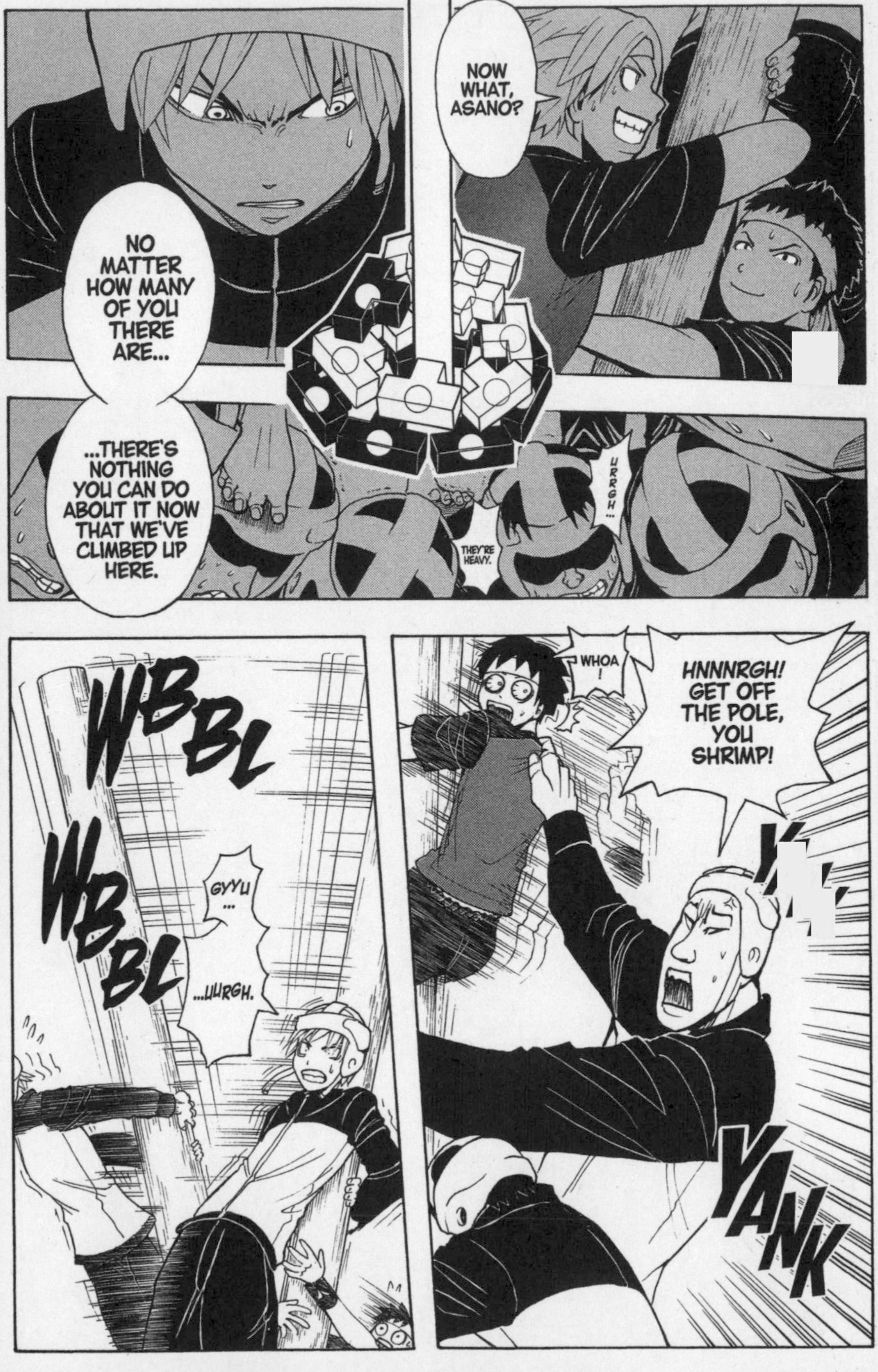
NOW WHAT, ASANO?
NO MATTER HOW MANY OF YOU THERE ARE...
...THERE'S NOTHING YOU CAN DO ABOUT IT NOW THAT WE'VE CLIMBED UP HERE.
URRGH...
THEY'RE HEAVY.
WHOA!
HNNNRGH! GET OFF THE POLE, YOU SHRIMP!
YANK
WBBL
WBBL
GYYU...
...UURGH.

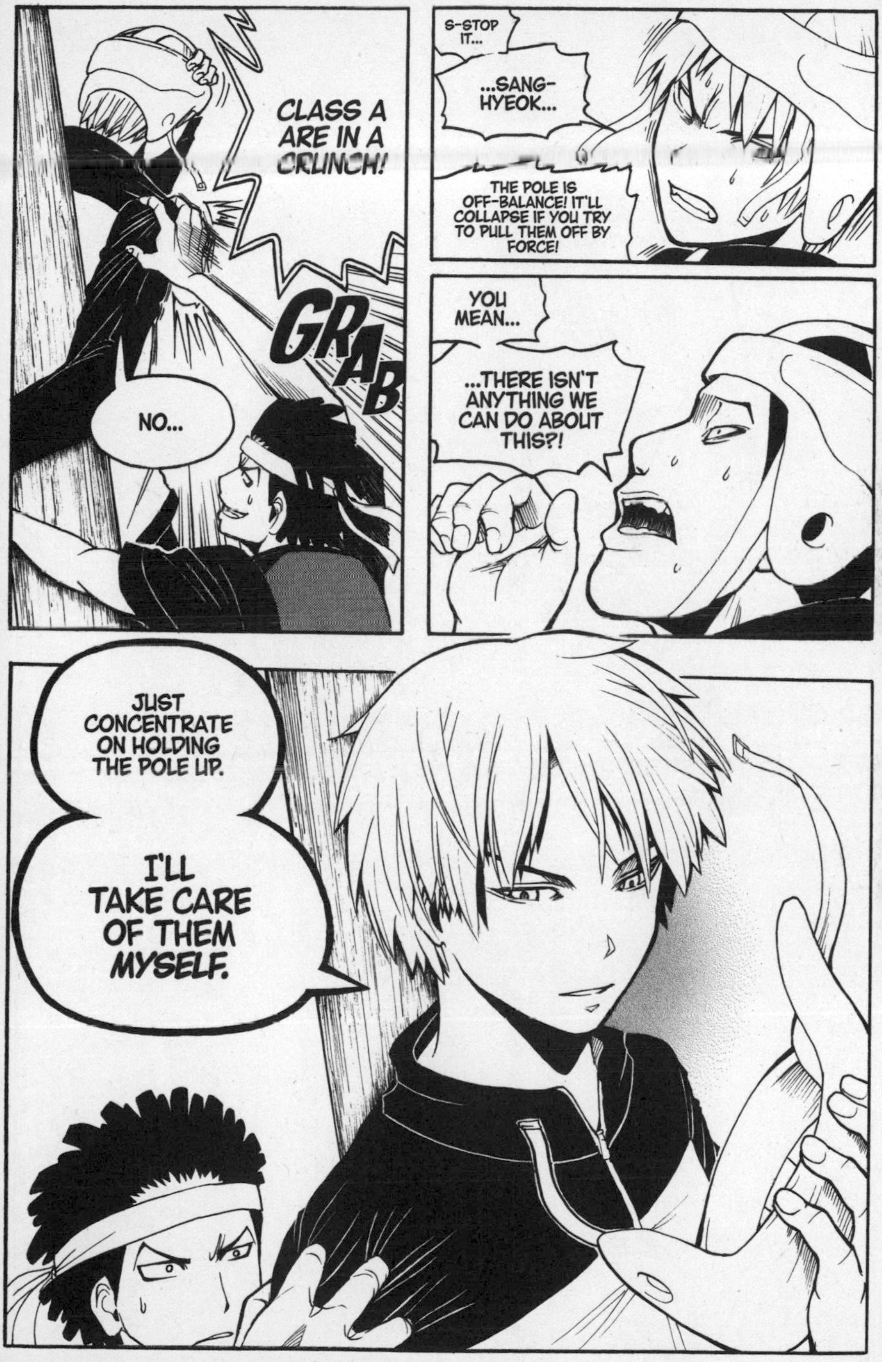
S-STOP IT...
...SANG-HYEOK...
THE POLE IS OFF-BALANCE! IT'LL COLLAPSE IF YOU TRY TO PULL THEM OFF BY FORCE!
YOU MEAN...
...THERE ISN'T ANYTHING WE CAN DO ABOUT THIS?!
CLASS A ARE IN A CRUNCH!
GRAB
NO...
JUST CONCENTRATE ON HOLDING THE POLE UP.
I'LL TAKE CARE OF THEM MYSELF.

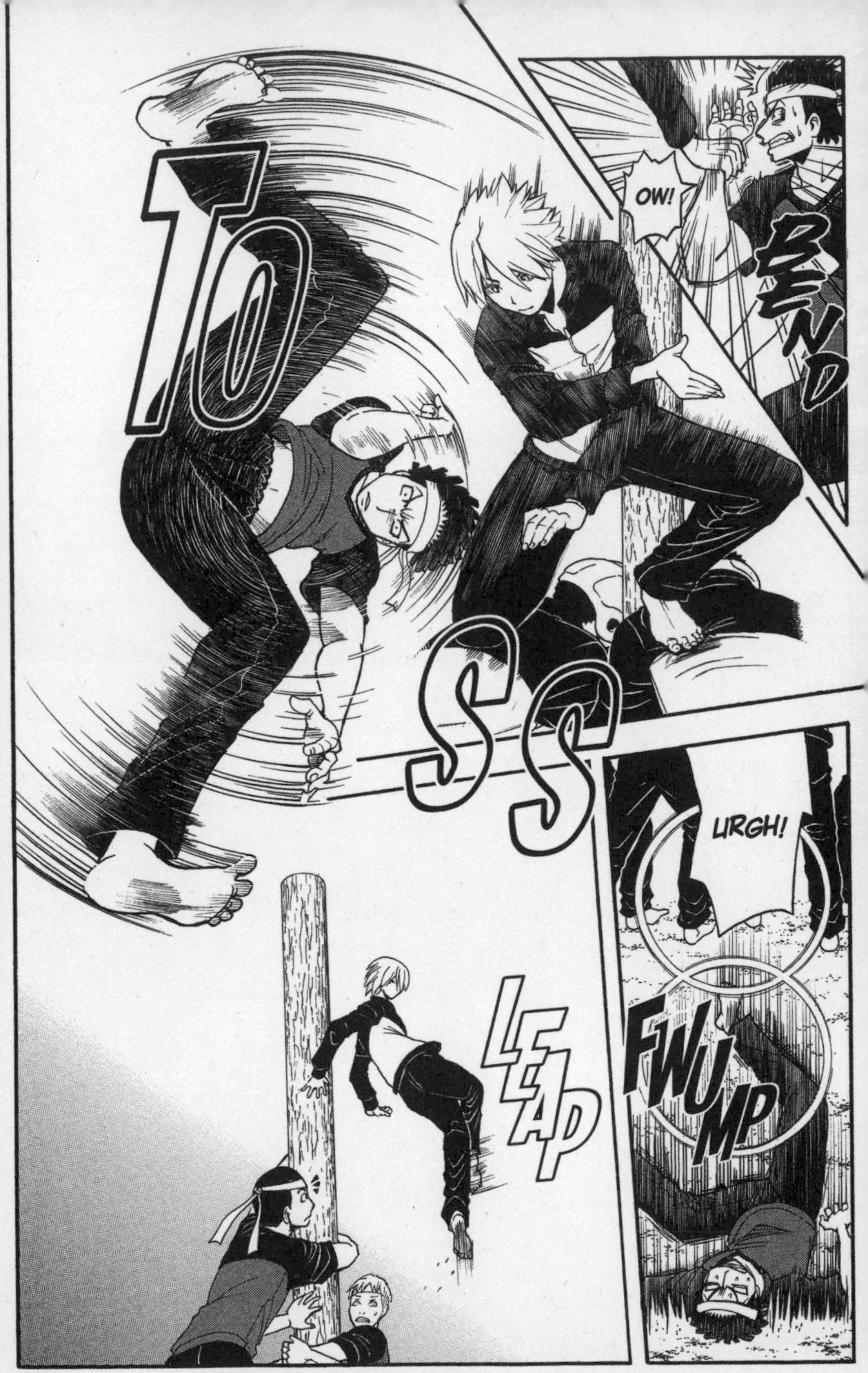
OW!
BEND
TOSS
URGH!
FWUMP
LEAP

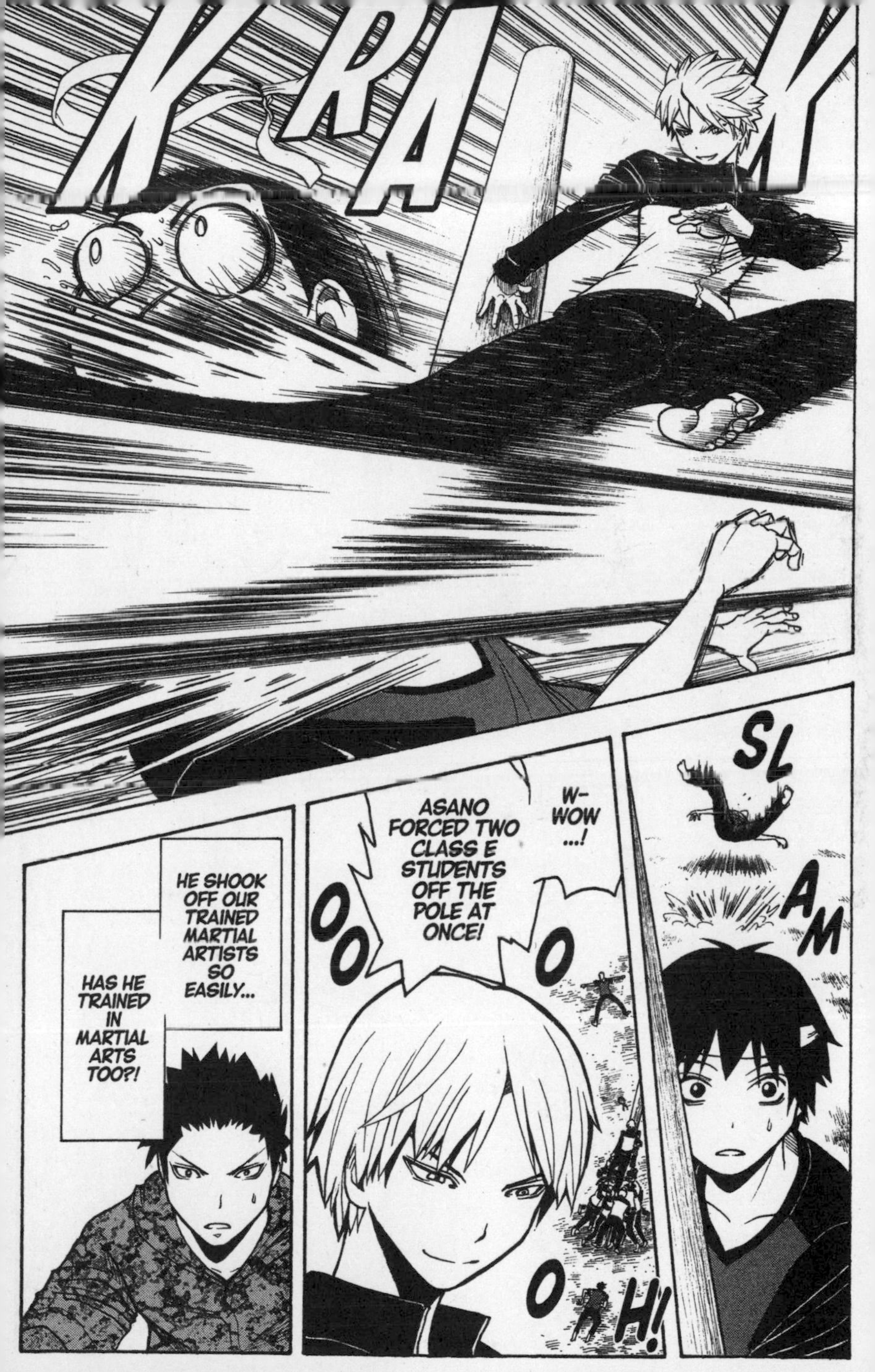
KRAK
SLAM
W-WOW...!
ASANO FORCED TWO CLASS E STUDENTS OFF THE POLE AT ONCE!
OOOOH!
HE SHOOK OFF OUR TRAINED MARTIAL ARTISTS SO EASILY...
HAS HE TRAINED IN MARTIAL ARTS TOO?!

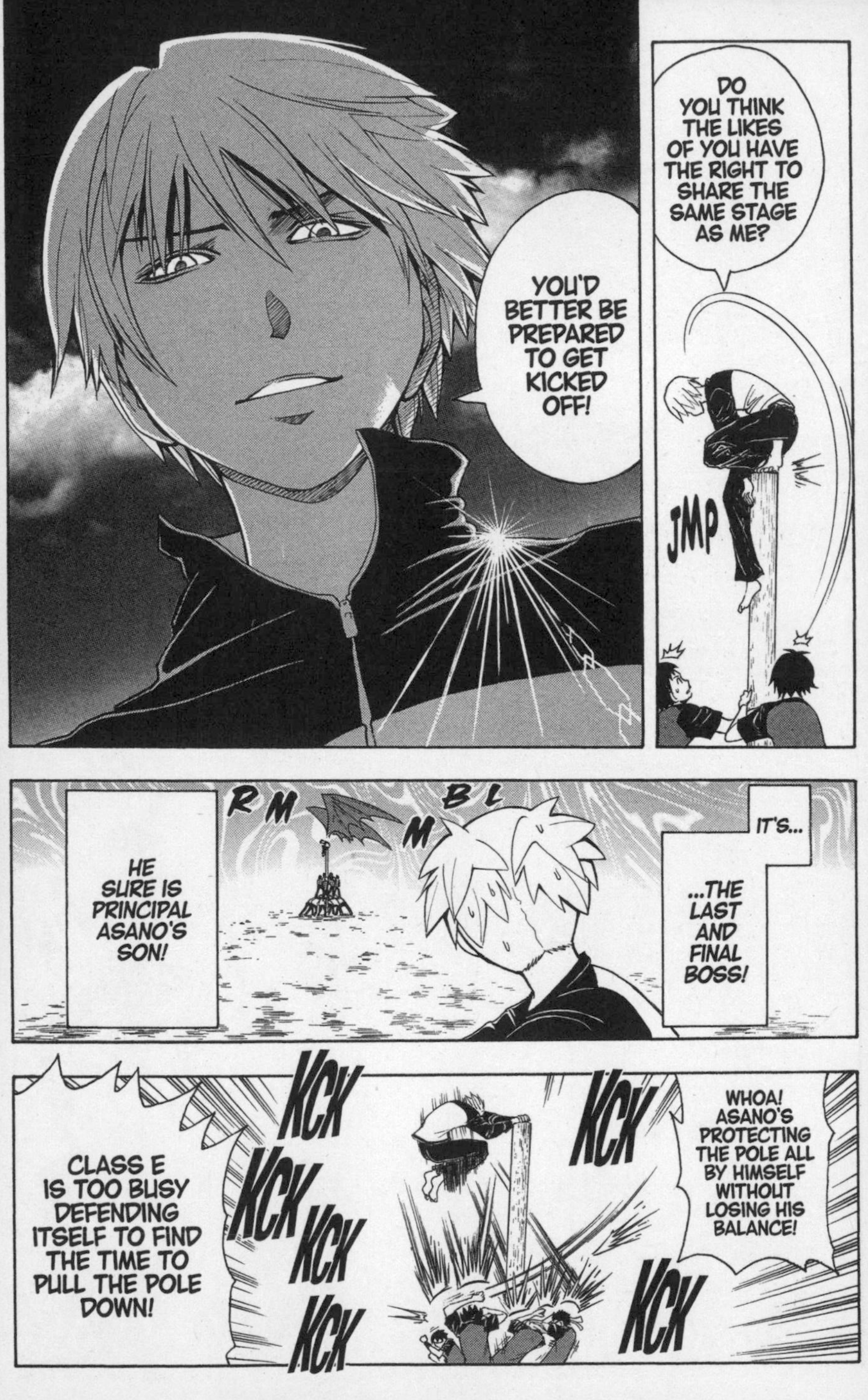
DO YOU THINK THE LIKES OF YOU HAVE THE RIGHT TO SHARE THE SAME STAGE AS ME?
JMP
YOU'D BETTER BE PREPARED TO GET KICKED OFF!
IT'S...
...THE LAST AND FINAL BOSS!
RMMBL
HE SURE IS PRINCIPAL ASANO'S SON!
WHOA! ASANO'S PROTECTING THE POLE ALL BY HIMSELF WITHOUT LOSING HIS BALANCE!
KCK
KCK
KCK
KCK
KCK
KCK
CLASS E IS TOO BUSY DEFENDING ITSELF TO FIND THE TIME TO PULL THE POLE DOWN!

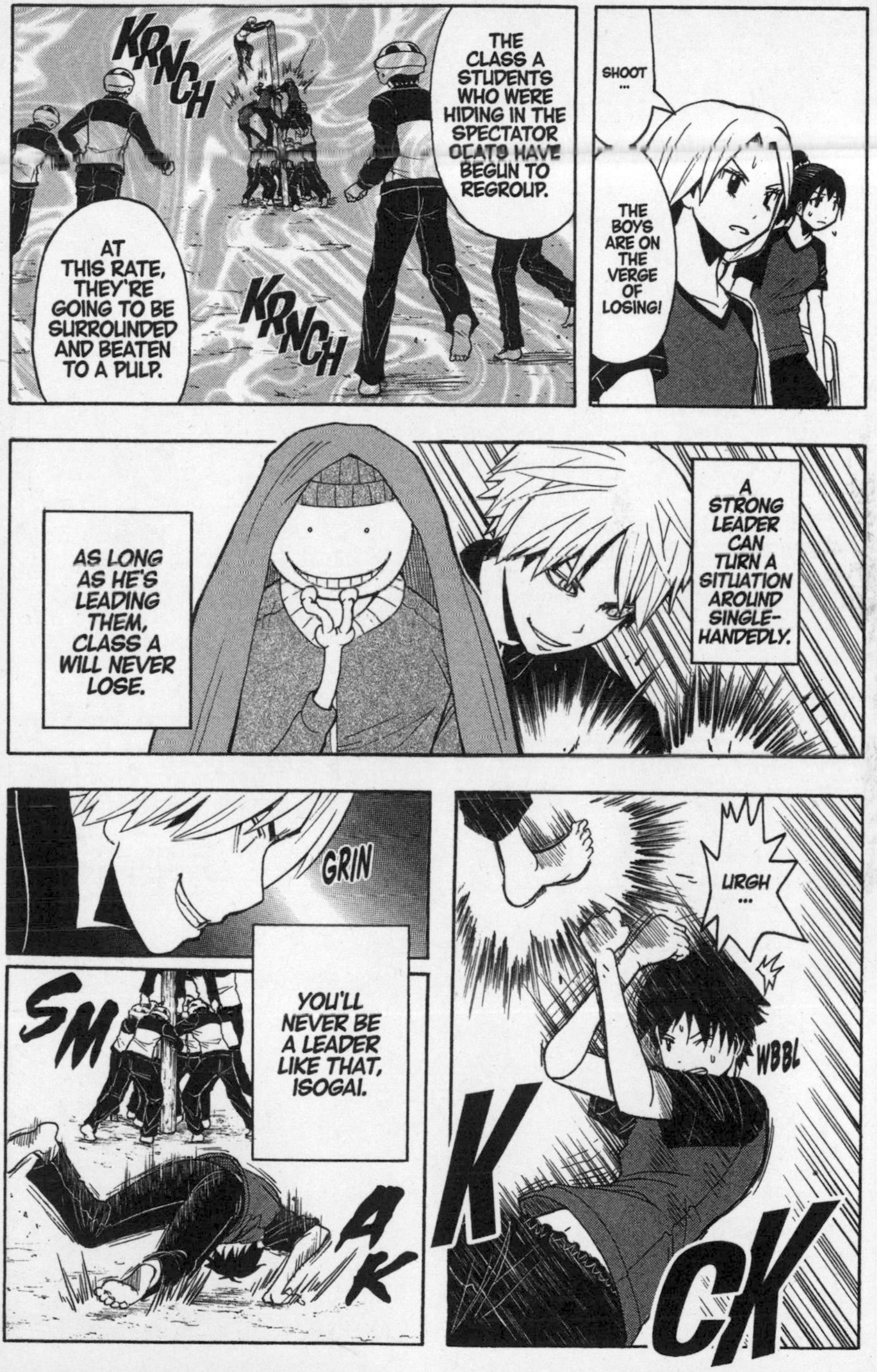
SHOOT ...
THE BOYS ARE ON THE VERGE OF LOSING!
THE CLASS A STUDENTS WHO WERE HIDING IN THE SPECTATOR SEATS HAVE BEGUN TO REGROUP.
KRNCH
AT THIS RATE, THEY'RE GOING TO BE SURROUNDED AND BEATEN TO A PULP.
KRNCH
A STRONG LEADER CAN TURN A SITUATION AROUND SINGLE-HANDEDLY.
AS LONG AS HE'S LEADING THEM, CLASS A WILL NEVER LOSE.
URGH ...
WBBL
KCK
GRIN
YOU'LL NEVER BE A LEADER LIKE THAT, ISOGAI.
SMAK

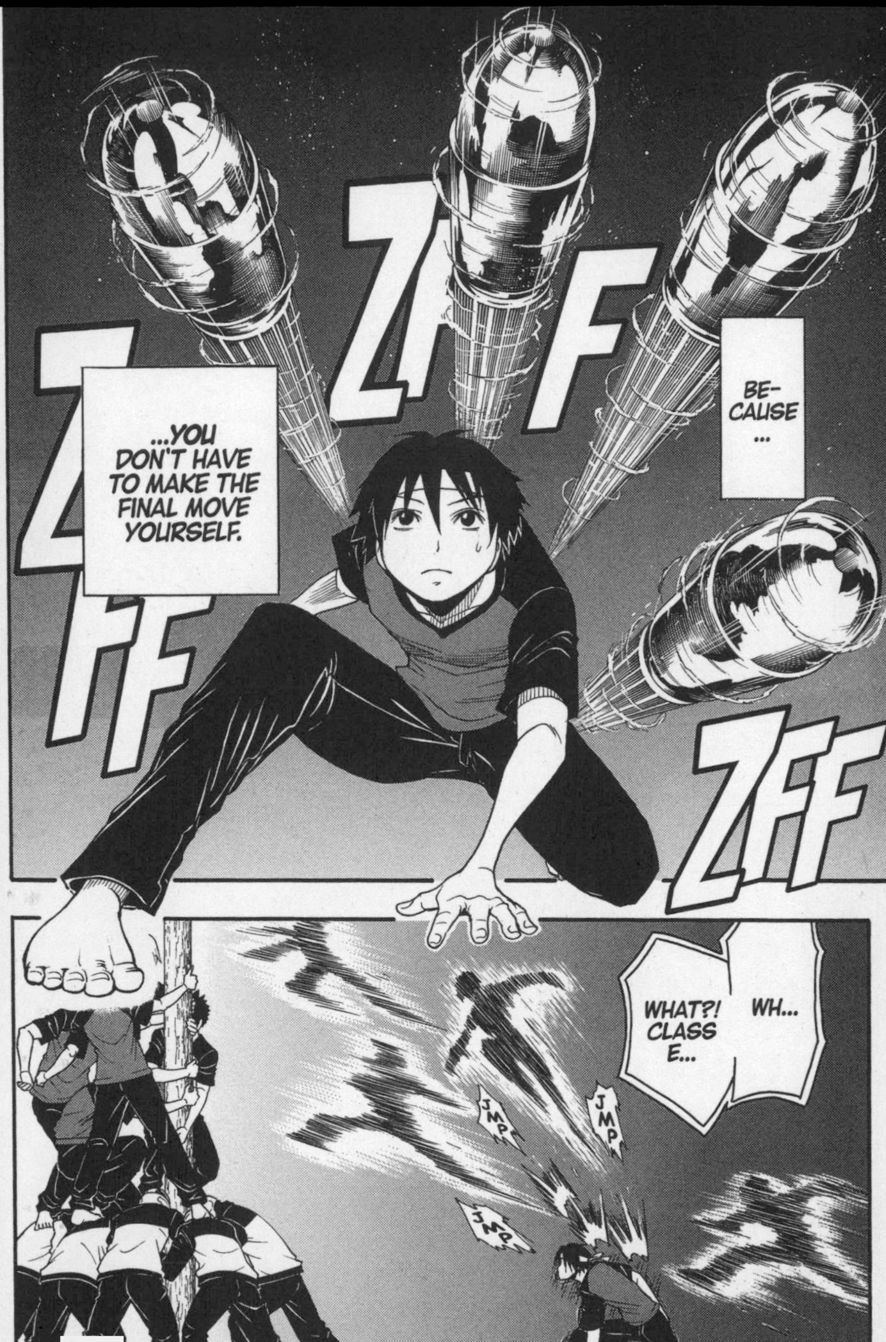
ZFF
BE-CAUSE...
ZFF
ZFF
...YOU DON'T HAVE TO MAKE THE FINAL MOVE YOURSELF.
ZFF
WH...
WHAT?! CLASS E...
JMP
JMP
JMP

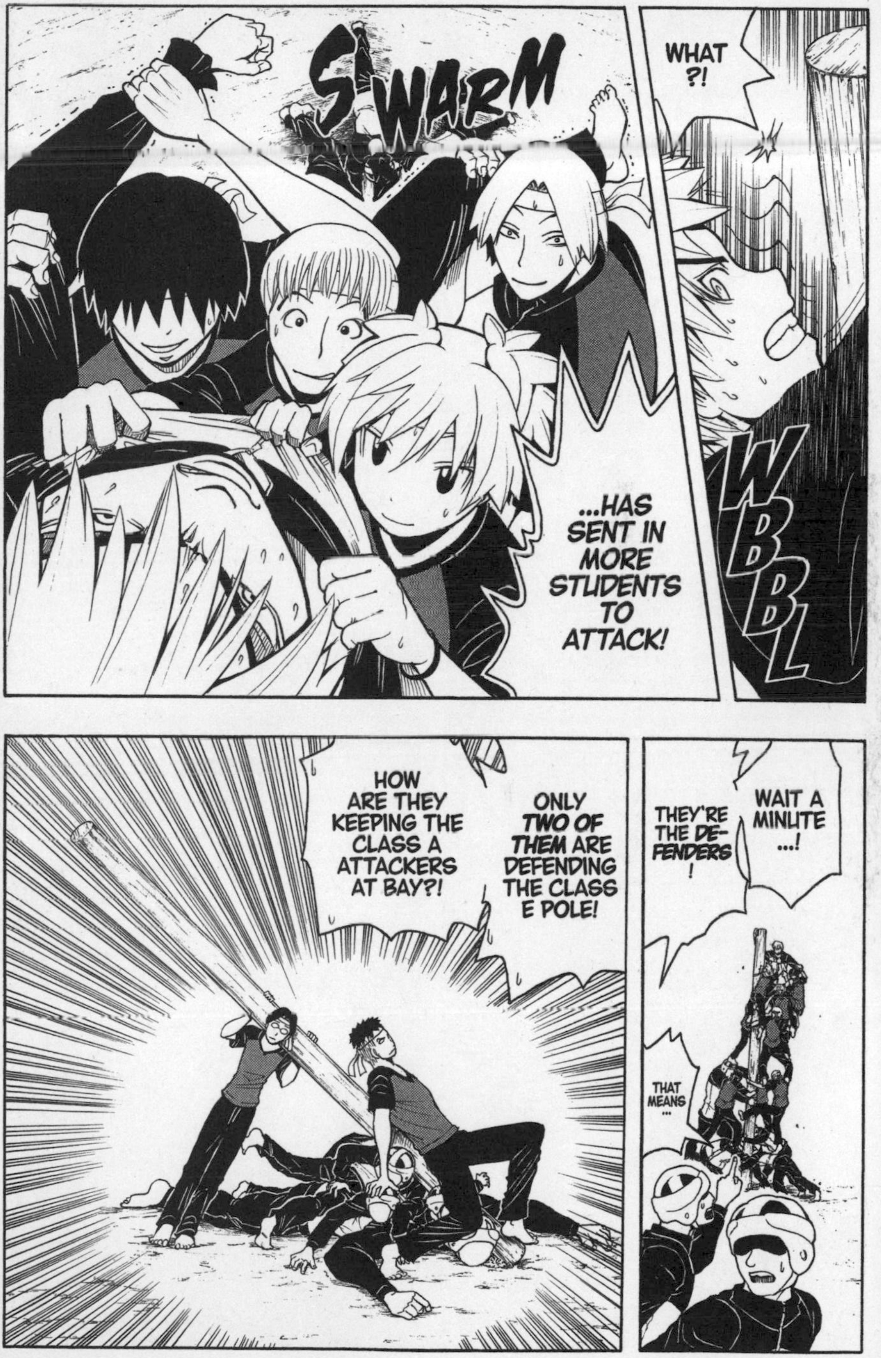
WHAT ?!
WBBL
SWARM
...HAS SENT IN MORE STUDENTS TO ATTACK!
WAIT A MINUTE ...!
THEY'RE THE DEFENDERS !
THAT MEANS ...
ONLY *TWO OF THEM* ARE DEFENDING THE CLASS E POLE!
HOW ARE THEY KEEPING THE CLASS A ATTACKERS AT BAY?!

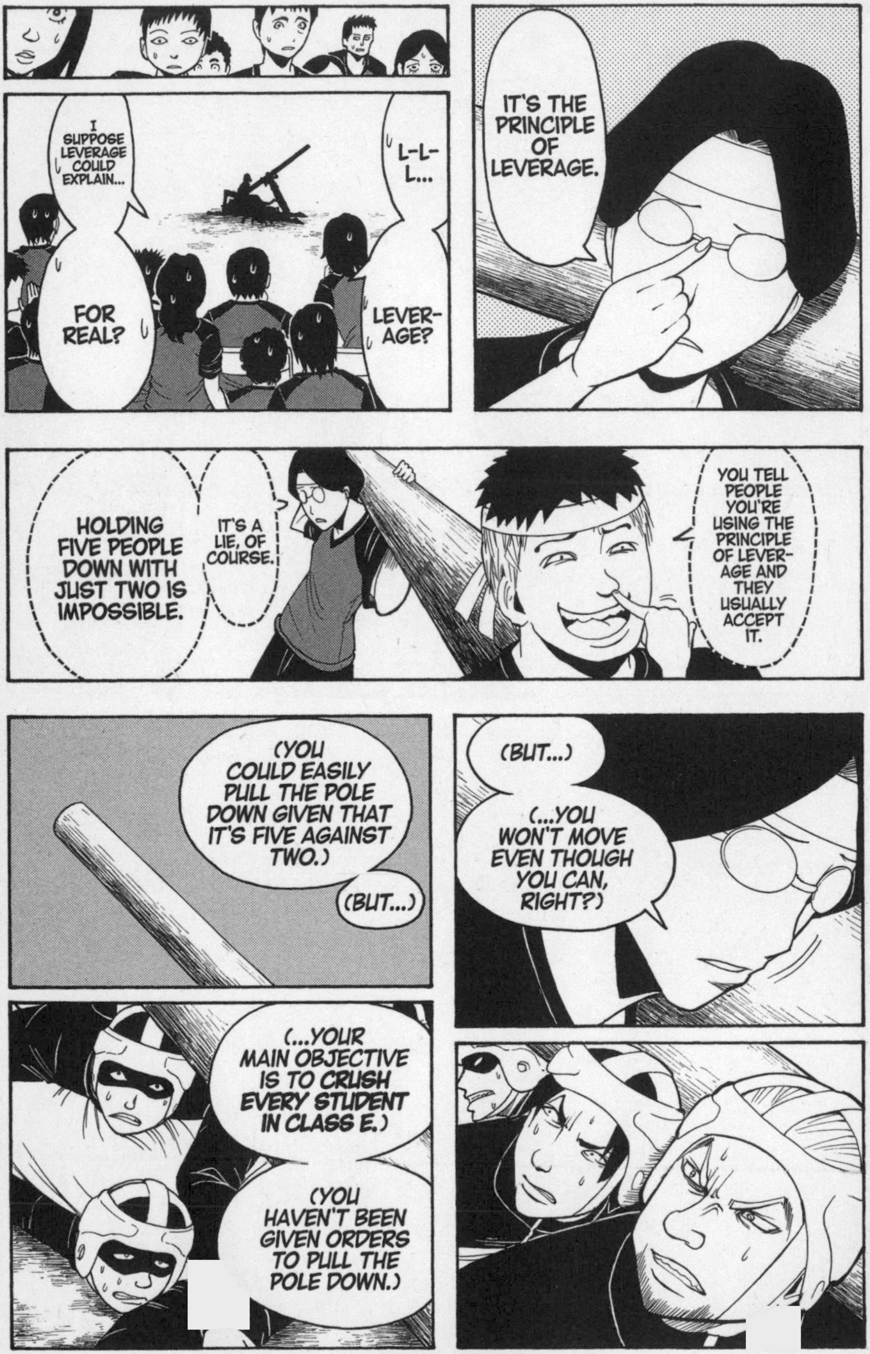
IT'S THE PRINCIPLE OF LEVERAGE.
L-L-L...
LEVER-AGE?
I SUPPOSE LEVERAGE COULD EXPLAIN...
FOR REAL?
YOU TELL PEOPLE YOU'RE USING THE PRINCIPLE OF LEVER-AGE AND THEY USUALLY ACCEPT IT.
IT'S A LIE, OF COURSE.
HOLDING FIVE PEOPLE DOWN WITH JUST TWO IS IMPOSSIBLE.
(BUT...)
(...YOU WON'T MOVE EVEN THOUGH YOU CAN, RIGHT?)
(YOU COULD EASILY PULL THE POLE DOWN GIVEN THAT IT'S FIVE AGAINST TWO.)
(BUT...)
(...YOUR MAIN OBJECTIVE IS TO CRUSH EVERY STUDENT IN CLASS E.)
(YOU HAVEN'T BEEN GIVEN ORDERS TO PULL THE POLE DOWN.)

(SPEAKING ENGLISH)

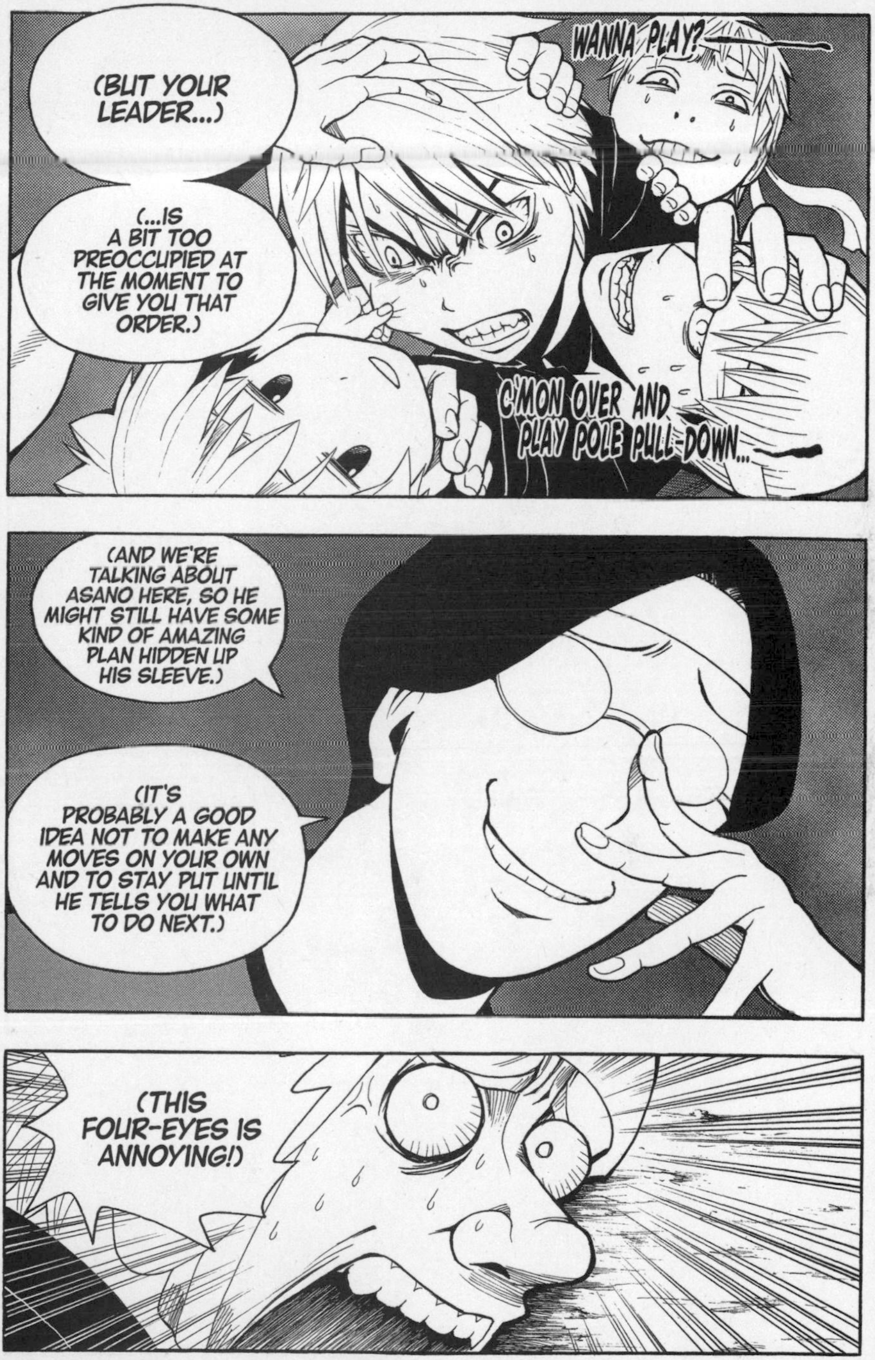
WANNA PLAY?
(BUT YOUR LEADER...)
(...IS A BIT TOO PREOCCUPIED AT THE MOMENT TO GIVE YOU THAT ORDER.)
C'MON OVER AND PLAY POLE PULL-DOWN...
(AND WE'RE TALKING ABOUT ASANO HERE, SO HE MIGHT STILL HAVE SOME KIND OF AMAZING PLAN HIDDEN UP HIS SLEEVE.)
(IT'S PROBABLY A GOOD IDEA NOT TO MAKE ANY MOVES ON YOUR OWN AND TO STAY PUT UNTIL HE TELLS YOU WHAT TO DO NEXT.)
(THIS FOUR-EYES IS ANNOYING!)

(SPEAKING ENGLISH)

THE KANJI FOR "PEOPLE" IS MADE UP OF TWO PEOPLE SUPPORTING EACH OTHER...
...AND TRAMPLING MORE PEOPLE BELOW THEM!
ON THE OTHER HAND, THE KANJI FOR "ENTER"...
...IS ALSO MADE UP OF PEOPLE TRAMPLING PEOPLE BELOW THEM!

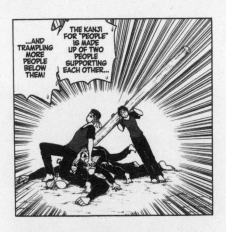

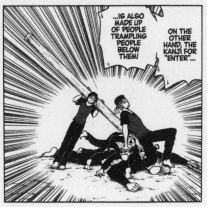

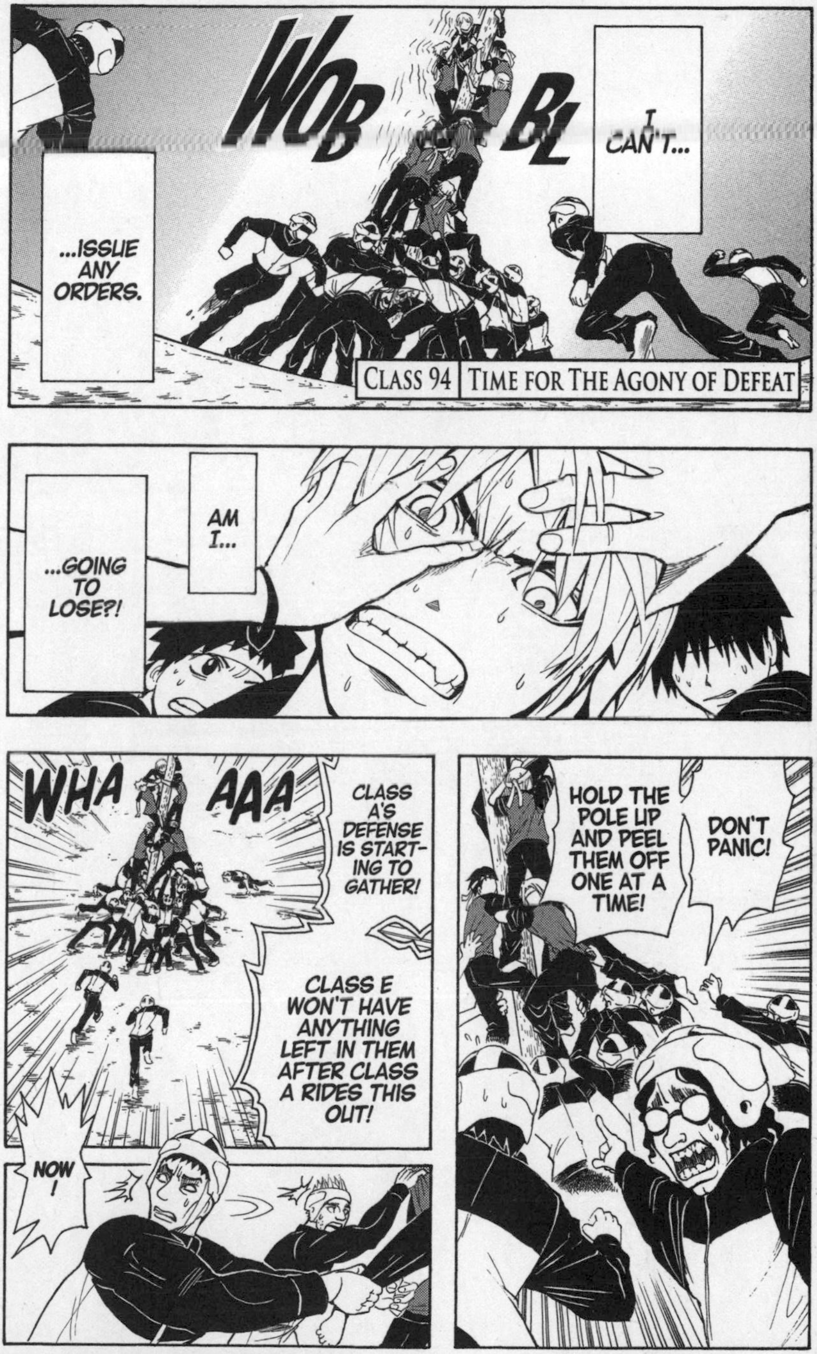
I CAN'T...
WOB BL
...ISSUE ANY ORDERS.
CLASS 94 TIME FOR THE AGONY OF DEFEAT
AM I...
...GOING TO LOSE?!
DON'T PANIC!
HOLD THE POLE UP AND PEEL THEM OFF ONE AT A TIME!
WHA AAA
CLASS A'S DEFENSE IS STARTING TO GATHER!
CLASS E WON'T HAVE ANYTHING LEFT IN THEM AFTER CLASS A RIDES THIS OUT!
NOW!

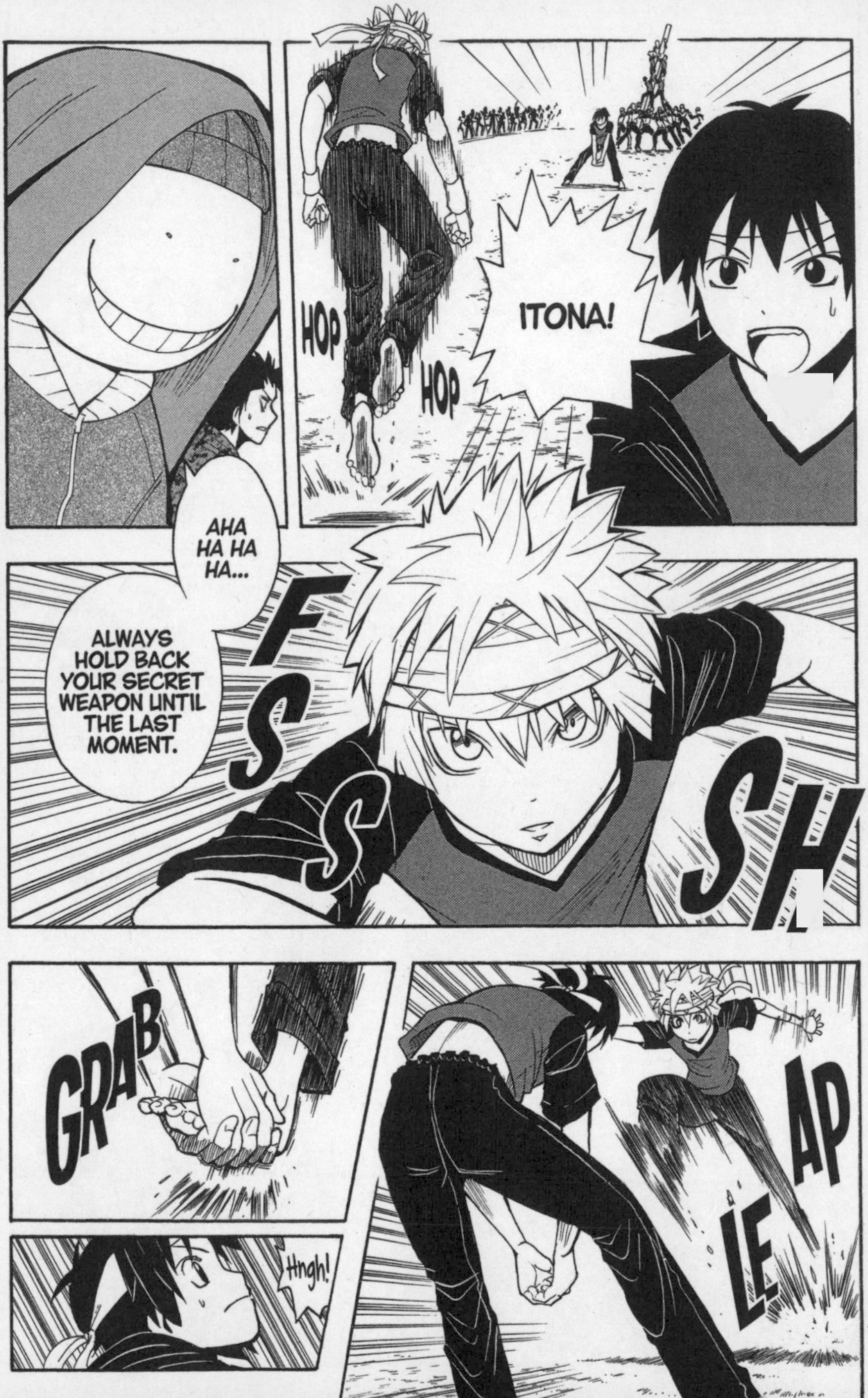
ITONA!
HOP
HOP
AHA HA HA HA...
ALWAYS HOLD BACK YOUR SECRET WEAPON UNTIL THE LAST MOMENT.
SH
FSSS
LEAP
GRAB
Hngh!

Class 94 Time for The Agony of Defeat

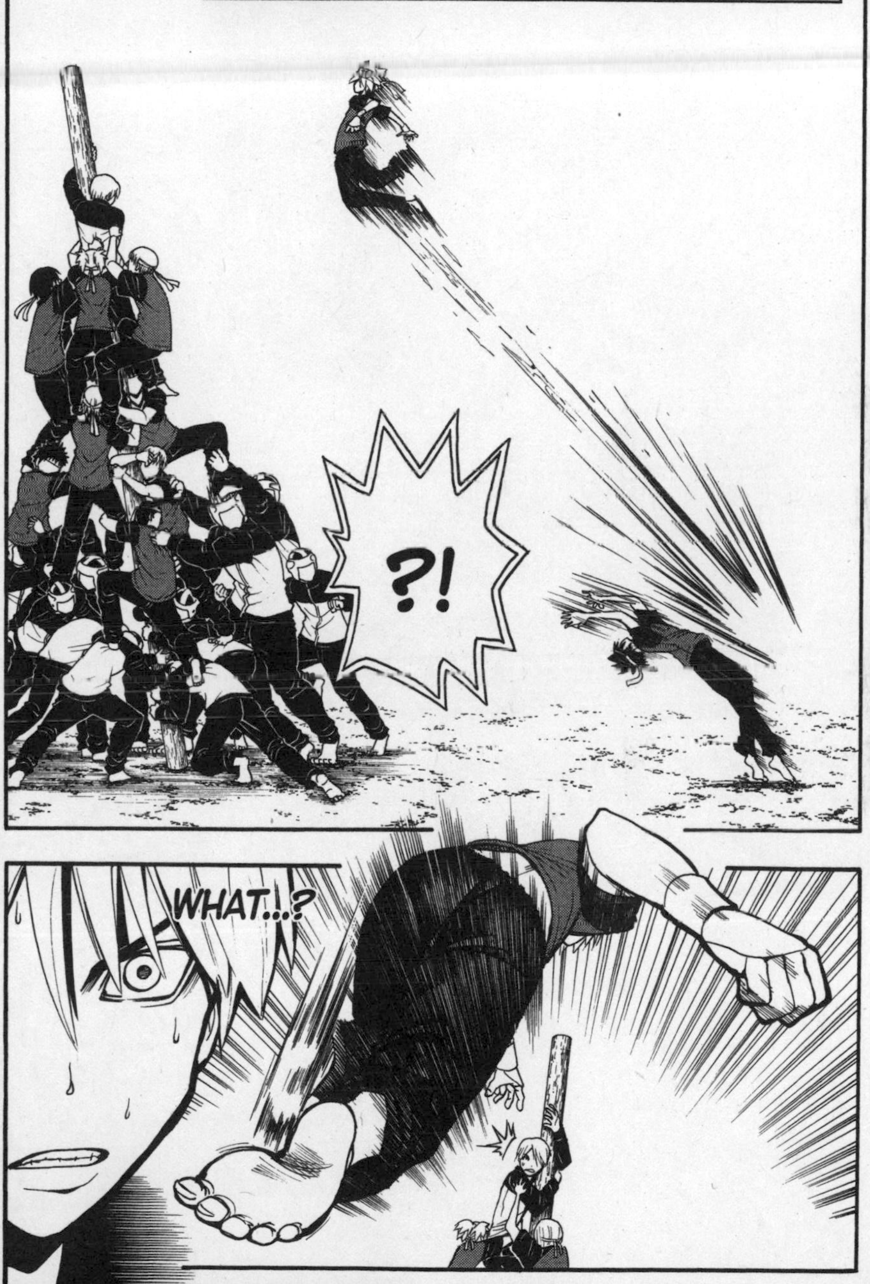
?!
WHAT...?

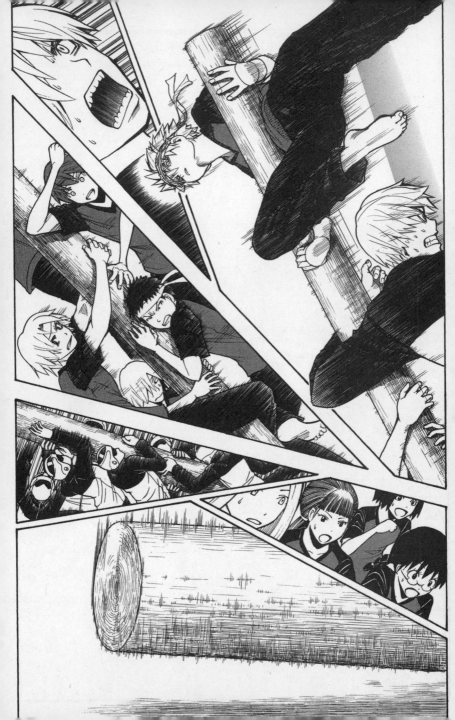

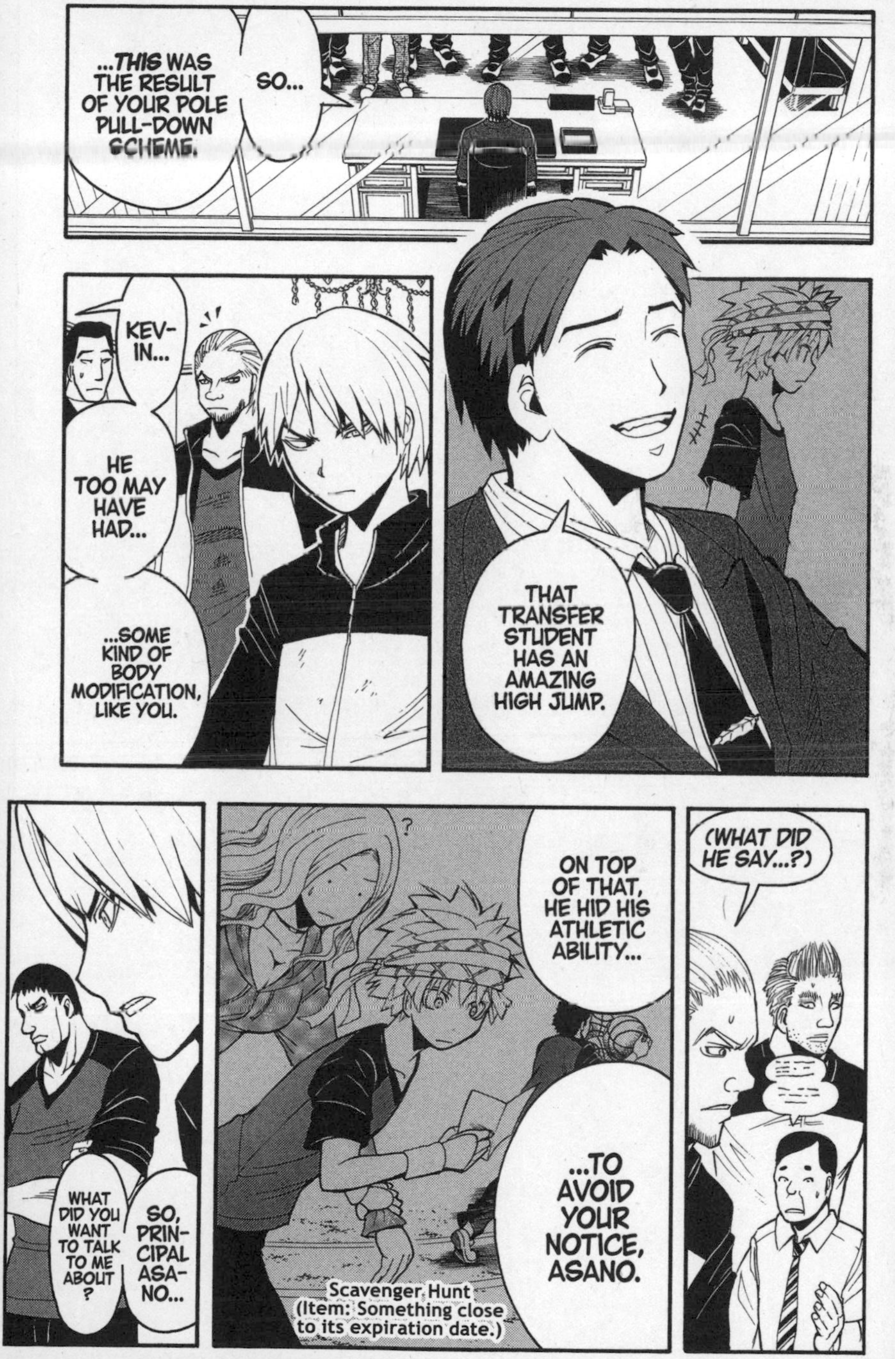
SO...
...THIS WAS THE RESULT OF YOUR POLE PULL-DOWN SCHEME.
THAT TRANSFER STUDENT HAS AN AMAZING HIGH JUMP.
KEV-IN...
HE TOO MAY HAVE HAD...
...SOME KIND OF BODY MODIFICATION, LIKE YOU.
(WHAT DID HE SAY...?)
ON TOP OF THAT, HE HID HIS ATHLETIC ABILITY...
...TO AVOID YOUR NOTICE, ASANO.
Scavenger Hunt (Item: Something close to its expiration date.)
SO, PRIN-CIPAL ASA-NO...
WHAT DID YOU WANT TO TALK TO ME ABOUT?

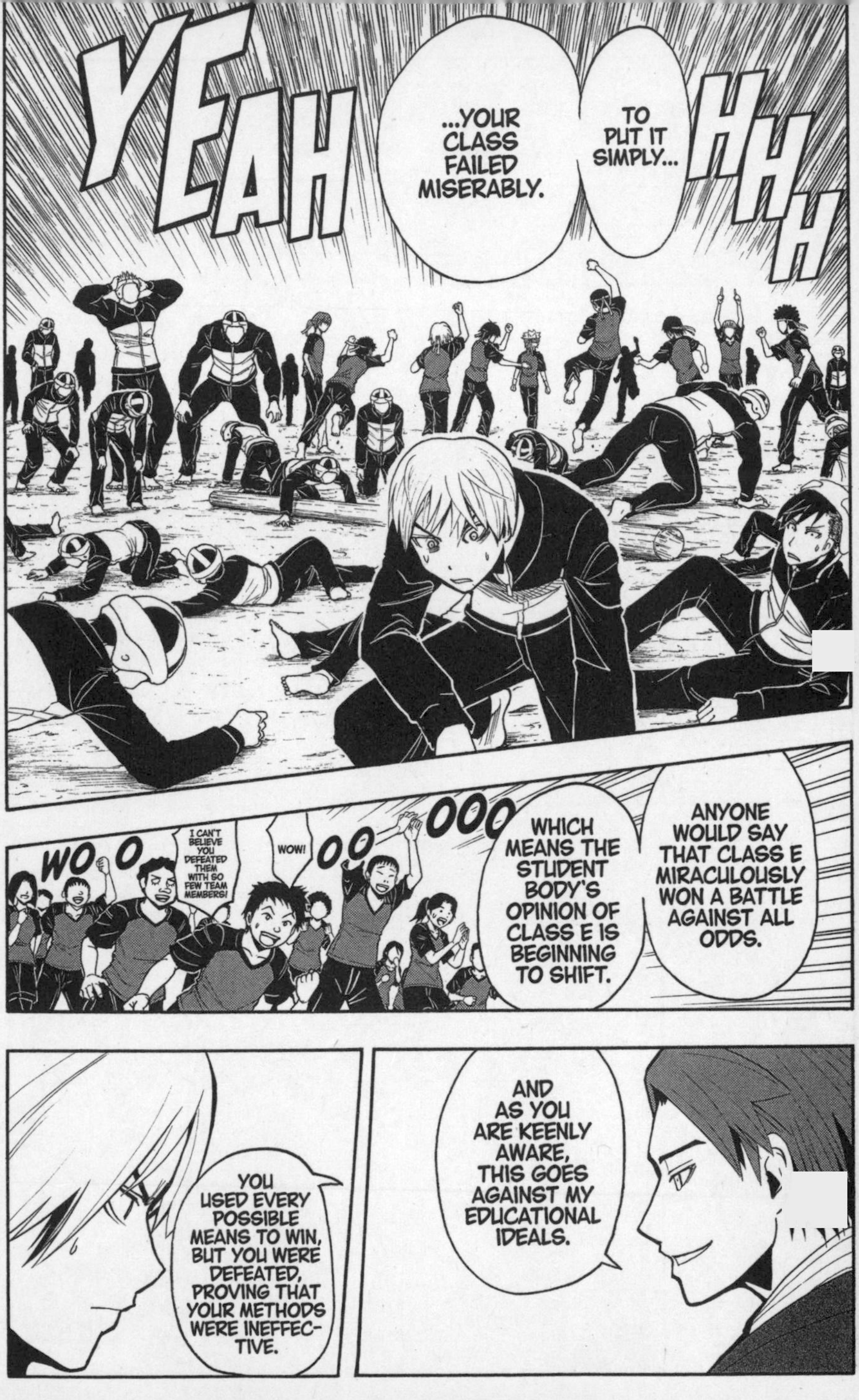
YEAHHHHH
TO PUT IT SIMPLY...
...YOUR CLASS FAILED MISERABLY.
ANYONE WOULD SAY THAT CLASS E MIRACULOUSLY WON A BATTLE AGAINST ALL ODDS.
WHICH MEANS THE STUDENT BODY'S OPINION OF CLASS E IS BEGINNING TO SHIFT.
WOOOOOOO
WOW!
I CAN'T BELIEVE YOU DEFEATED THEM WITH SO FEW TEAM MEMBERS!
AND AS YOU ARE KEENLY AWARE, THIS GOES AGAINST MY EDUCATIONAL IDEALS.
YOU USED EVERY POSSIBLE MEANS TO WIN, BUT YOU WERE DEFEATED, PROVING THAT YOUR METHODS WERE INEFFEC-TIVE.

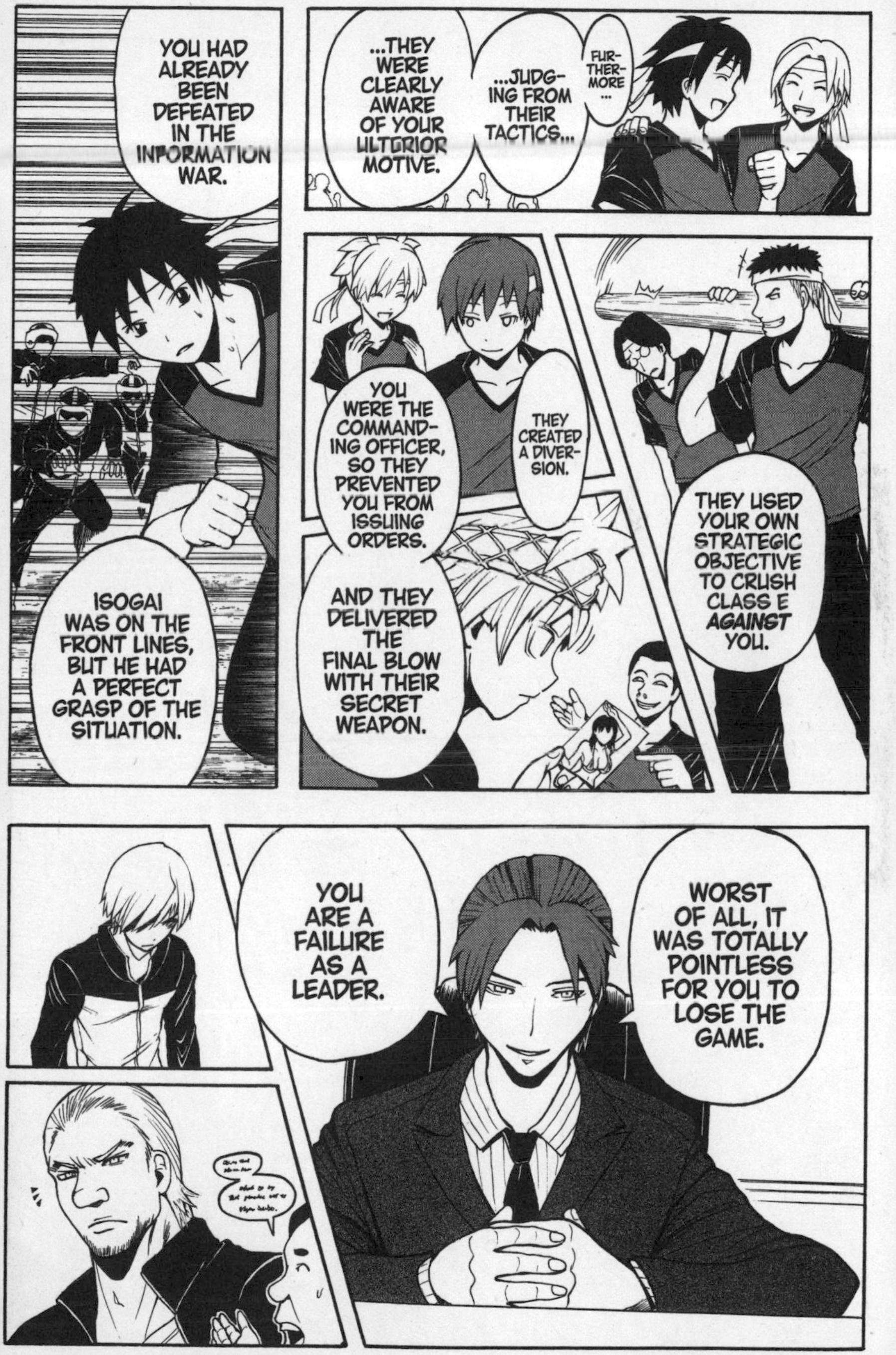
FUR-THER-MORE...
...JUDG-ING FROM THEIR TACTICS...
...THEY WERE CLEARLY AWARE OF YOUR ULTERIOR MOTIVE.
THEY USED YOUR OWN STRATEGIC OBJECTIVE TO CRUSH CLASS E AGAINST YOU.
THEY CREATED A DIVER-SION.
YOU WERE THE COMMAND-ING OFFICER, SO THEY PREVENTED YOU FROM ISSUING ORDERS.
AND THEY DELIVERED THE FINAL BLOW WITH THEIR SECRET WEAPON.
YOU HAD ALREADY BEEN DEFEATED IN THE INFORMATION WAR.
ISOGAI WAS ON THE FRONT LINES, BUT HE HAD A PERFECT GRASP OF THE SITUATION.
WORST OF ALL, IT WAS TOTALLY POINTLESS FOR YOU TO LOSE THE GAME.
YOU ARE A FAILURE AS A LEADER.

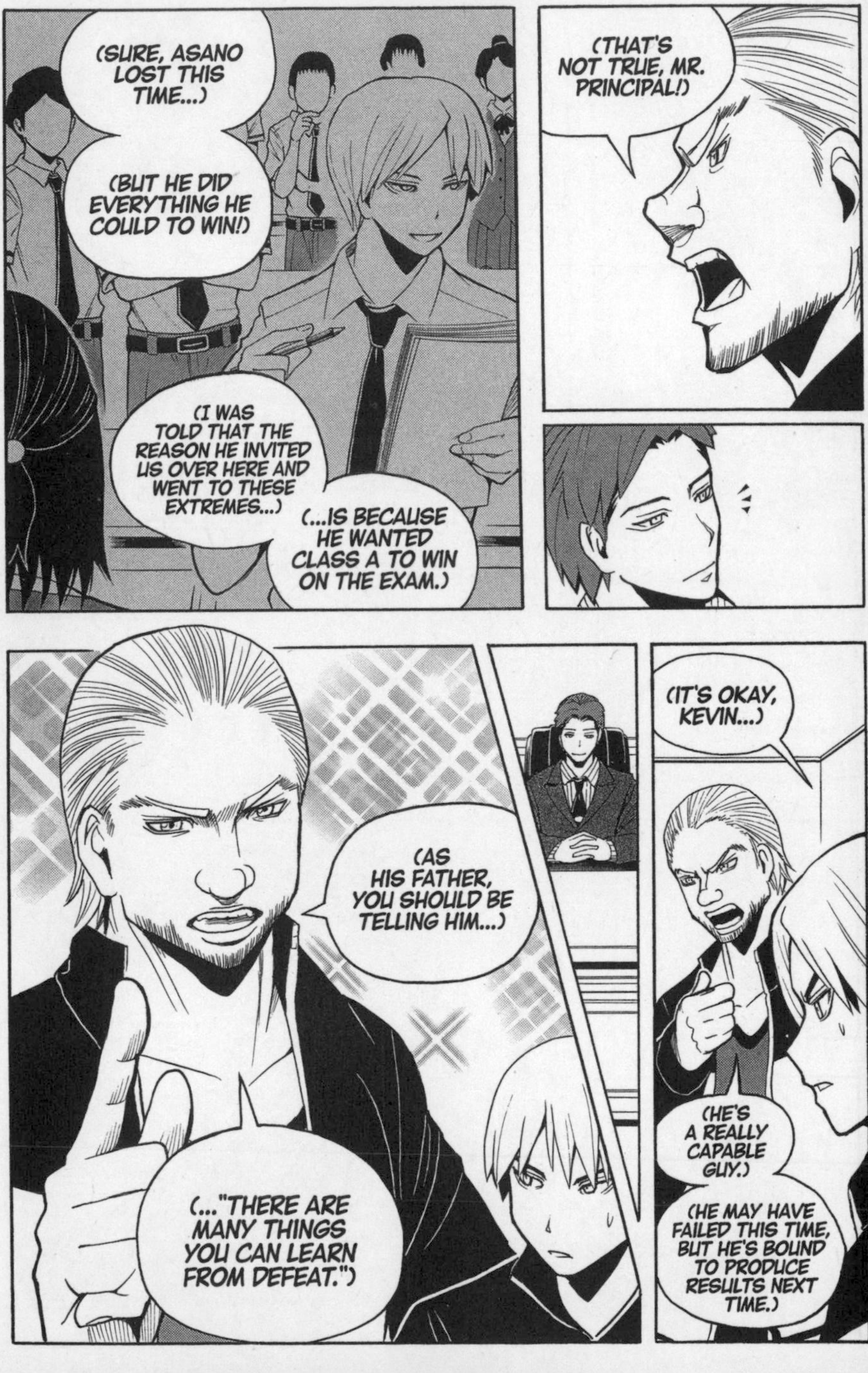
(THAT'S NOT TRUE, MR. PRINCIPAL!)
(SURE, ASANO LOST THIS TIME...)
(BUT HE DID EVERYTHING HE COULD TO WIN!)
(I WAS TOLD THAT THE REASON HE INVITED US OVER HERE AND WENT TO THESE EXTREMES...)
(...IS BECAUSE HE WANTED CLASS A TO WIN ON THE EXAM.)
(IT'S OKAY, KEVIN...)
(HE'S A REALLY CAPABLE GUY.)
(HE MAY HAVE FAILED THIS TIME, BUT HE'S BOUND TO PRODUCE RESULTS NEXT TIME.)
(AS HIS FATHER, YOU SHOULD BE TELLING HIM...)
(..."THERE ARE MANY THINGS YOU CAN LEARN FROM DEFEAT.")

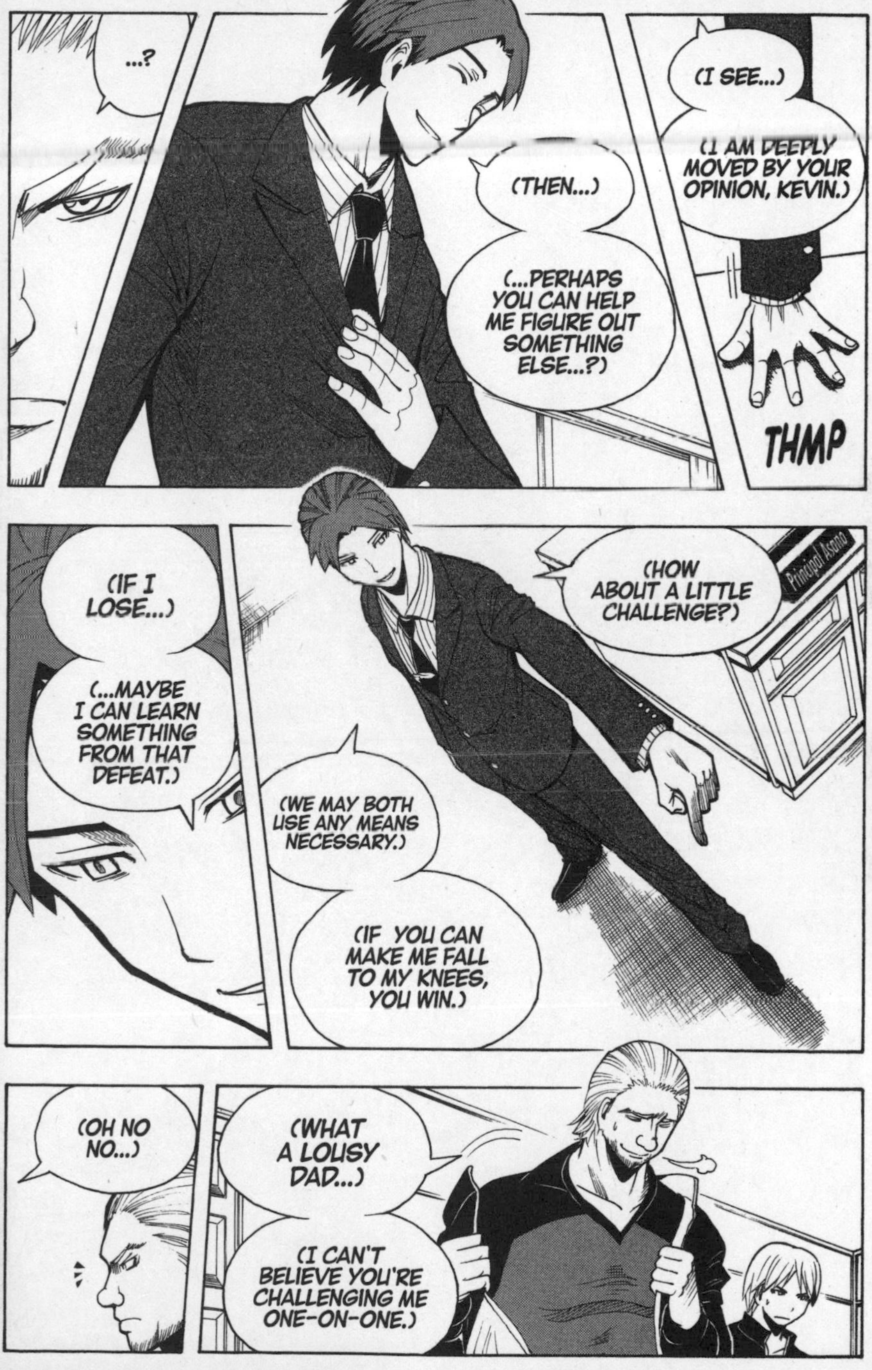
(I SEE...)
(I AM DEEPLY MOVED BY YOUR OPINION, KEVIN.)
THMP
(THEN...)
(...PERHAPS YOU CAN HELP ME FIGURE OUT SOMETHING ELSE...?)
...?
Principal Asano
(HOW ABOUT A LITTLE CHALLENGE?)
(WE MAY BOTH USE ANY MEANS NECESSARY.)
(IF YOU CAN MAKE ME FALL TO MY KNEES, YOU WIN.)
(IF I LOSE...)
(...MAYBE I CAN LEARN SOMETHING FROM THAT DEFEAT.)
(WHAT A LOUSY DAD...)
(I CAN'T BELIEVE YOU'RE CHALLENGING ME ONE-ON-ONE.)
(OH NO NO...)

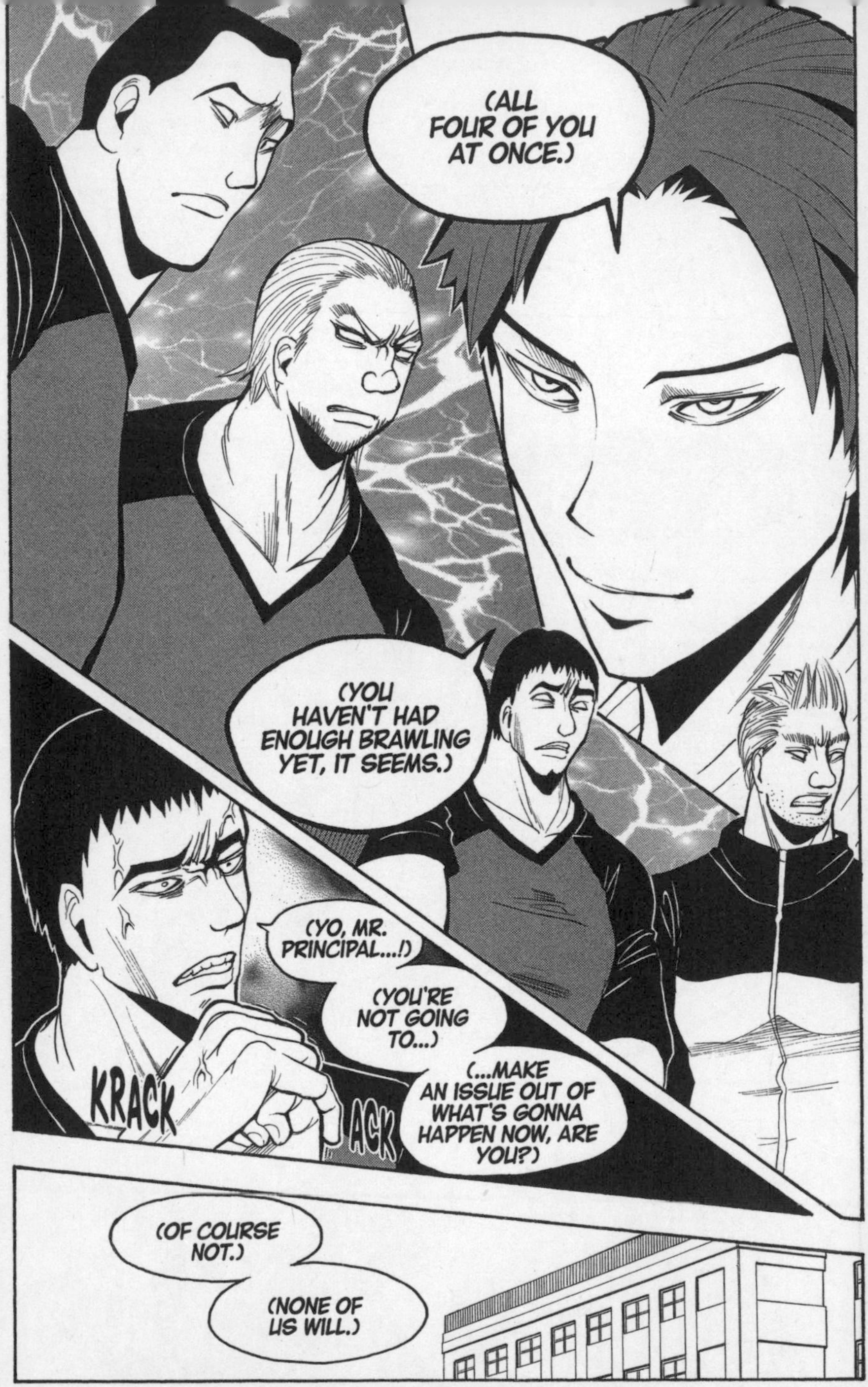
(ALL FOUR OF YOU AT ONCE.)
(YOU HAVEN'T HAD ENOUGH BRAWLING YET, IT SEEMS.)
(YO, MR. PRINCIPAL...!)
(YOU'RE NOT GOING TO...)
(...MAKE AN ISSUE OUT OF WHAT'S GONNA HAPPEN NOW, ARE YOU?)
KRACK
ACK
(OF COURSE NOT.)
(NONE OF US WILL.)

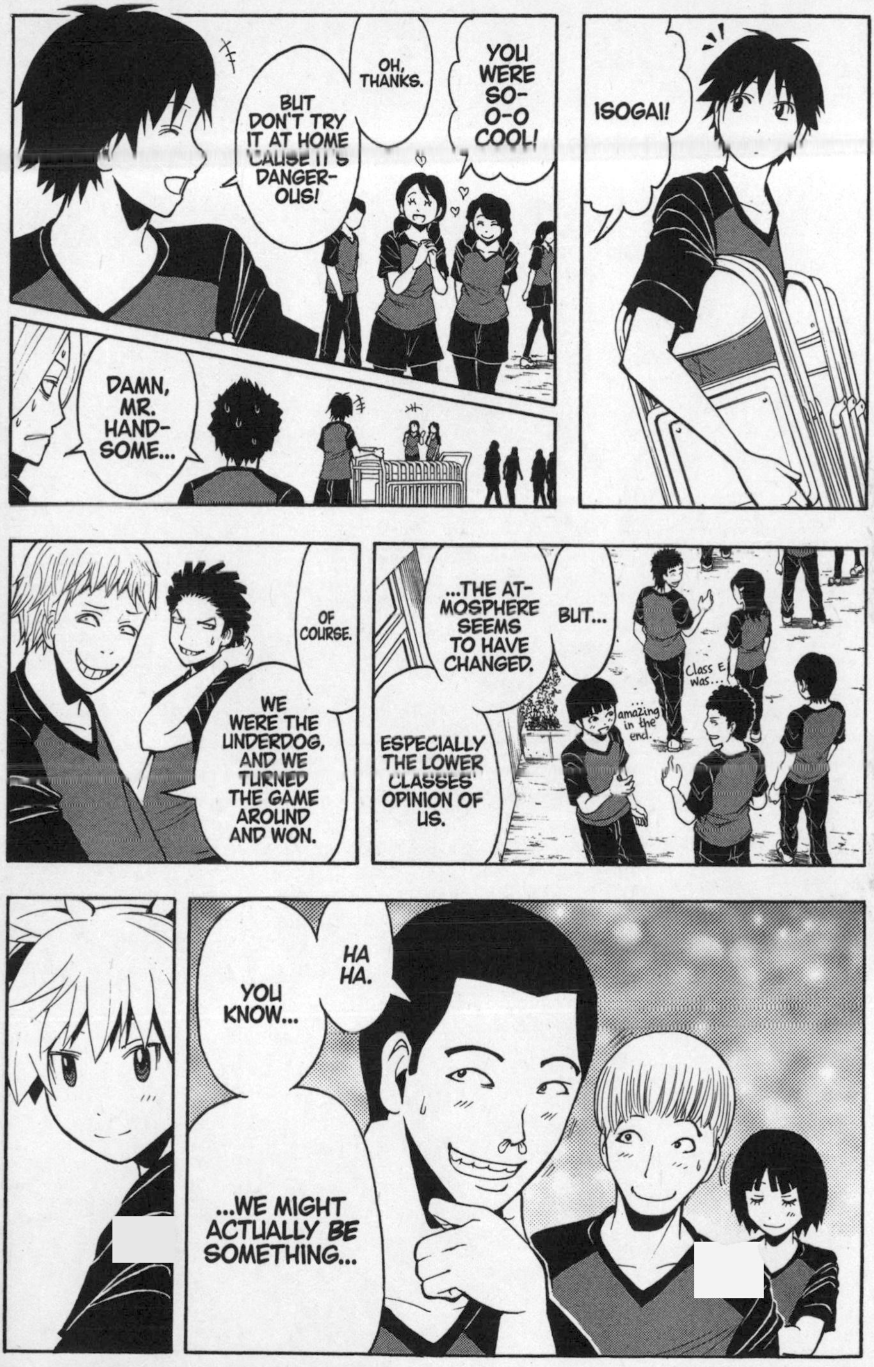
ISOGAI!
YOU WERE SO-O-O COOL!
OH, THANKS.
BUT DON'T TRY IT AT HOME CAUSE IT'S DANGER-OUS!
DAMN, MR. HAND-SOME...
BUT...
...THE AT-MOSPHERE SEEMS TO HAVE CHANGED.
ESPECIALLY THE LOWER CLASSES' OPINION OF US.
Class E was...
...amazing in the end.
OF COURSE.
WE WERE THE UNDERDOG, AND WE TURNED THE GAME AROUND AND WON.
HA HA.
YOU KNOW...
...WE MIGHT ACTUALLY BE SOMETHING...

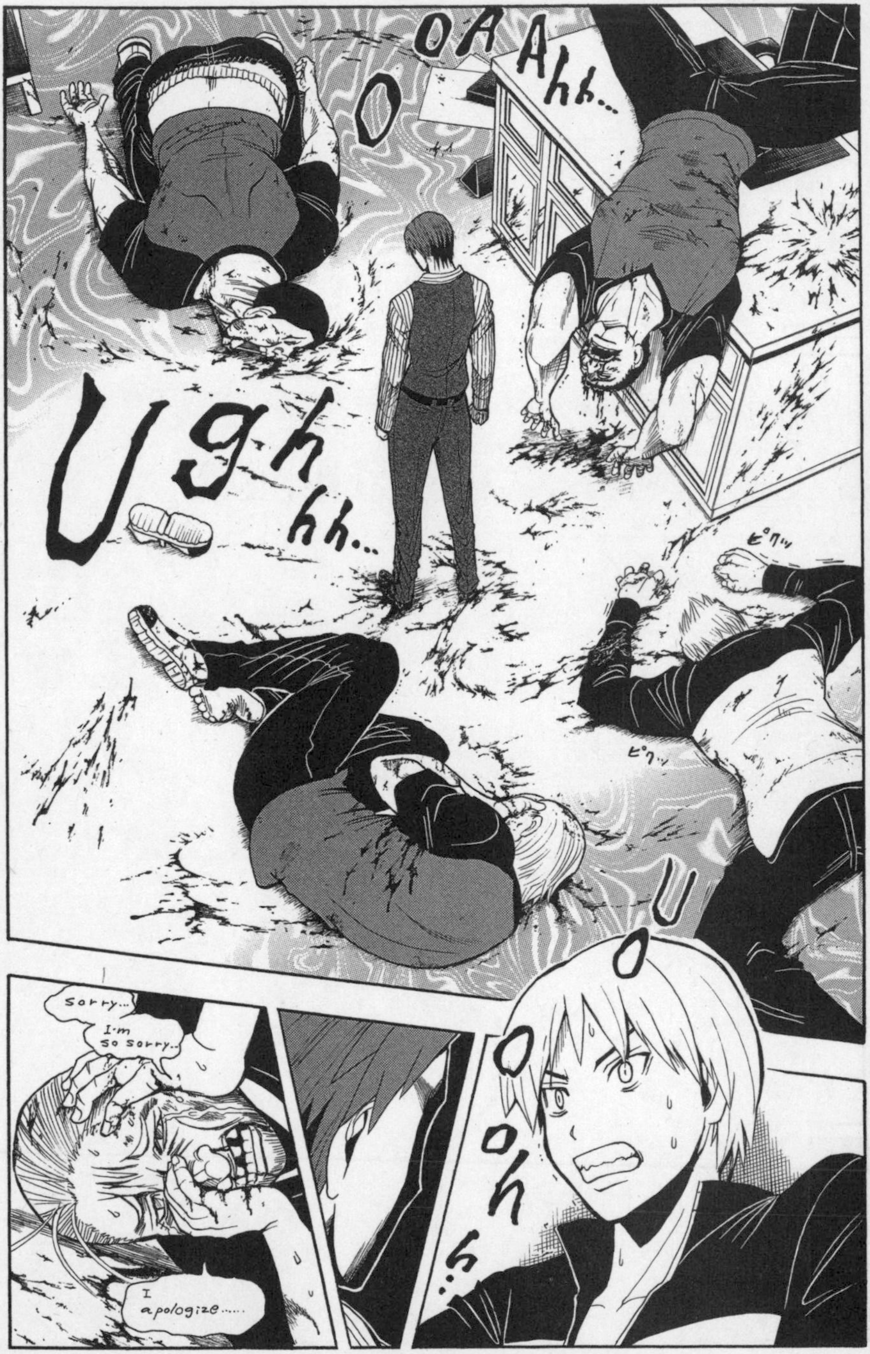

OOAAAhh...
Ughhh...
ピクッ
ピクッ
UOOohs...
Sorry...
I'm so sorry...
I apologize......

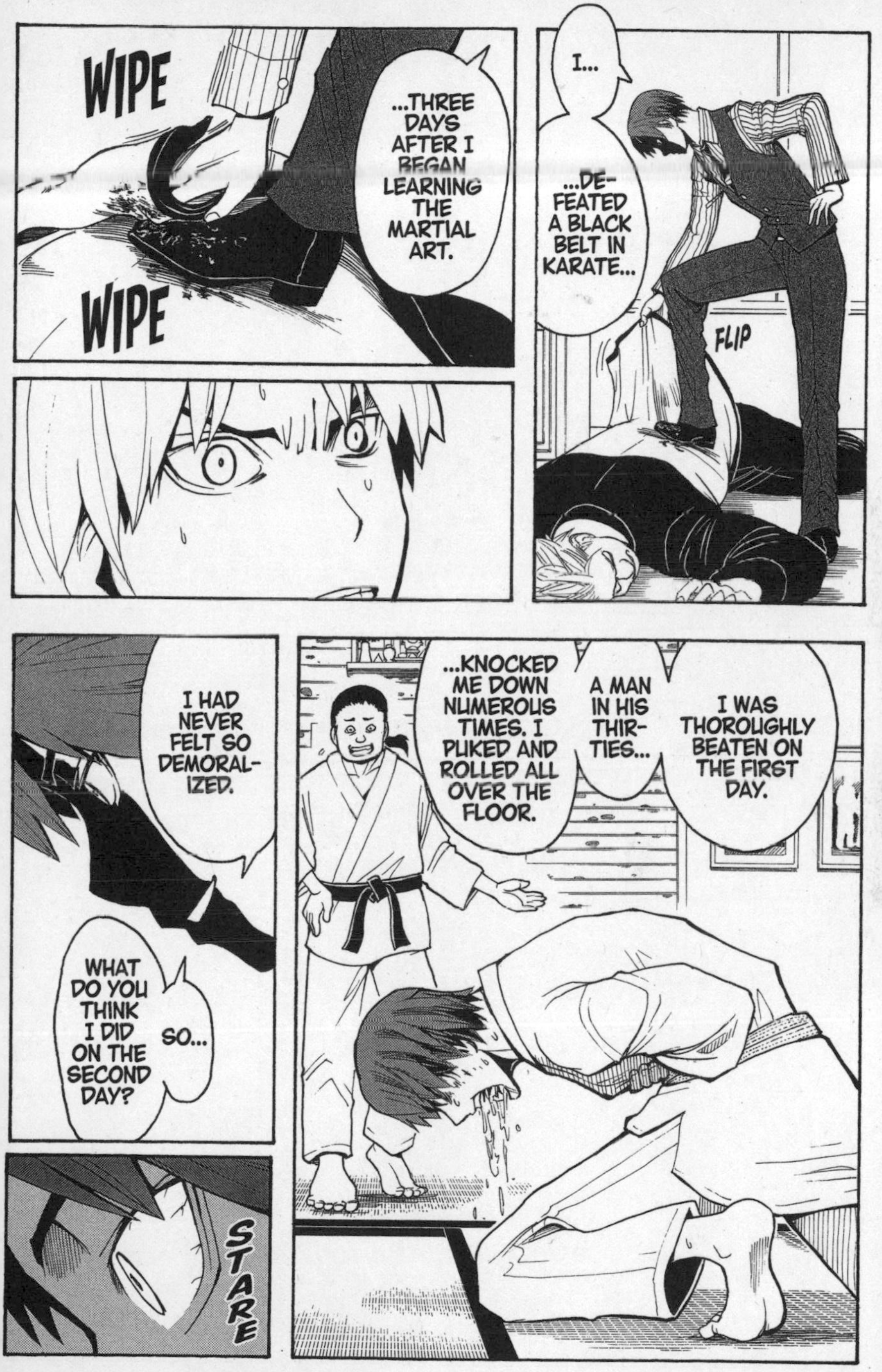
I...
...DE-FEATED A BLACK BELT IN KARATE...
FLIP
WIPE
...THREE DAYS AFTER I BEGAN LEARNING THE MARTIAL ART.
WIPE
I WAS THOROUGHLY BEATEN ON THE FIRST DAY.
A MAN IN HIS THIR-TIES...
...KNOCKED ME DOWN NUMEROUS TIMES. I PUKED AND ROLLED ALL OVER THE FLOOR.
I HAD NEVER FELT SO DEMORAL-IZED.
SO...
WHAT DO YOU THINK I DID ON THE SECOND DAY?
STARE

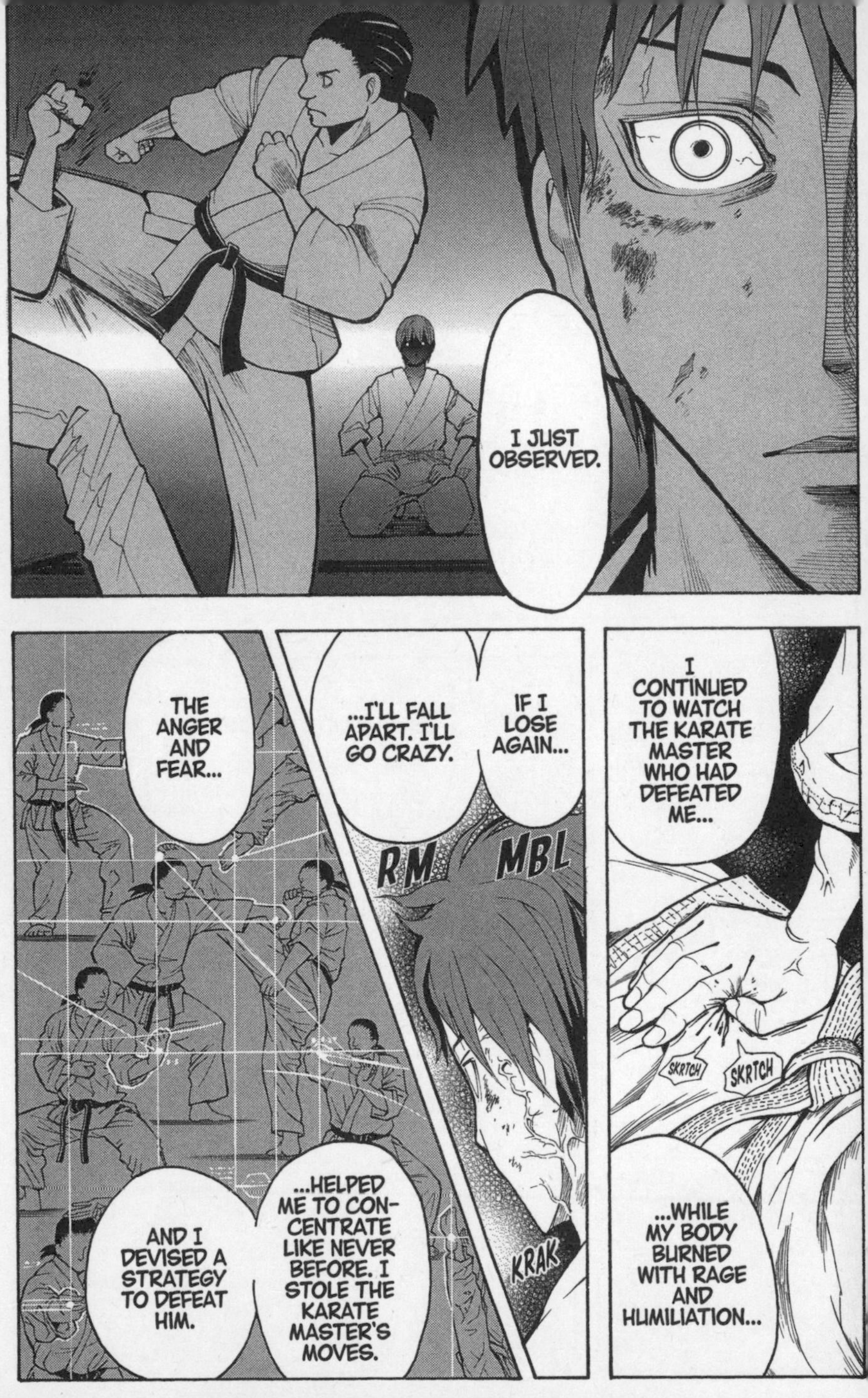
I JUST OBSERVED.
I CONTINUED TO WATCH THE KARATE MASTER WHO HAD DEFEATED ME...
SKRTCH
SKRTCH
...WHILE MY BODY BURNED WITH RAGE AND HUMILIATION...
IF I LOSE AGAIN...
...I'LL FALL APART. I'LL GO CRAZY.
RM MBL
KRAK
THE ANGER AND FEAR...
...HELPED ME TO CON-CENTRATE LIKE NEVER BEFORE. I STOLE THE KARATE MASTER'S MOVES.
AND I DEVISED A STRATEGY TO DEFEAT HIM.

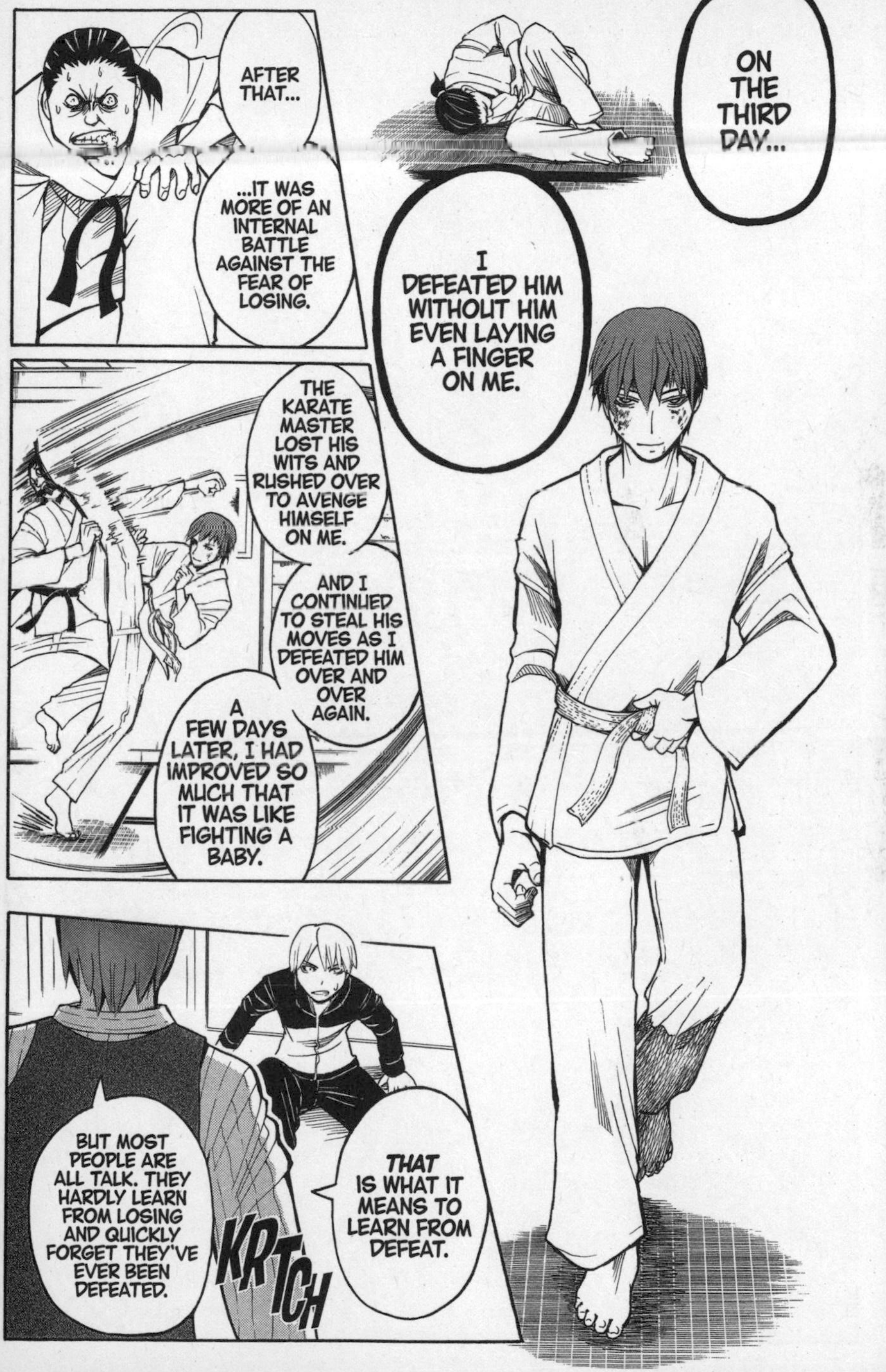
ON THE THIRD DAY...
I DEFEATED HIM WITHOUT HIM EVEN LAYING A FINGER ON ME.
AFTER THAT...
...IT WAS MORE OF AN INTERNAL BATTLE AGAINST THE FEAR OF LOSING.
THE KARATE MASTER LOST HIS WITS AND RUSHED OVER TO AVENGE HIMSELF ON ME.
AND I CONTINUED TO STEAL HIS MOVES AS I DEFEATED HIM OVER AND OVER AGAIN.
A FEW DAYS LATER, I HAD IMPROVED SO MUCH THAT IT WAS LIKE FIGHTING A BABY.
THAT IS WHAT IT MEANS TO LEARN FROM DEFEAT.
KRTCH
BUT MOST PEOPLE ARE ALL TALK. THEY HARDLY LEARN FROM LOSING AND QUICKLY FORGET THEY'VE EVER BEEN DEFEATED.

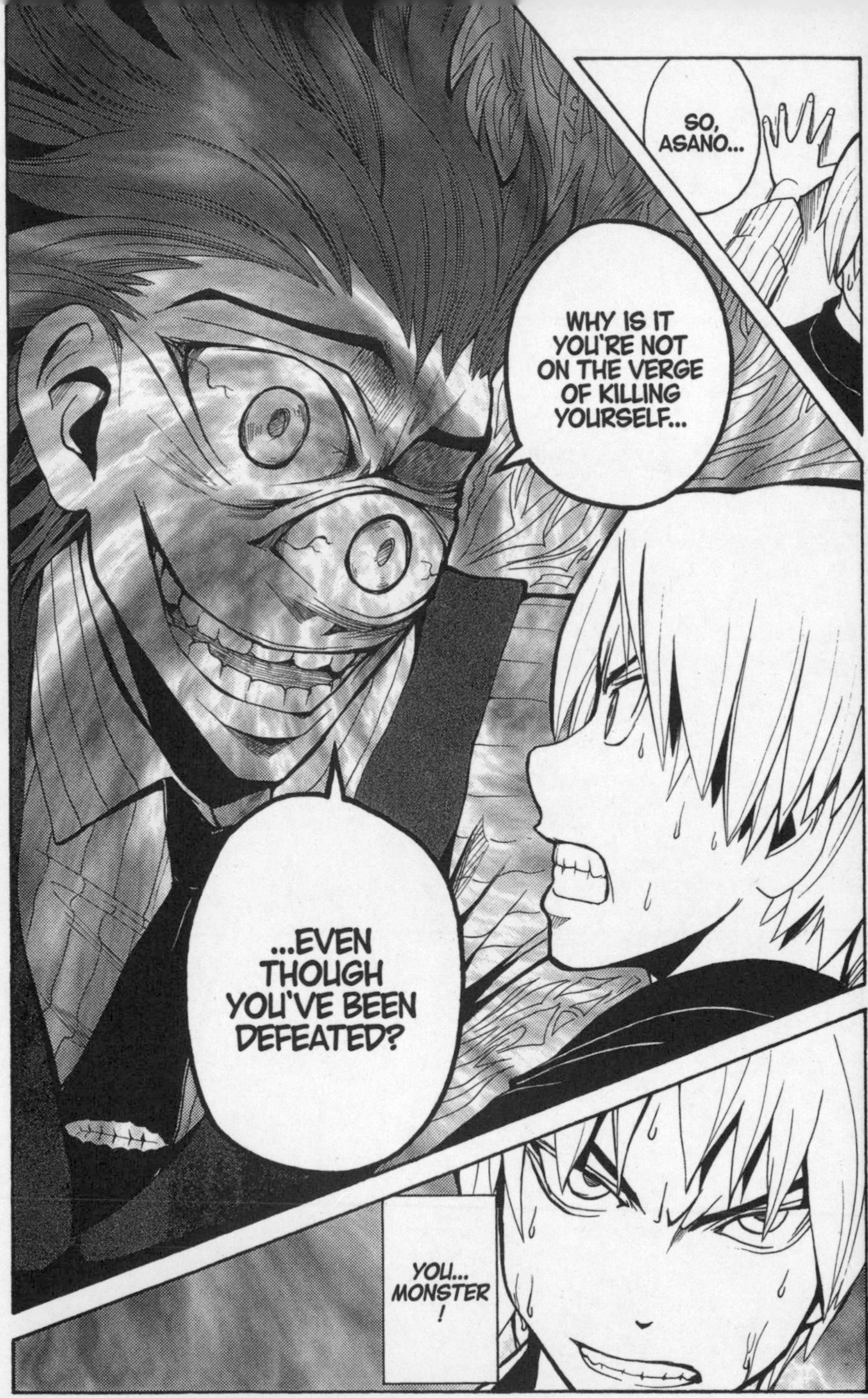
SO, ASANO...
WHY IS IT YOU'RE NOT ON THE VERGE OF KILLING YOURSELF...
...EVEN THOUGH YOU'VE BEEN DEFEATED?
YOU... MONSTER!

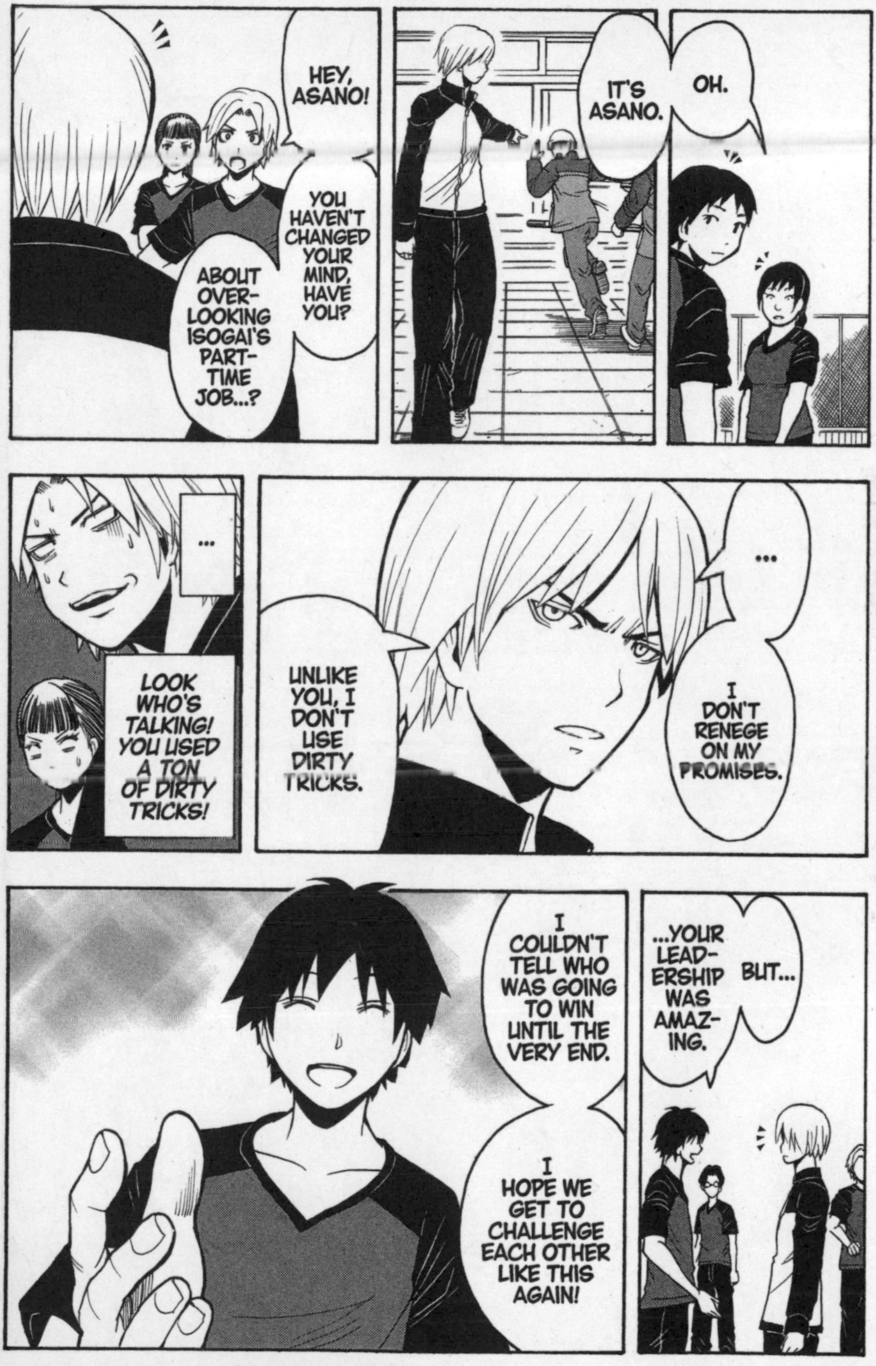
OH.
IT'S ASANO.
HEY, ASANO!
YOU HAVEN'T CHANGED YOUR MIND, HAVE YOU?
ABOUT OVER-LOOKING ISOGAI'S PART-TIME JOB...?
...
I DON'T RENEGE ON MY PROMISES.
UNLIKE YOU, I DON'T USE DIRTY TRICKS.
...
LOOK WHO'S TALKING! YOU USED A TON OF DIRTY TRICKS!
BUT...
...YOUR LEAD-ERSHIP WAS AMAZ-ING.
I COULDN'T TELL WHO WAS GOING TO WIN UNTIL THE VERY END.
I HOPE WE GET TO CHALLENGE EACH OTHER LIKE THIS AGAIN!

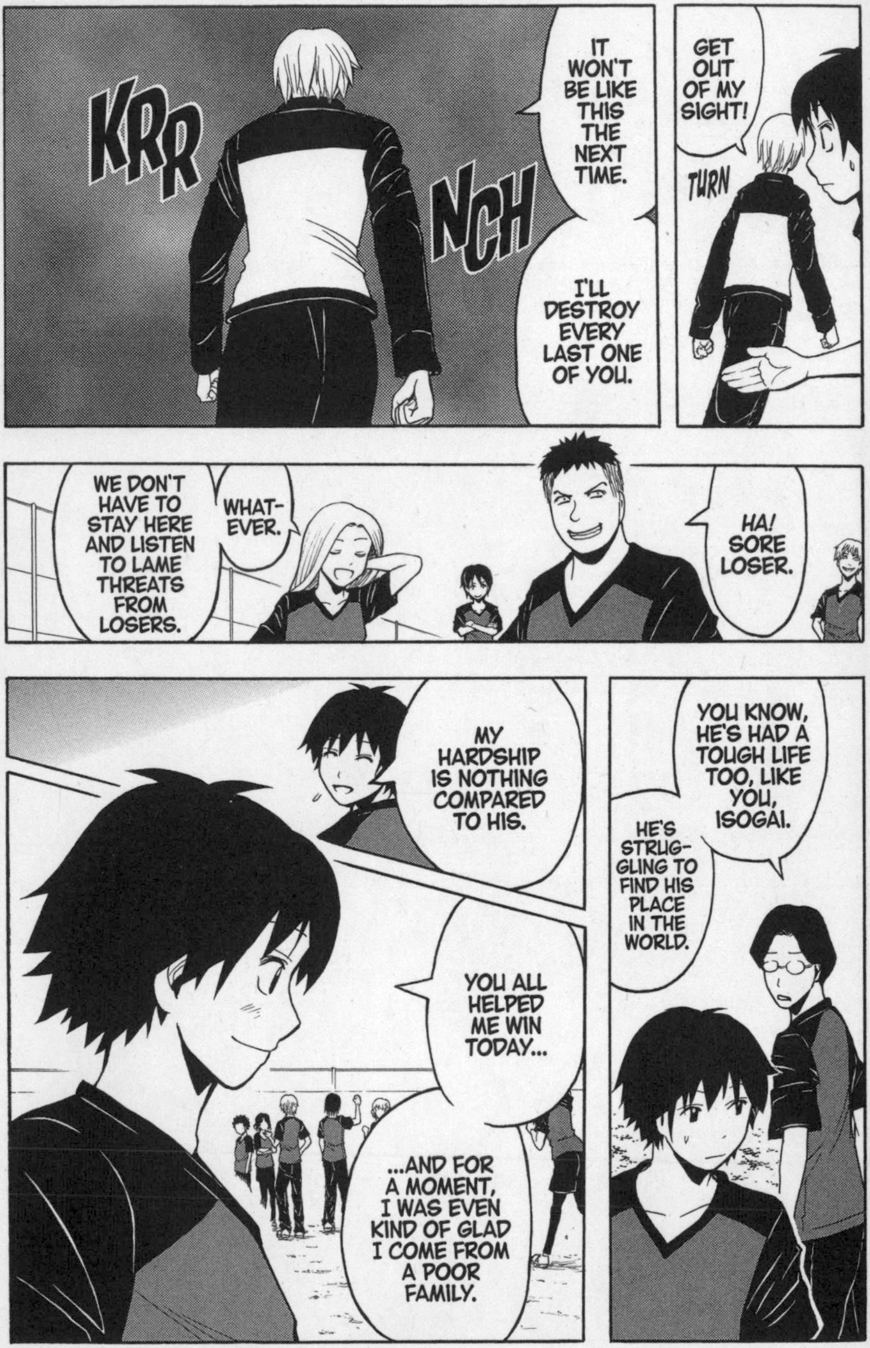
GET OUT OF MY SIGHT!
TURN
IT WON'T BE LIKE THIS THE NEXT TIME.
KRRNCH
I'LL DESTROY EVERY LAST ONE OF YOU.
HA! SORE LOSER.
WHAT-EVER.
WE DON'T HAVE TO STAY HERE AND LISTEN TO LAME THREATS FROM LOSERS.
YOU KNOW, HE'S HAD A TOUGH LIFE TOO, LIKE YOU, ISOGAI.
HE'S STRUG-GLING TO FIND HIS PLACE IN THE WORLD.
MY HARDSHIP IS NOTHING COMPARED TO HIS.
YOU ALL HELPED ME WIN TODAY...
...AND FOR A MOMENT, I WAS EVEN KIND OF GLAD I COME FROM A POOR FAMILY.

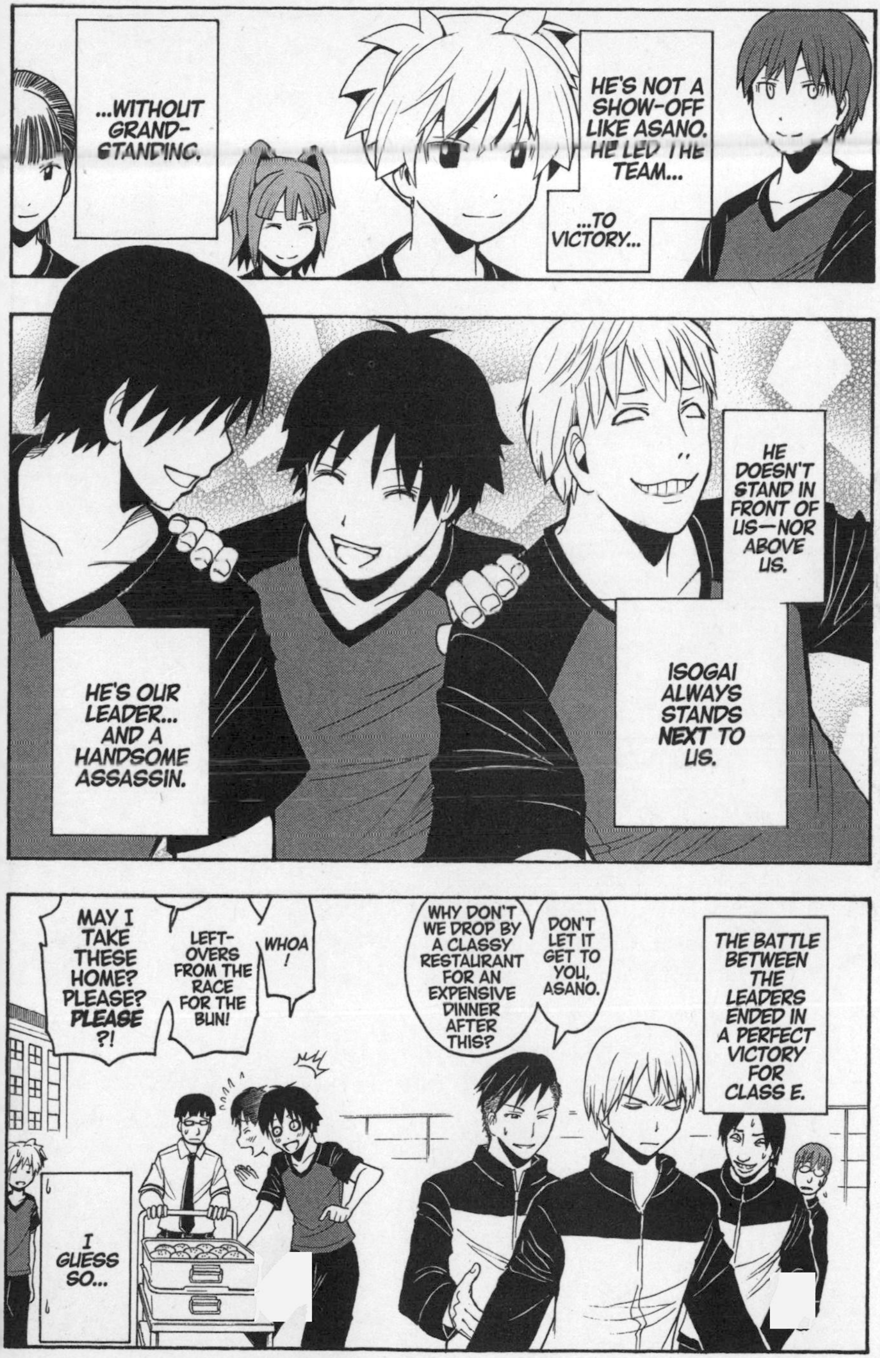
HE'S NOT A SHOW-OFF LIKE ASANO. HE LED THE TEAM...
...TO VICTORY...
...WITHOUT GRAND-STANDING.
HE DOESN'T STAND IN FRONT OF US—NOR ABOVE US.
ISOGAI ALWAYS STANDS NEXT TO US.
HE'S OUR LEADER... AND A HANDSOME ASSASSIN.
THE BATTLE BETWEEN THE LEADERS ENDED IN A PERFECT VICTORY FOR CLASS E.
DON'T LET IT GET TO YOU, ASANO.
WHY DON'T WE DROP BY A CLASSY RESTAURANT FOR AN EXPENSIVE DINNER AFTER THIS?
WHOA!
LEFT-OVERS FROM THE RACE FOR THE BUN!
MAY I TAKE THESE HOME? PLEASE? PLEASE?!
I GUESS SO...

A-1 GAKUSHU ASANO

- 😊 BIRTHDAY: JANUARY 1
- 😊 HEIGHT: 5' 9"
- 😊 WEIGHT: 141 LBS.
- 😊 FAVORITE SUBJECT: ALL MAJOR SUBJECTS
- 😊 LEAST FAVORITE SUBJECT: ETHICS
- 😊 HOBBY/SKILL: LEADERSHIP
- 😊 FUTURE GOAL: TO BE IN A POSITION WHERE HE CAN DELEGATE EVERY TASK TO ANOTHER PERSON
- 😊 WHAT HIS FATHER'S JOB WILL BE THEN: TO WARM MY SLIPPERS INSIDE HIS SHIRT AND HAND THEM TO ME WHEN I GO OUT (BUT I WON'T WEAR THEM)

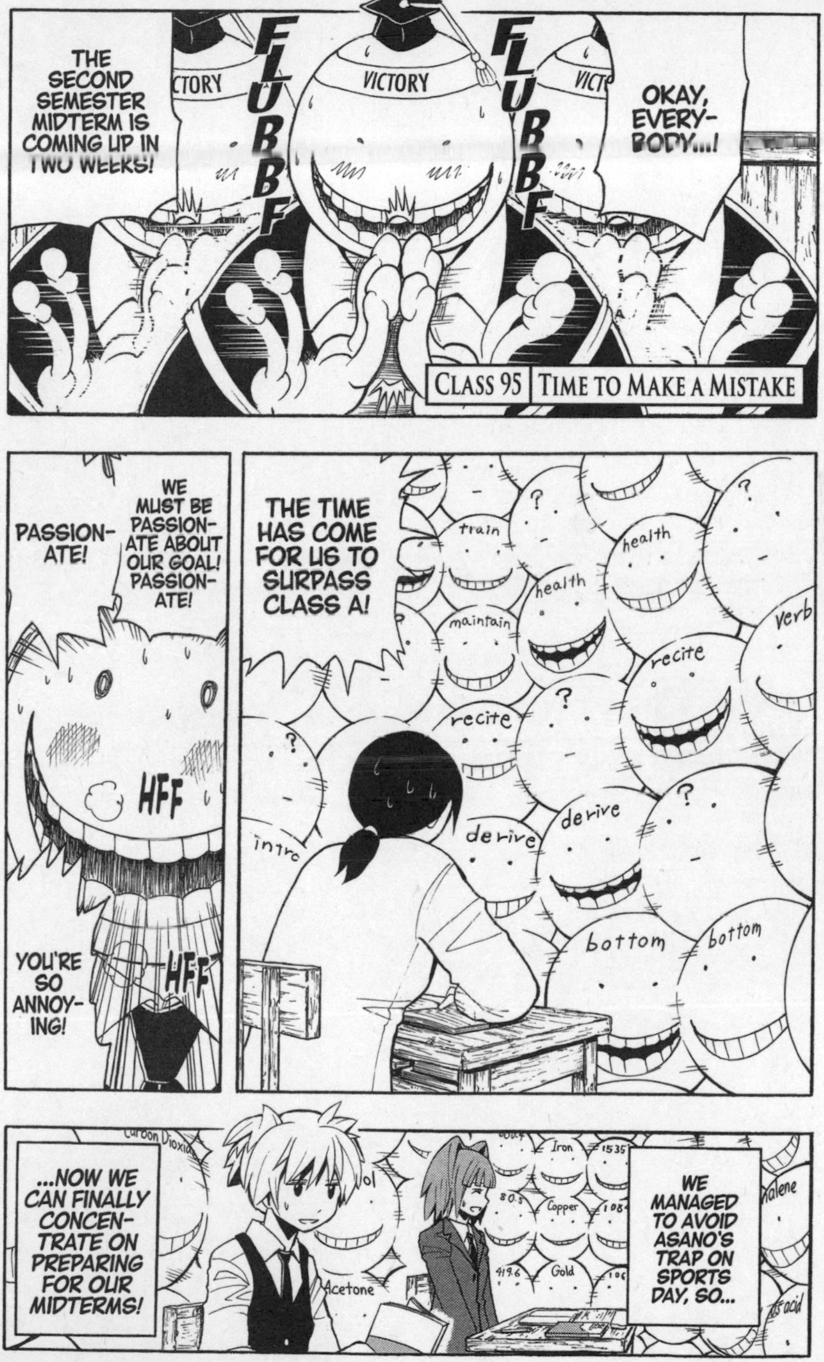
OKAY, EVERYBODY...!
FLUBB
VICTORY
FLUBB
THE SECOND SEMESTER MIDTERM IS COMING UP IN TWO WEEKS!
CLASS 95 TIME TO MAKE A MISTAKE
THE TIME HAS COME FOR US TO SURPASS CLASS A!
health
verb
recite
derive
bottom
train
maintain
WE MUST BE PASSIONATE ABOUT OUR GOAL! PASSIONATE!
PASSIONATE!
HFF
HFF
YOU'RE SO ANNOYING!
WE MANAGED TO AVOID ASANO'S TRAP ON SPORTS DAY, SO...
Iron
1535
Copper
1084
Gold
80.5
419.6
Acetone
...NOW WE CAN FINALLY CONCENTRATE ON PREPARING FOR OUR MIDTERMS!

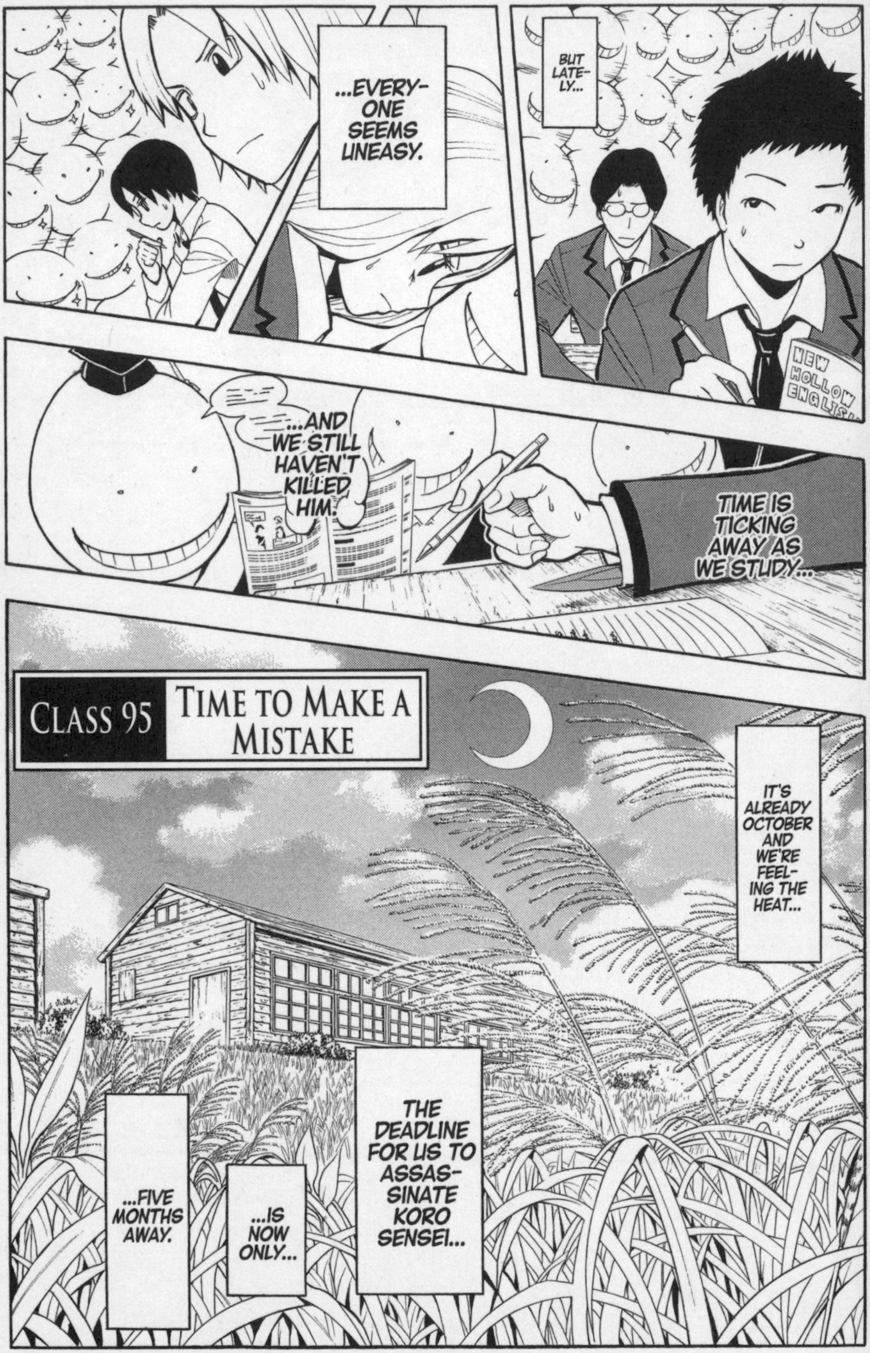
BUT LATELY...
...EVERY-ONE SEEMS UNEASY.
NEW HOLLOW ENGLIS
TIME IS TICKING AWAY AS WE STUDY...
...AND WE STILL HAVEN'T KILLED HIM.
CLASS 95
TIME TO MAKE A MISTAKE
IT'S ALREADY OCTOBER AND WE'RE FEEL-ING THE HEAT...
THE DEADLINE FOR US TO ASSAS-SINATE KORO SENSEI...
...IS NOW ONLY...
...FIVE MONTHS AWAY.

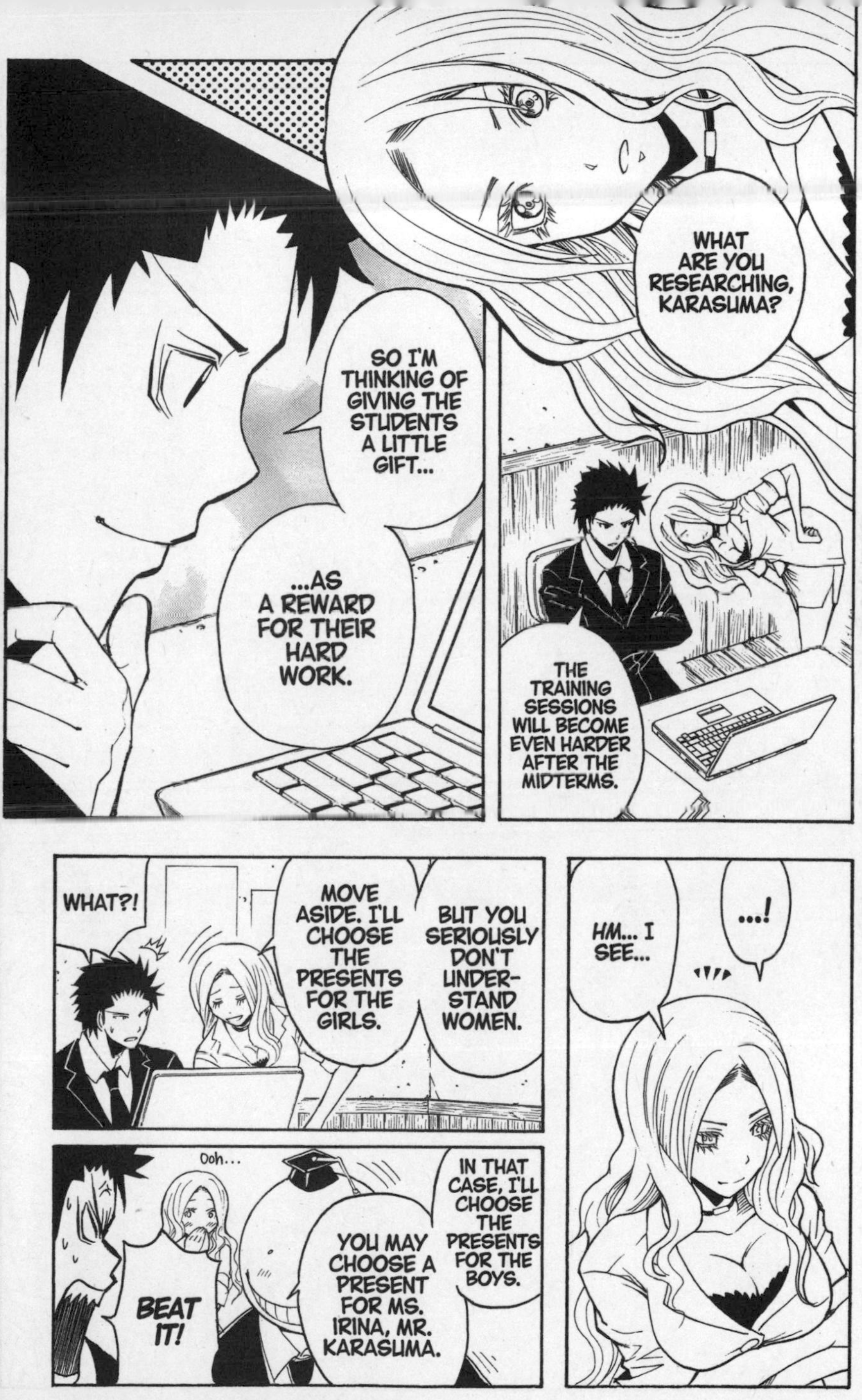
WHAT ARE YOU RESEARCHING, KARASUMA?
THE TRAINING SESSIONS WILL BECOME EVEN HARDER AFTER THE MIDTERMS.
SO I'M THINKING OF GIVING THE STUDENTS A LITTLE GIFT...
...AS A REWARD FOR THEIR HARD WORK.
...!
HM... I SEE...
BUT YOU SERIOUSLY DON'T UNDER-STAND WOMEN.
MOVE ASIDE. I'LL CHOOSE THE PRESENTS FOR THE GIRLS.
WHAT?!
IN THAT CASE, I'LL CHOOSE THE PRESENTS FOR THE BOYS.
YOU MAY CHOOSE A PRESENT FOR MS. IRINA, MR. KARASUMA.
Ooh...
BEAT IT!

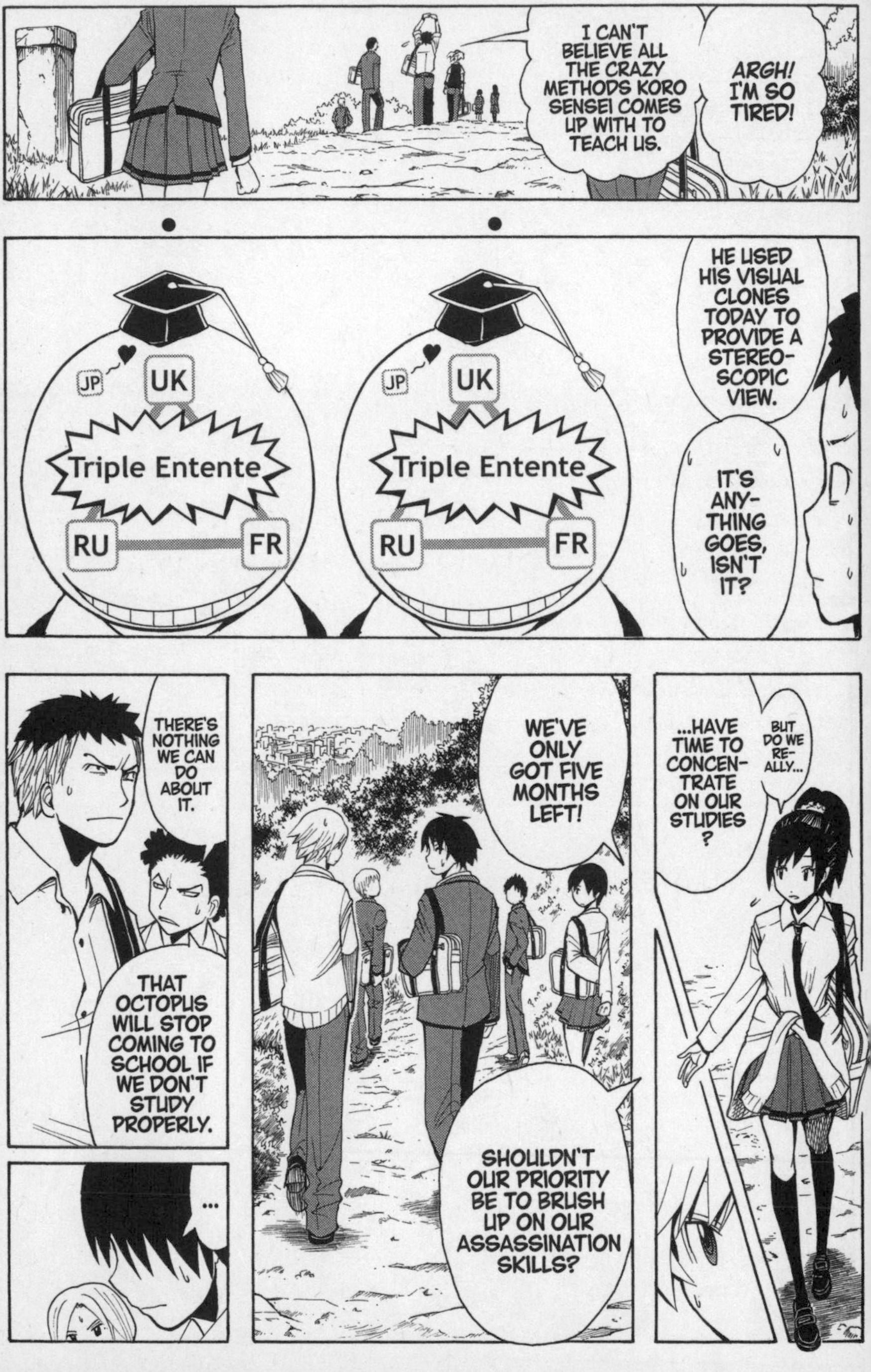
ARGH! I'M SO TIRED!
I CAN'T BELIEVE ALL THE CRAZY METHODS KORO SENSEI COMES UP WITH TO TEACH US.
HE USED HIS VISUAL CLONES TODAY TO PROVIDE A STEREO-SCOPIC VIEW.
IT'S ANY-THING GOES, ISN'T IT?
JP
UK
Triple Entente
RU
FR
JP
UK
Triple Entente
RU
FR
BUT DO WE RE-ALLY...
...HAVE TIME TO CONCEN-TRATE ON OUR STUDIES?
WE'VE ONLY GOT FIVE MONTHS LEFT!
SHOULDN'T OUR PRIORITY BE TO BRUSH UP ON OUR ASSASSINATION SKILLS?
THERE'S NOTHING WE CAN DO ABOUT IT.
THAT OCTOPUS WILL STOP COMING TO SCHOOL IF WE DON'T STUDY PROPERLY.
...

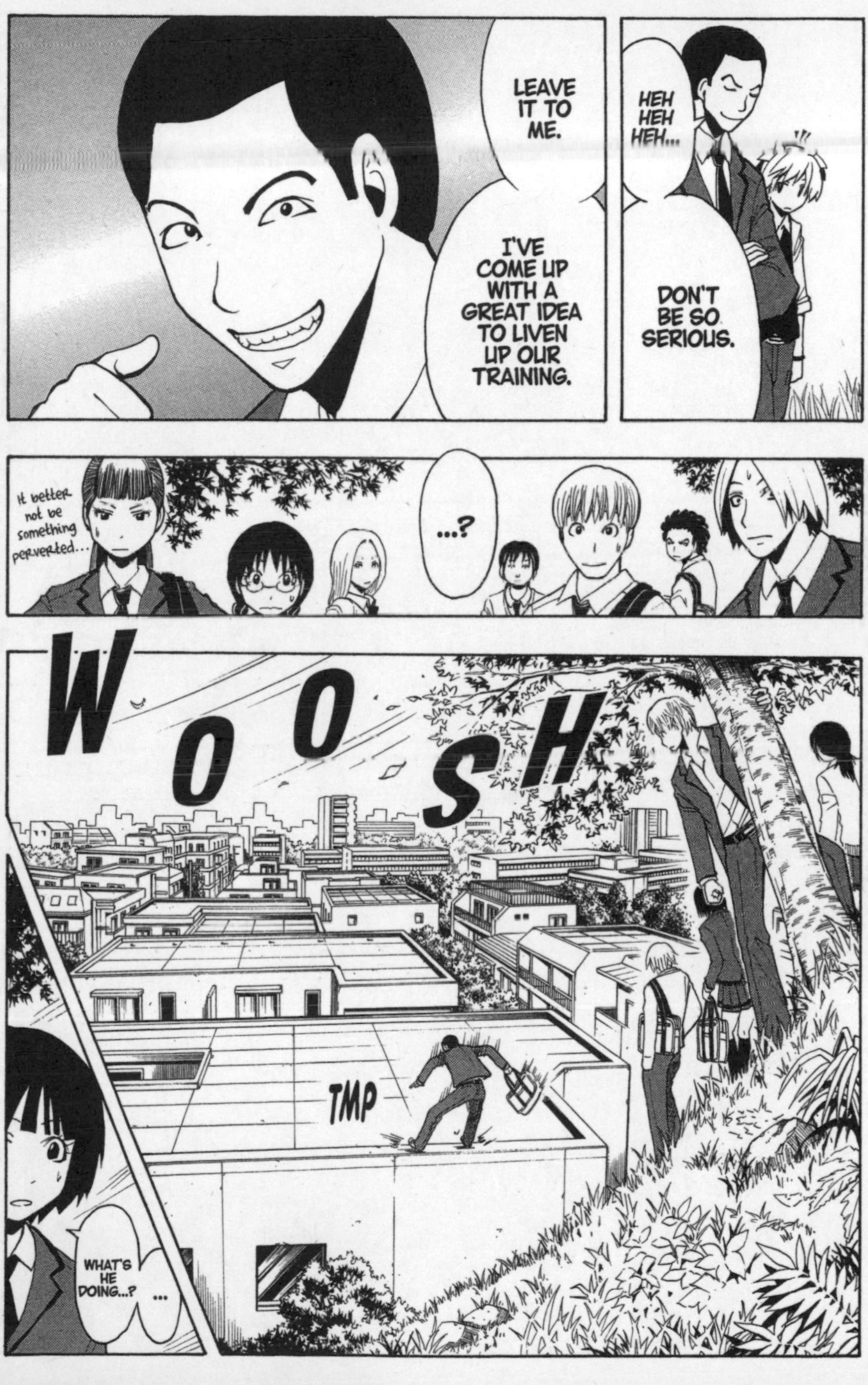
HEH HEH HEH...
DON'T BE SO SERIOUS.
LEAVE IT TO ME.
I'VE COME UP WITH A GREAT IDEA TO LIVEN UP OUR TRAINING.
...?
It better not be something perverted...
WOOSH
TMP
...
WHAT'S HE DOING...?

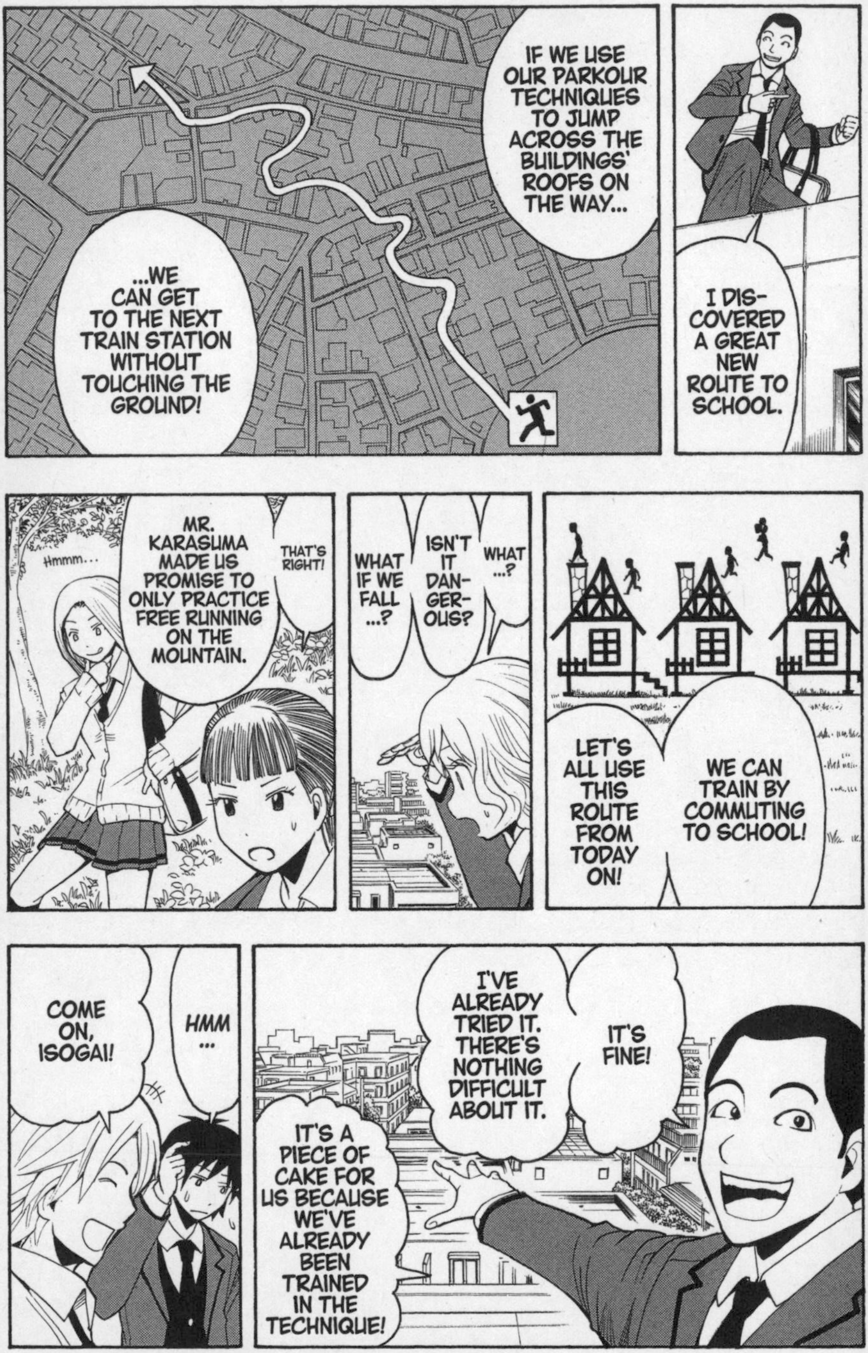
I DISCOVERED A GREAT NEW ROUTE TO SCHOOL.
IF WE USE OUR PARKOUR TECHNIQUES TO JUMP ACROSS THE BUILDINGS' ROOFS ON THE WAY...
...WE CAN GET TO THE NEXT TRAIN STATION WITHOUT TOUCHING THE GROUND!
WE CAN TRAIN BY COMMUTING TO SCHOOL!
LET'S ALL USE THIS ROUTE FROM TODAY ON!
WHAT ...?
ISN'T IT DANGEROUS?
WHAT IF WE FALL ...?
THAT'S RIGHT!
MR. KARASUMA MADE US PROMISE TO ONLY PRACTICE FREE RUNNING ON THE MOUNTAIN.
Hmmm...
IT'S FINE!
I'VE ALREADY TRIED IT. THERE'S NOTHING DIFFICULT ABOUT IT.
IT'S A PIECE OF CAKE FOR US BECAUSE WE'VE ALREADY BEEN TRAINED IN THE TECHNIQUE!
HMM ...
COME ON, ISOGAI!

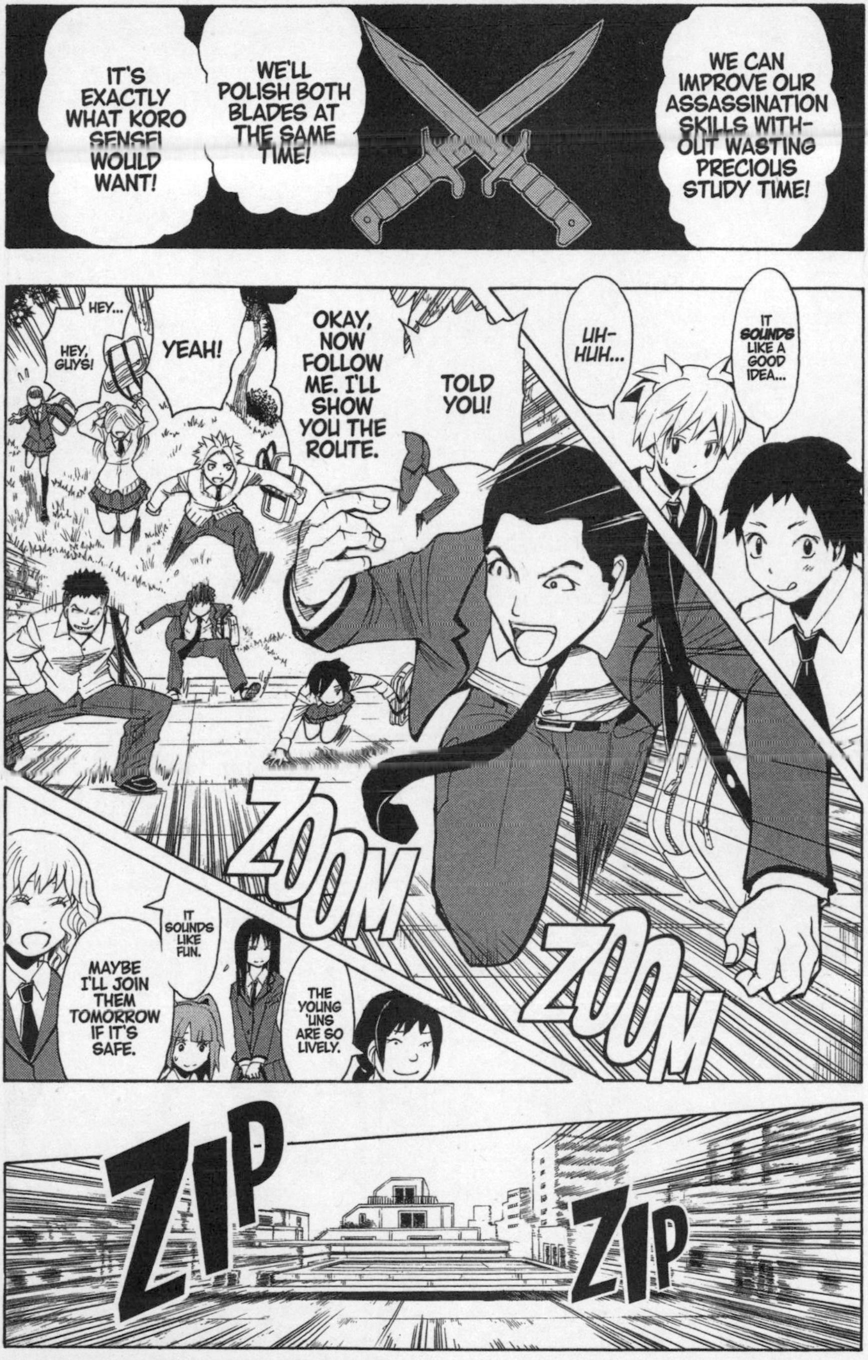
WE CAN IMPROVE OUR ASSASSINATION SKILLS WITH-OUT WASTING PRECIOUS STUDY TIME!
WE'LL POLISH BOTH BLADES AT THE SAME TIME!
IT'S EXACTLY WHAT KORO SENSEI WOULD WANT!
IT SOUNDS LIKE A GOOD IDEA...
UH-HUH...
TOLD YOU!
OKAY, NOW FOLLOW ME. I'LL SHOW YOU THE ROUTE.
YEAH!
HEY...
HEY, GUYS!
ZOOM
ZOOM
THE YOUNG 'UNS ARE SO LIVELY.
IT SOUNDS LIKE FUN.
MAYBE I'LL JOIN THEM TOMORROW IF IT'S SAFE.
ZIP-
ZIP

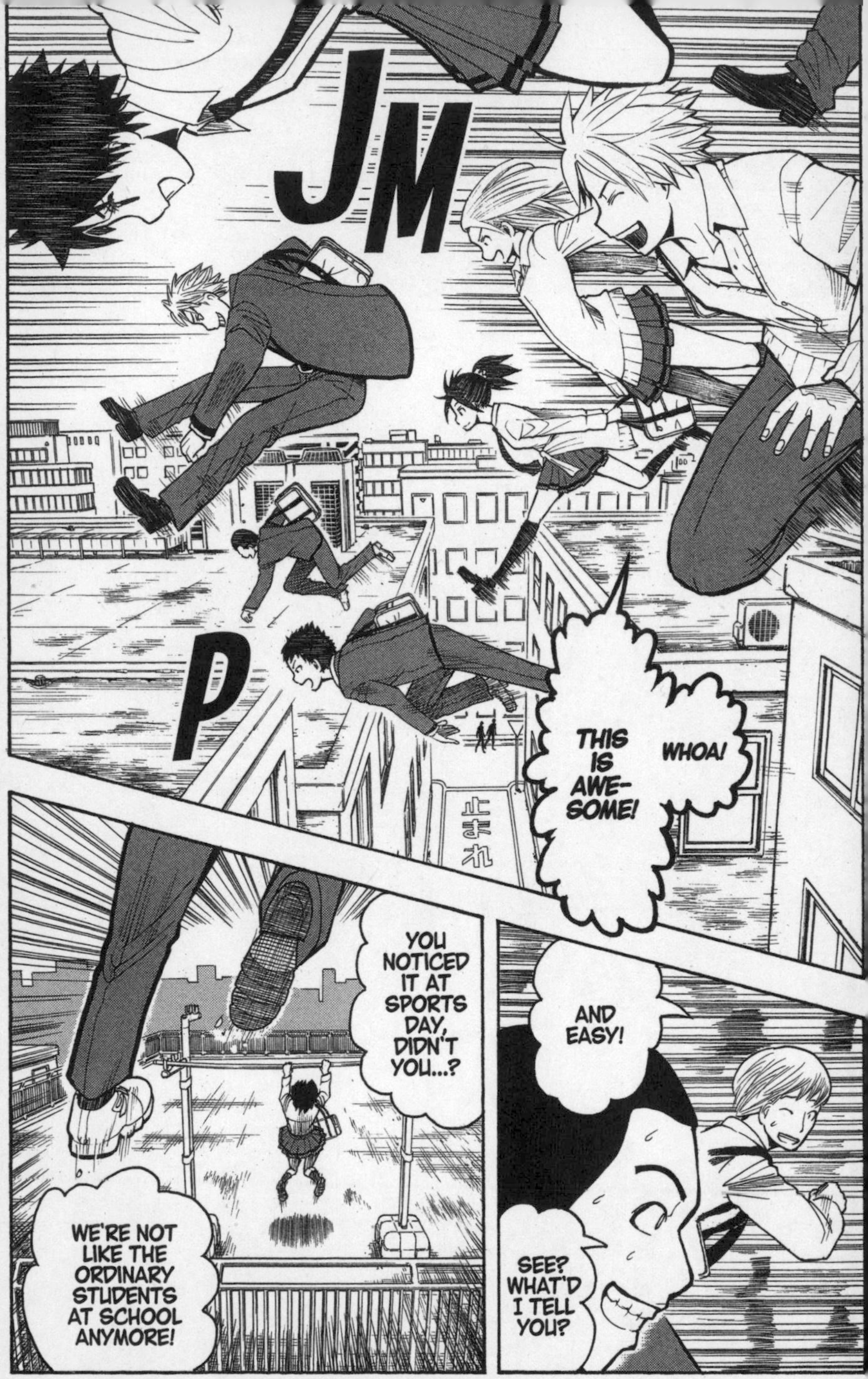
JM
P
WHOA! THIS IS AWESOME!
止まれ
AND EASY!
SEE? WHAT'D I TELL YOU?
YOU NOTICED IT AT SPORTS DAY, DIDN'T YOU...?
WE'RE NOT LIKE THE ORDINARY STUDENTS AT SCHOOL ANYMORE!

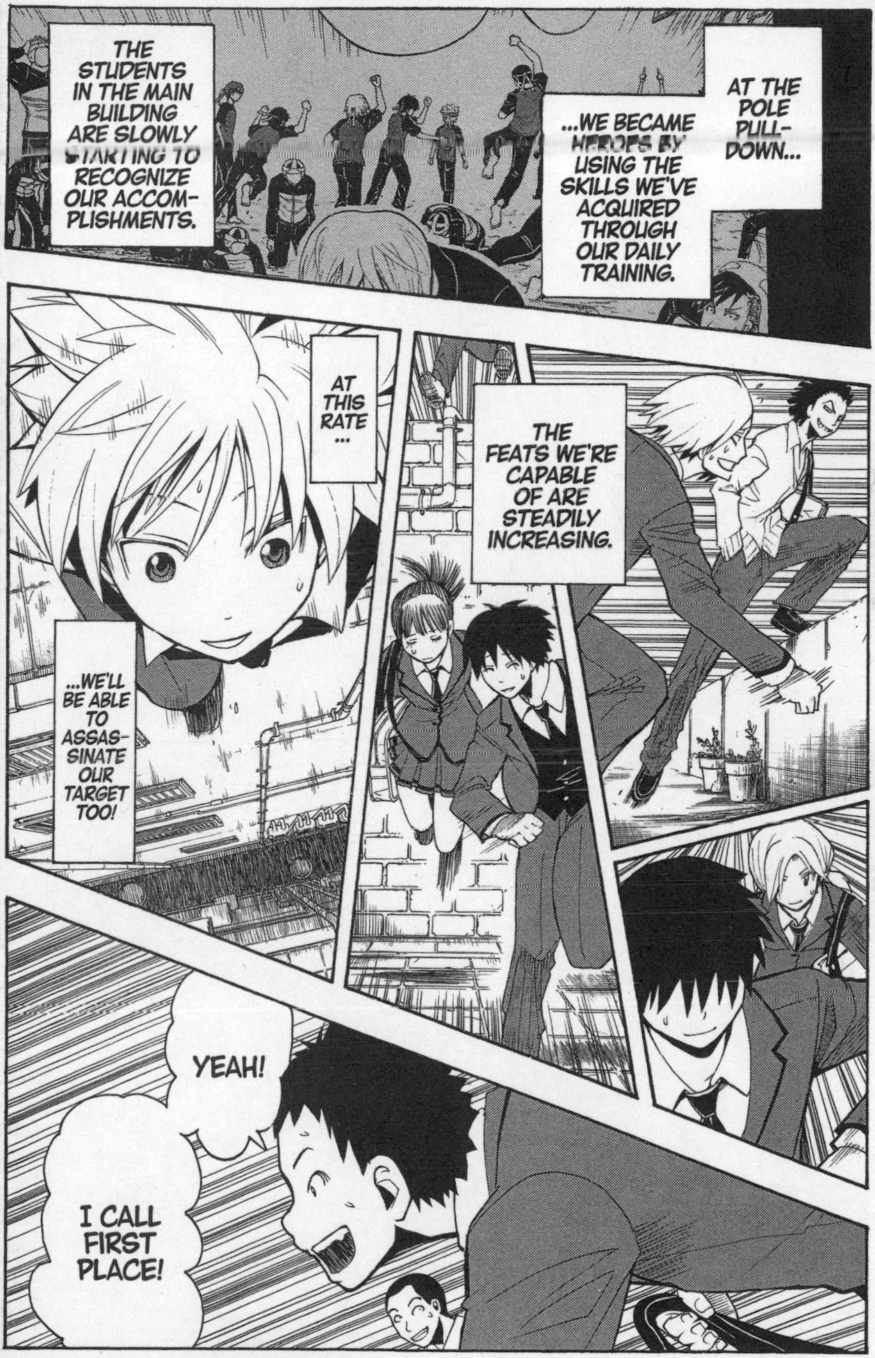
AT THE POLE PULL-DOWN...
...WE BECAME HEROES BY USING THE SKILLS WE'VE ACQUIRED THROUGH OUR DAILY TRAINING.
THE STUDENTS IN THE MAIN BUILDING ARE SLOWLY STARTING TO RECOGNIZE OUR ACCOMPLISHMENTS.
THE FEATS WE'RE CAPABLE OF ARE STEADILY INCREASING.
AT THIS RATE...
...WE'LL BE ABLE TO ASSASSINATE OUR TARGET TOO!
YEAH!
I CALL FIRST PLACE!

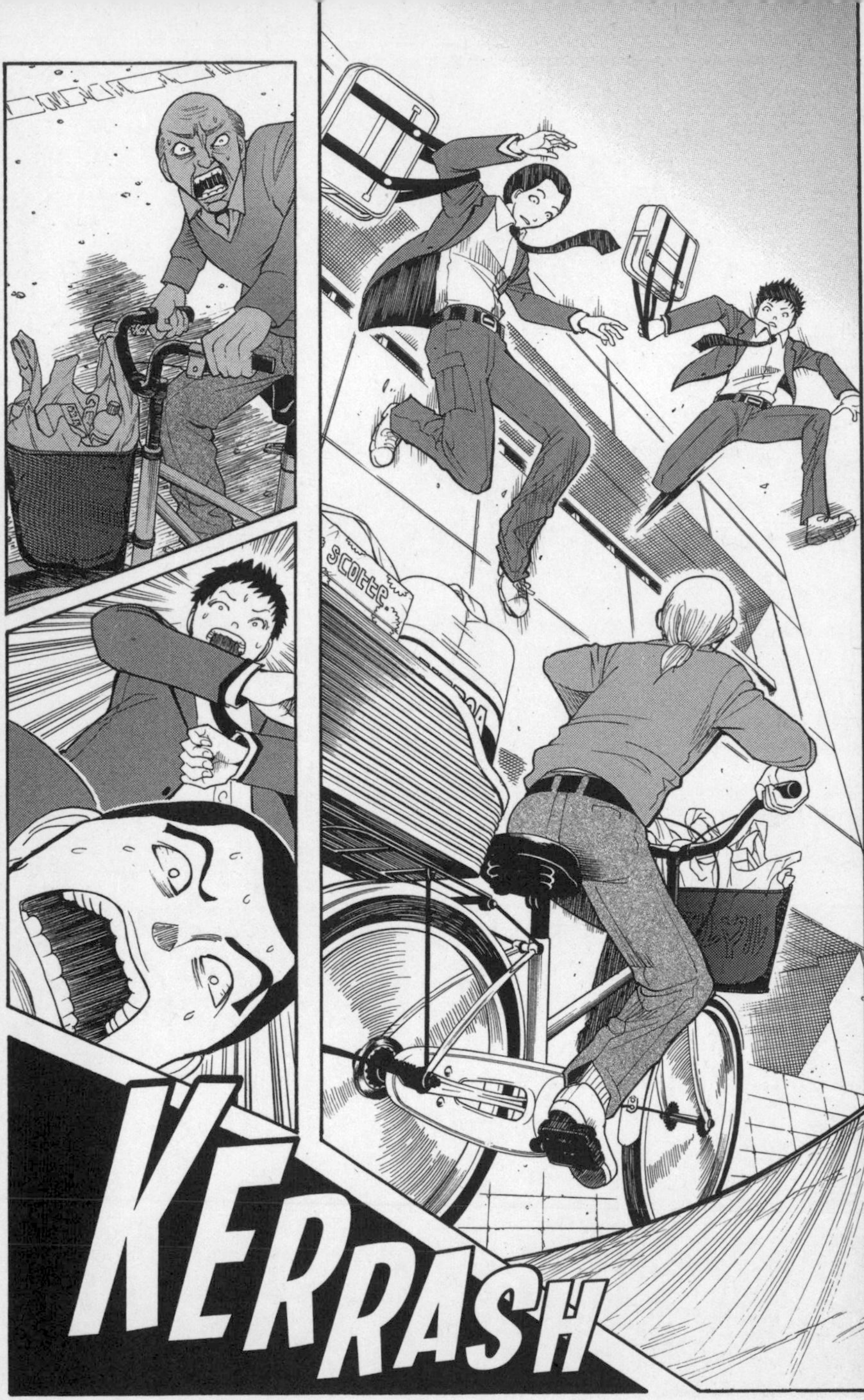
scotte
KERRASH

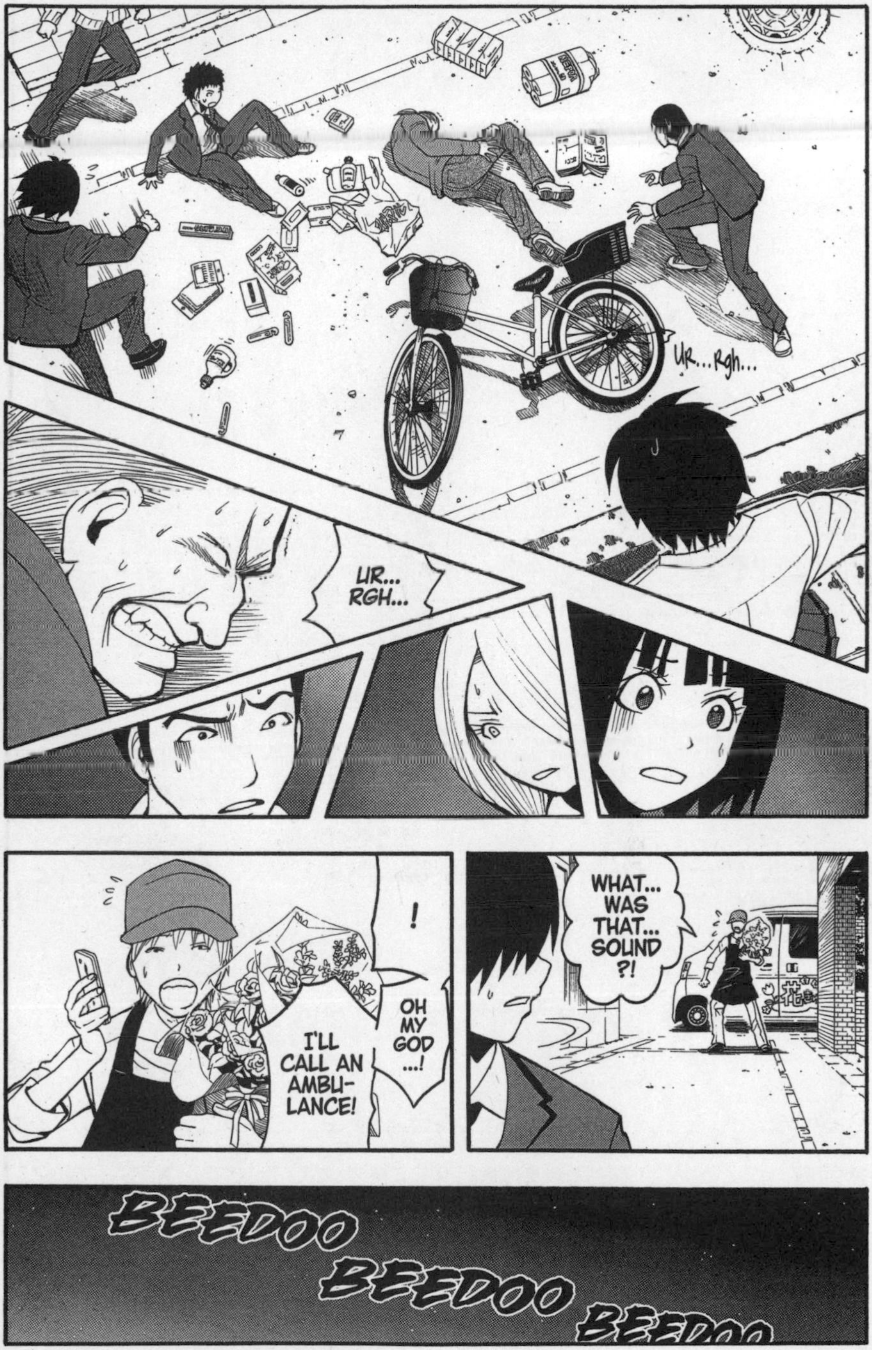
UR...Rgh...
UR... RGH...
WHAT... WAS THAT... SOUND ?!
!
OH MY GOD ...!
I'LL CALL AN AMBULANCE!
BEEDOO
BEEDOO
BEEDOO

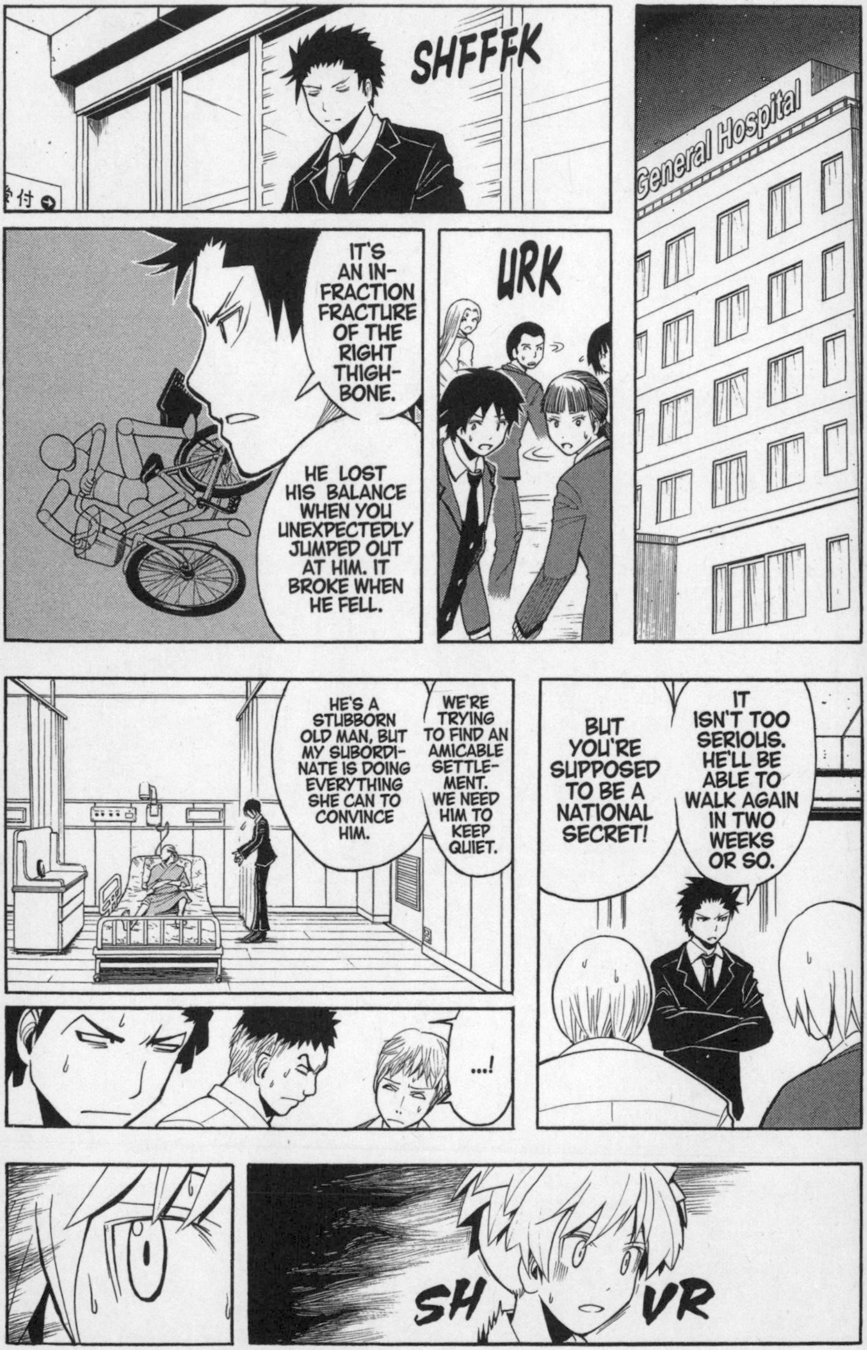
General Hospital
SHFFFK
URK
IT'S AN IN-FRACTION FRACTURE OF THE RIGHT THIGH-BONE.
HE LOST HIS BALANCE WHEN YOU UNEXPECTEDLY JUMPED OUT AT HIM. IT BROKE WHEN HE FELL.
IT ISN'T TOO SERIOUS. HE'LL BE ABLE TO WALK AGAIN IN TWO WEEKS OR SO.
BUT YOU'RE SUPPOSED TO BE A NATIONAL SECRET!
WE'RE TRYING TO FIND AN AMICABLE SETTLE-MENT. WE NEED HIM TO KEEP QUIET.
HE'S A STUBBORN OLD MAN, BUT MY SUBORDI-NATE IS DOING EVERYTHING SHE CAN TO CONVINCE HIM.
...!
SH VR

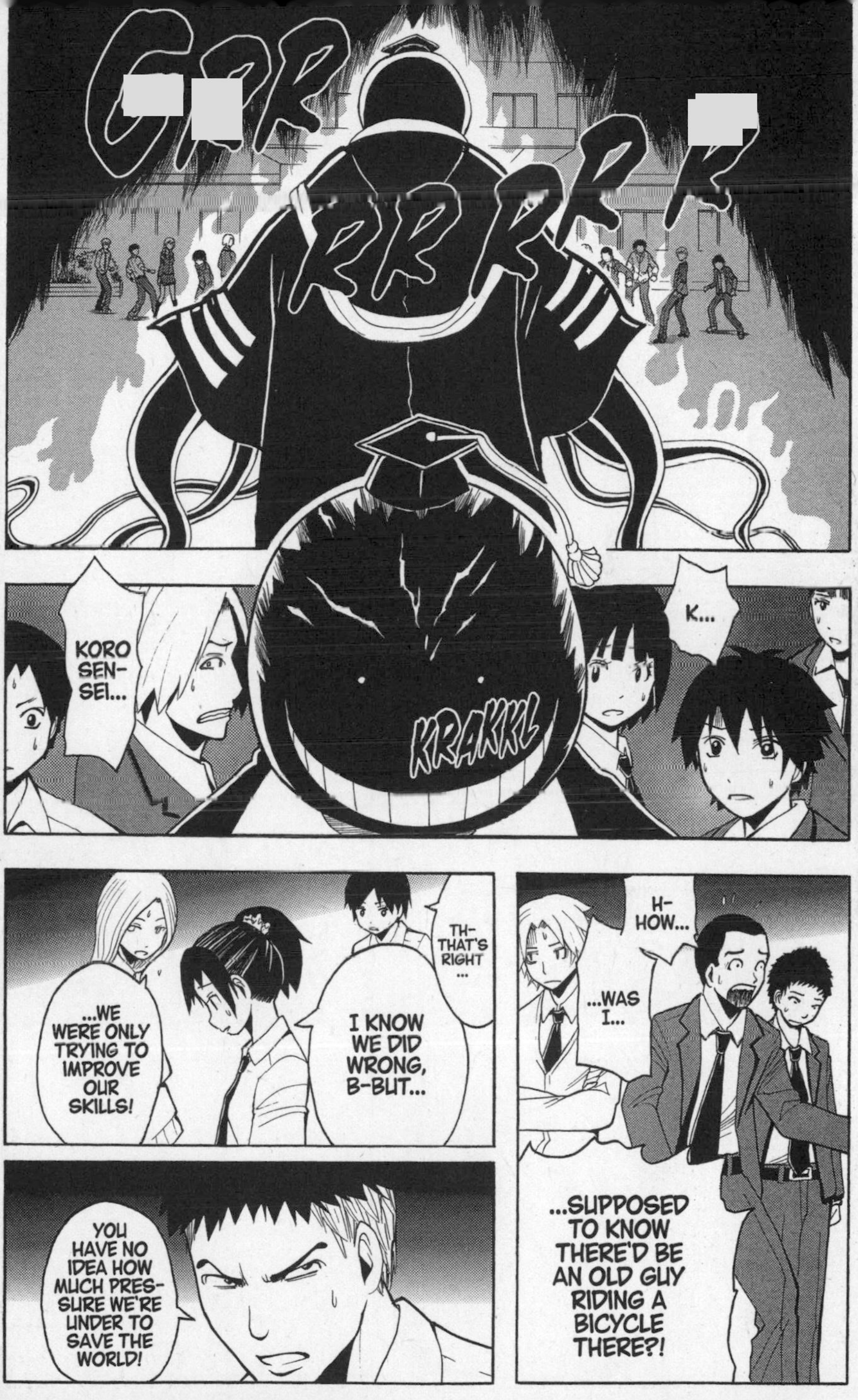
K...
KORO SENSEI...
KRAKKL
H-HOW...
...WAS I...
...SUPPOSED TO KNOW THERE'D BE AN OLD GUY RIDING A BICYCLE THERE?!
TH-THAT'S RIGHT...
I KNOW WE DID WRONG, B-BUT...
...WE WERE ONLY TRYING TO IMPROVE OUR SKILLS!
YOU HAVE NO IDEA HOW MUCH PRESSURE WE'RE UNDER TO SAVE THE WORLD!

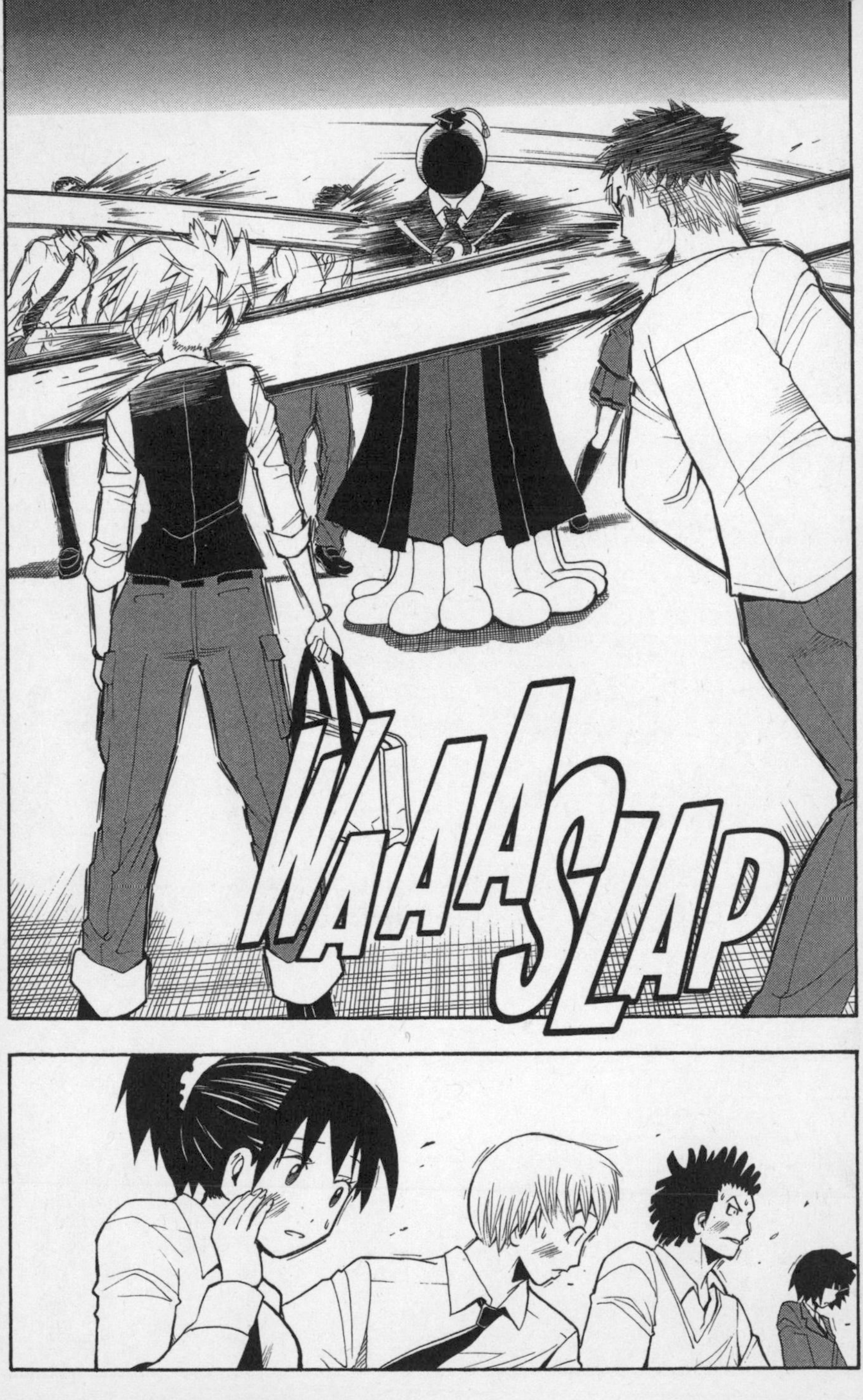
WAAAASLAP

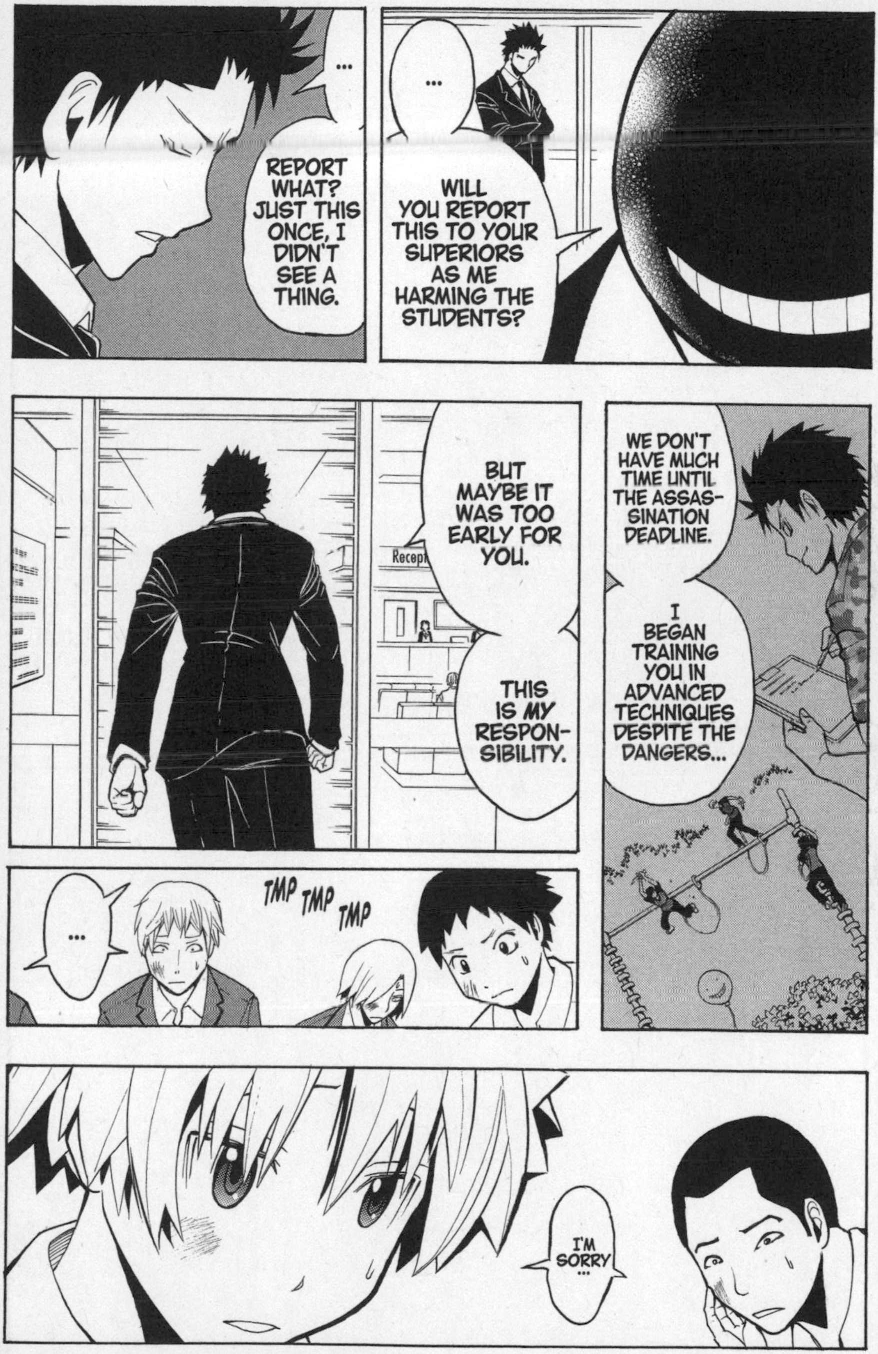
...
WILL YOU REPORT THIS TO YOUR SUPERIORS AS ME HARMING THE STUDENTS?
...
REPORT WHAT? JUST THIS ONCE, I DIDN'T SEE A THING.
WE DON'T HAVE MUCH TIME UNTIL THE ASSASSINATION DEADLINE.
I BEGAN TRAINING YOU IN ADVANCED TECHNIQUES DESPITE THE DANGERS...
BUT MAYBE IT WAS TOO EARLY FOR YOU.
THIS IS MY RESPONSIBILITY.
TMP TMP TMP
...
I'M SORRY...

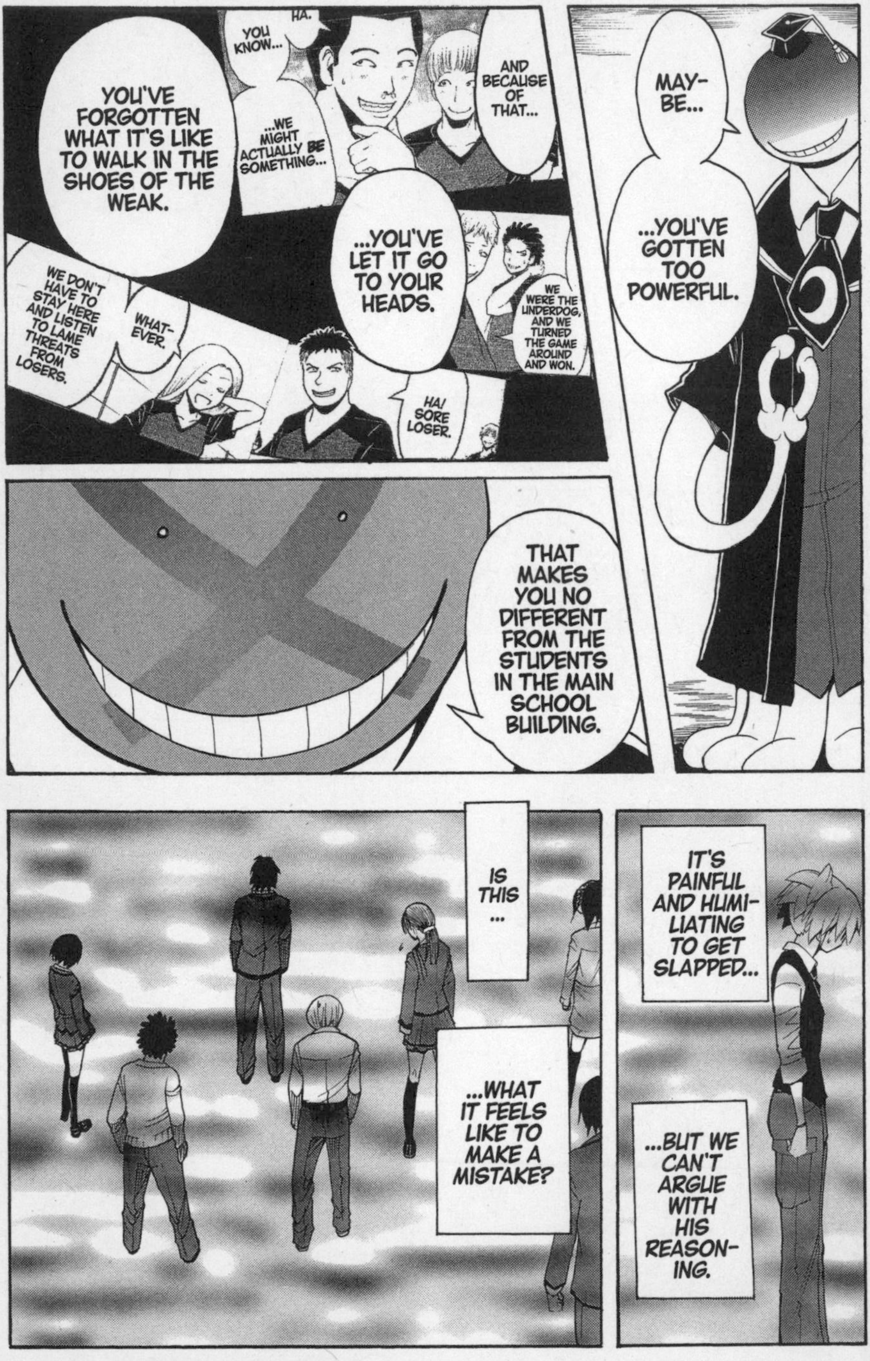
MAY-BE...
...YOU'VE GOTTEN TOO POWERFUL.
AND BECAUSE OF THAT...
HA.
YOU KNOW...
...WE MIGHT ACTUALLY BE SOMETHING...
YOU'VE FORGOTTEN WHAT IT'S LIKE TO WALK IN THE SHOES OF THE WEAK.
...YOU'VE LET IT GO TO YOUR HEADS.
WE WERE THE UNDERDOG, AND WE TURNED THE GAME AROUND AND WON.
HA! SORE LOSER.
WHAT-EVER.
WE DON'T HAVE TO STAY HERE AND LISTEN TO LAME THREATS FROM LOSERS.
THAT MAKES YOU NO DIFFERENT FROM THE STUDENTS IN THE MAIN SCHOOL BUILDING.
IT'S PAINFUL AND HUMILIATING TO GET SLAPPED...
...BUT WE CAN'T ARGUE WITH HIS REASON-ING.
IS THIS ...
...WHAT IT FEELS LIKE TO MAKE A MISTAKE?

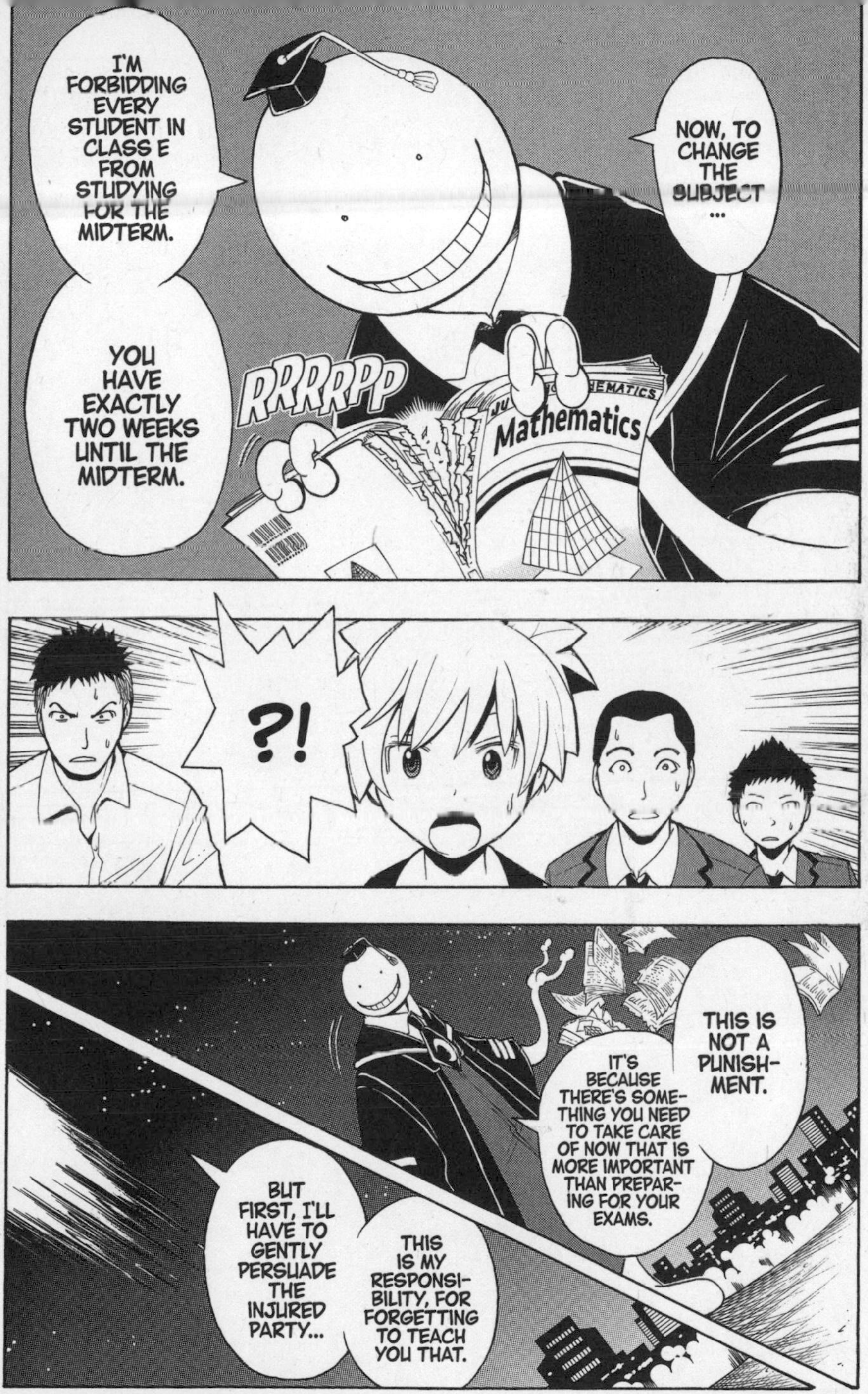
NOW, TO CHANGE THE SUBJECT ...
I'M FORBIDDING EVERY STUDENT IN CLASS E FROM STUDYING FOR THE MIDTERM.
YOU HAVE EXACTLY TWO WEEKS UNTIL THE MIDTERM.
RRRRPP
Mathematics
?!
THIS IS NOT A PUNISHMENT.
IT'S BECAUSE THERE'S SOMETHING YOU NEED TO TAKE CARE OF NOW THAT IS MORE IMPORTANT THAN PREPARING FOR YOUR EXAMS.
THIS IS MY RESPONSIBILITY, FOR FORGETTING TO TEACH YOU THAT.
BUT FIRST, I'LL HAVE TO GENTLY PERSUADE THE INJURED PARTY...

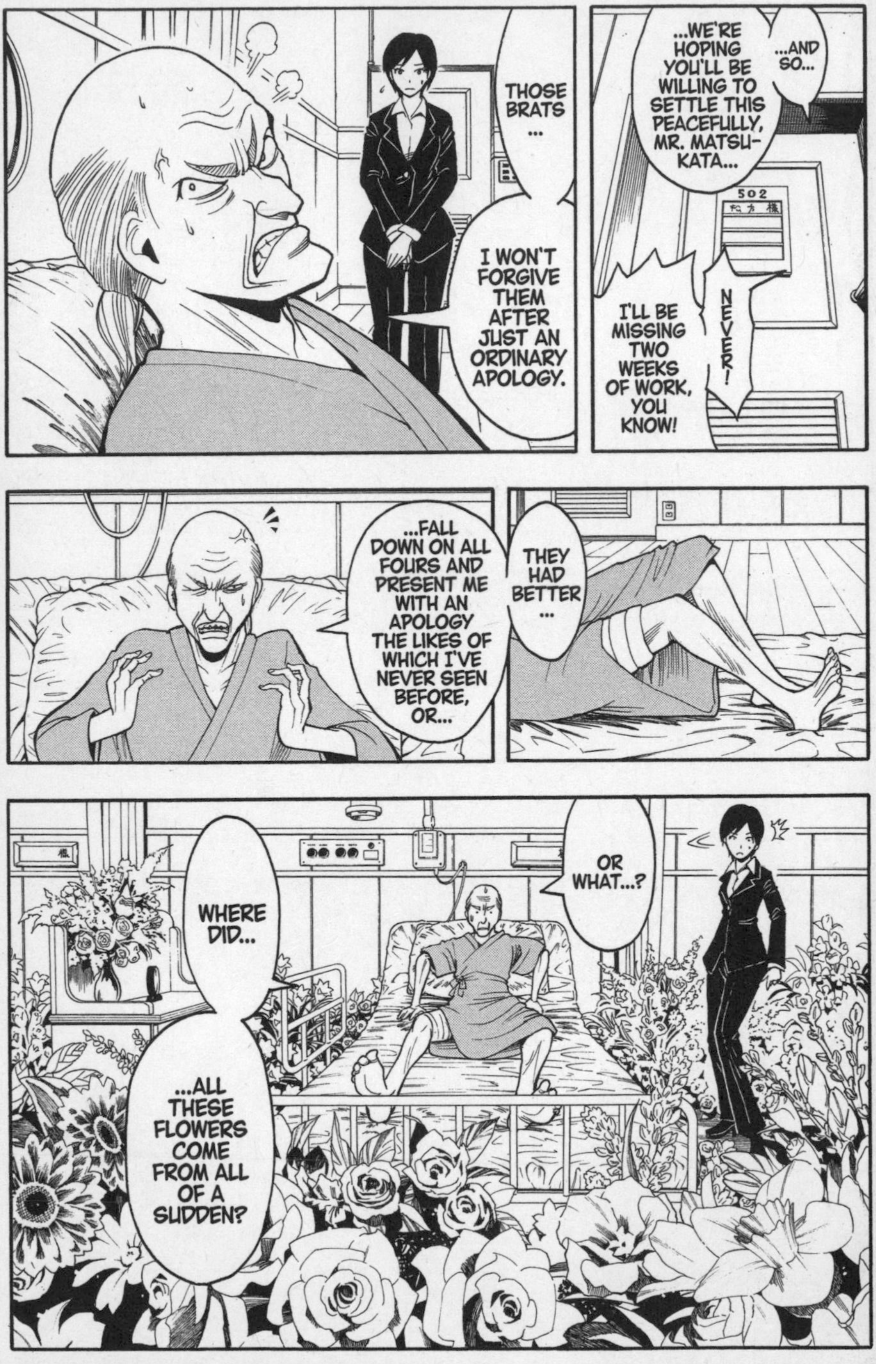
...AND SO...
...WE'RE HOPING YOU'LL BE WILLING TO SETTLE THIS PEACEFULLY, MR. MATSU-KATA...
NEVER!
I'LL BE MISSING TWO WEEKS OF WORK, YOU KNOW!
THOSE BRATS ...
I WON'T FORGIVE THEM AFTER JUST AN ORDINARY APOLOGY.
THEY HAD BETTER ...
...FALL DOWN ON ALL FOURS AND PRESENT ME WITH AN APOLOGY THE LIKES OF WHICH I'VE NEVER SEEN BEFORE, OR...
OR WHAT...?
WHERE DID...
...ALL THESE FLOWERS COME FROM ALL OF A SUDDEN?

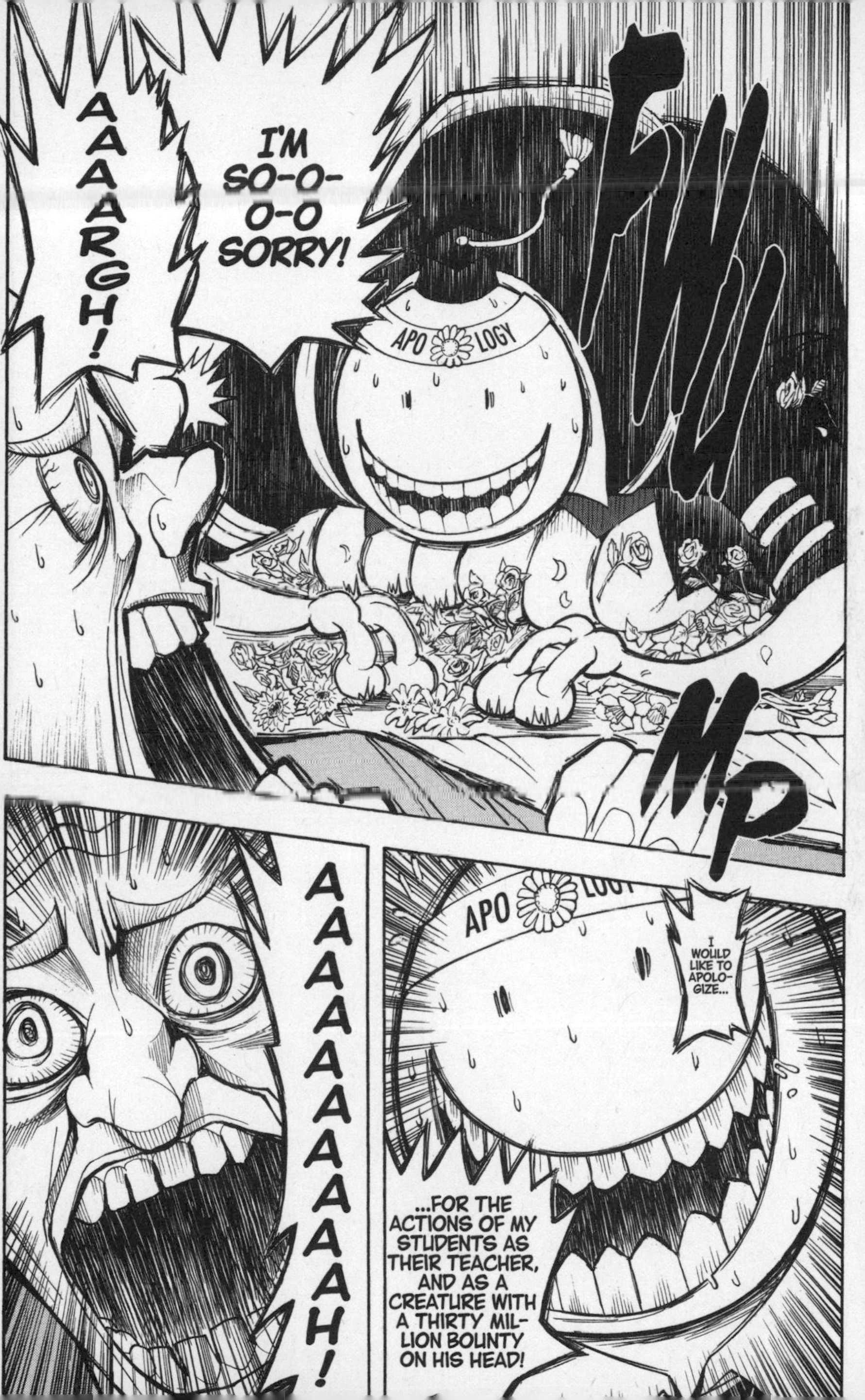
FWUMP
APO LOGY
I'M SO-O-O-O-O SORRY!
AAAARGH!
APO LOGY
I WOULD LIKE TO APOLOGIZE...
...FOR THE ACTIONS OF MY STUDENTS AS THEIR TEACHER, AND AS A CREATURE WITH A THIRTY MILLION BOUNTY ON HIS HEAD!
AAAAAAAAAAH!

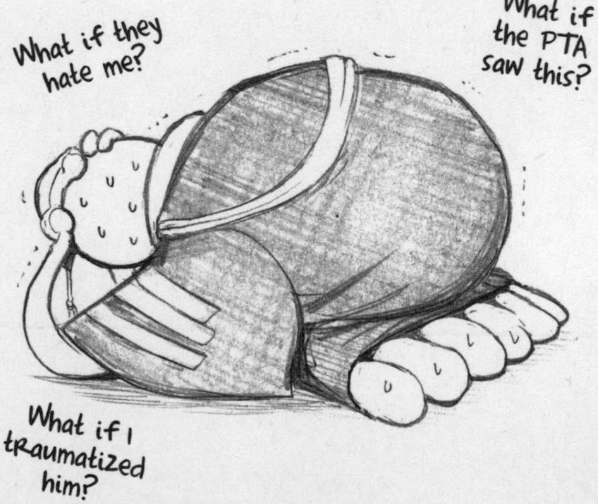
What if the PTA saw this?
What if they hate me?
What if I traumatized him?

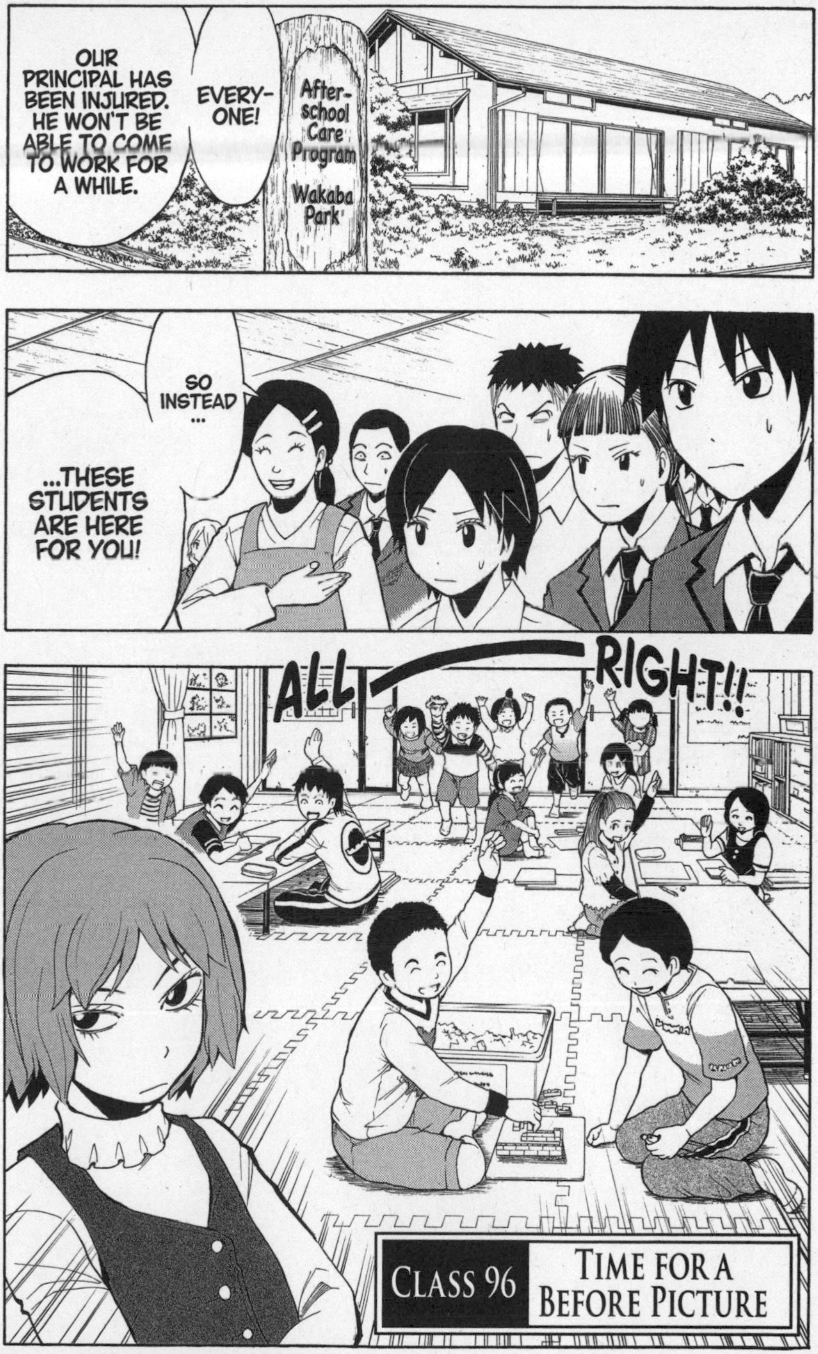
After-school Care Program
Wakaba Park
EVERY-ONE!
OUR PRINCIPAL HAS BEEN INJURED. HE WON'T BE ABLE TO COME TO WORK FOR A WHILE.
SO INSTEAD ...
...THESE STUDENTS ARE HERE FOR YOU!
ALL——RIGHT!!
CLASS 96
TIME FOR A BEFORE PICTURE

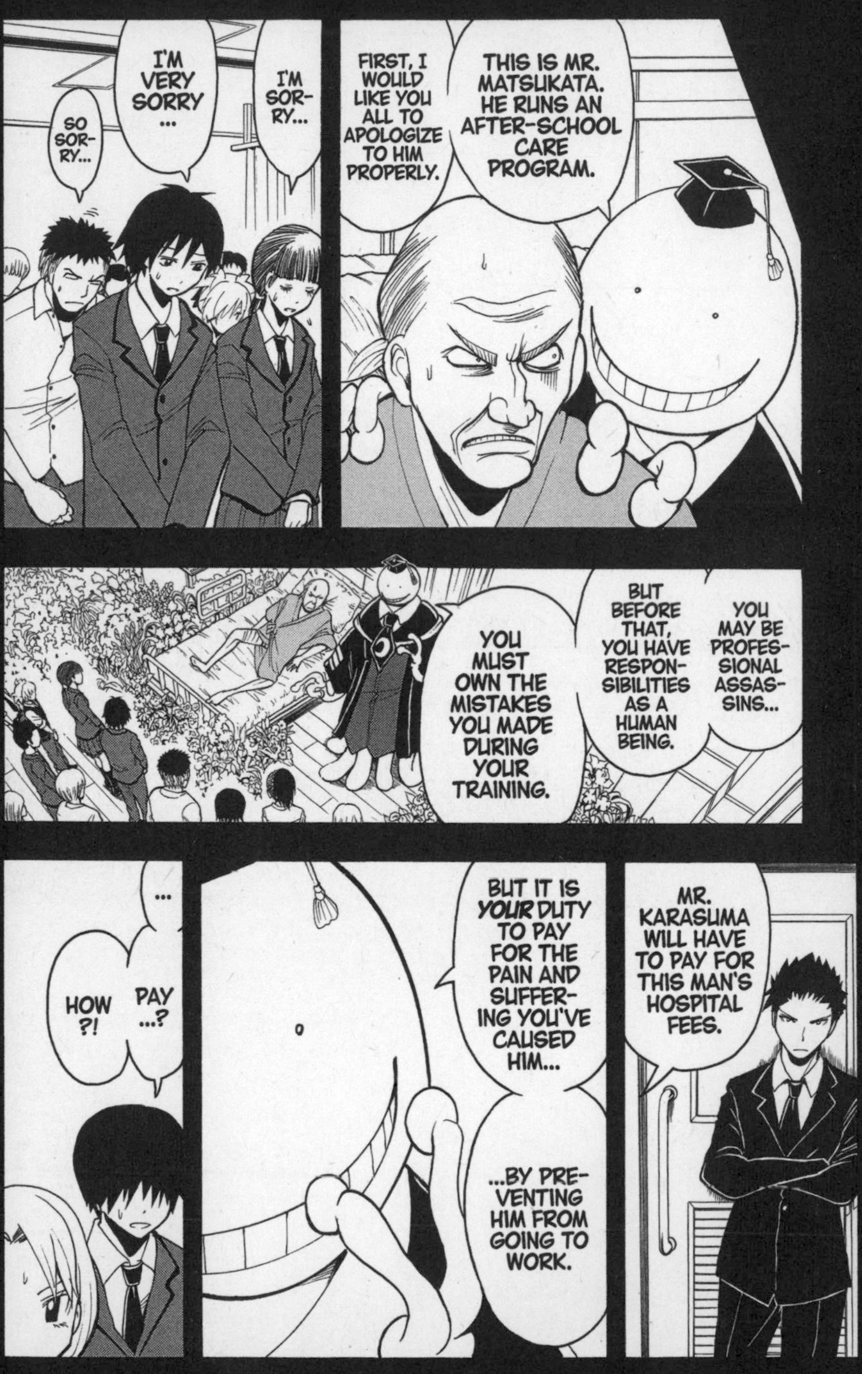
THIS IS MR. MATSUKATA. HE RUNS AN AFTER-SCHOOL CARE PROGRAM.
FIRST, I WOULD LIKE YOU ALL TO APOLOGIZE TO HIM PROPERLY.
I'M SORRY...
I'M VERY SORRY ...
SO SORRY...
YOU MAY BE PROFESSIONAL ASSASSINS...
BUT BEFORE THAT, YOU HAVE RESPONSIBILITIES AS A HUMAN BEING.
YOU MUST OWN THE MISTAKES YOU MADE DURING YOUR TRAINING.
MR. KARASUMA WILL HAVE TO PAY FOR THIS MAN'S HOSPITAL FEES.
BUT IT IS *YOUR* DUTY TO PAY FOR THE PAIN AND SUFFERING YOU'VE CAUSED HIM...
...BY PREVENTING HIM FROM GOING TO WORK.
...
PAY ...?
HOW ?!

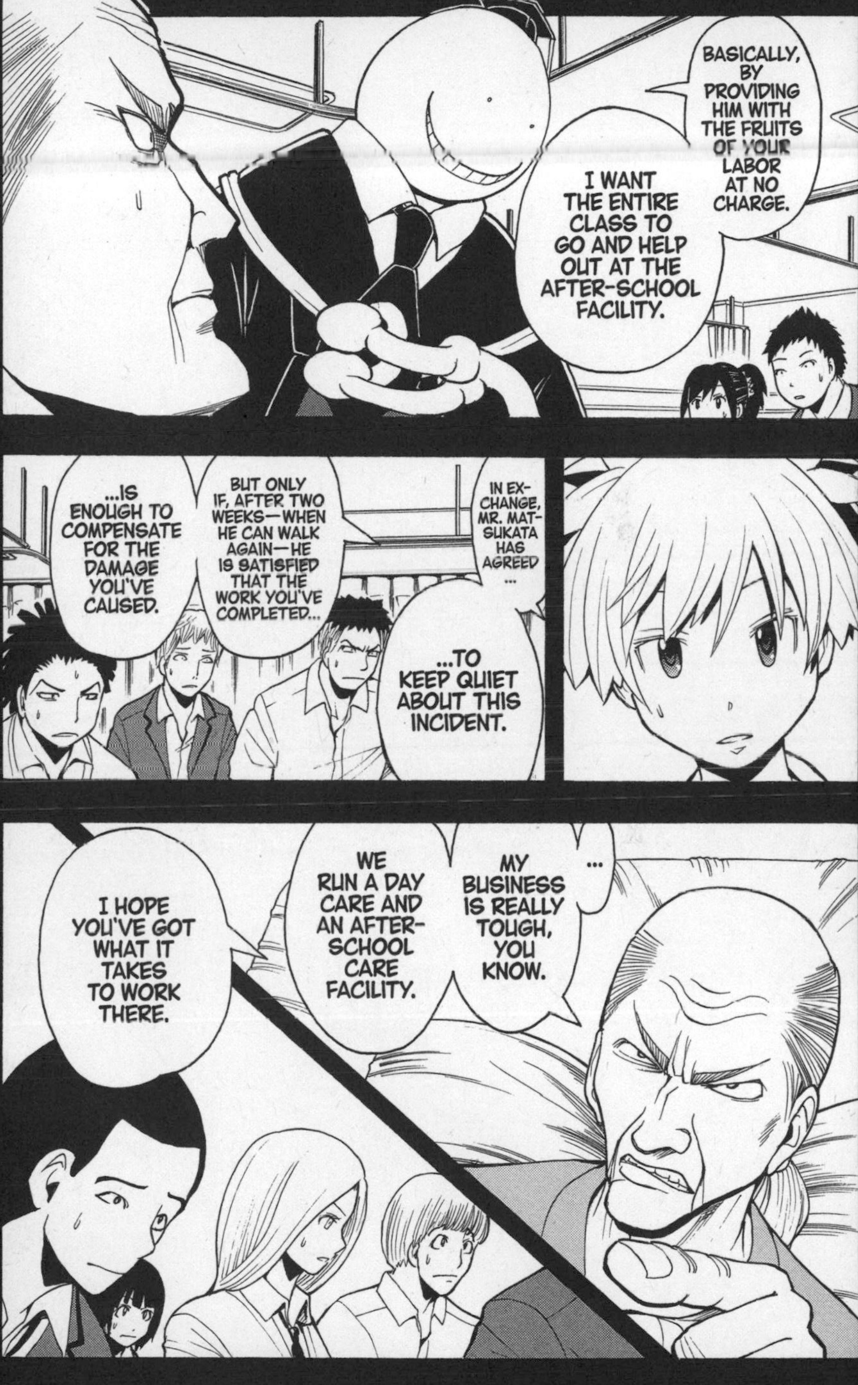
BASICALLY, BY PROVIDING HIM WITH THE FRUITS OF YOUR LABOR AT NO CHARGE.
I WANT THE ENTIRE CLASS TO GO AND HELP OUT AT THE AFTER-SCHOOL FACILITY.
IN EX-CHANGE, MR. MAT-SUKATA HAS AGREED ...
...TO KEEP QUIET ABOUT THIS INCIDENT.
BUT ONLY IF, AFTER TWO WEEKS—WHEN HE CAN WALK AGAIN—HE IS SATISFIED THAT THE WORK YOU'VE COMPLETED...
...IS ENOUGH TO COMPENSATE FOR THE DAMAGE YOU'VE CAUSED.
...
MY BUSINESS IS REALLY TOUGH, YOU KNOW.
WE RUN A DAY CARE AND AN AFTER-SCHOOL CARE FACILITY.
I HOPE YOU'VE GOT WHAT IT TAKES TO WORK THERE.

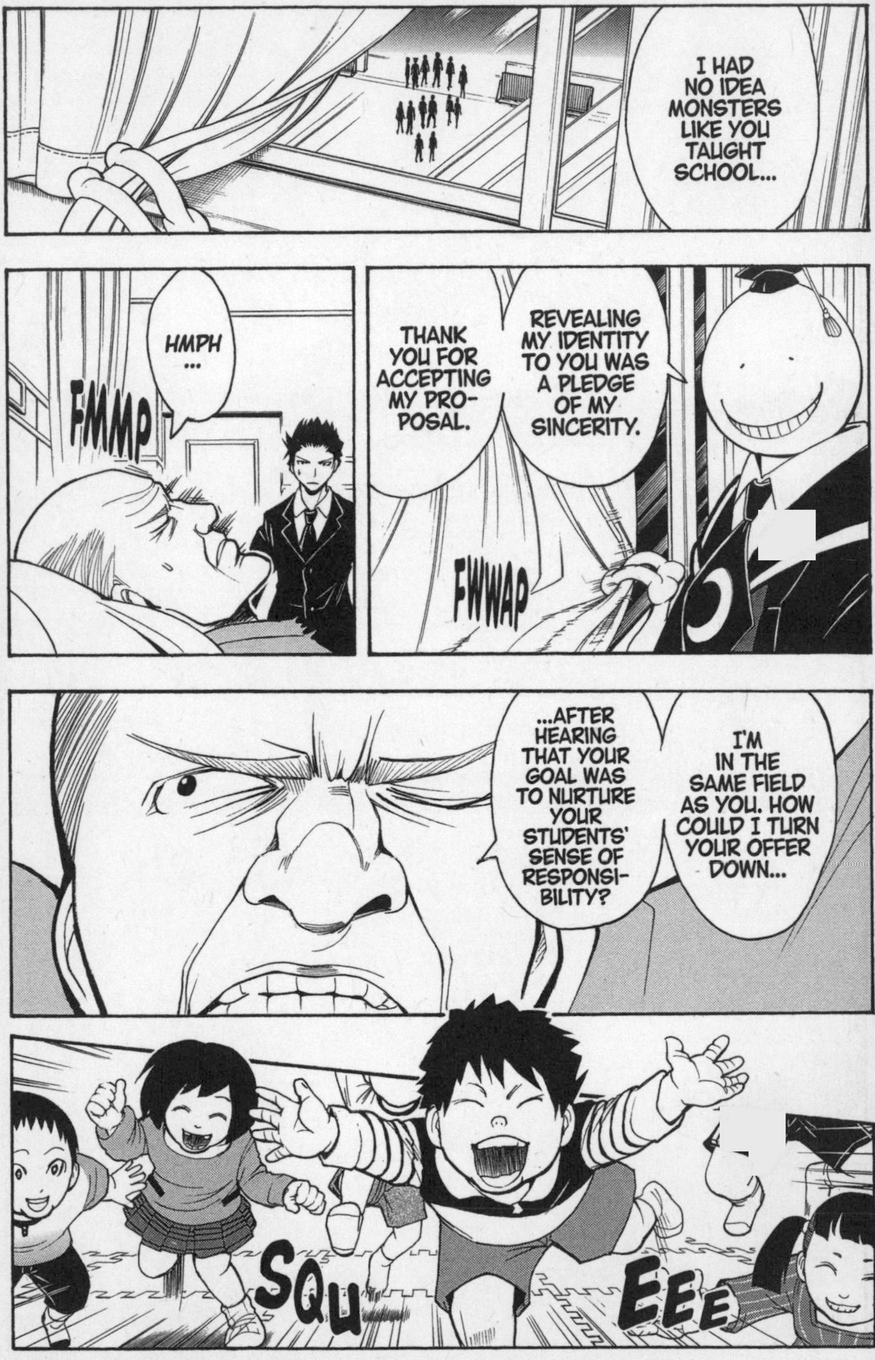
I HAD NO IDEA MONSTERS LIKE YOU TAUGHT SCHOOL...
REVEALING MY IDENTITY TO YOU WAS A PLEDGE OF MY SINCERITY.
THANK YOU FOR ACCEPTING MY PRO-POSAL.
FWWAP
HMPH ...
FMMP
I'M IN THE SAME FIELD AS YOU. HOW COULD I TURN YOUR OFFER DOWN...
...AFTER HEARING THAT YOUR GOAL WAS TO NURTURE YOUR STUDENTS' SENSE OF RESPONSI-BILITY?
SQUEEE

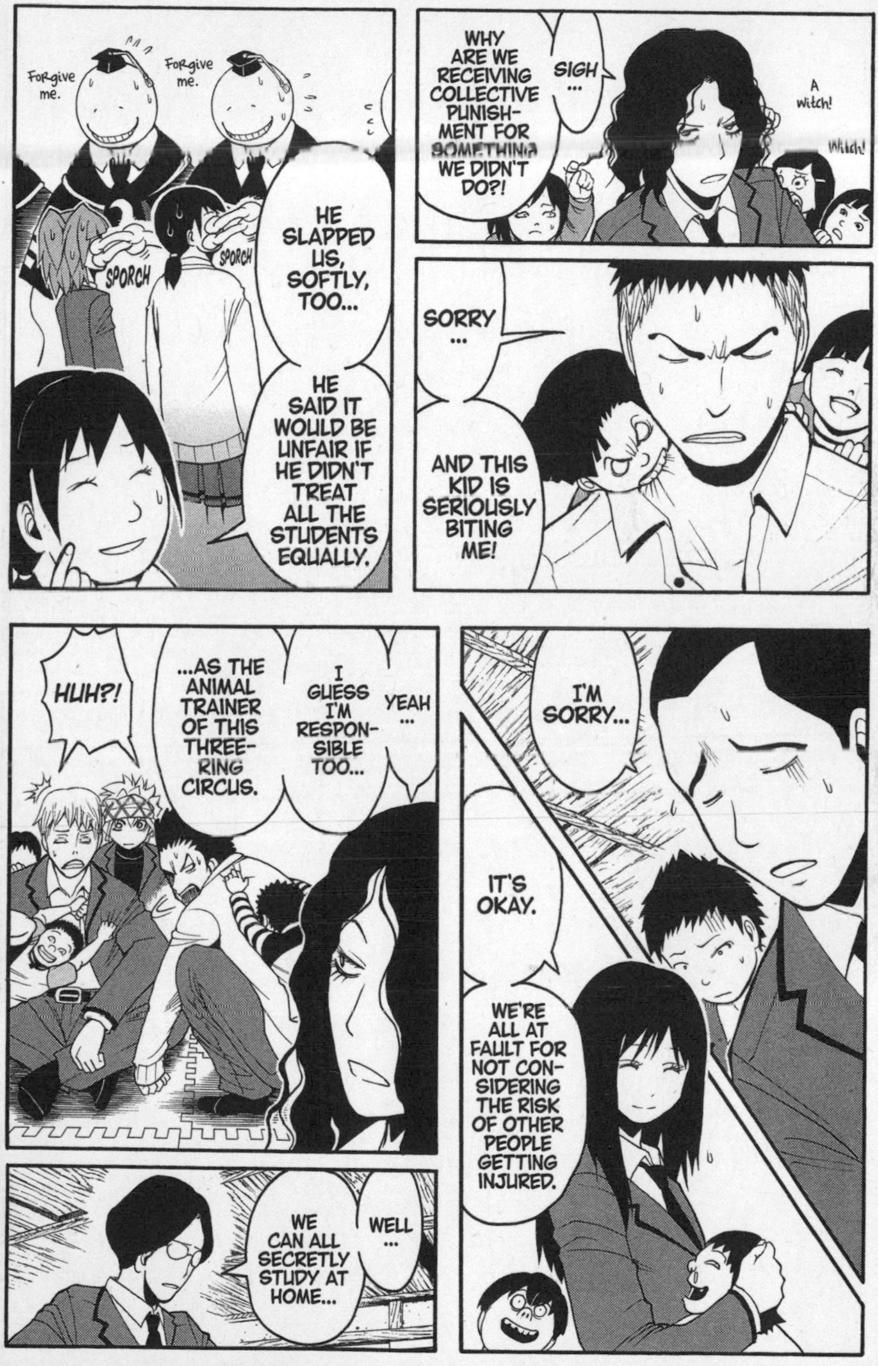
WHY ARE WE RECEIVING COLLECTIVE PUNISHMENT FOR SOMETHING WE DIDN'T DO?!
SIGH ...
A witch!
Witch!
SORRY ...
AND THIS KID IS SERIOUSLY BITING ME!
Forgive me.
Forgive me.
SPORCH
SPORCH
HE SLAPPED US, SOFTLY, TOO...
HE SAID IT WOULD BE UNFAIR IF HE DIDN'T TREAT ALL THE STUDENTS EQUALLY.
I'M SORRY...
IT'S OKAY.
WE'RE ALL AT FAULT FOR NOT CONSIDERING THE RISK OF OTHER PEOPLE GETTING INJURED.
YEAH ...
I GUESS I'M RESPONSIBLE TOO...
...AS THE ANIMAL TRAINER OF THIS THREE-RING CIRCUS.
HUH?!
WELL ...
WE CAN ALL SECRETLY STUDY AT HOME...

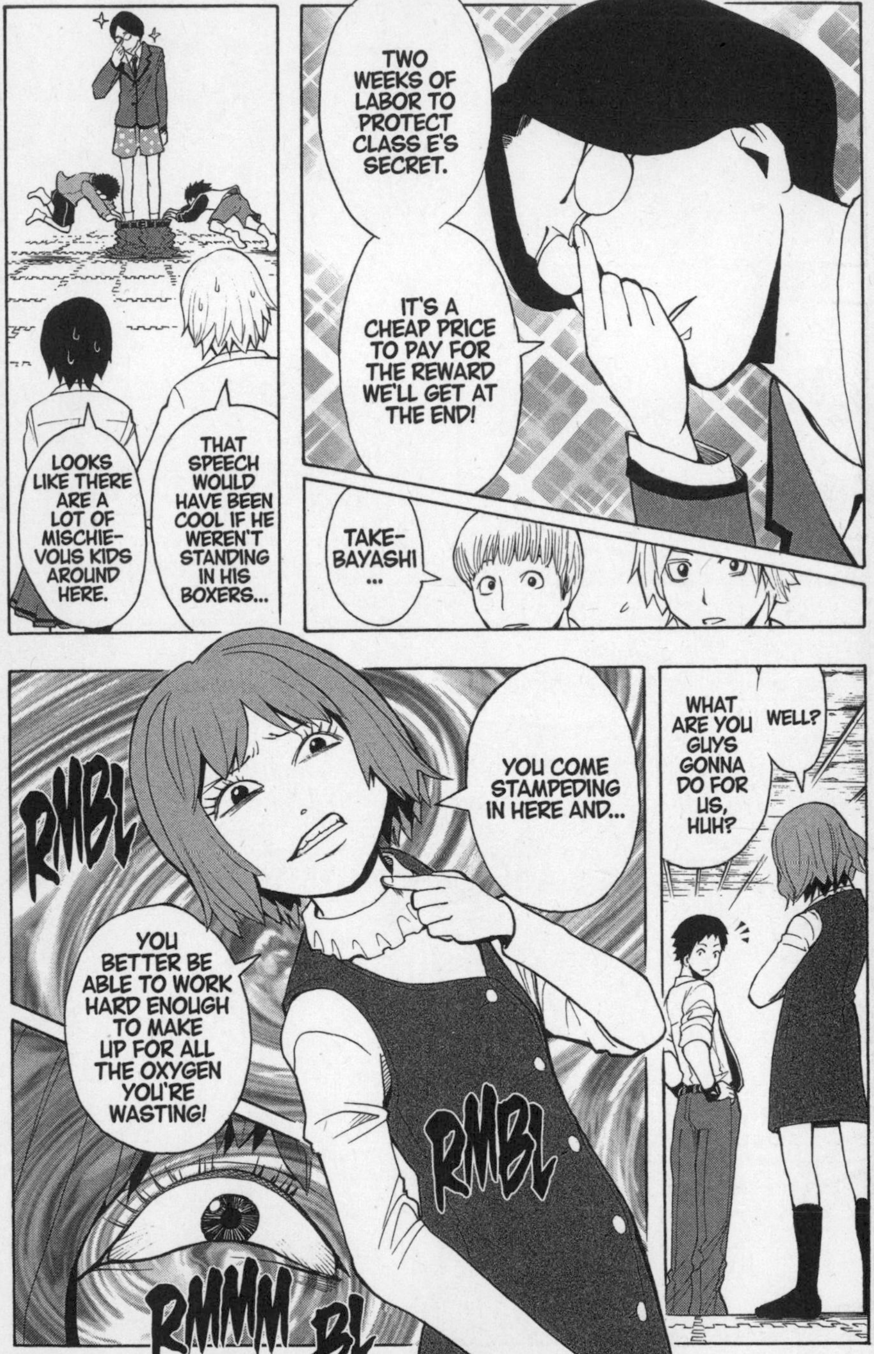
TWO WEEKS OF LABOR TO PROTECT CLASS E'S SECRET.
IT'S A CHEAP PRICE TO PAY FOR THE REWARD WE'LL GET AT THE END!
TAKE-BAYASHI...
THAT SPEECH WOULD HAVE BEEN COOL IF HE WEREN'T STANDING IN HIS BOXERS...
LOOKS LIKE THERE ARE A LOT OF MISCHIE-VOUS KIDS AROUND HERE.
WELL?
WHAT ARE YOU GUYS GONNA DO FOR US, HUH?
YOU COME STAMPEDING IN HERE AND...
RMBL
YOU BETTER BE ABLE TO WORK HARD ENOUGH TO MAKE UP FOR ALL THE OXYGEN YOU'RE WASTING!
RMBL
RMMM BL

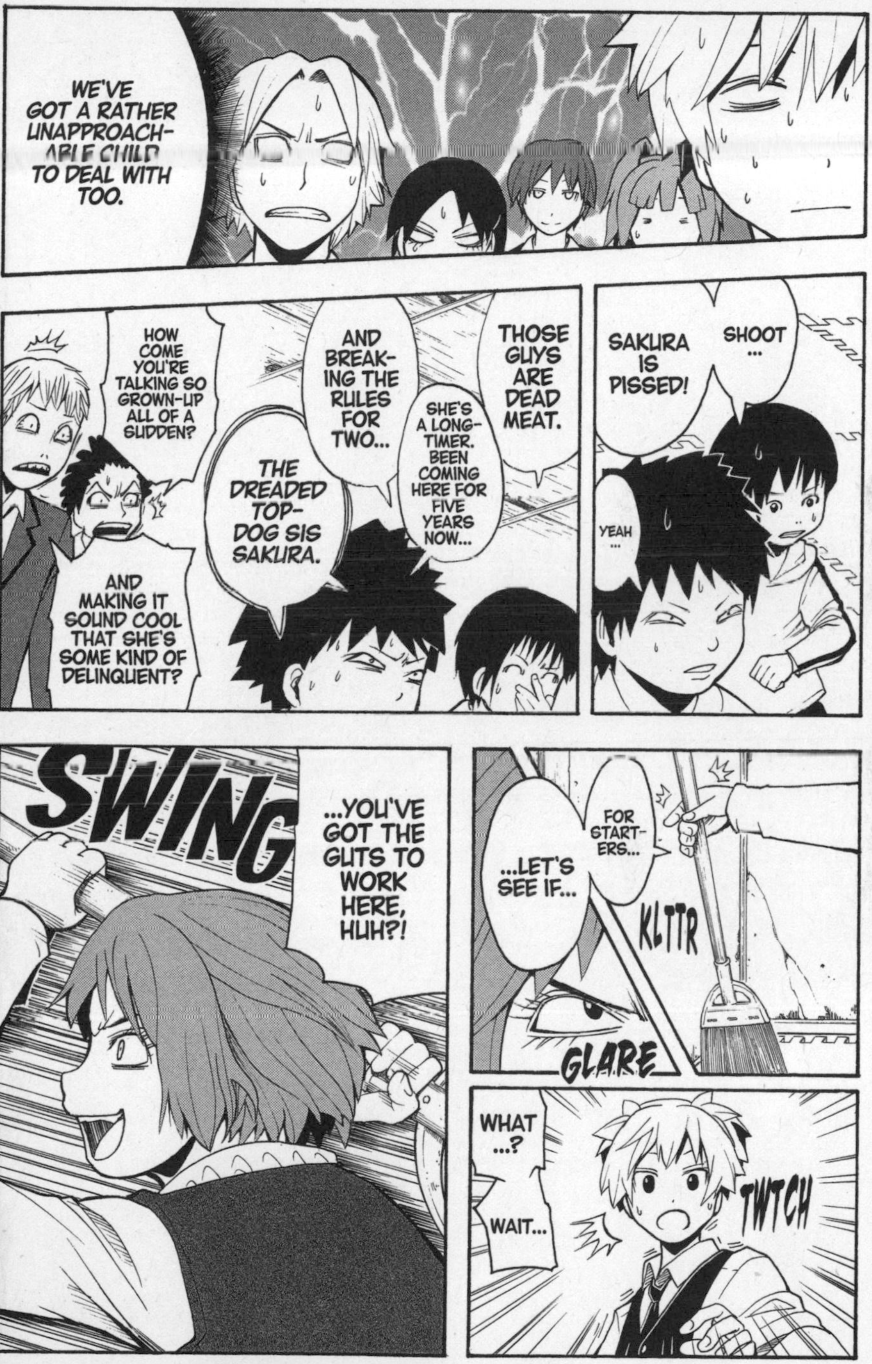
WE'VE GOT A RATHER UNAPPROACH-ABLE CHILD TO DEAL WITH TOO.
SHOOT ...
SAKURA IS PISSED!
YEAH ...
THOSE GUYS ARE DEAD MEAT.
SHE'S A LONG-TIMER. BEEN COMING HERE FOR FIVE YEARS NOW...
AND BREAK-ING THE RULES FOR TWO...
THE DREADED TOP-DOG SIS SAKURA.
HOW COME YOU'RE TALKING SO GROWN-UP ALL OF A SUDDEN?
AND MAKING IT SOUND COOL THAT SHE'S SOME KIND OF DELINQUENT?
FOR START-ERS...
...LET'S SEE IF...
KLTTR
GLARE
WHAT ...?
TWTCH
WAIT...
SWING
...YOU'VE GOT THE GUTS TO WORK HERE, HUH?!

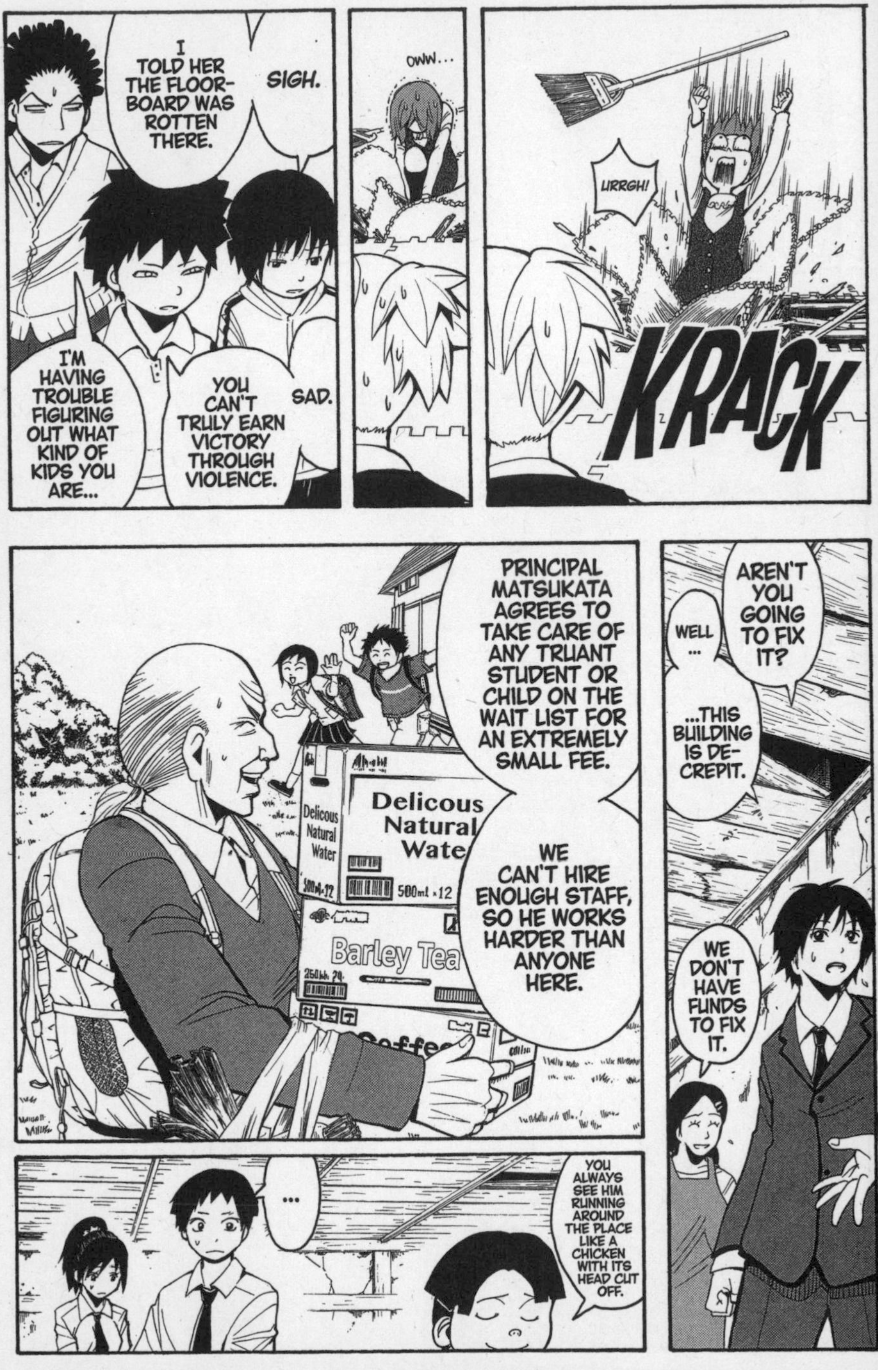
URRGH!
KRACK
OWW...
SIGH.
I TOLD HER THE FLOOR-BOARD WAS ROTTEN THERE.
SAD.
YOU CAN'T TRULY EARN VICTORY THROUGH VIOLENCE.
I'M HAVING TROUBLE FIGURING OUT WHAT KIND OF KIDS YOU ARE...
AREN'T YOU GOING TO FIX IT?
WELL ...
...THIS BUILDING IS DE-CREPIT.
WE DON'T HAVE FUNDS TO FIX IT.
PRINCIPAL MATSUKATA AGREES TO TAKE CARE OF ANY TRUANT STUDENT OR CHILD ON THE WAIT LIST FOR AN EXTREMELY SMALL FEE.
WE CAN'T HIRE ENOUGH STAFF, SO HE WORKS HARDER THAN ANYONE HERE.
Delicous Natural Water
Delicous Natural Water
500ml ×12
Barley Tea
YOU ALWAYS SEE HIM RUNNING AROUND THE PLACE LIKE A CHICKEN WITH ITS HEAD CUT OFF.
...

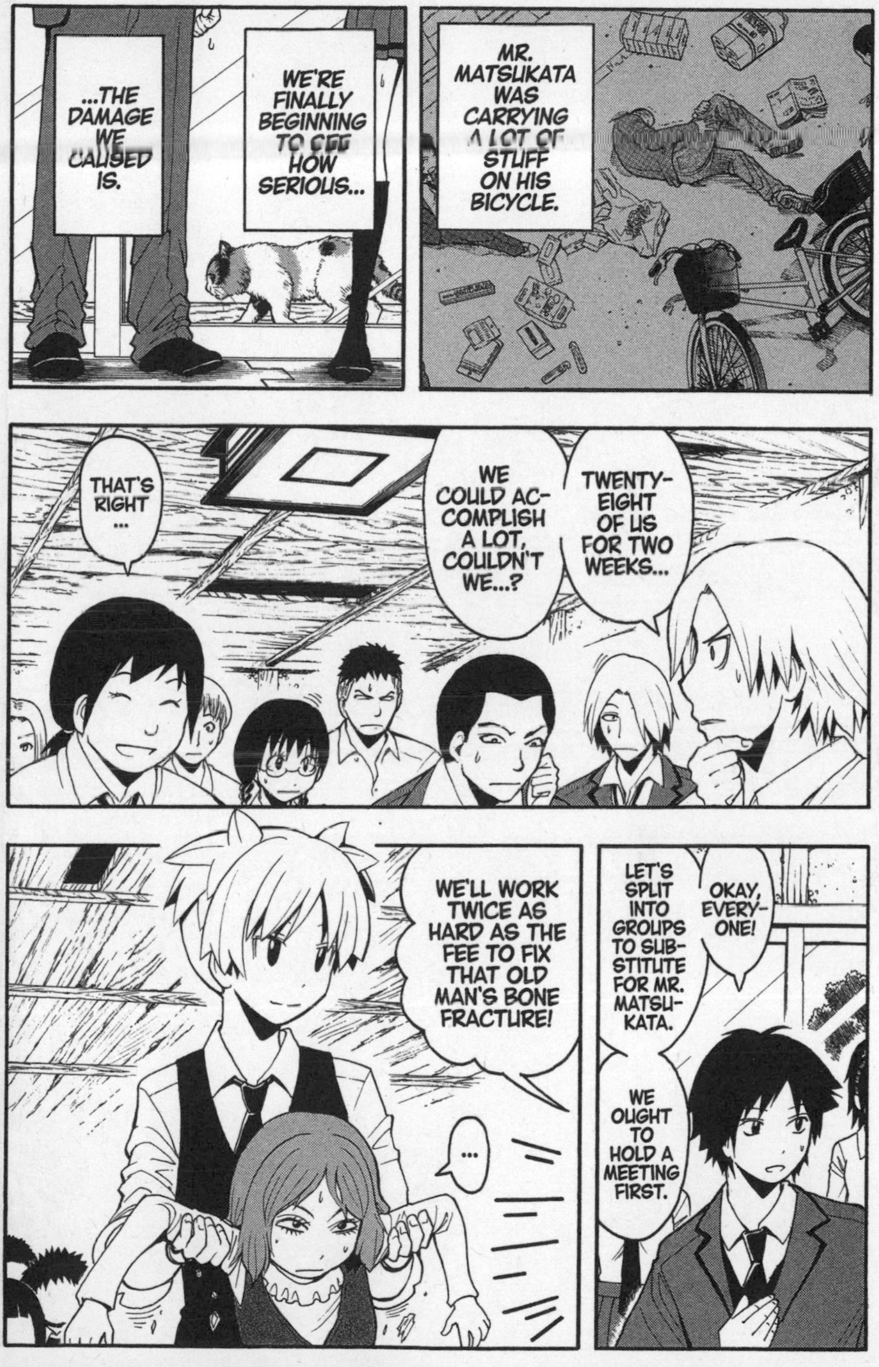
MR. MATSUKATA WAS CARRYING A LOT OF STUFF ON HIS BICYCLE.
WE'RE FINALLY BEGINNING TO SEE HOW SERIOUS...
...THE DAMAGE WE CAUSED IS.
TWENTY-EIGHT OF US FOR TWO WEEKS...
WE COULD ACCOMPLISH A LOT, COULDN'T WE...?
THAT'S RIGHT ...
OKAY, EVERYONE!
LET'S SPLIT INTO GROUPS TO SUBSTITUTE FOR MR. MATSUKATA.
WE OUGHT TO HOLD A MEETING FIRST.
WE'LL WORK TWICE AS HARD AS THE FEE TO FIX THAT OLD MAN'S BONE FRACTURE!
...

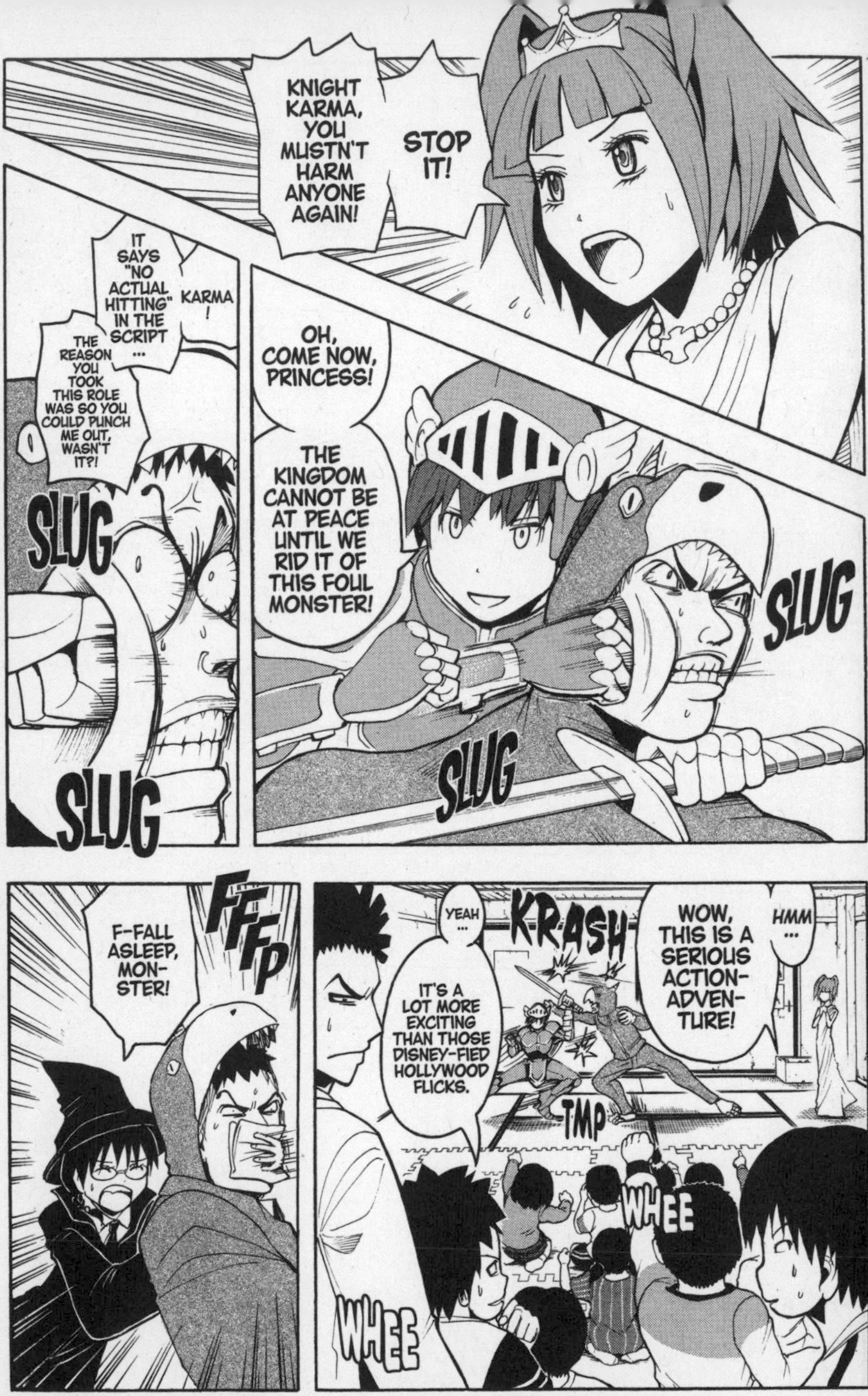
STOP IT!
KNIGHT KARMA, YOU MUSTN'T HARM ANYONE AGAIN!
OH, COME NOW, PRINCESS!
THE KINGDOM CANNOT BE AT PEACE UNTIL WE RID IT OF THIS FOUL MONSTER!
SLUG
SLUG
KARMA!
IT SAYS "NO ACTUAL HITTING" IN THE SCRIPT...
THE REASON YOU TOOK THIS ROLE WAS SO YOU COULD PUNCH ME OUT, WASN'T IT?!
SLUG
SLUG
HMM...
WOW, THIS IS A SERIOUS ACTION-ADVENTURE!
KRASH
YEAH...
IT'S A LOT MORE EXCITING THAN THOSE DISNEY-FIED HOLLYWOOD FLICKS.
TMP
WHEE
WHEE
FFFP
F-FALL ASLEEP, MON-STER!

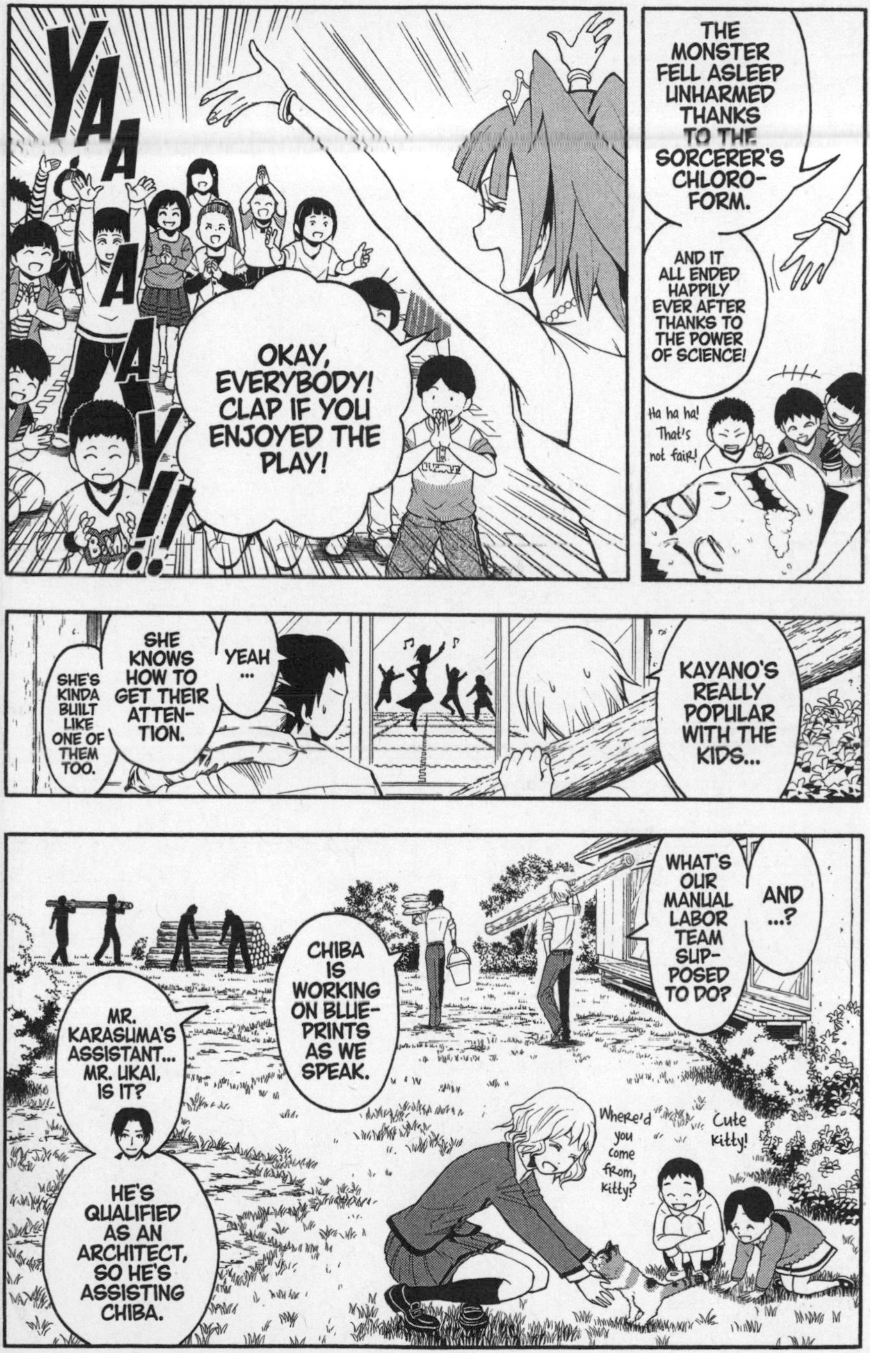
THE MONSTER FELL ASLEEP UNHARMED THANKS TO THE SORCERER'S CHLOROFORM.
AND IT ALL ENDED HAPPILY EVER AFTER THANKS TO THE POWER OF SCIENCE!
Ha ha ha! That's not fair!
YAAAAY!!
OKAY, EVERYBODY! CLAP IF YOU ENJOYED THE PLAY!
KAYANO'S REALLY POPULAR WITH THE KIDS...
YEAH...
SHE KNOWS HOW TO GET THEIR ATTENTION.
SHE'S KINDA BUILT LIKE ONE OF THEM TOO.
AND...?
WHAT'S OUR MANUAL LABOR TEAM SUPPOSED TO DO?
CHIBA IS WORKING ON BLUEPRINTS AS WE SPEAK.
MR. KARASUMA'S ASSISTANT... MR. UKAI, IS IT?
HE'S QUALIFIED AS AN ARCHITECT, SO HE'S ASSISTING CHIBA.
Cute kitty!
Where'd you come from, kitty?

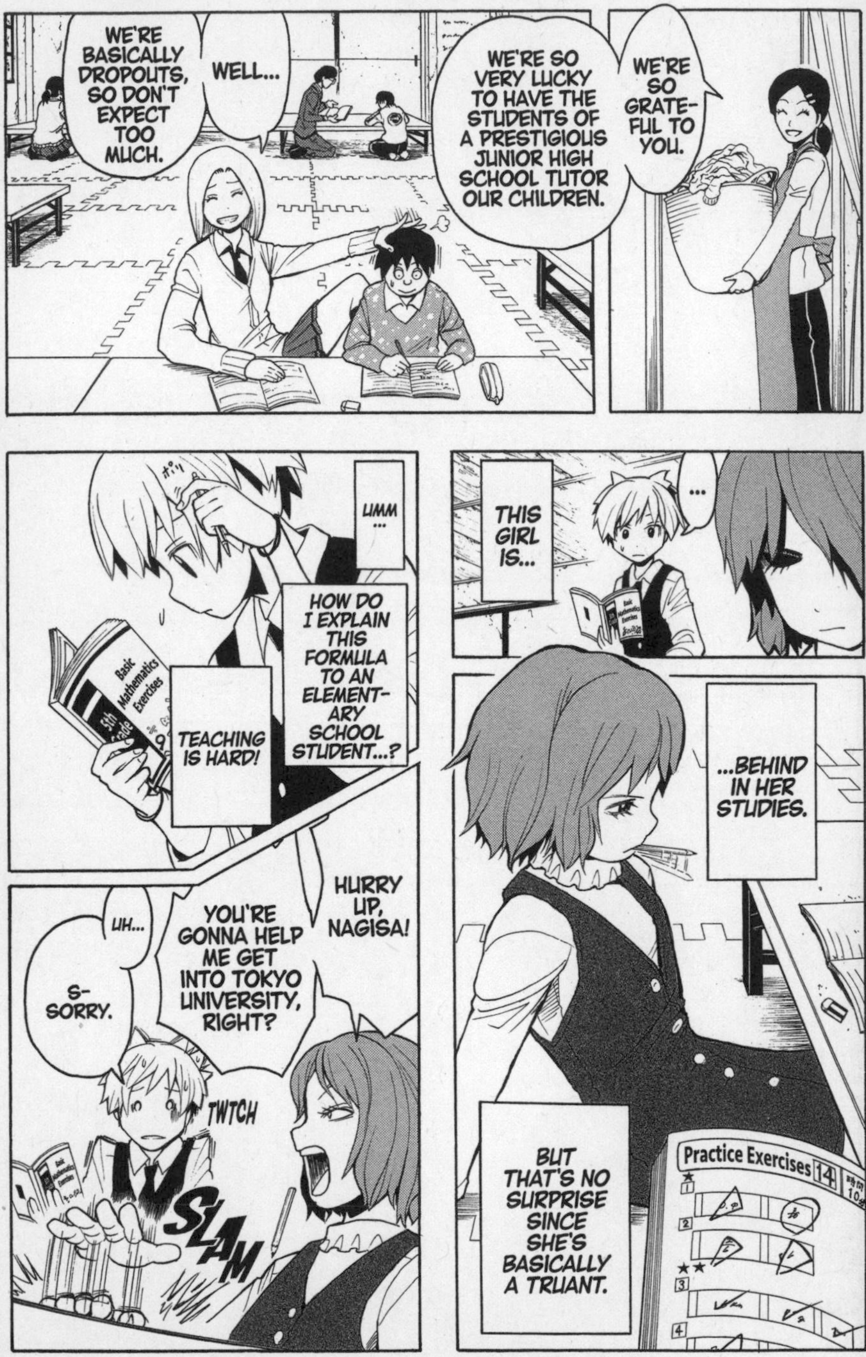
WE'RE SO GRATEFUL TO YOU.
WE'RE SO VERY LUCKY TO HAVE THE STUDENTS OF A PRESTIGIOUS JUNIOR HIGH SCHOOL TUTOR OUR CHILDREN.
WELL...
WE'RE BASICALLY DROPOUTS, SO DON'T EXPECT TOO MUCH.
...
THIS GIRL IS...
Basic Mathematics Exercises
...BEHIND IN HER STUDIES.
BUT THAT'S NO SURPRISE SINCE SHE'S BASICALLY A TRUANT.
Practice Exercises 14
UMM...
HOW DO I EXPLAIN THIS FORMULA TO AN ELEMENTARY SCHOOL STUDENT...?
Basic Mathematics Exercises
5th Grade
TEACHING IS HARD!
HURRY UP, NAGISA!
YOU'RE GONNA HELP ME GET INTO TOKYO UNIVERSITY, RIGHT?
UH...
S-SORRY.
TWTCH
SLAM

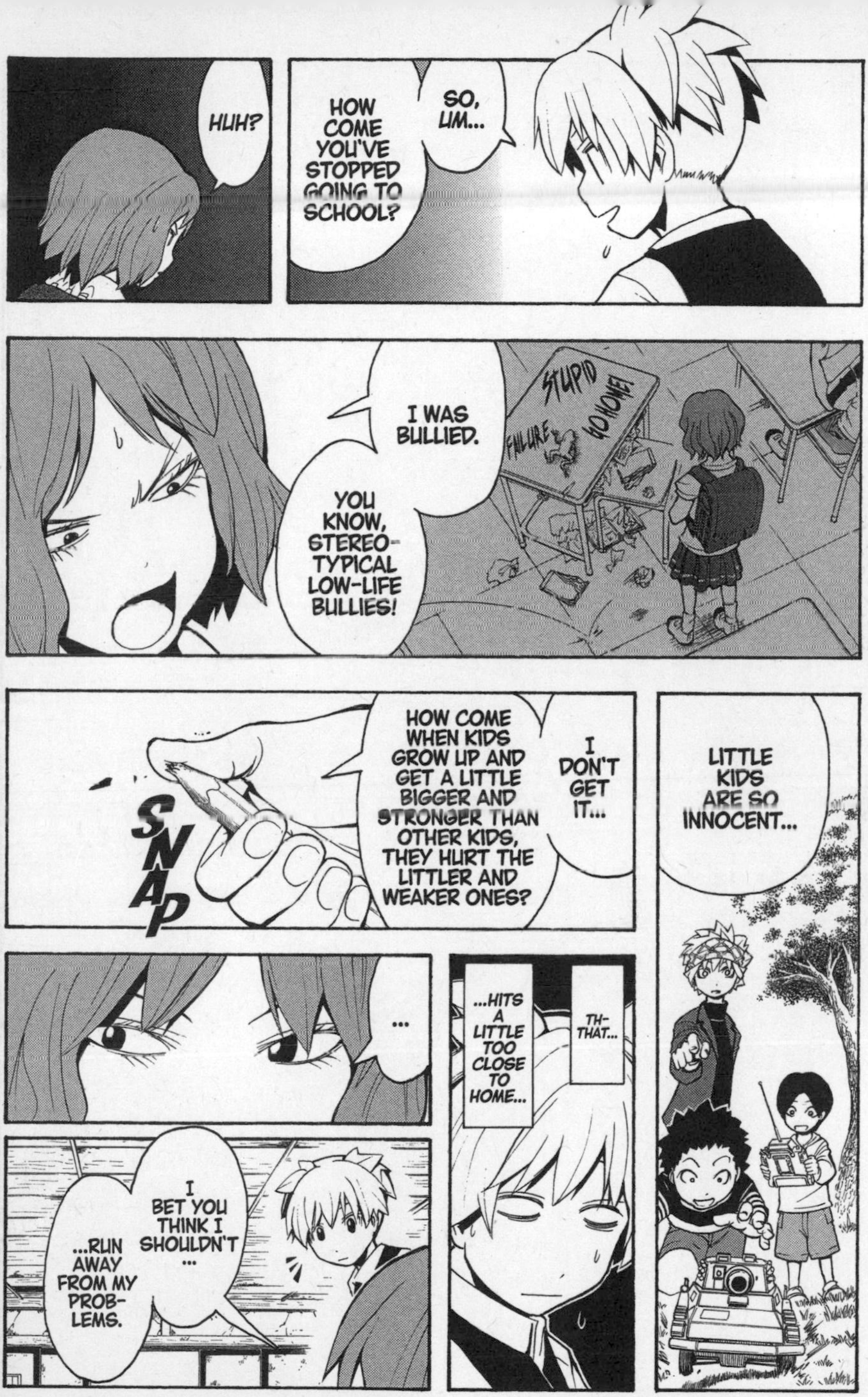
SO, UM...
HOW COME YOU'VE STOPPED GOING TO SCHOOL?
HUH?
STUPID
GO HOME!
FAILURE
I WAS BULLIED.
YOU KNOW, STEREO-TYPICAL LOW-LIFE BULLIES!
LITTLE KIDS ARE SO INNOCENT...
I DON'T GET IT...
HOW COME WHEN KIDS GROW UP AND GET A LITTLE BIGGER AND STRONGER THAN OTHER KIDS, THEY HURT THE LITTLER AND WEAKER ONES?
SNAP
TH-THAT...
...HITS A LITTLE TOO CLOSE TO HOME...
...
I BET YOU THINK I SHOULDN'T ...
...RUN AWAY FROM MY PROB-LEMS.

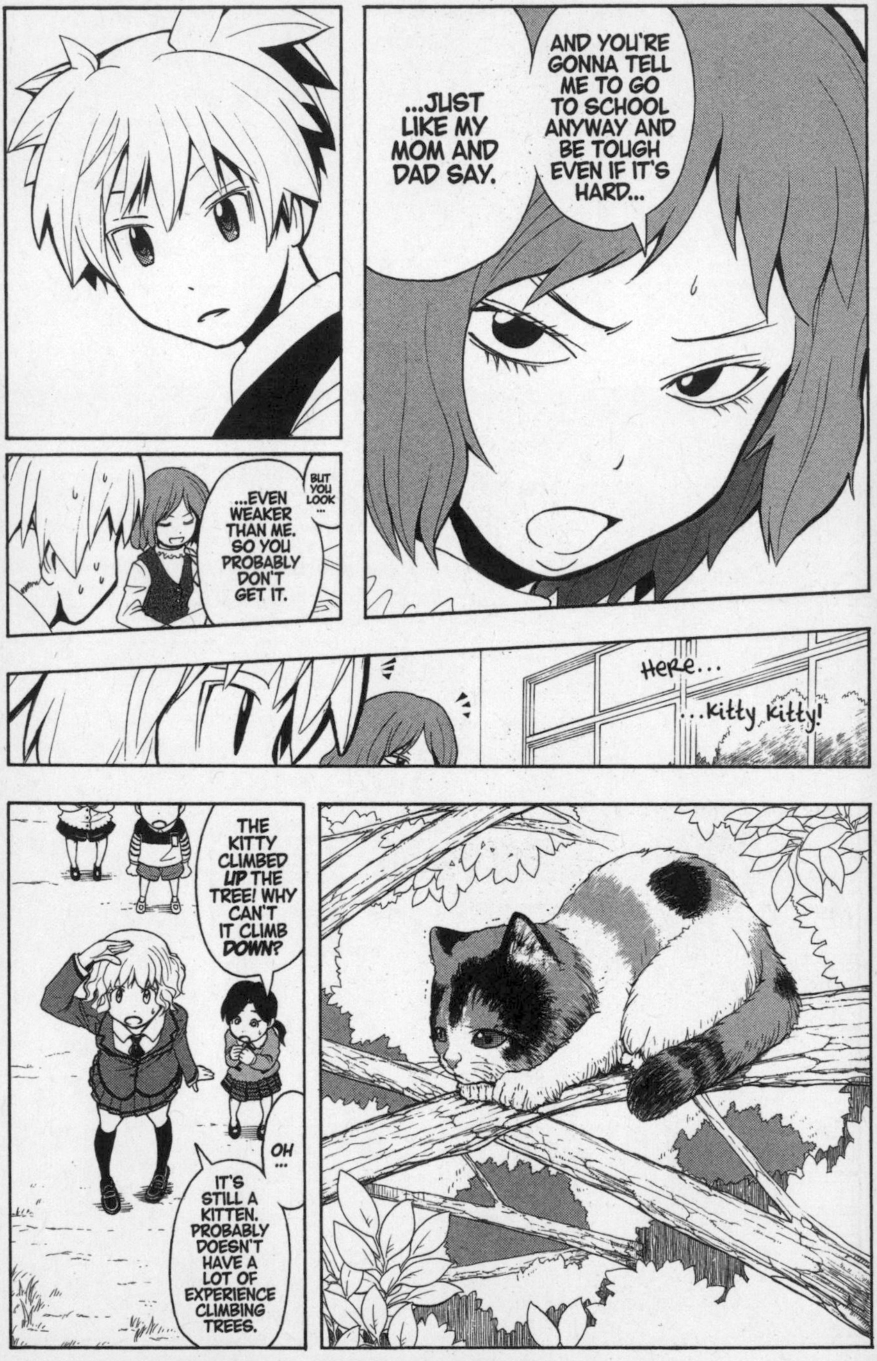
AND YOU'RE GONNA TELL ME TO GO TO SCHOOL ANYWAY AND BE TOUGH EVEN IF IT'S HARD...
...JUST LIKE MY MOM AND DAD SAY.
BUT YOU LOOK...
...EVEN WEAKER THAN ME. SO YOU PROBABLY DON'T GET IT.
Here...
...kitty kitty!
THE KITTY CLIMBED *UP* THE TREE! WHY CAN'T IT CLIMB *DOWN*?
OH...
IT'S STILL A KITTEN. PROBABLY DOESN'T HAVE A LOT OF EXPERIENCE CLIMBING TREES.

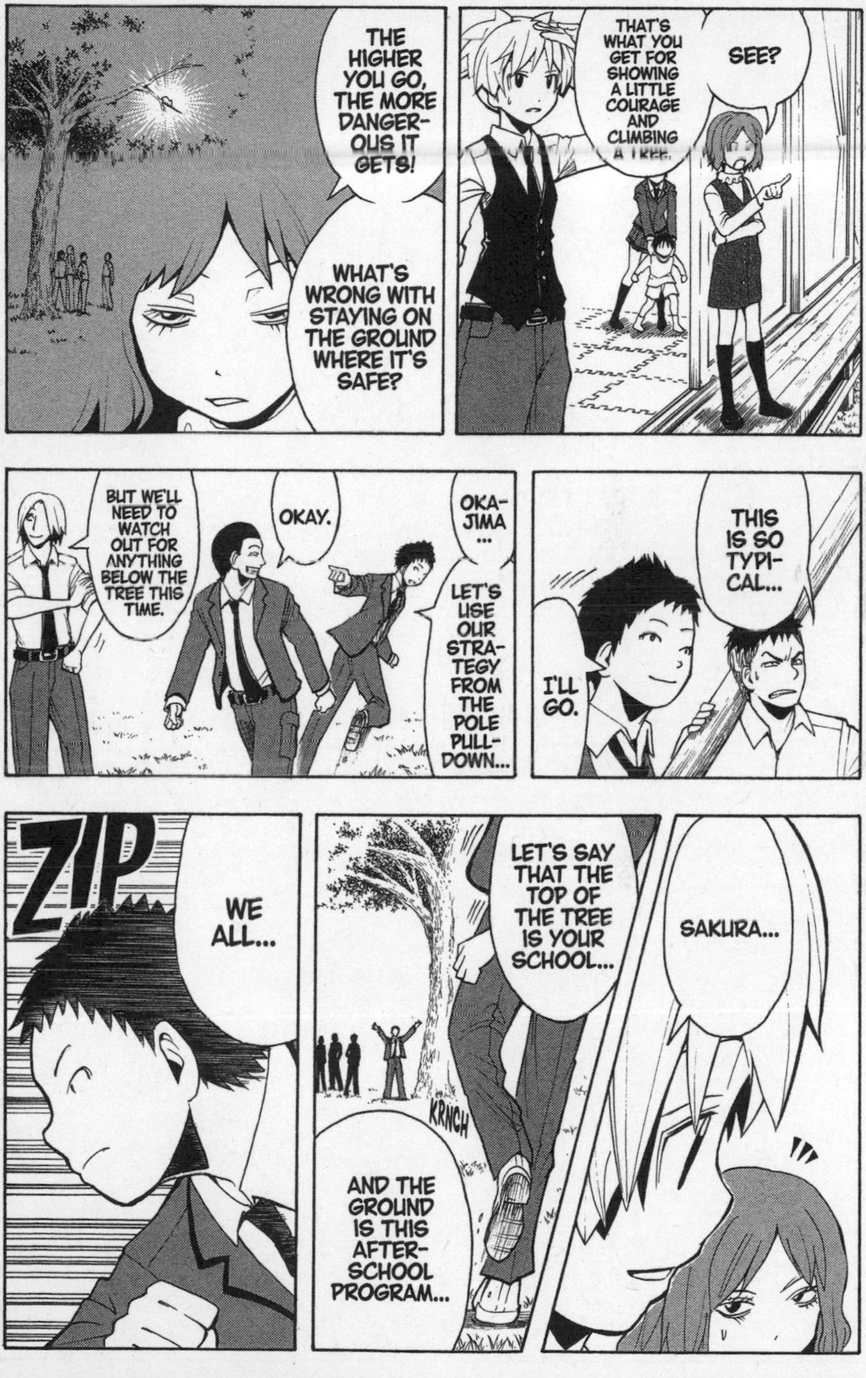
SEE?
THAT'S WHAT YOU GET FOR SHOWING A LITTLE COURAGE AND CLIMBING A TREE.
THE HIGHER YOU GO, THE MORE DANGEROUS IT GETS!
WHAT'S WRONG WITH STAYING ON THE GROUND WHERE IT'S SAFE?
THIS IS SO TYPICAL...
I'LL GO.
OKAJIMA...
LET'S USE OUR STRATEGY FROM THE POLE PULLDOWN...
OKAY.
BUT WE'LL NEED TO WATCH OUT FOR ANYTHING BELOW THE TREE THIS TIME.
SAKURA...
LET'S SAY THAT THE TOP OF THE TREE IS YOUR SCHOOL...
KRNCH
AND THE GROUND IS THIS AFTER-SCHOOL PROGRAM...
ZIP
WE ALL...

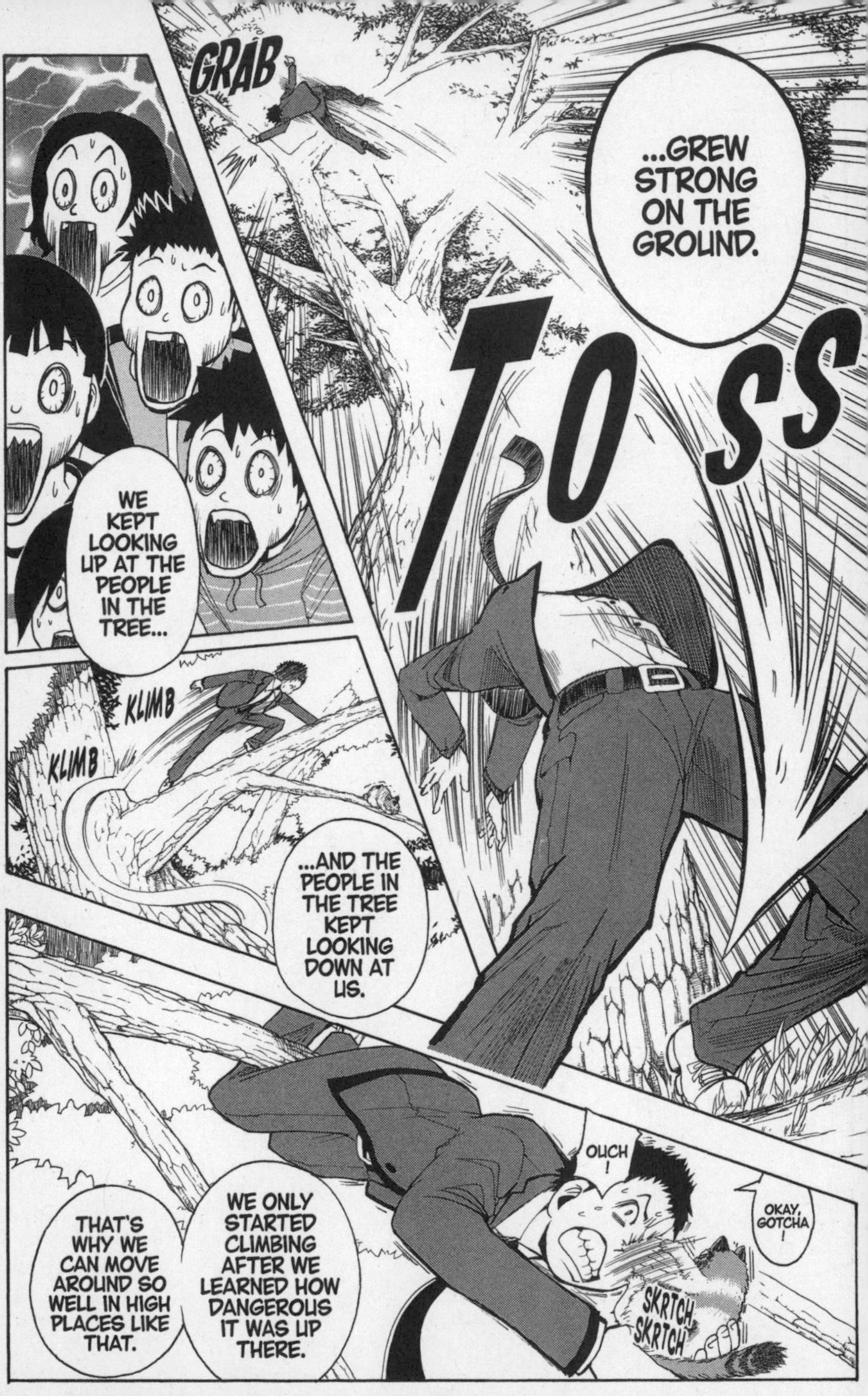
GRAB
...GREW STRONG ON THE GROUND.
TOSS
WE KEPT LOOKING UP AT THE PEOPLE IN THE TREE...
KLIMB
KLIMB
...AND THE PEOPLE IN THE TREE KEPT LOOKING DOWN AT US.
OKAY, GOTCHA!
SKRTCH, SKRTCH
OUCH!
WE ONLY STARTED CLIMBING AFTER WE LEARNED HOW DANGEROUS IT WAS UP THERE.
THAT'S WHY WE CAN MOVE AROUND SO WELL IN HIGH PLACES LIKE THAT.

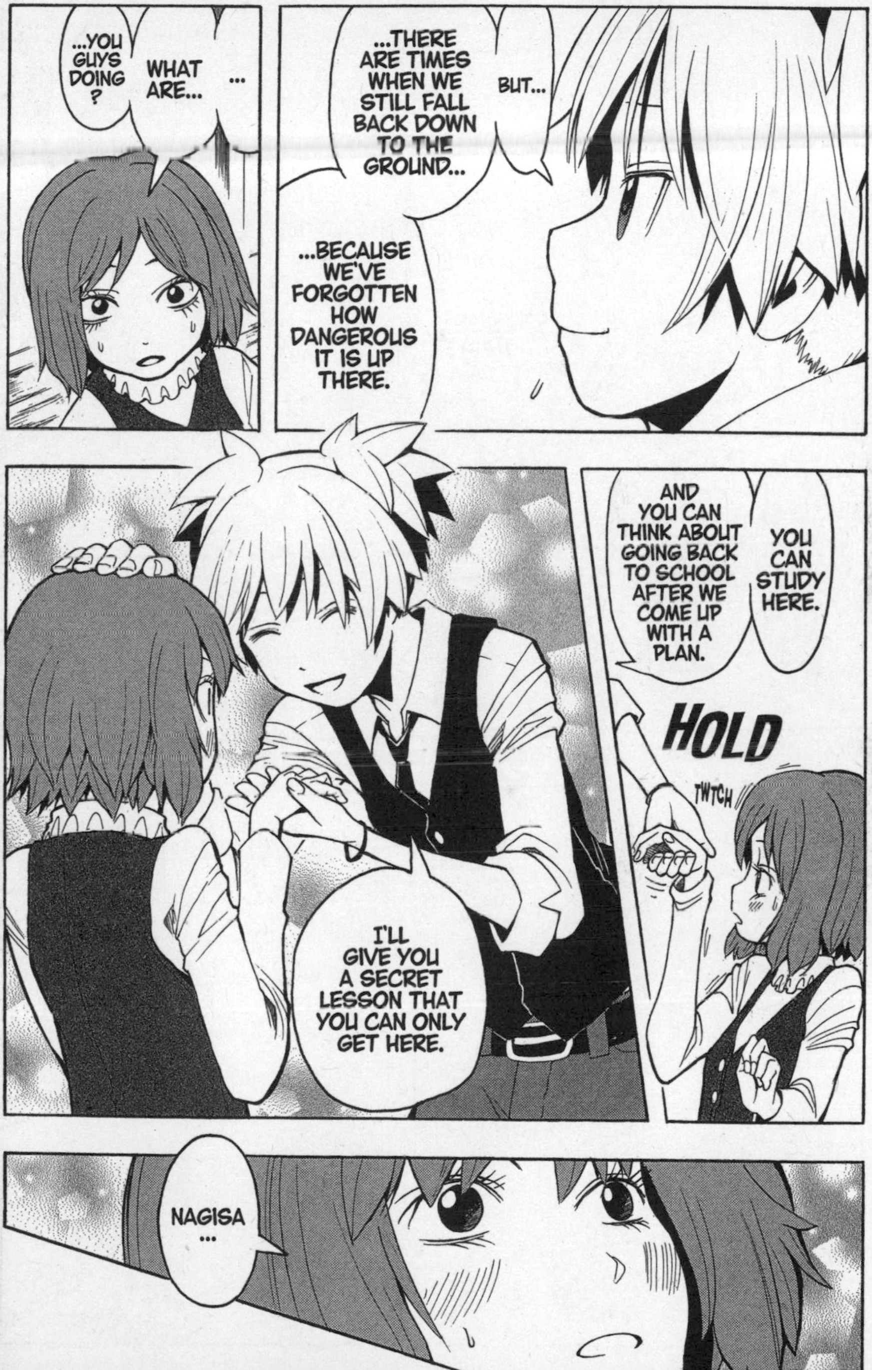
BUT...
...THERE ARE TIMES WHEN WE STILL FALL BACK DOWN TO THE GROUND...
...BECAUSE WE'VE FORGOTTEN HOW DANGEROUS IT IS UP THERE.
...
WHAT ARE...
...YOU GUYS DOING?
YOU CAN STUDY HERE.
AND YOU CAN THINK ABOUT GOING BACK TO SCHOOL AFTER WE COME UP WITH A PLAN.
HOLD
TWTCH
I'LL GIVE YOU A SECRET LESSON THAT YOU CAN ONLY GET HERE.
NAGISA...

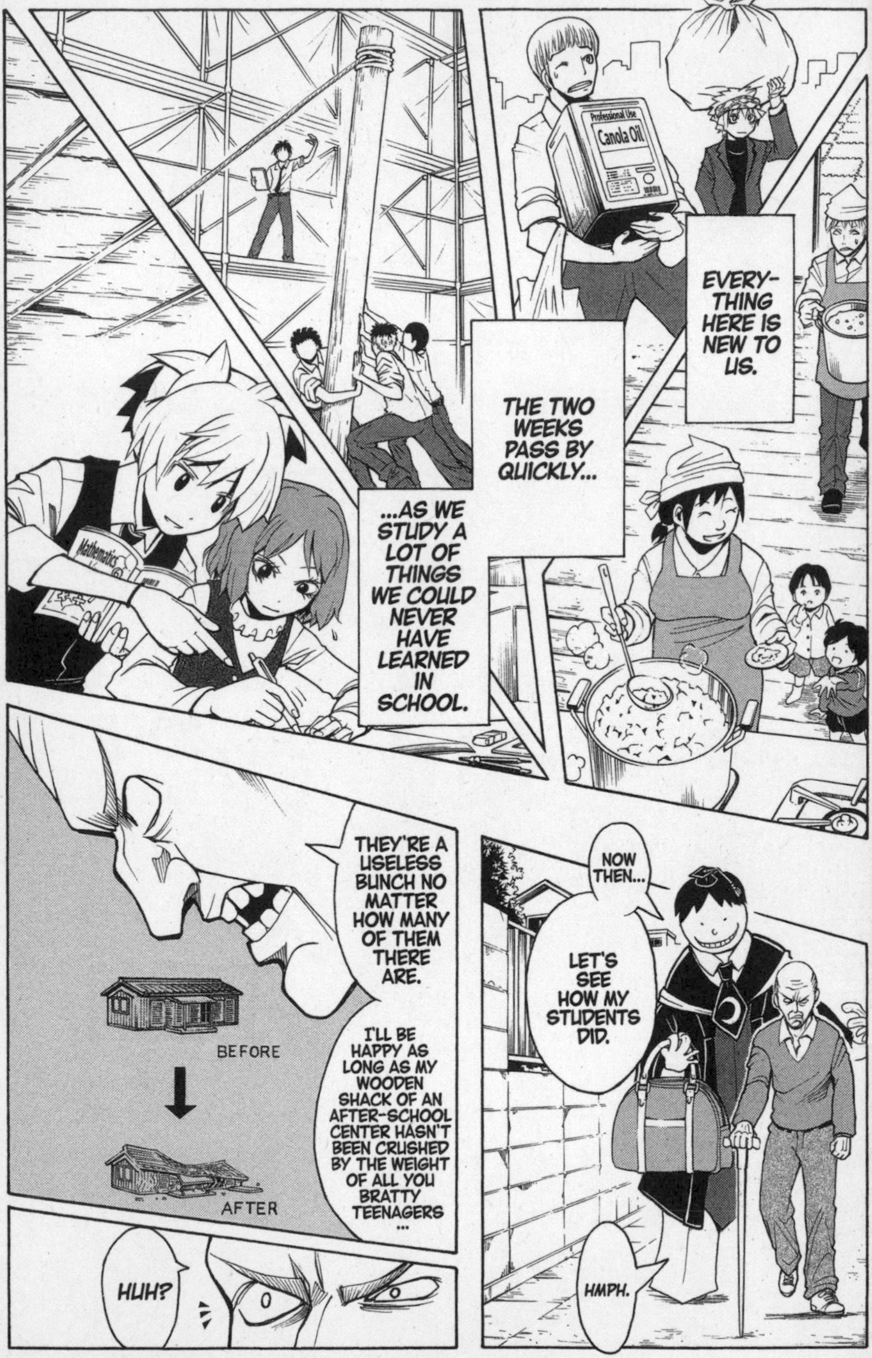
Professional Use
Canola Oil
EVERY-THING HERE IS NEW TO US.
THE TWO WEEKS PASS BY QUICKLY...
...AS WE STUDY A LOT OF THINGS WE COULD NEVER HAVE LEARNED IN SCHOOL.
Mathematics
NOW THEN...
LET'S SEE HOW MY STUDENTS DID.
HMPH.
THEY'RE A USELESS BUNCH NO MATTER HOW MANY OF THEM THERE ARE.
I'LL BE HAPPY AS LONG AS MY WOODEN SHACK OF AN AFTER-SCHOOL CENTER HASN'T BEEN CRUSHED BY THE WEIGHT OF ALL YOU BRATTY TEENAGERS...
BEFORE
AFTER
HUH?

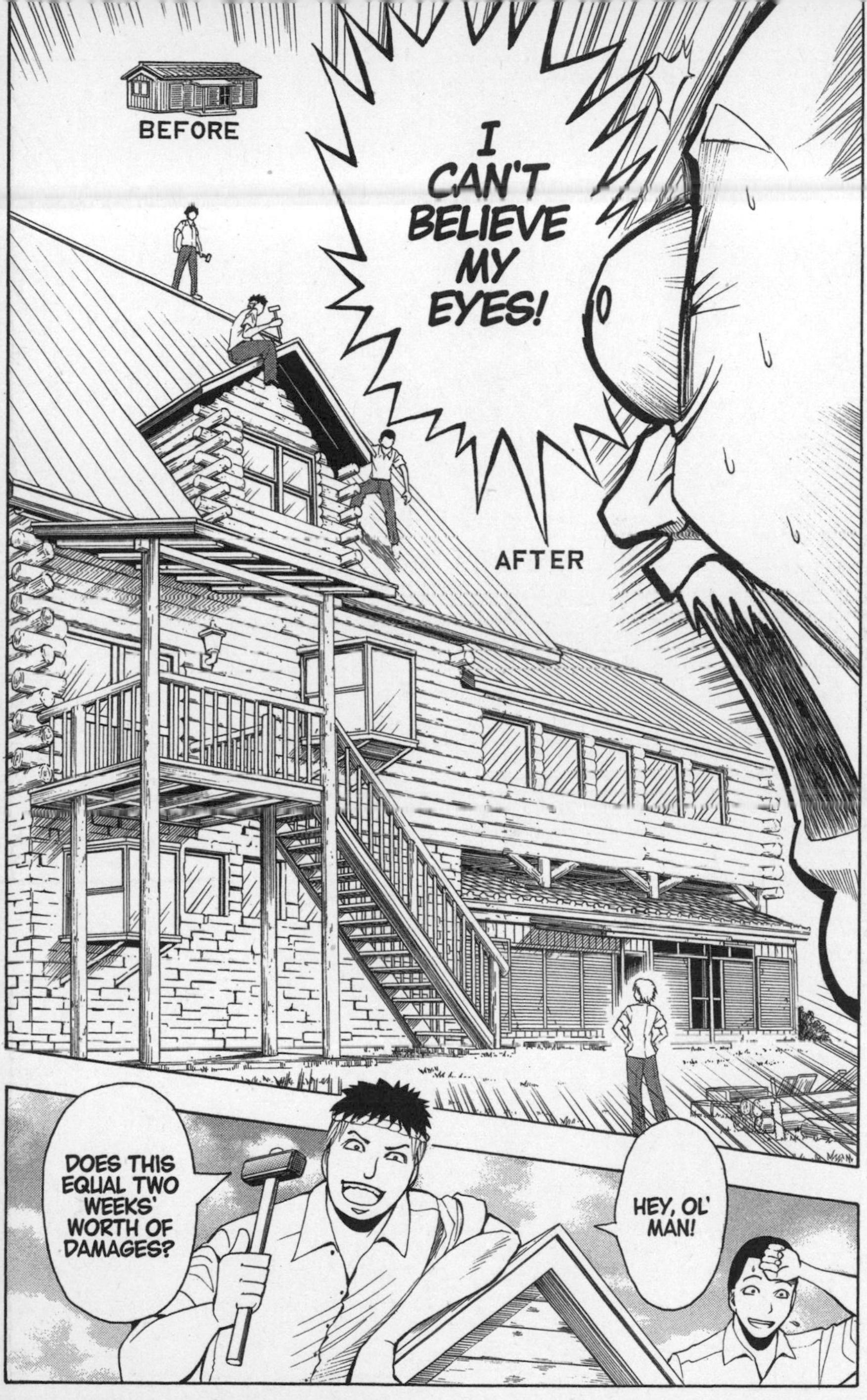
I CAN'T BELIEVE MY EYES!
BEFORE
AFTER
HEY, OL' MAN!
DOES THIS EQUAL TWO WEEKS' WORTH OF DAMAGES?

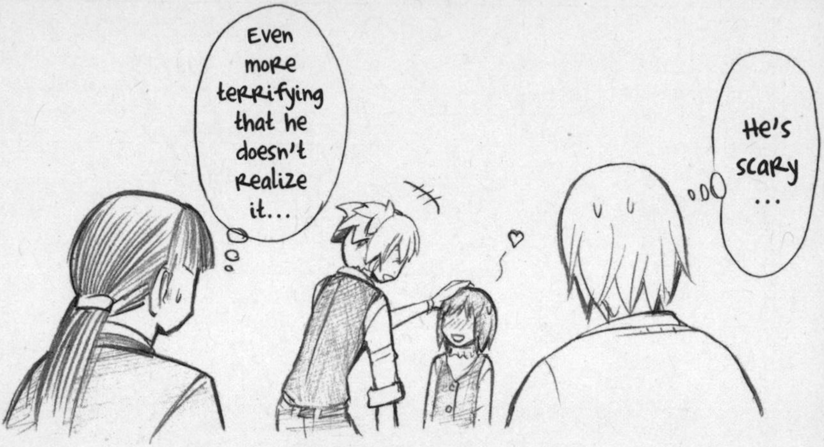
He's scary...
Even more terrifying that he doesn't realize it...

Everyone's beginning to see how dangerous he is.

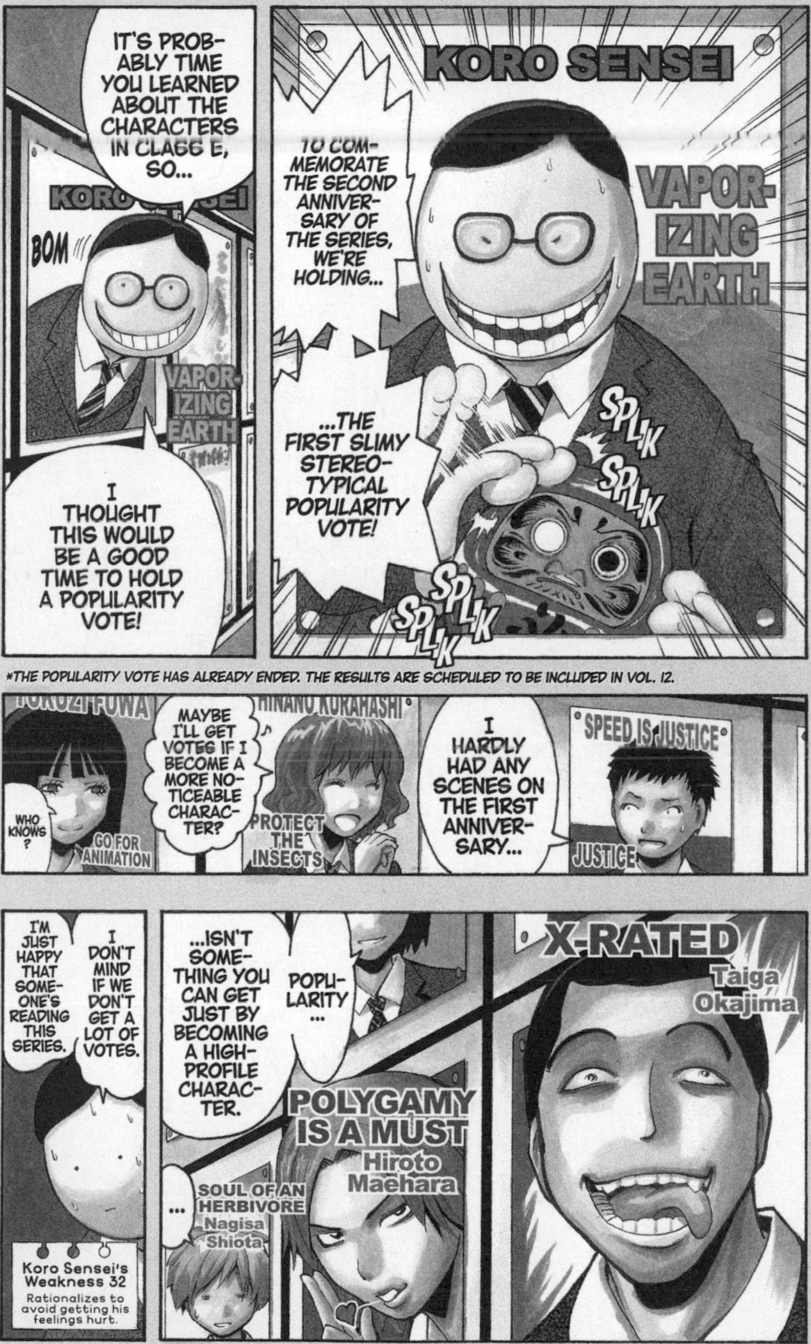
KORO SENSEI
VAPORIZING EARTH
TO COMMEMORATE THE SECOND ANNIVERSARY OF THE SERIES, WE'RE HOLDING...
...THE FIRST SLIMY STEREOTYPICAL POPULARITY VOTE!
SPLIK SPLIK SPLIK SPLIK
IT'S PROBABLY TIME YOU LEARNED ABOUT THE CHARACTERS IN CLASS E, SO...
KORO SENSEI
BOM
VAPORIZING EARTH
I THOUGHT THIS WOULD BE A GOOD TIME TO HOLD A POPULARITY VOTE!
*THE POPULARITY VOTE HAS ALREADY ENDED. THE RESULTS ARE SCHEDULED TO BE INCLUDED IN VOL. 12.
"SPEED IS JUSTICE"
I HARDLY HAD ANY SCENES ON THE FIRST ANNIVERSARY...
JUSTICE
HINANO KURAHASHI
MAYBE I'LL GET VOTES IF I BECOME A MORE NOTICEABLE CHARACTER?
PROTECT THE INSECTS
YUZUKI FUWA
WHO KNOWS?
GO FOR ANIMATION
X-RATED
Taiga Okajima
POPULARITY...
...ISN'T SOMETHING YOU CAN GET JUST BY BECOMING A HIGH-PROFILE CHARACTER.
POLYGAMY IS A MUST
Hiroto Maehara
SOUL OF AN HERBIVORE
Nagisa Shiota
...
I DON'T MIND IF WE DON'T GET A LOT OF VOTES.
I'M JUST HAPPY THAT SOMEONE'S READING THIS SERIES.
Koro Sensei's Weakness 32
Rationalizes to avoid getting his feelings hurt.

CLASS 97 TIME FOR AN AFTER PICTURE

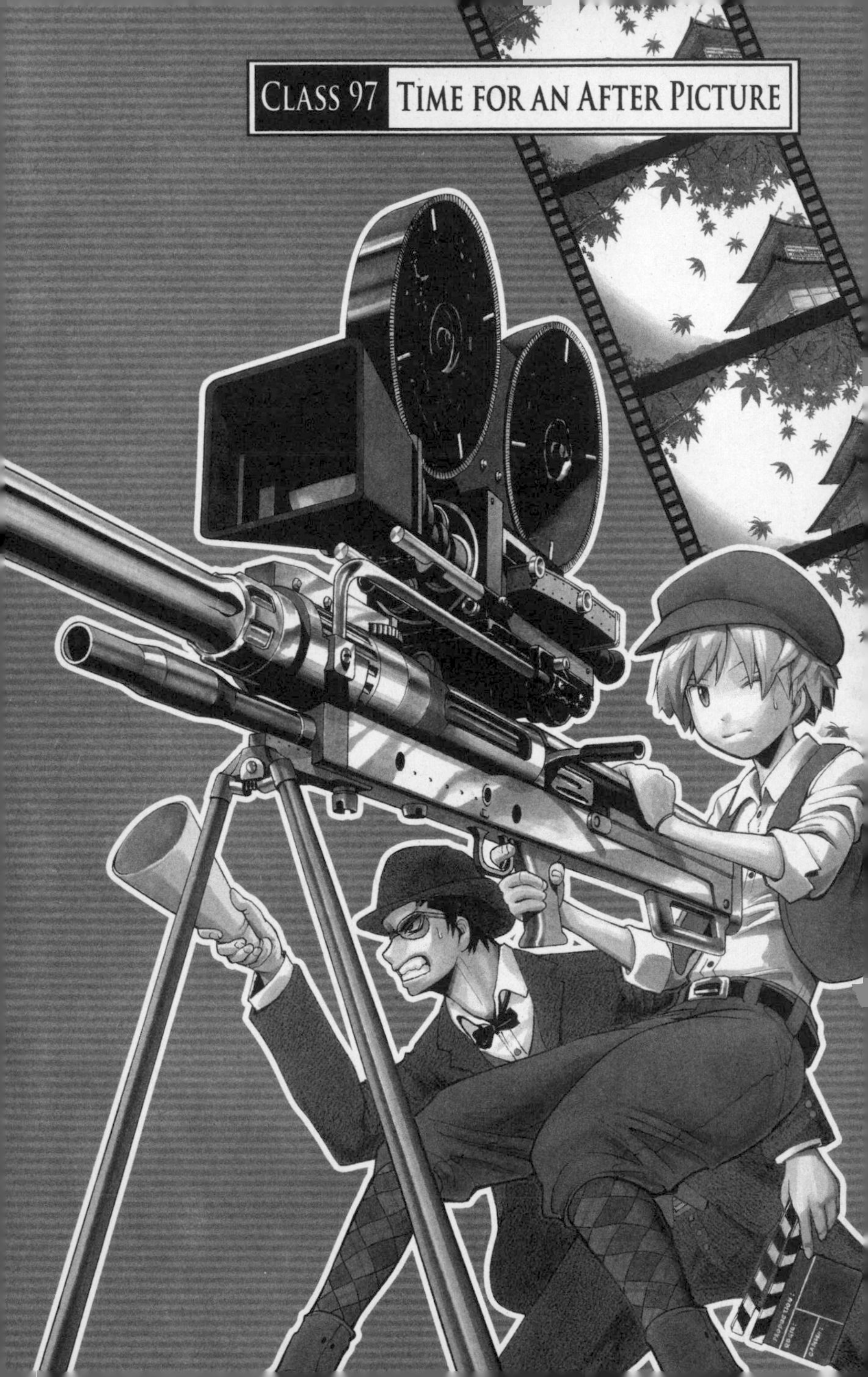

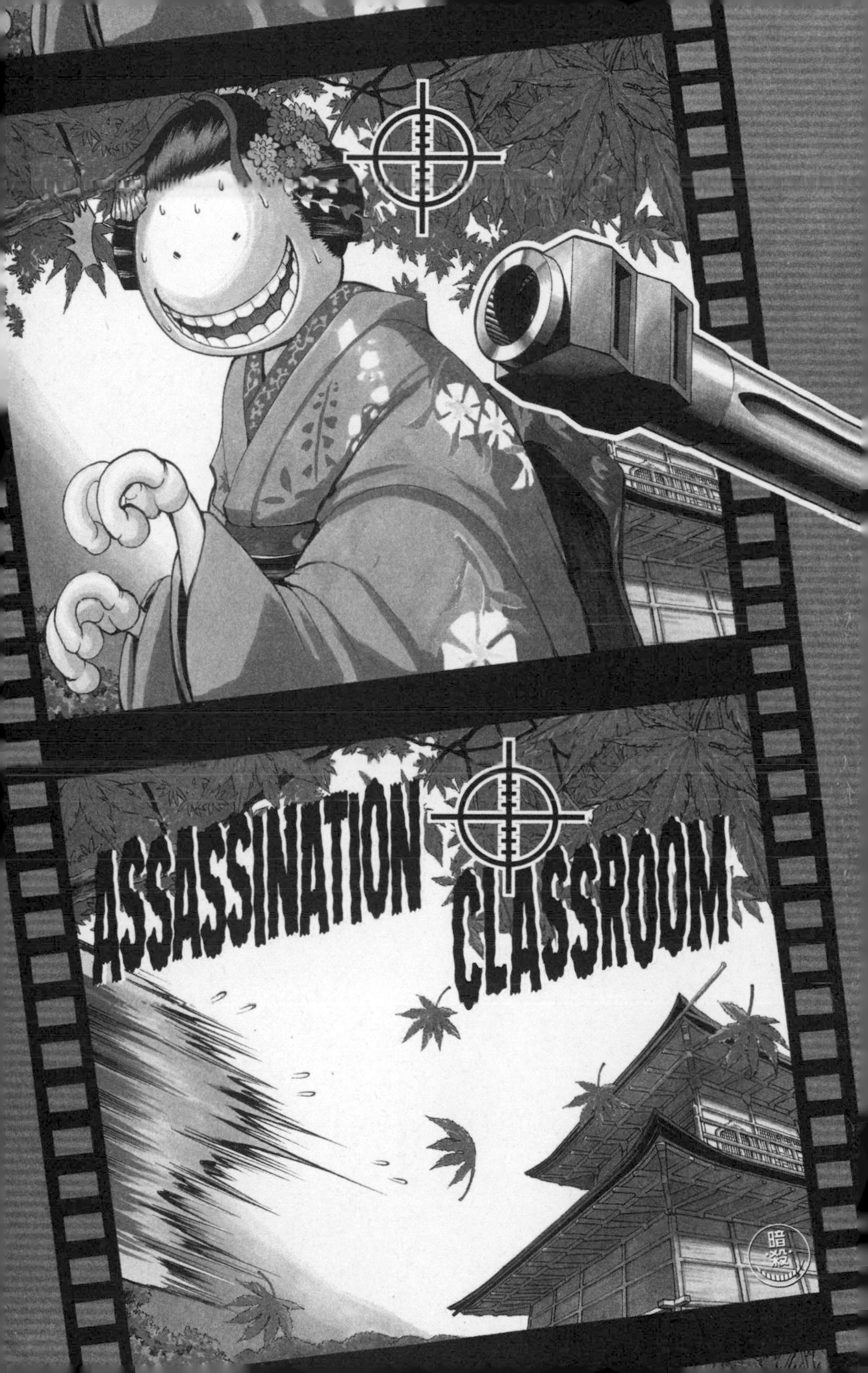
ASSASSINATION CLASSROOM
暗殺

Don't forget to watch the Assassination Classroom anime and live-action movie!

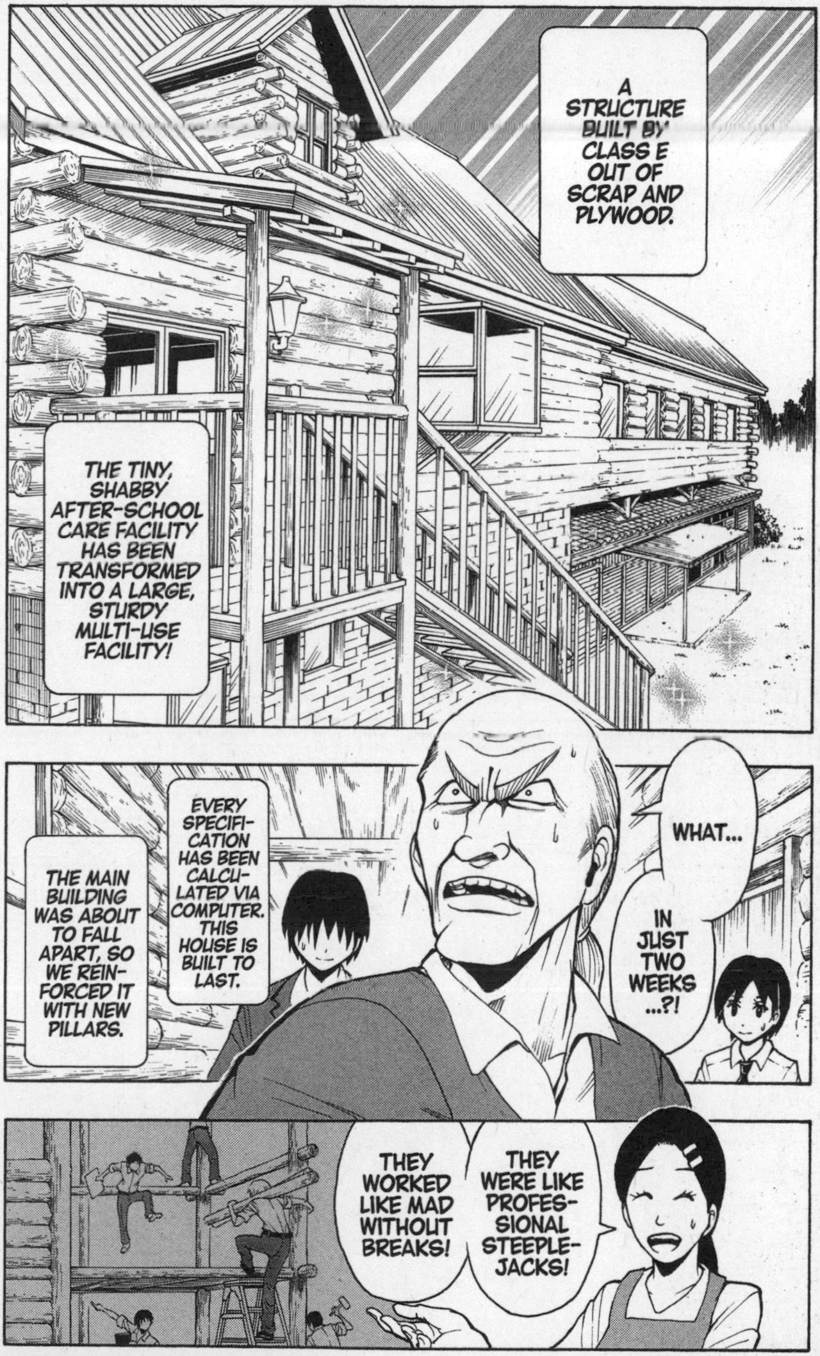
A STRUCTURE BUILT BY CLASS E OUT OF SCRAP AND PLYWOOD.
THE TINY, SHABBY AFTER-SCHOOL CARE FACILITY HAS BEEN TRANSFORMED INTO A LARGE, STURDY MULTI-USE FACILITY!
WHAT...
IN JUST TWO WEEKS...?!
EVERY SPECIFICATION HAS BEEN CALCULATED VIA COMPUTER. THIS HOUSE IS BUILT TO LAST.
THE MAIN BUILDING WAS ABOUT TO FALL APART, SO WE REINFORCED IT WITH NEW PILLARS.
THEY WERE LIKE PROFESSIONAL STEEPLEJACKS!
THEY WORKED LIKE MAD WITHOUT BREAKS!

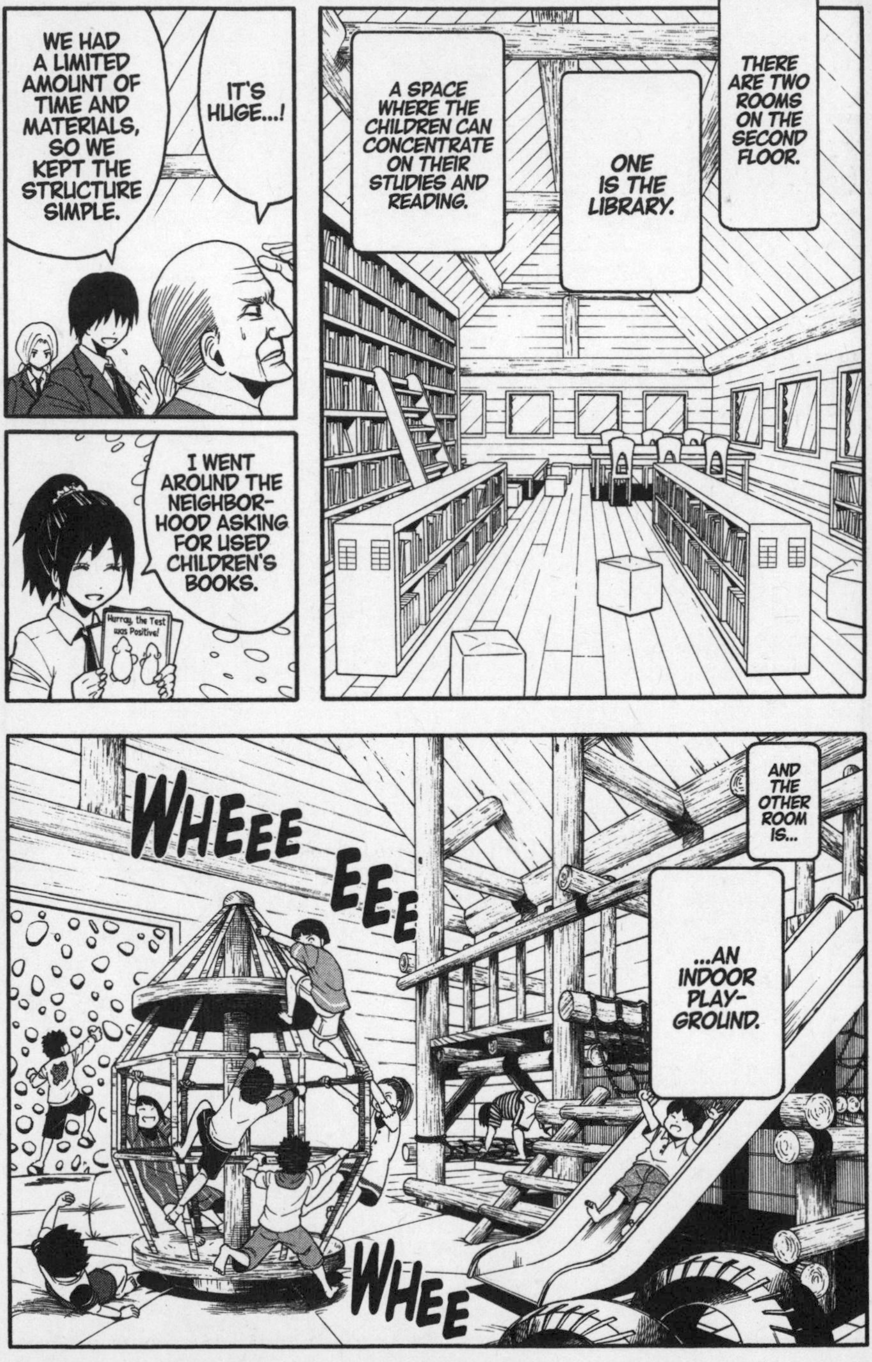
THERE ARE TWO ROOMS ON THE SECOND FLOOR.
ONE IS THE LIBRARY.
A SPACE WHERE THE CHILDREN CAN CONCENTRATE ON THEIR STUDIES AND READING.
IT'S HUGE...!
WE HAD A LIMITED AMOUNT OF TIME AND MATERIALS, SO WE KEPT THE STRUCTURE SIMPLE.
I WENT AROUND THE NEIGHBOR-HOOD ASKING FOR USED CHILDREN'S BOOKS.
Hurray, the Test was Positive!
AND THE OTHER ROOM IS...
...AN INDOOR PLAY-GROUND.
WHEEE
EEE
WHEE

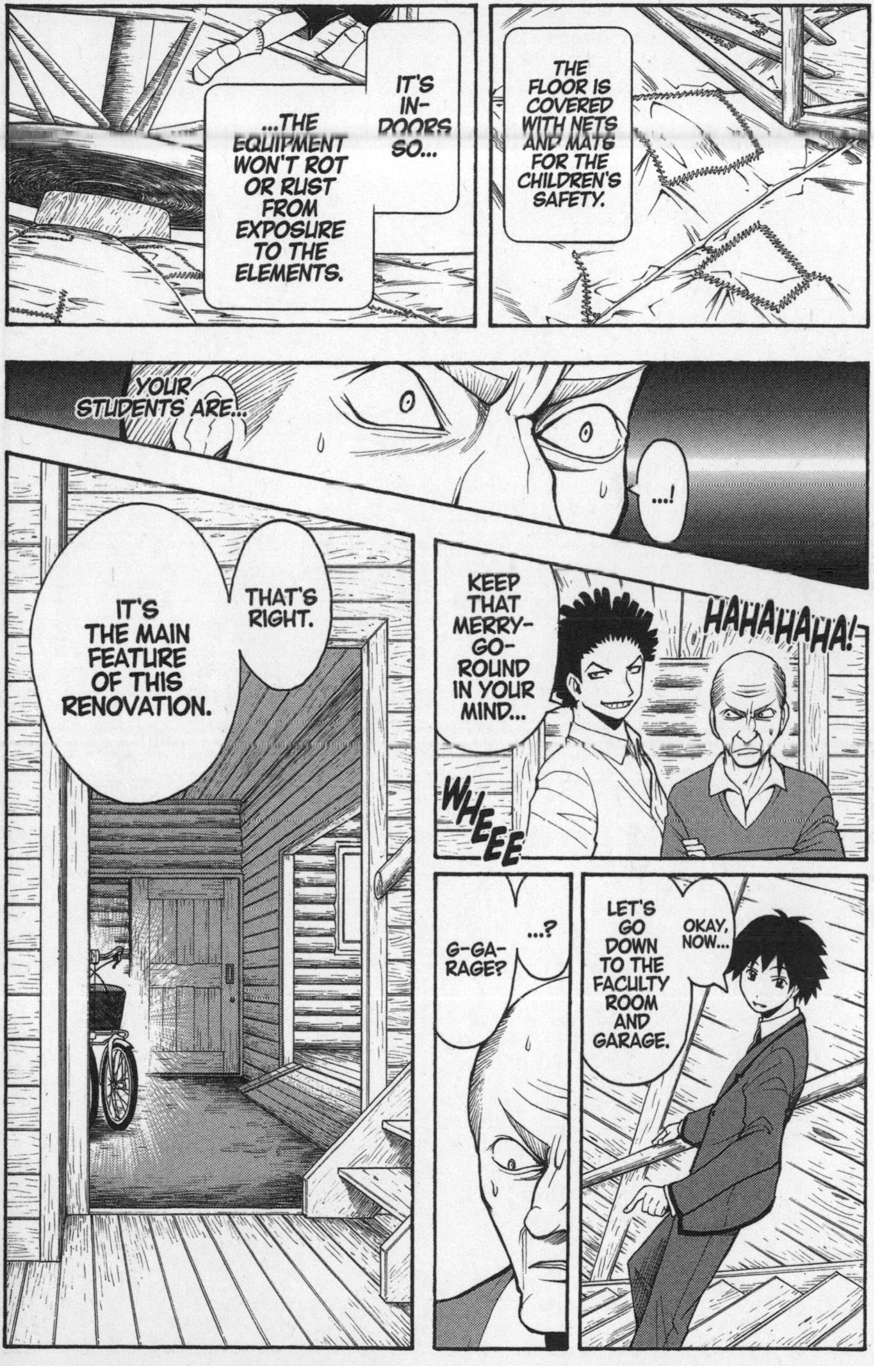
THE FLOOR IS COVERED WITH NETS AND MATS FOR THE CHILDREN'S SAFETY.
IT'S IN-DOORS SO...
...THE EQUIPMENT WON'T ROT OR RUST FROM EXPOSURE TO THE ELEMENTS.
YOUR STUDENTS ARE...
...!
THAT'S RIGHT.
IT'S THE MAIN FEATURE OF THIS RENOVATION.
HAHAHAHA!
KEEP THAT MERRY-GO-ROUND IN YOUR MIND...
WHEEE
OKAY, NOW...
LET'S GO DOWN TO THE FACULTY ROOM AND GARAGE.
...?
G-GA-RAGE?

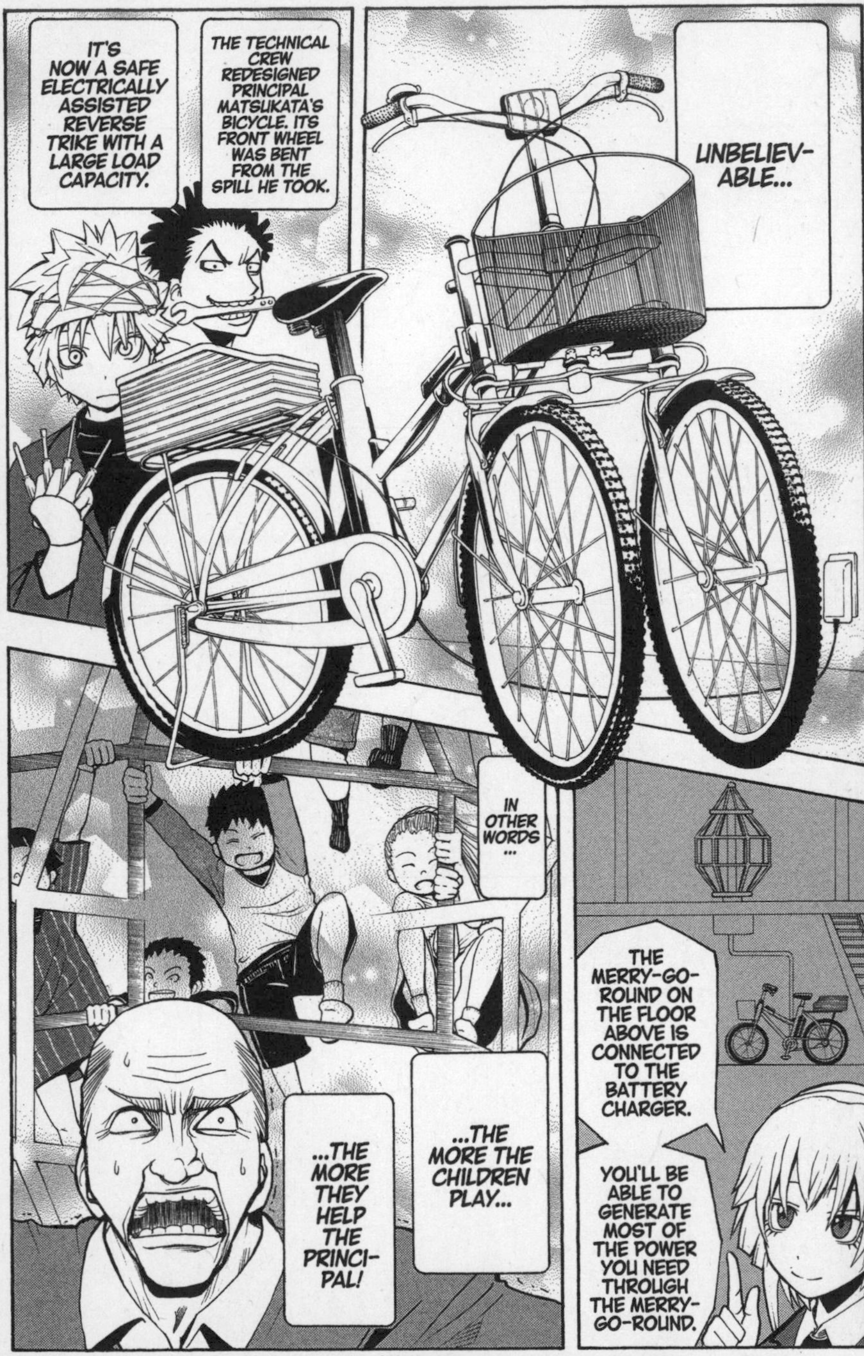
UNBELIEVABLE...
THE TECHNICAL CREW REDESIGNED PRINCIPAL MATSUKATA'S BICYCLE. ITS FRONT WHEEL WAS BENT FROM THE SPILL HE TOOK.
IT'S NOW A SAFE ELECTRICALLY ASSISTED REVERSE TRIKE WITH A LARGE LOAD CAPACITY.
THE MERRY-GO-ROUND ON THE FLOOR ABOVE IS CONNECTED TO THE BATTERY CHARGER.
YOU'LL BE ABLE TO GENERATE MOST OF THE POWER YOU NEED THROUGH THE MERRY-GO-ROUND.
IN OTHER WORDS...
...THE MORE THE CHILDREN PLAY...
...THE MORE THEY HELP THE PRINCIPAL!

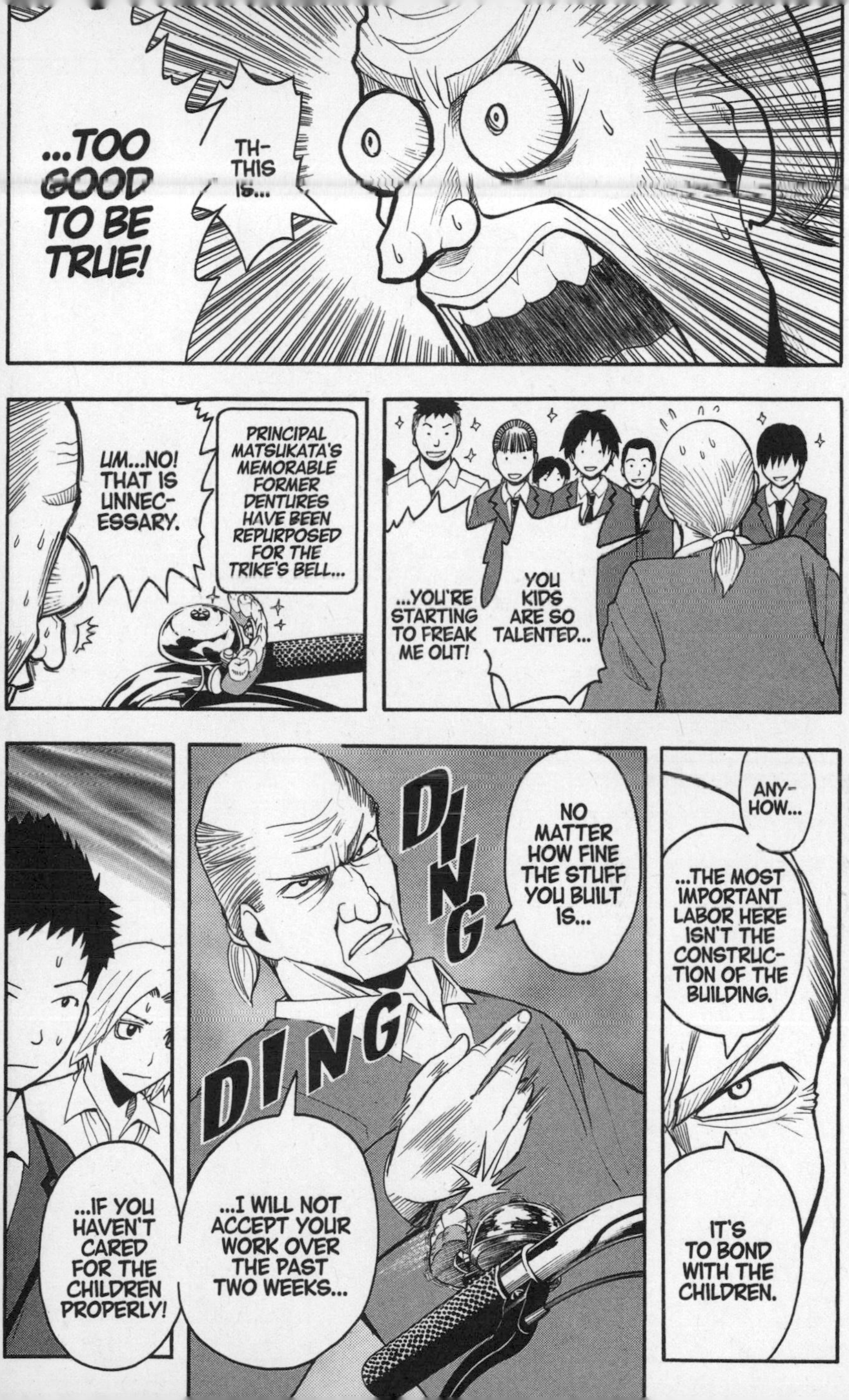
TH-THIS IS...
...TOO GOOD TO BE TRUE!
YOU KIDS ARE SO TALENTED...
...YOU'RE STARTING TO FREAK ME OUT!
PRINCIPAL MATSUKATA'S MEMORABLE FORMER DENTURES HAVE BEEN REPURPOSED FOR THE TRIKE'S BELL...
UM...NO! THAT IS UNNEC-ESSARY.
ANY-HOW...
...THE MOST IMPORTANT LABOR HERE ISN'T THE CONSTRUC-TION OF THE BUILDING.
IT'S TO BOND WITH THE CHILDREN.
DING
NO MATTER HOW FINE THE STUFF YOU BUILT IS...
DING
...I WILL NOT ACCEPT YOUR WORK OVER THE PAST TWO WEEKS...
...IF YOU HAVEN'T CARED FOR THE CHILDREN PROPERLY!

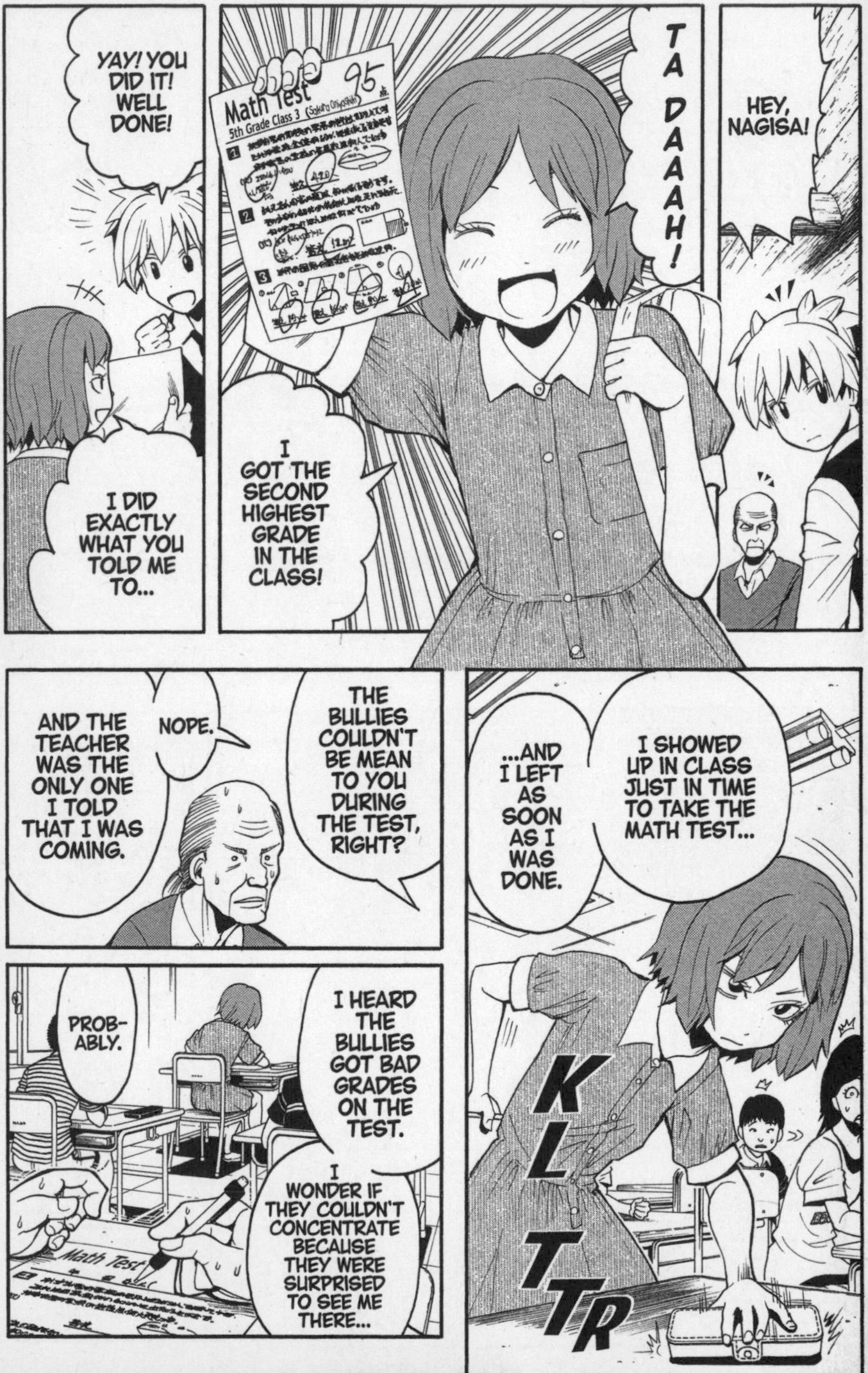
HEY, NAGISA!
TA DAAAAH!
Math Test
5th Grade Class 3
95
I GOT THE SECOND HIGHEST GRADE IN THE CLASS!
YAY! YOU DID IT! WELL DONE!
I DID EXACTLY WHAT YOU TOLD ME TO...
I SHOWED UP IN CLASS JUST IN TIME TO TAKE THE MATH TEST...
...AND I LEFT AS SOON AS I WAS DONE.
KLTTR
THE BULLIES COULDN'T BE MEAN TO YOU DURING THE TEST, RIGHT?
NOPE.
AND THE TEACHER WAS THE ONLY ONE I TOLD THAT I WAS COMING.
I HEARD THE BULLIES GOT BAD GRADES ON THE TEST.
I WONDER IF THEY COULDN'T CONCENTRATE BECAUSE THEY WERE SURPRISED TO SEE ME THERE...
PROB-ABLY.
Math Test

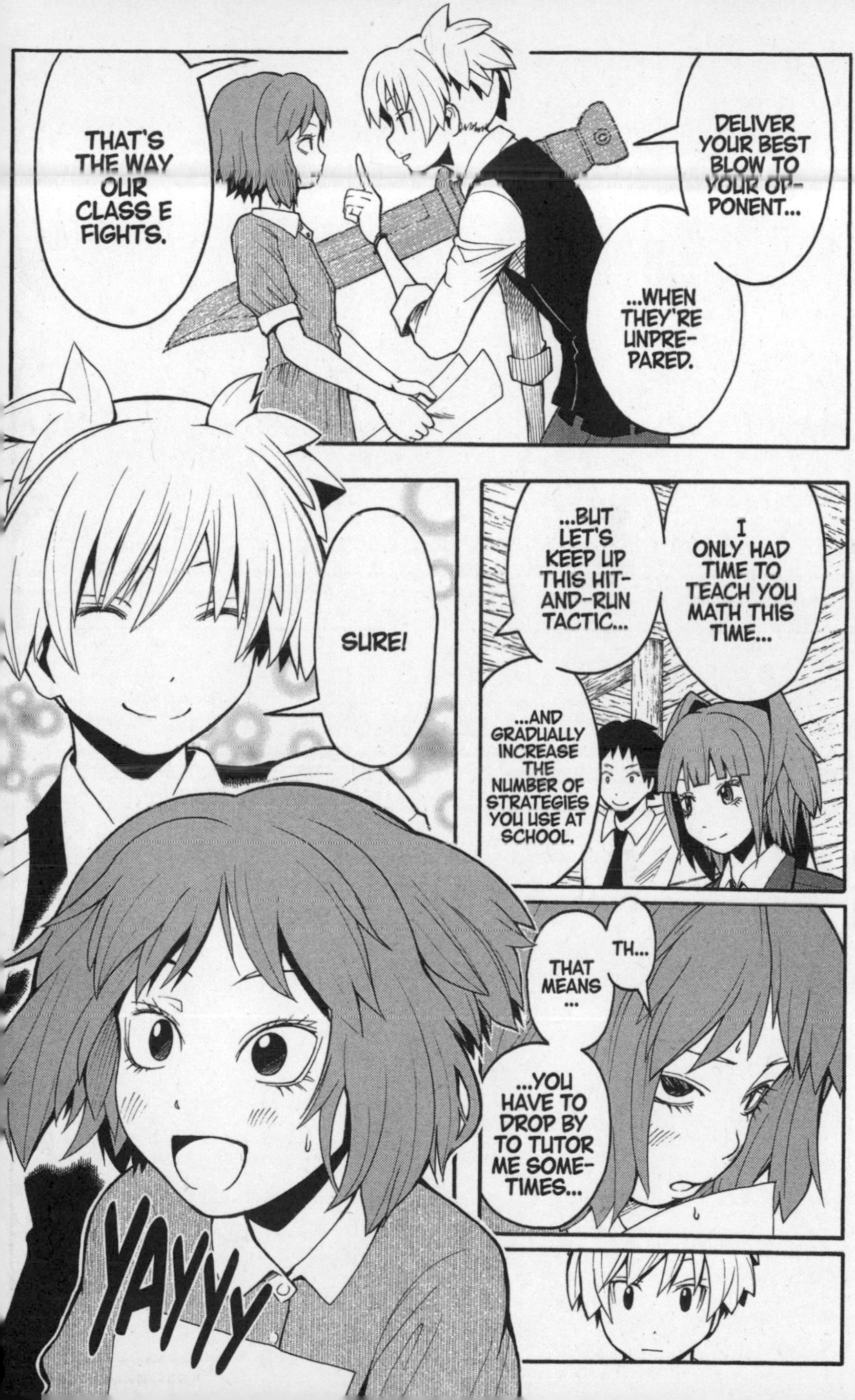
DELIVER YOUR BEST BLOW TO YOUR OP-PONENT...
...WHEN THEY'RE UNPRE-PARED.
THAT'S THE WAY OUR CLASS E FIGHTS.
I ONLY HAD TIME TO TEACH YOU MATH THIS TIME...
...BUT LET'S KEEP UP THIS HIT-AND-RUN TACTIC...
...AND GRADUALLY INCREASE THE NUMBER OF STRATEGIES YOU USE AT SCHOOL.
SURE!
TH... THAT MEANS...
...YOU HAVE TO DROP BY TO TUTOR ME SOME-TIMES...
YAYYY

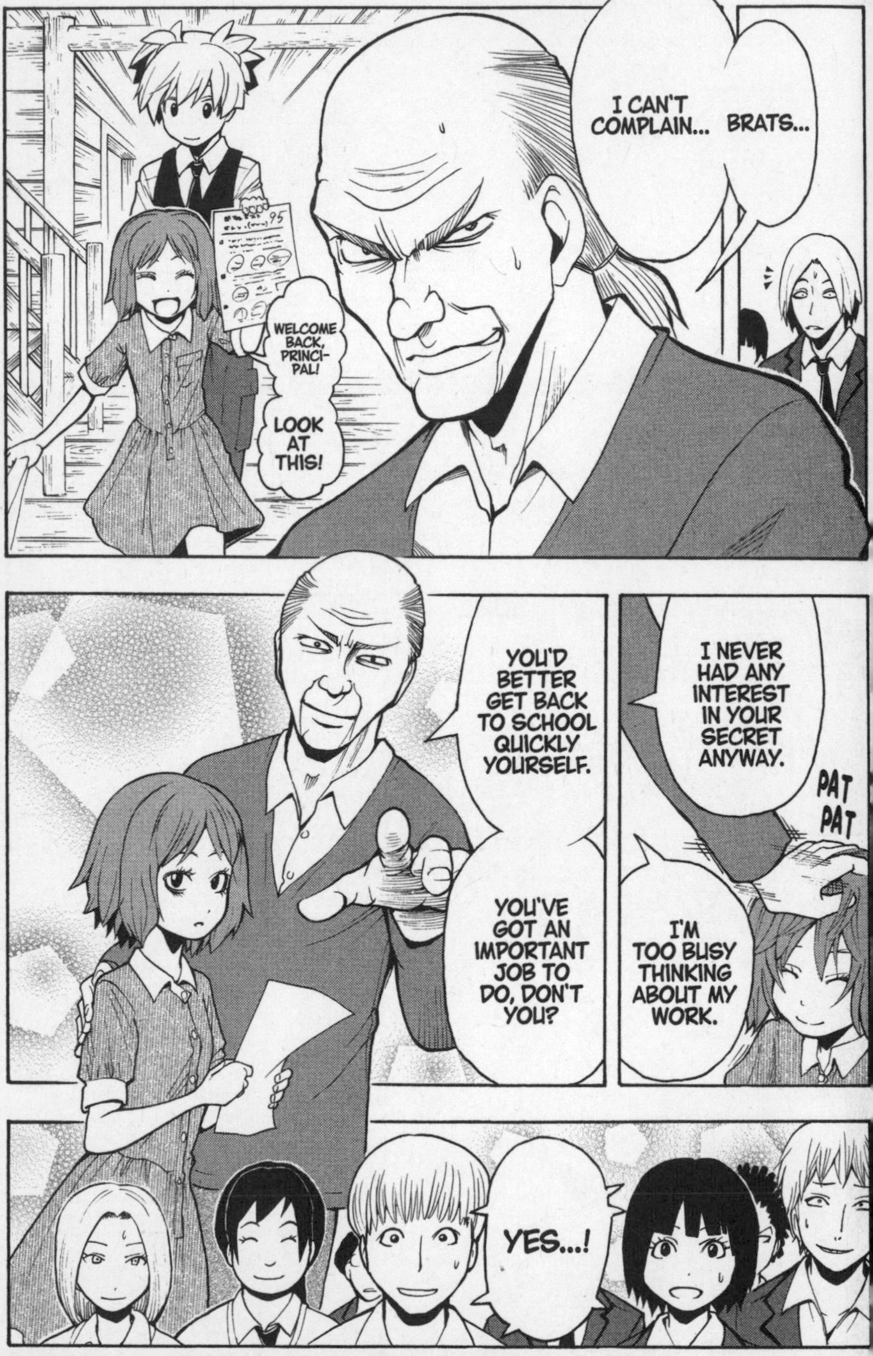
BRATS...
I CAN'T COMPLAIN...
WELCOME BACK, PRINCI-PAL!
LOOK AT THIS!
95
PAT PAT
I NEVER HAD ANY INTEREST IN YOUR SECRET ANYWAY.
I'M TOO BUSY THINKING ABOUT MY WORK.
YOU'D BETTER GET BACK TO SCHOOL QUICKLY YOURSELF.
YOU'VE GOT AN IMPORTANT JOB TO DO, DON'T YOU?
YES...!

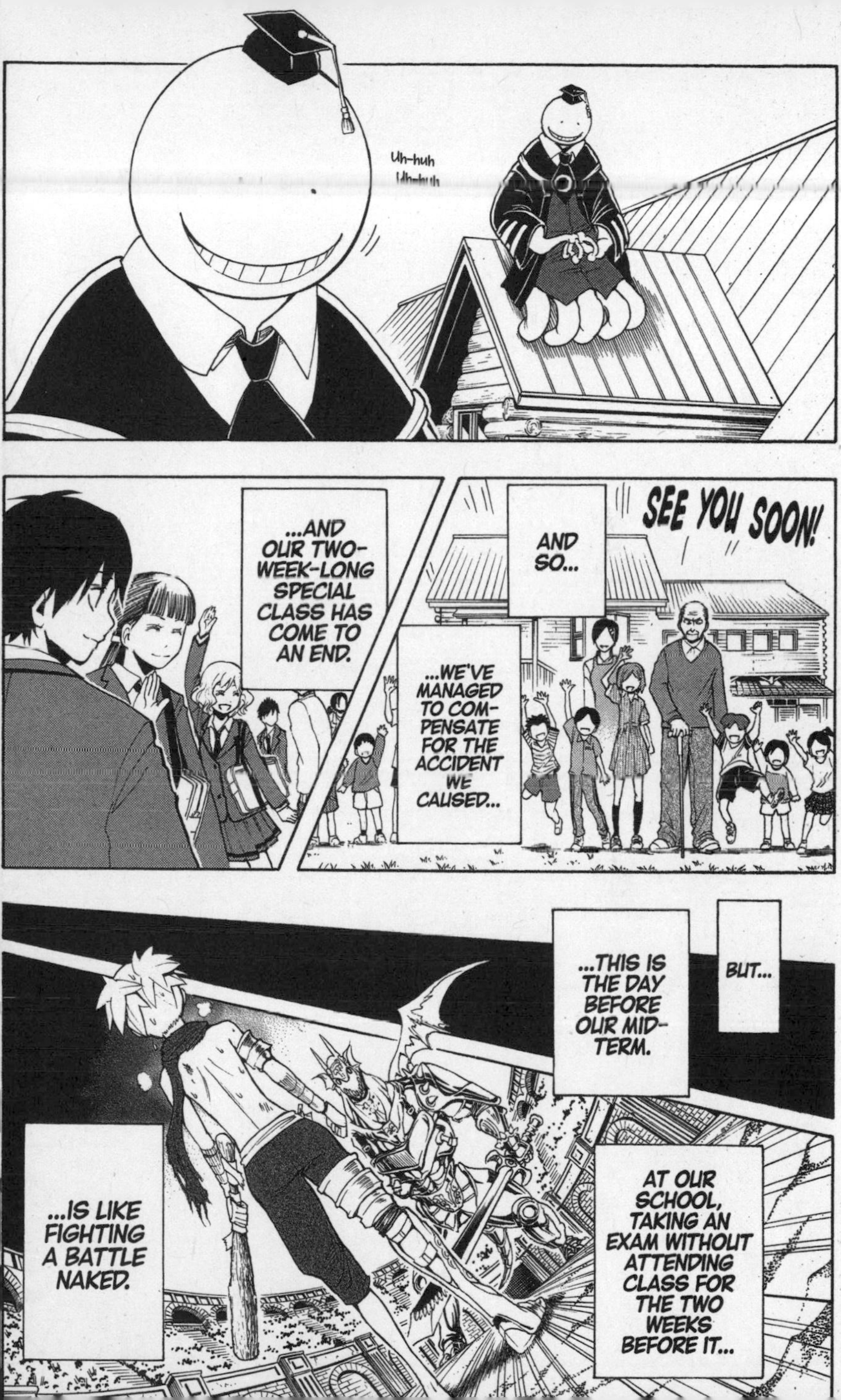
Uh-huh
Uh-huh
SEE YOU SOON!
AND SO...
...WE'VE MANAGED TO COMPENSATE FOR THE ACCIDENT WE CAUSED...
...AND OUR TWO-WEEK-LONG SPECIAL CLASS HAS COME TO AN END.
BUT...
...THIS IS THE DAY BEFORE OUR MID-TERM.
AT OUR SCHOOL, TAKING AN EXAM WITHOUT ATTENDING CLASS FOR THE TWO WEEKS BEFORE IT...
...IS LIKE FIGHTING A BATTLE NAKED.

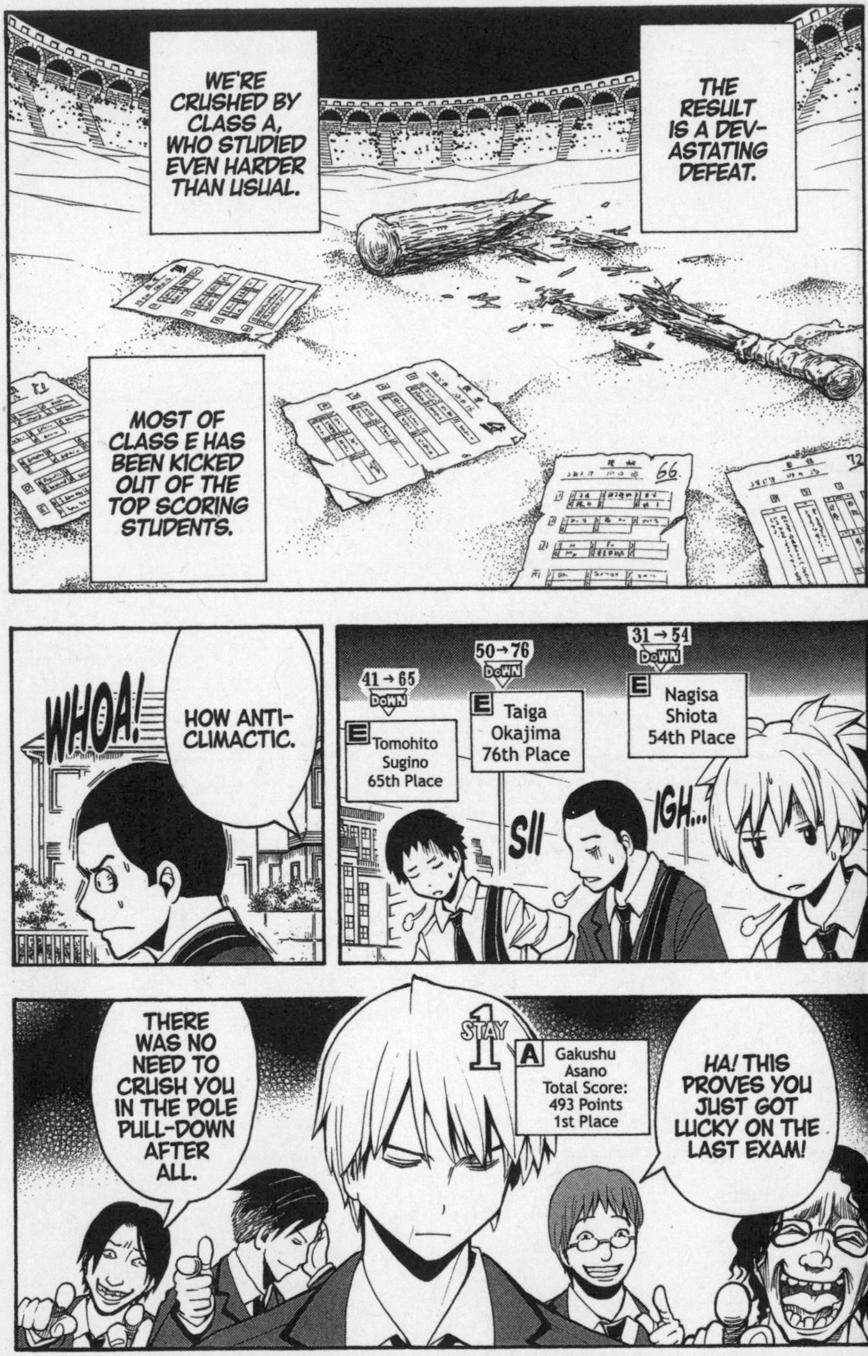
THE RESULT IS A DEV-ASTATING DEFEAT.
WE'RE CRUSHED BY CLASS A, WHO STUDIED EVEN HARDER THAN USUAL.
MOST OF CLASS E HAS BEEN KICKED OUT OF THE TOP SCORING STUDENTS.
31 → 54 DOWN
E Nagisa Shiota 54th Place
IGH...
50 → 76 DOWN
E Taiga Okajima 76th Place
SII
41 → 65 DOWN
E Tomohito Sugino 65th Place
HOW ANTI-CLIMACTIC.
WHOA!
HA! THIS PROVES YOU JUST GOT LUCKY ON THE LAST EXAM!
STAY 1
A Gakushu Asano Total Score: 493 Points 1st Place
THERE WAS NO NEED TO CRUSH YOU IN THE POLE PULL-DOWN AFTER ALL.

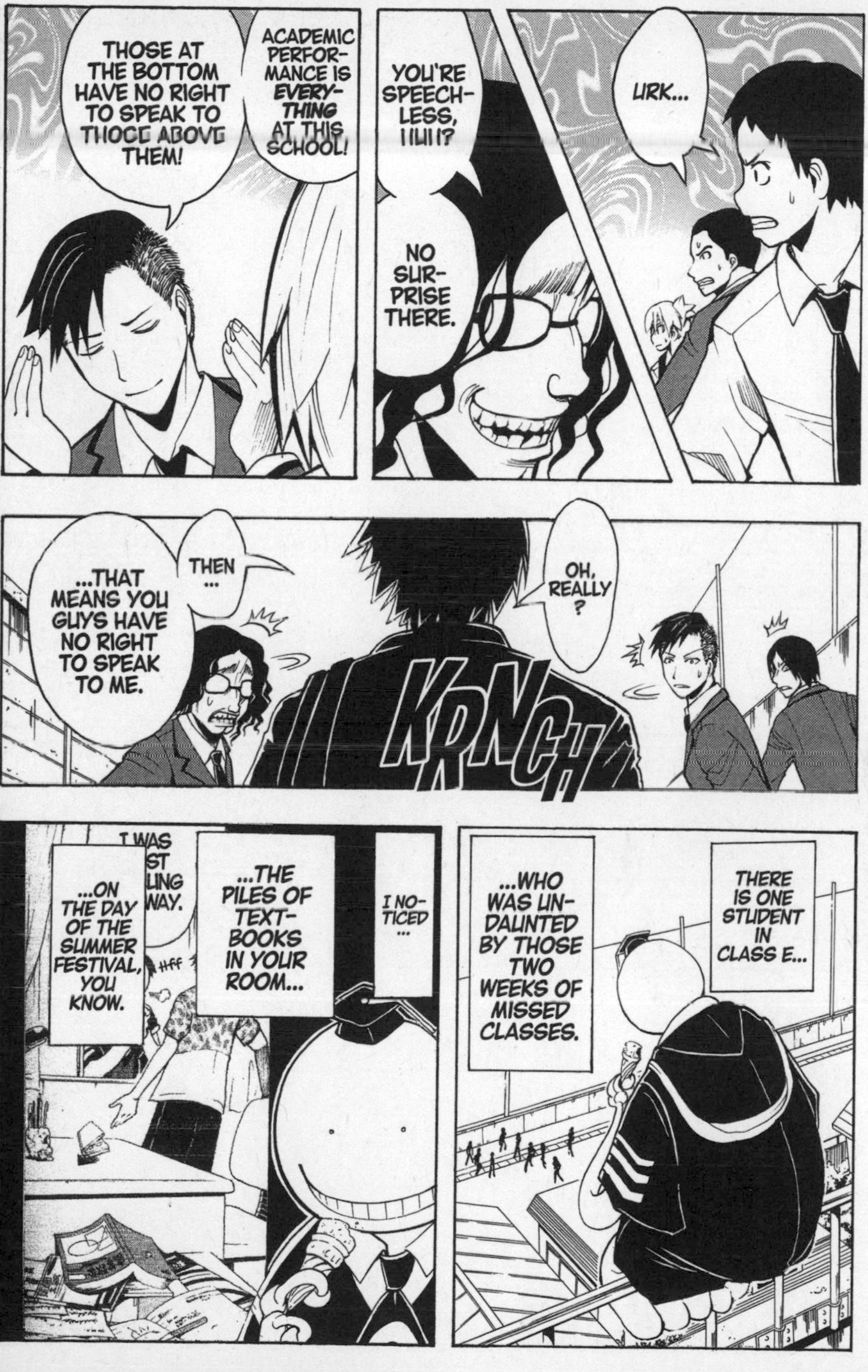
URK...
YOU'RE SPEECHLESS, HUH?
NO SURPRISE THERE.
ACADEMIC PERFORMANCE IS EVERYTHING AT THIS SCHOOL!
THOSE AT THE BOTTOM HAVE NO RIGHT TO SPEAK TO THOSE ABOVE THEM!
OH, REALLY?
THEN...
...THAT MEANS YOU GUYS HAVE NO RIGHT TO SPEAK TO ME.
KRNCH
THERE IS ONE STUDENT IN CLASS E...
...WHO WAS UNDAUNTED BY THOSE TWO WEEKS OF MISSED CLASSES.
I NOTICED...
...THE PILES OF TEXTBOOKS IN YOUR ROOM...
...ON THE DAY OF THE SUMMER FESTIVAL, YOU KNOW.

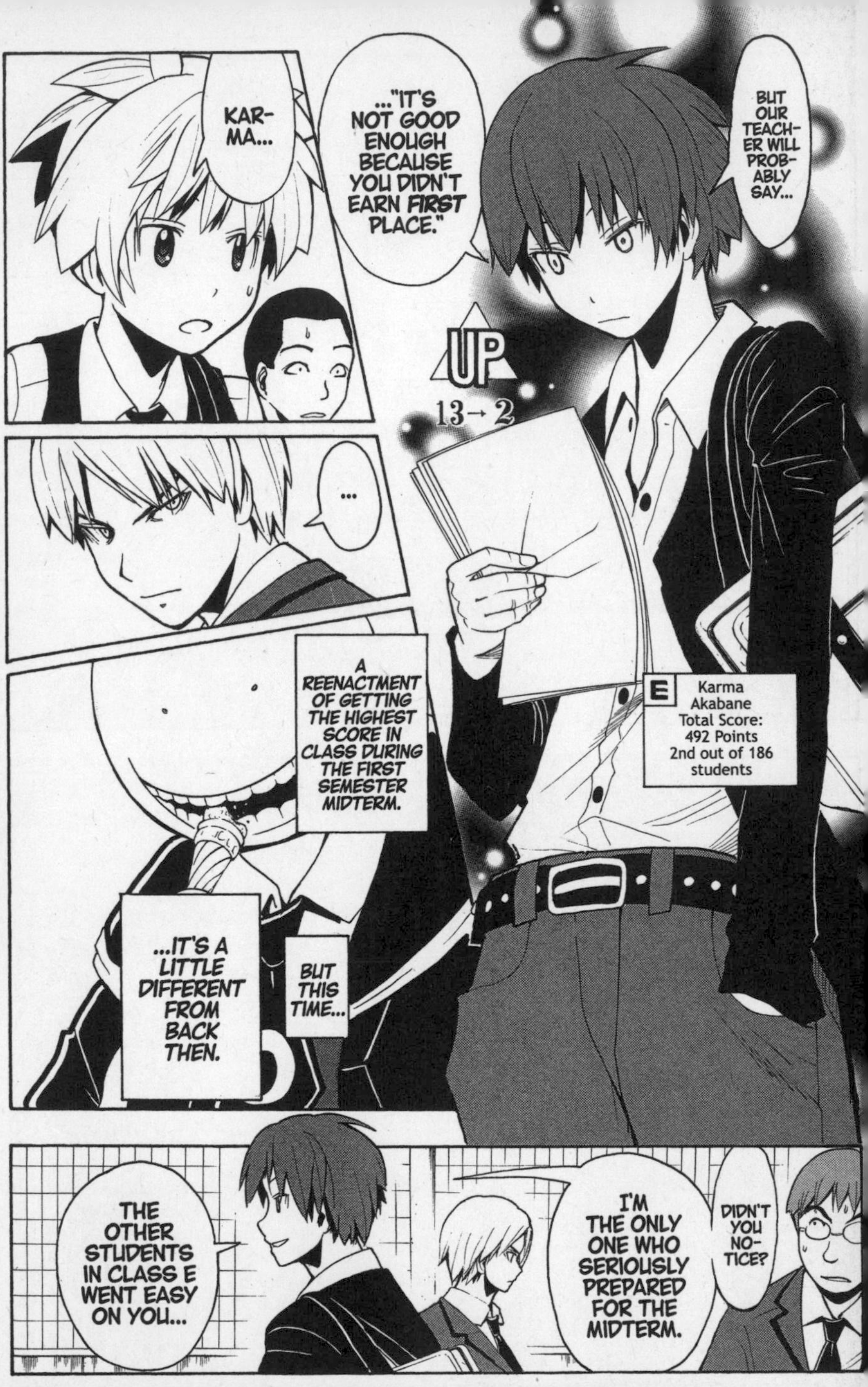
BUT OUR TEACHER WILL PROBABLY SAY...
..."IT'S NOT GOOD ENOUGH BECAUSE YOU DIDN'T EARN FIRST PLACE."
UP
13→2
E
Karma Akabane Total Score: 492 Points 2nd out of 186 students
KARMA...
...
A REENACTMENT OF GETTING THE HIGHEST SCORE IN CLASS DURING THE FIRST SEMESTER MIDTERM.
BUT THIS TIME...
...IT'S A LITTLE DIFFERENT FROM BACK THEN.
DIDN'T YOU NOTICE?
I'M THE ONLY ONE WHO SERIOUSLY PREPARED FOR THE MIDTERM.
THE OTHER STUDENTS IN CLASS E WENT EASY ON YOU...

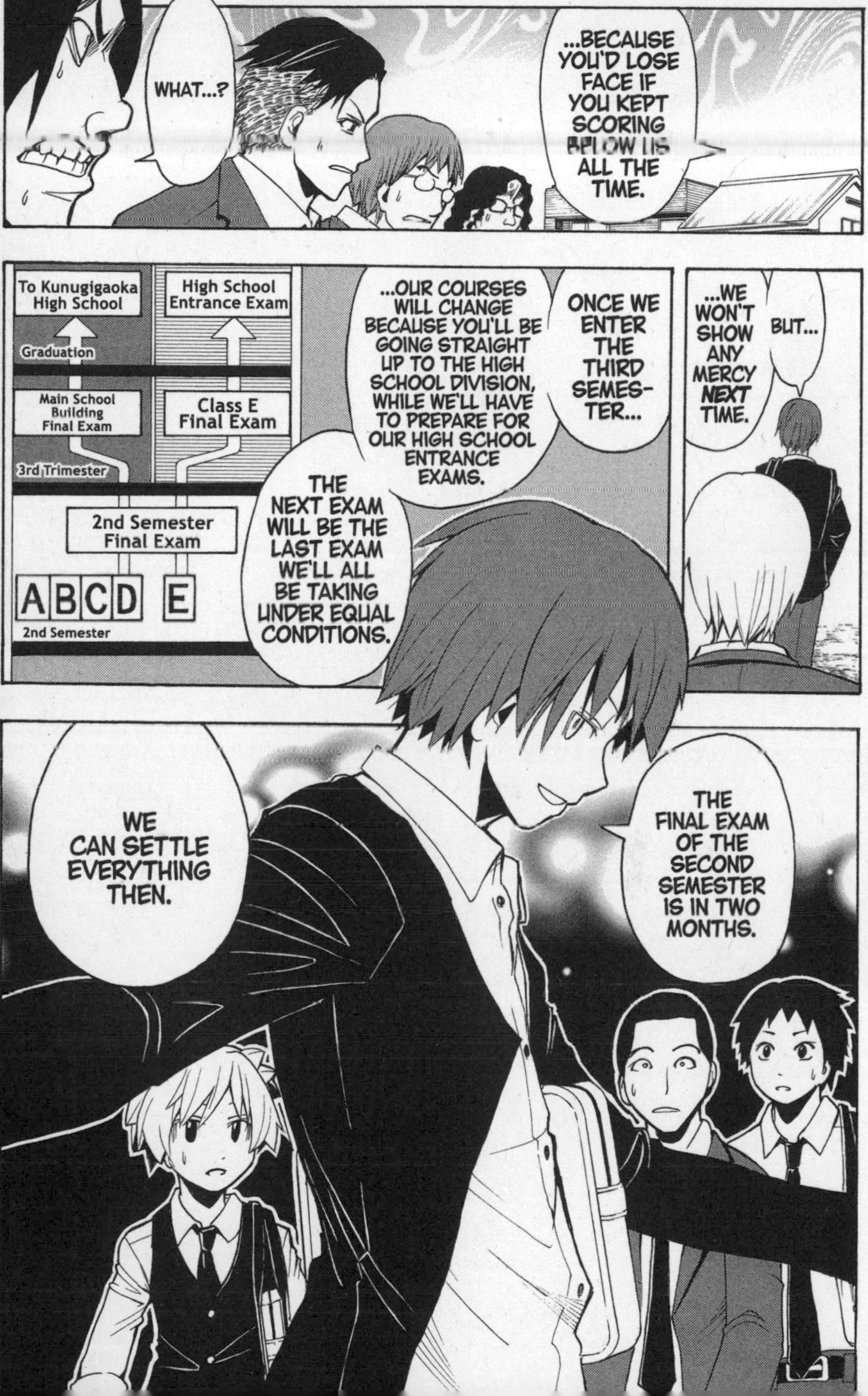
...BECAUSE YOU'D LOSE FACE IF YOU KEPT SCORING BELOW US ALL THE TIME.
WHAT...?
BUT...
...WE WON'T SHOW ANY MERCY NEXT TIME.
ONCE WE ENTER THE THIRD SEMESTER...
...OUR COURSES WILL CHANGE BECAUSE YOU'LL BE GOING STRAIGHT UP TO THE HIGH SCHOOL DIVISION, WHILE WE'LL HAVE TO PREPARE FOR OUR HIGH SCHOOL ENTRANCE EXAMS.
THE NEXT EXAM WILL BE THE LAST EXAM WE'LL ALL BE TAKING UNDER EQUAL CONDITIONS.
To Kunugigaoka High School
High School Entrance Exam
Graduation
Main School Building Final Exam
Class E Final Exam
3rd Trimester
2nd Semester Final Exam
ABCD
E
2nd Semester
THE FINAL EXAM OF THE SECOND SEMESTER IS IN TWO MONTHS.
WE CAN SETTLE EVERYTHING THEN.

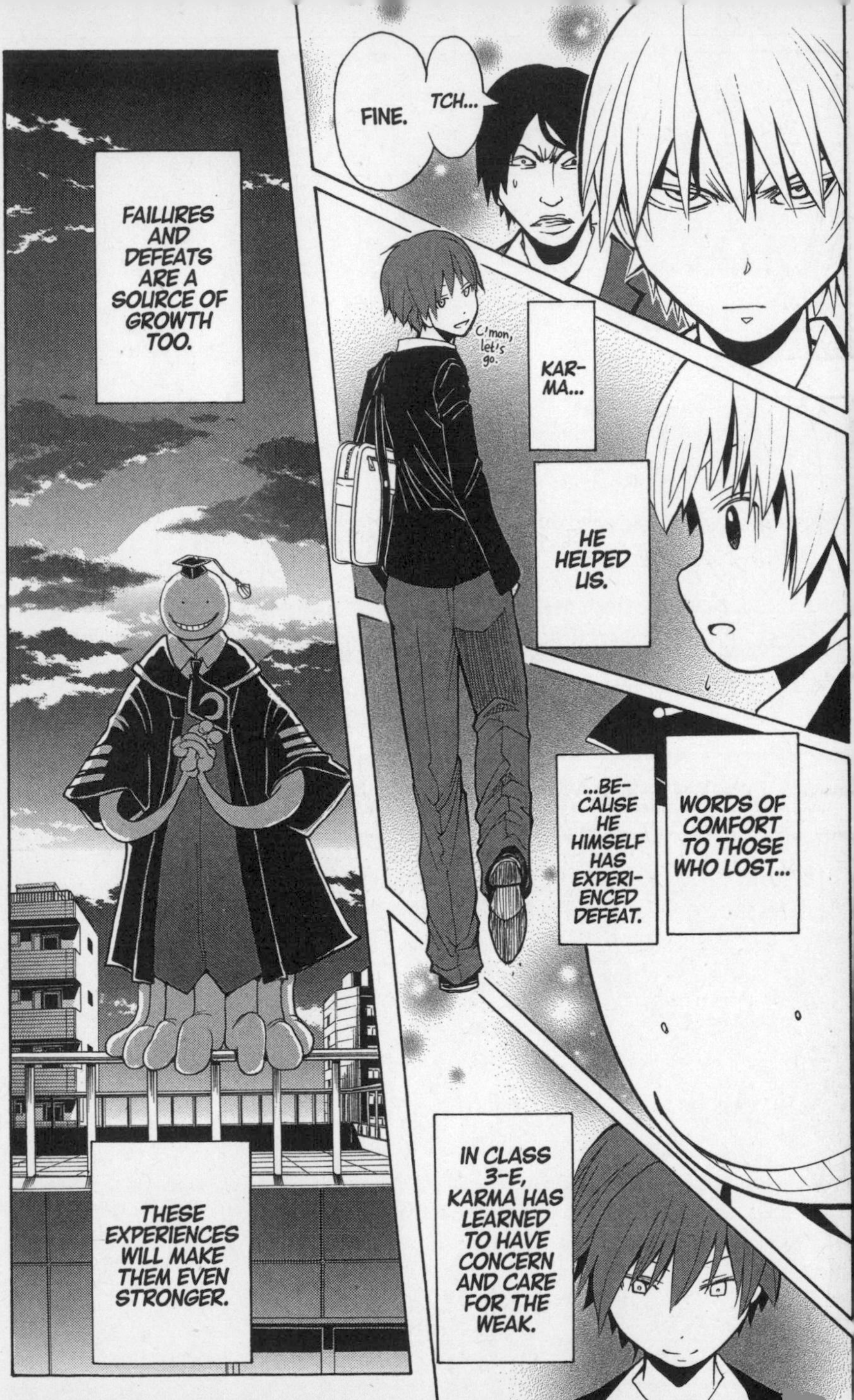
TCH...
FINE.
C'mon, let's go.
KARMA...
HE HELPED US.
WORDS OF COMFORT TO THOSE WHO LOST...
...BECAUSE HE HIMSELF HAS EXPERIENCED DEFEAT.
IN CLASS 3-E, KARMA HAS LEARNED TO HAVE CONCERN AND CARE FOR THE WEAK.
FAILURES AND DEFEATS ARE A SOURCE OF GROWTH TOO.
THESE EXPERIENCES WILL MAKE THEM EVEN STRONGER.

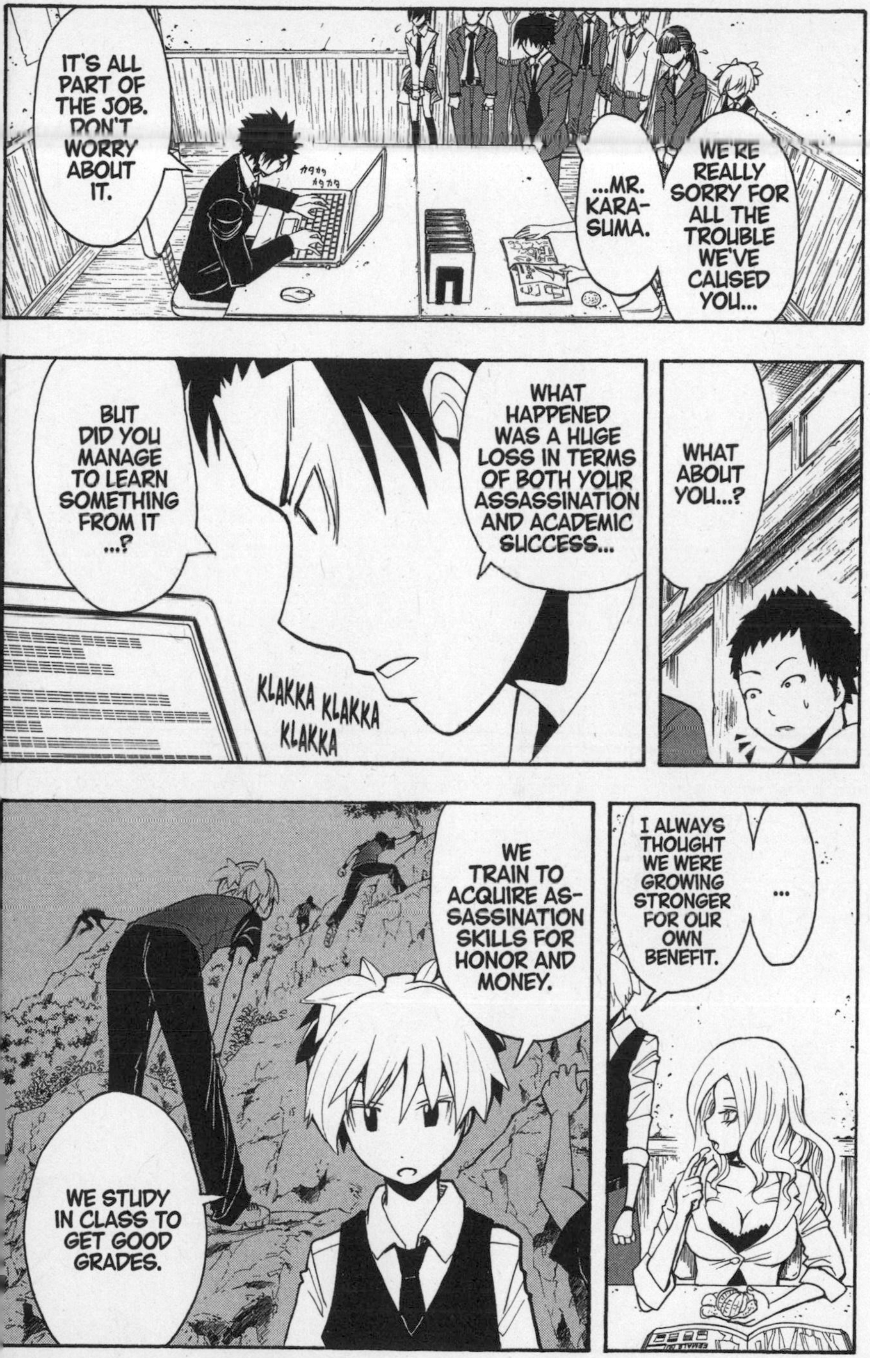
WE'RE REALLY SORRY FOR ALL THE TROUBLE WE'VE CAUSED YOU...
...MR. KARA-SUMA.
IT'S ALL PART OF THE JOB. DON'T WORRY ABOUT IT.
WHAT ABOUT YOU...?
WHAT HAPPENED WAS A HUGE LOSS IN TERMS OF BOTH YOUR ASSASSINATION AND ACADEMIC SUCCESS...
BUT DID YOU MANAGE TO LEARN SOMETHING FROM IT ...?
KLAKKA KLAKKA KLAKKA
I ALWAYS THOUGHT WE WERE GROWING STRONGER FOR OUR OWN BENEFIT.
...
WE TRAIN TO ACQUIRE AS-SASSINATION SKILLS FOR HONOR AND MONEY.
WE STUDY IN CLASS TO GET GOOD GRADES.

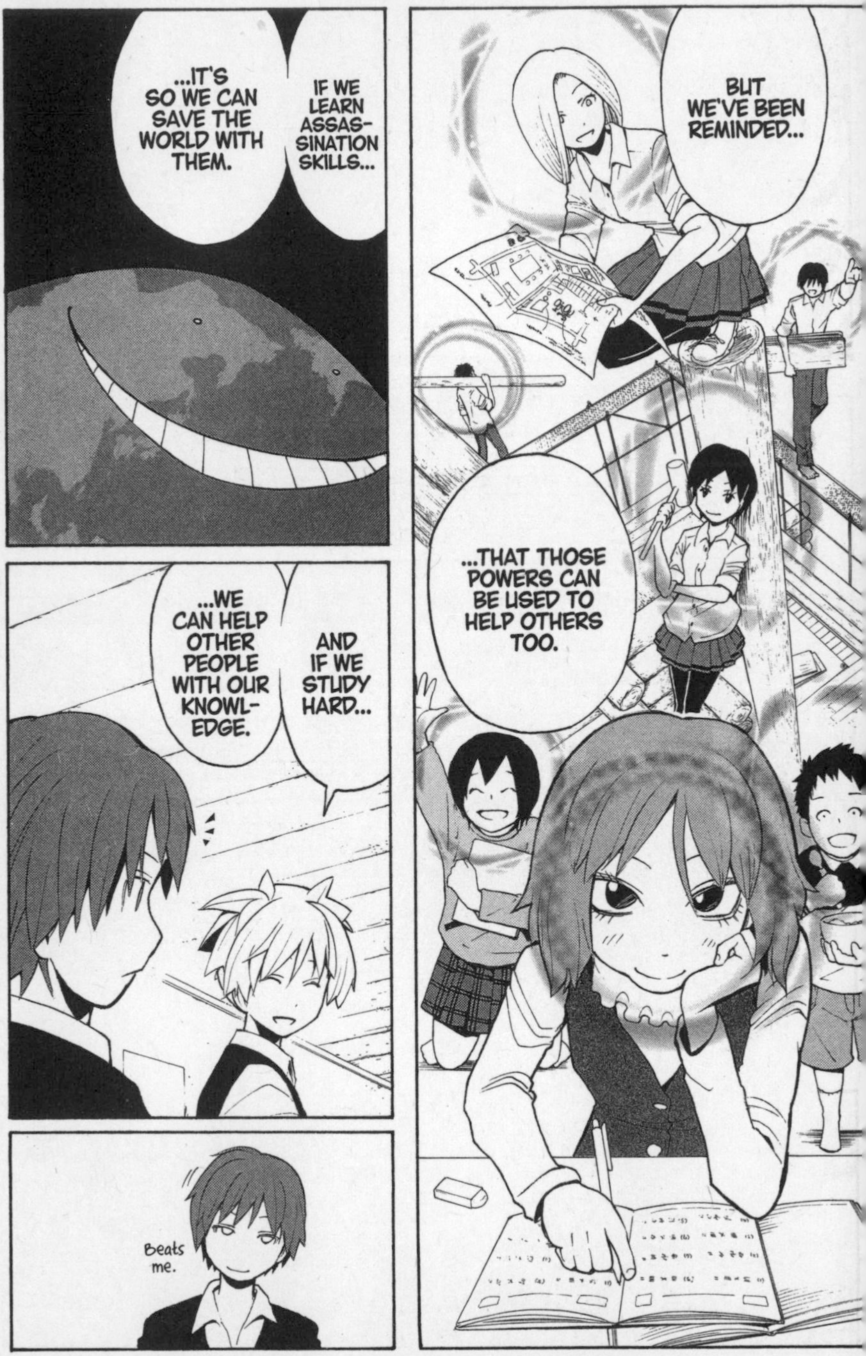
BUT WE'VE BEEN REMINDED...
...THAT THOSE POWERS CAN BE USED TO HELP OTHERS TOO.
IF WE LEARN ASSAS-SINATION SKILLS...
...IT'S SO WE CAN SAVE THE WORLD WITH THEM.
AND IF WE STUDY HARD...
...WE CAN HELP OTHER PEOPLE WITH OUR KNOWL-EDGE.
Beats me.

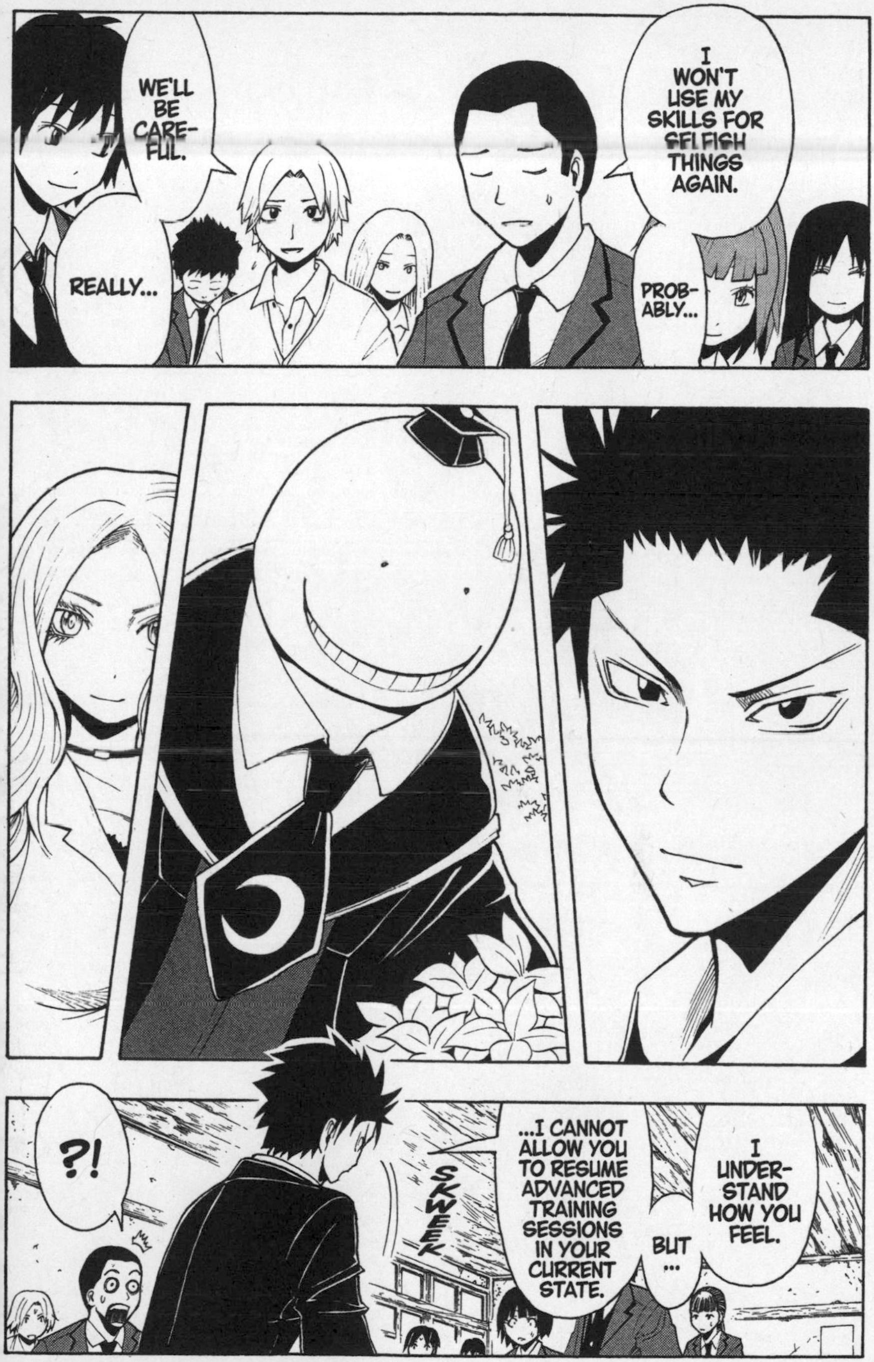
I WON'T USE MY SKILLS FOR SELFISH THINGS AGAIN.
PROBABLY...
WE'LL BE CAREFUL.
REALLY...
I UNDERSTAND HOW YOU FEEL.
BUT...
...I CANNOT ALLOW YOU TO RESUME ADVANCED TRAINING SESSIONS IN YOUR CURRENT STATE.
SKWEEK
?!

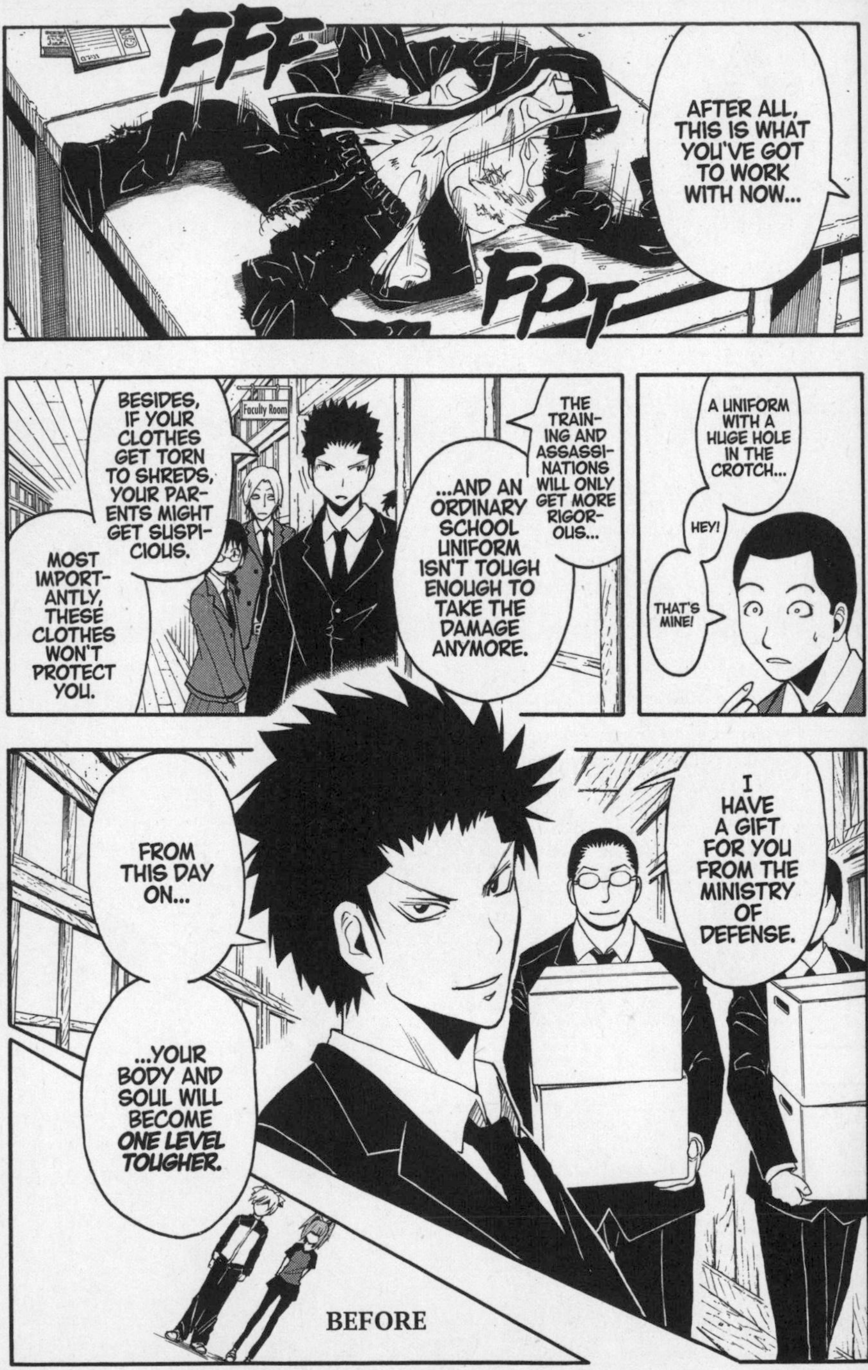
FFF
AFTER ALL, THIS IS WHAT YOU'VE GOT TO WORK WITH NOW...
FPT
A UNIFORM WITH A HUGE HOLE IN THE CROTCH...
HEY!
THAT'S MINE!
THE TRAINING AND ASSASSINATIONS WILL ONLY GET MORE RIGOROUS...
...AND AN ORDINARY SCHOOL UNIFORM ISN'T TOUGH ENOUGH TO TAKE THE DAMAGE ANYMORE.
Faculty Room
BESIDES, IF YOUR CLOTHES GET TORN TO SHREDS, YOUR PARENTS MIGHT GET SUSPICIOUS.
MOST IMPORTANTLY, THESE CLOTHES WON'T PROTECT YOU.
I HAVE A GIFT FOR YOU FROM THE MINISTRY OF DEFENSE.
FROM THIS DAY ON...
...YOUR BODY AND SOUL WILL BECOME *ONE LEVEL TOUGHER.*
BEFORE

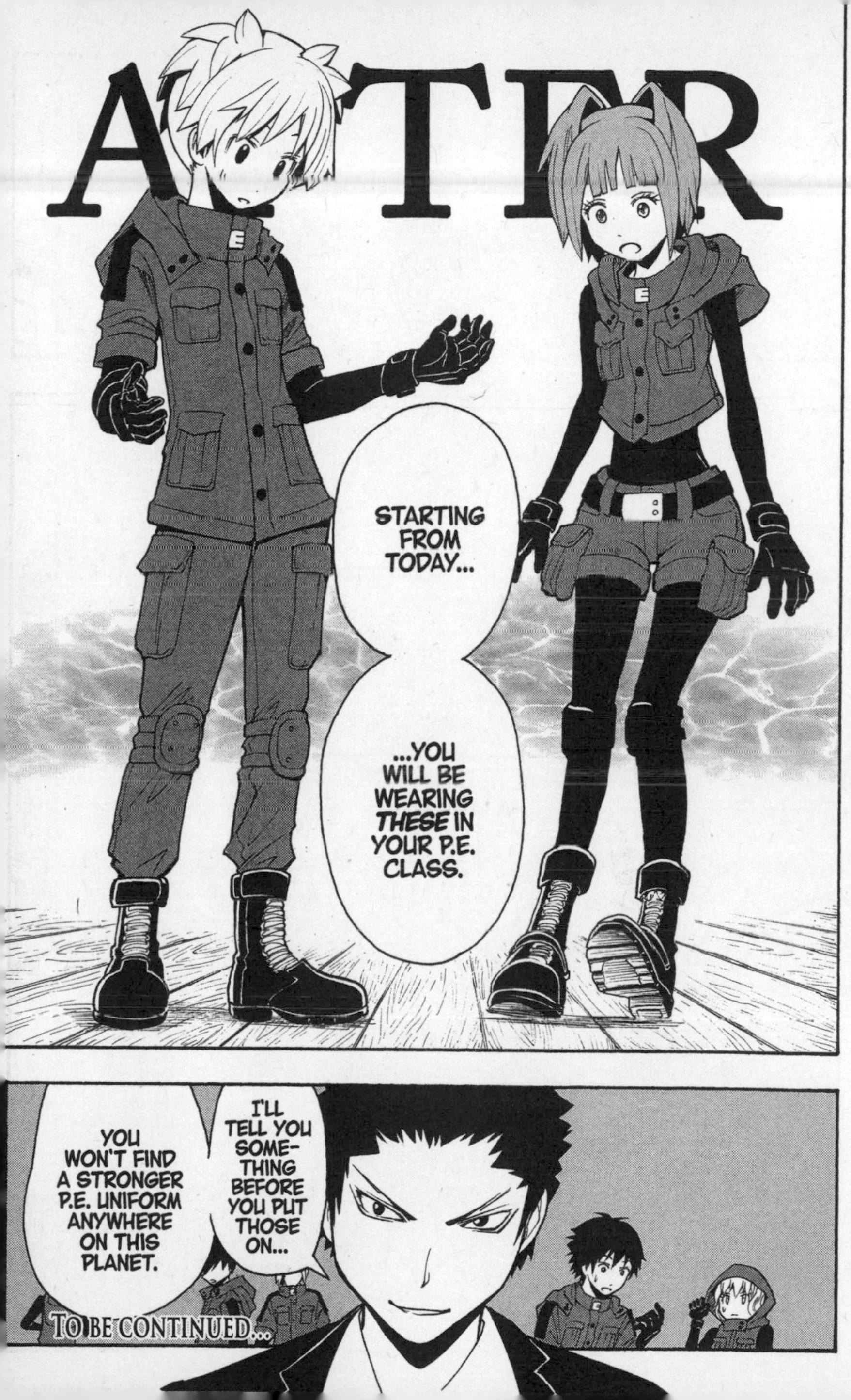
STARTING FROM TODAY...
...YOU WILL BE WEARING *THESE* IN YOUR P.E. CLASS.
I'LL TELL YOU SOME-THING BEFORE YOU PUT THOSE ON...
YOU WON'T FIND A STRONGER P.E. UNIFORM ANYWHERE ON THIS PLANET.
TO BE CONTINUED...

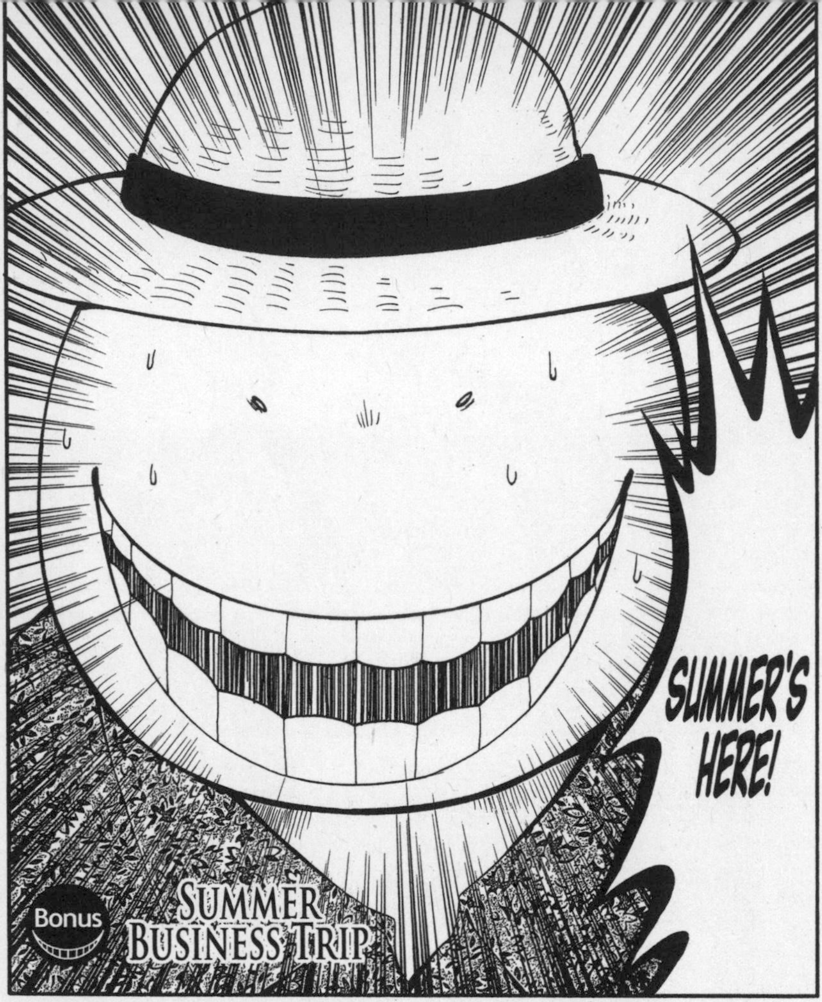
SUMMER'S HERE!
Bonus
SUMMER BUSINESS TRIP

*THIS WAS SPECIALLY DRAWN FOR THE FREE GIVEAWAY BOOK AT JUMP VICTORY CARNIVAL 2014.

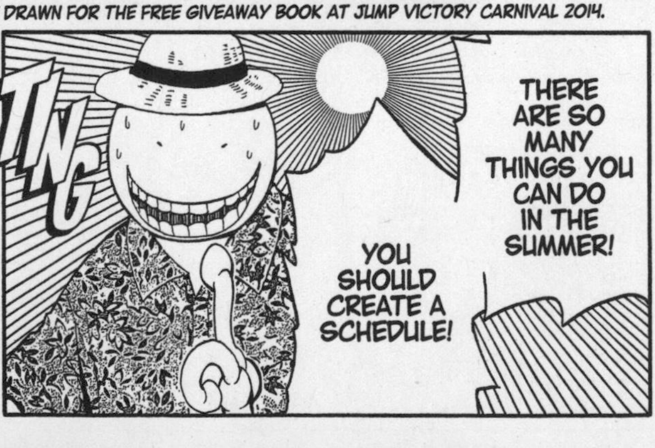
THERE ARE SO MANY THINGS YOU CAN DO IN THE SUMMER!
TING
YOU SHOULD CREATE A SCHEDULE!

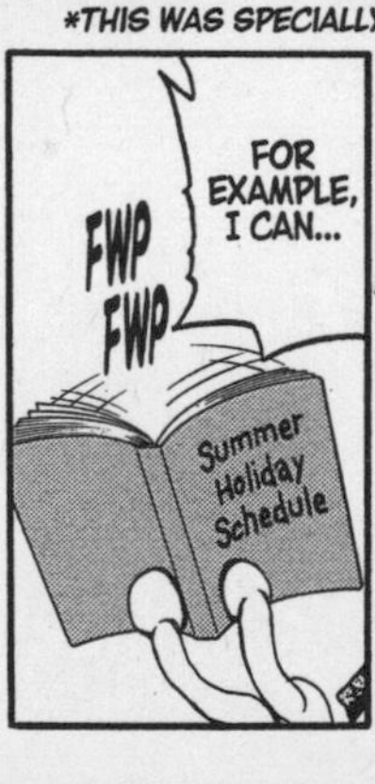
FOR EXAMPLE, I CAN...
FWP FWP
Summer Holiday Schedule

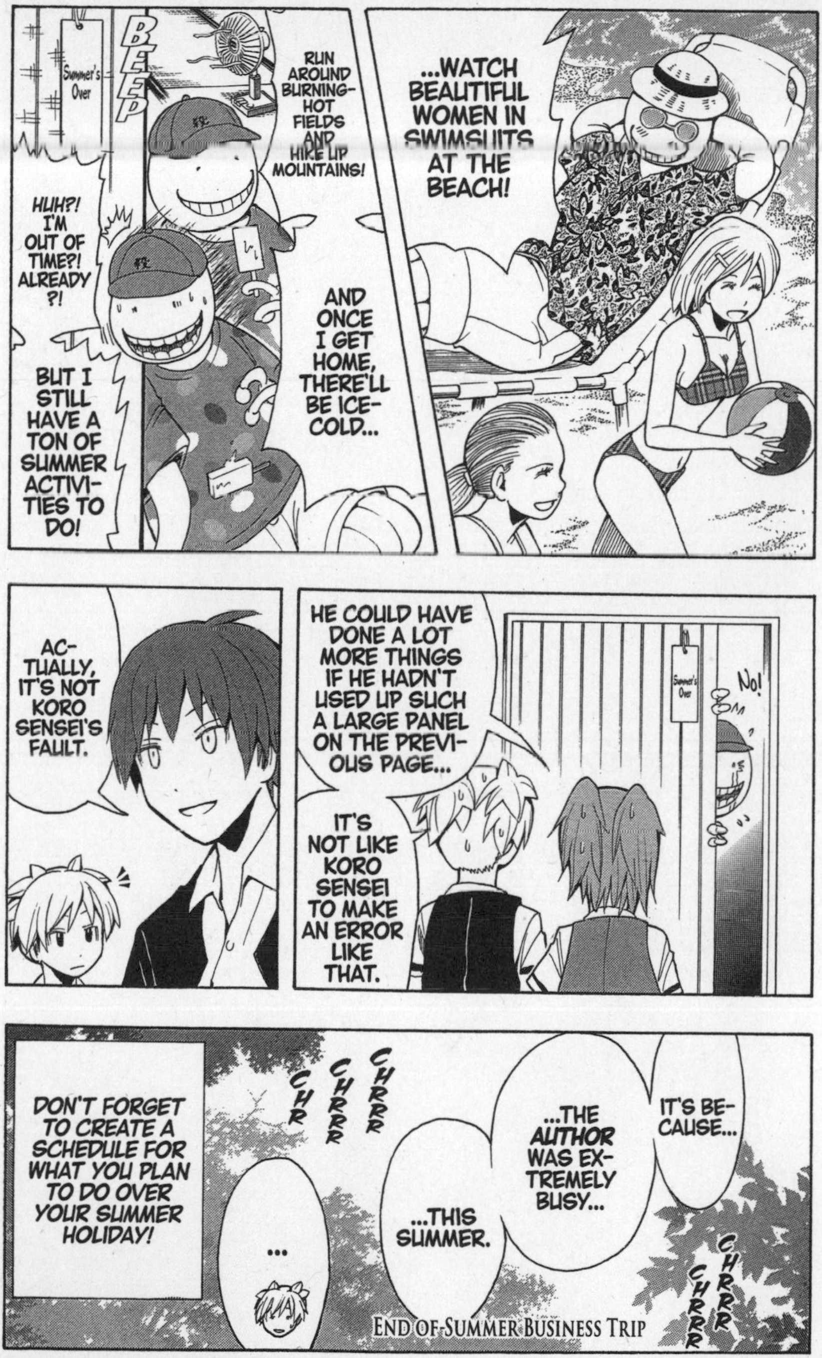
...WATCH BEAUTIFUL WOMEN IN SWIMSUITS AT THE BEACH!
RUN AROUND BURNING-HOT FIELDS AND HIKE UP MOUNTAINS!
AND ONCE I GET HOME, THERE'LL BE ICE-COLD...
BEEP
Summer's Over
HUH?! I'M OUT OF TIME?! ALREADY?!
BUT I STILL HAVE A TON OF SUMMER ACTIVITIES TO DO!
HE COULD HAVE DONE A LOT MORE THINGS IF HE HADN'T USED UP SUCH A LARGE PANEL ON THE PREVIOUS PAGE...
IT'S NOT LIKE KORO SENSEI TO MAKE AN ERROR LIKE THAT.
Summer's Over
No!
ACTUALLY, IT'S NOT KORO SENSEI'S FAULT.
IT'S BECAUSE...
...THE AUTHOR WAS EXTREMELY BUSY...
...THIS SUMMER.
...
CHRRR
CHRRR
CHRRR
CHRRR
CHR
DON'T FORGET TO CREATE A SCHEDULE FOR WHAT YOU PLAN TO DO OVER YOUR SUMMER HOLIDAY!
END OF SUMMER BUSINESS TRIP

♪
ARE
you...

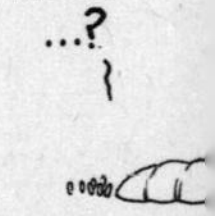
...my mother ...?

As the manga artist of this series, I would love for you to compare the Assassination Classroom anime to the live action movie version. The reason is that the CGI in the live action movie is so well done and the anime also makes Koro Sensei seem real!

The anime is most enjoyable if you sympathize with the students. But when watching the live action movie, I'd like you to jump into Class E as if you really were a student being taught by Koro Sensei.

The staff of the anime and live-action movie were both very dedicated, and I could tell they truly cared about the original series. Given that, I'll have no complaints, no matter how the anime and movie turn out in the end. I'm excited and looking forward to seeing them!

—Yusei Matsui

Yusei Matsui was born on the last day of January in Saitama Prefecture, Japan. He has been drawing manga since elementary school. Some of his favorite manga series are *Bobobo-bo Bo-bobo*, *JoJo's Bizarre Adventure* and *Ultimate Muscle*. Matsui learned his trade working as an assistant to manga artist Yoshio Sawai, creator of *Bobobo-bo Bo-bobo*. In 2005, Matsui debuted his original manga *Neuro: Supernatural Detective* in *Weekly Shonen Jump*. In 2007, *Neuro* was adapted into an anime. In 2012, *Assassination Classroom* began serialization in *Weekly Shonen Jump*.

VICTORY!

This new blue color appears during tests and when he uses his head. It is similar to the color of Bikkuriman's Protector sticker,* so he calls it "Protector Blue." Use it as a good luck charm when taking tests and as a cover for your textbooks.

*Bikkuriman was a popular chocolate snack in the late eighties.
It came with a collectible Angel, Demon or Protector sticker.

ASSASSINATION
CLASSROOM

YUSEI MATSUI

TIME FOR SPORTS DAY

A MOMENT OF TENTACLE ZEN

I got a slime,
I got a slime,
I got a grateful slime.

– Dragon Slime

ASSASSINATION CLASSROOM

Volume 11
SHONEN JUMP ADVANCED Manga Edition

Story and Art by YUSEI MATSUI

Translation/Tetsuichiro Miyaki
English Adaptation/Bryant Turnage
Touch-up Art & Lettering/Stephen Dutro
Cover & Interior Design/Sam Elzway
Editor/Annette Roman

Printed in the U.S.A.

Published by VIZ Media, LLC
P.O. Box 77010
San Francisco, CA 94107

10 9 8 7 6 5 4 3 2 1
First printing, August 2016

www.viz.com

www.shonenjump.com

RATED T+ FOR OLDER TEEN

PARENTAL ADVISORY
ASSASSINATION CLASSROOM is rated T+ for Older Teen and is recommended for ages 16 and up. It contains realistic violence and suggestive situations.

ratings.viz.com

Syllabus for
Assassination Classroom, Vol. 12

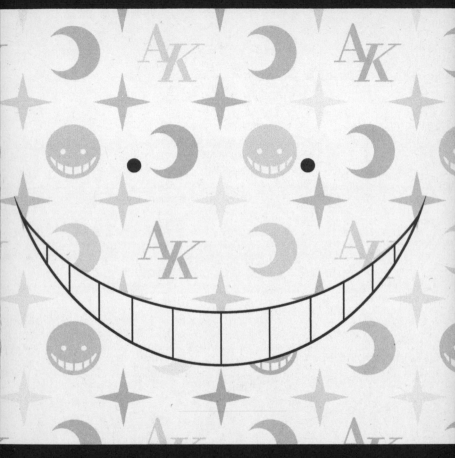

Mr. Karasuma gives the 3–E students super-powered uniforms...with great results. What feats can they perform in their snazzy new outfits? Then, Mr. Karasuma gives Ms. Vitch a bouquet for her birthday...with disastrous results. Next, a 3–E teacher is kidnapped by master assassin Death, who threatens to kill his hostage if the students tell anyone. Their rescue attempt goes horribly awry, and soon they are the ones in need of rescuing! But at what cost to the world ...?

Available October 2016!

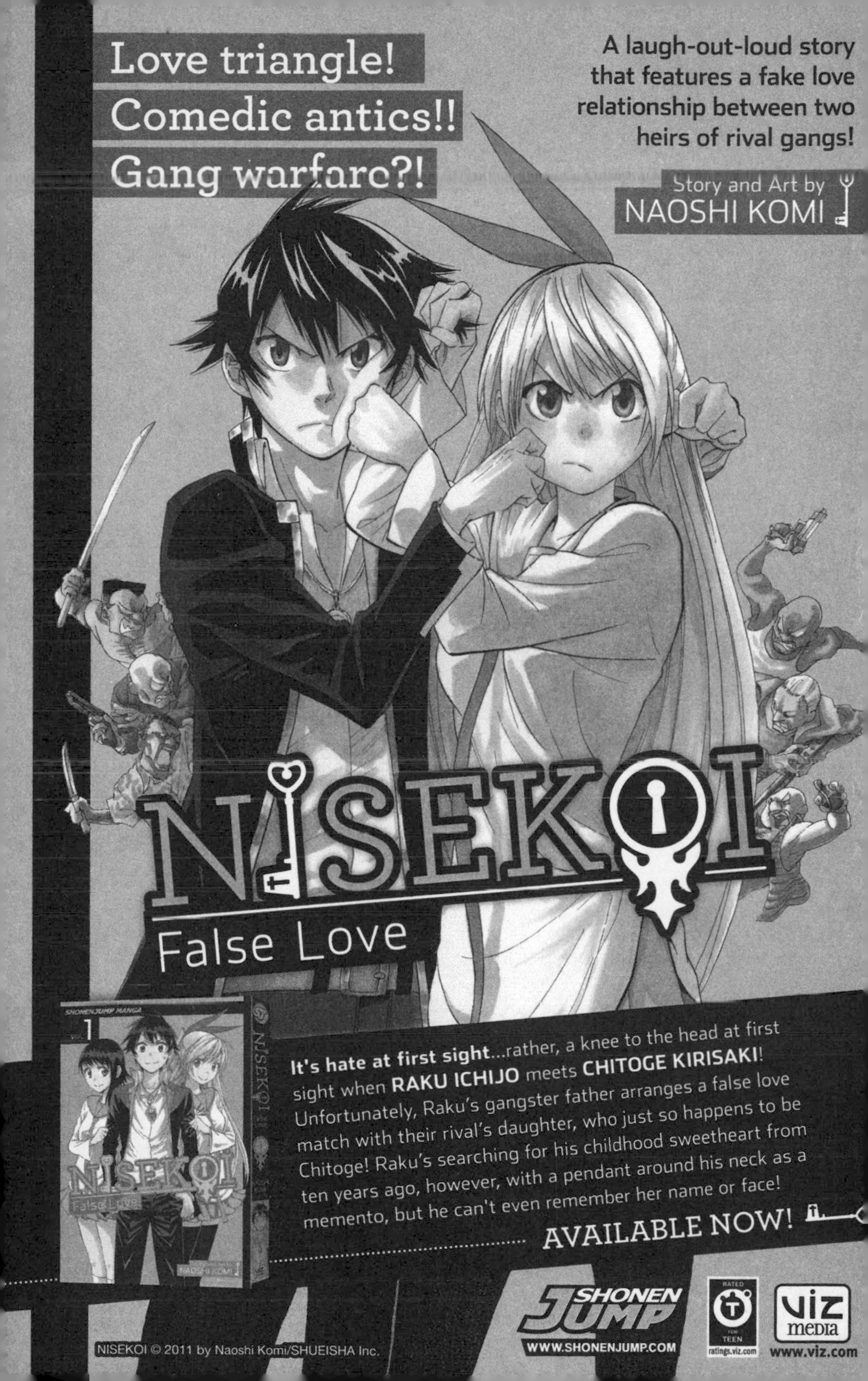

Love triangle!
Comedic antics!!
Gang warfare?!
A laugh-out-loud story that features a fake love relationship between two heirs of rival gangs!
Story and Art by
NAOSHI KOMI
NISEKOI
False Love
SHONENJUMP MANGA
VOL 1
NISEKOI
False Love
NAOSHI KOMI
It's hate at first sight...rather, a knee to the head at first sight when RAKU ICHIJO meets CHITOGE KIRISAKI! Unfortunately, Raku's gangster father arranges a false love match with their rival's daughter, who just so happens to be Chitoge! Raku's searching for his childhood sweetheart from ten years ago, however, with a pendant around his neck as a memento, but he can't even remember her name or face!
AVAILABLE NOW!
SHONEN JUMP
WWW.SHONENJUMP.COM
RATED T FOR TEEN
ratings.viz.com
viz media
www.viz.com
NISEKOI © 2011 by Naoshi Komi/SHUEISHA Inc.

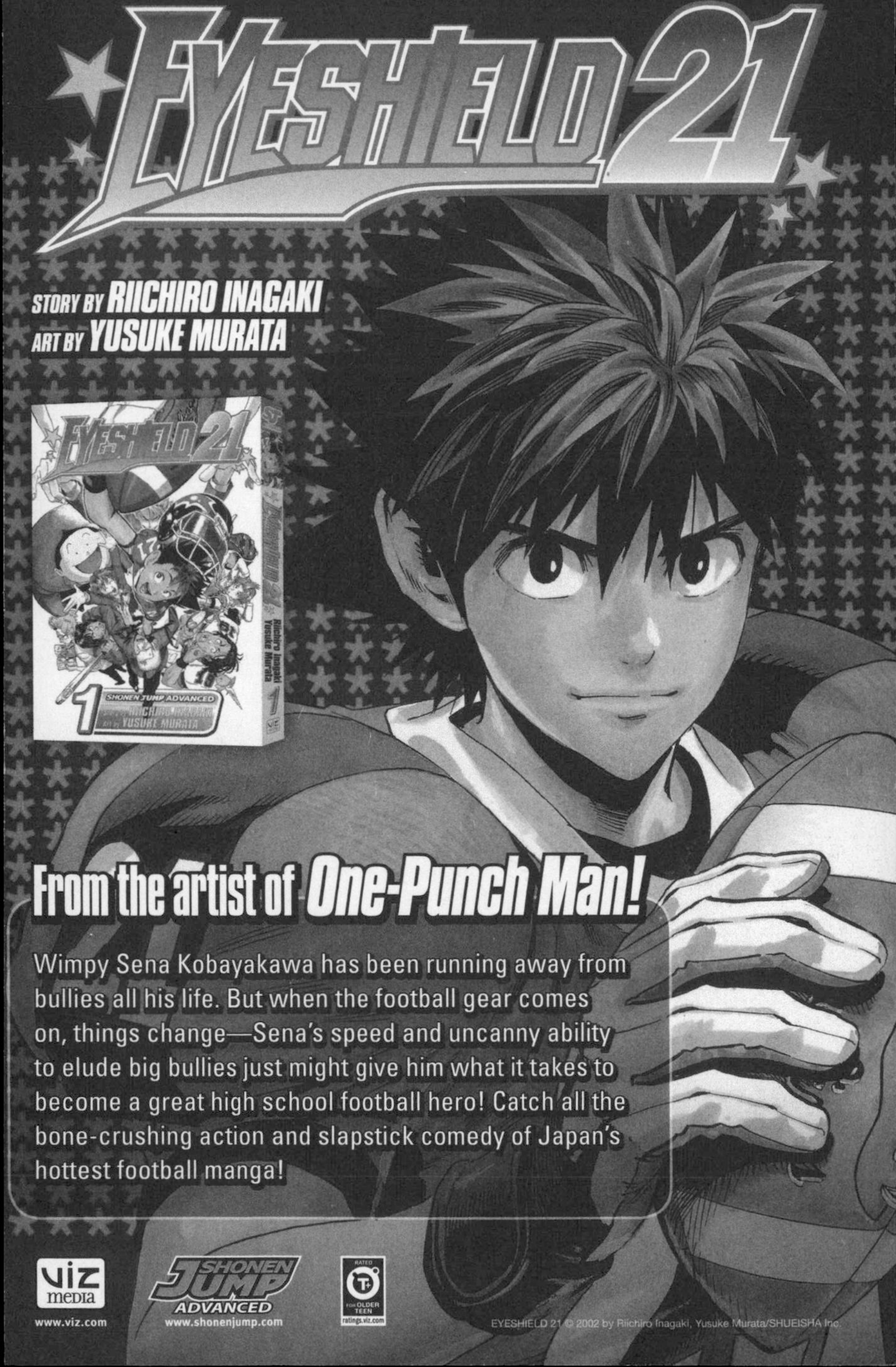
EYESHIELD 21
STORY BY RIICHIRO INAGAKI
ART BY YUSUKE MURATA
From the artist of One-Punch Man!
Wimpy Sena Kobayakawa has been running away from bullies all his life. But when the football gear comes on, things change—Sena's speed and uncanny ability to elude big bullies just might give him what it takes to become a great high school football hero! Catch all the bone-crushing action and slapstick comedy of Japan's hottest football manga!
VIZ media
www.viz.com
SHONEN JUMP ADVANCED
www.shonenjump.com
RATED T+ FOR OLDER TEEN
ratings.viz.com
EYESHIELD 21 © 2002 by Riichiro Inagaki, Yusuke Murata/SHUEISHA Inc.

Twin★Star Exorcists

ONMYOJI

STORY AND ART BY **Yoshiaki Sukeno**

The action-packed romantic comedy from the creator of *Good Luck Girl!*

Rokuro dreams of becoming *anything* but an exorcist!
Then mysterious Benio turns up. The pair are dubbed the
"Twin Star Exorcists" and learn they are fated to marry...

Can Rokuro escape both fates?

www.viz.com

You're Reading in the Wrong Direction!!

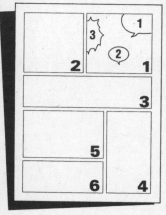

Whoops! Guess what? You're starting at the wrong end of the comic!

...It's true! In keeping with the original Japanese format, **Assassination Classroom** is meant to be read from right to left, starting in the upper-right corner.

Unlike English, which is read from left to right, Japanese is read from right to left, meaning that action, sound effects and word-balloon order are completely reversed... something which can make readers unfamiliar with Japanese feel pretty backwards themselves. For this reason, manga or Japanese comics published in the U.S. in English have sometimes been published "flopped"—that is, printed in exact reverse order, as though seen from the other side of a mirror.

By flopping pages, U.S. publishers can avoid confusing readers, but the compromise is not without its downside. For one thing, a character in a flopped manga series who once wore in the original Japanese version a T-shirt emblazoned with "M A Y" (as in "the merry month of") now wears one which reads "Y A M"! Additionally, many manga creators in Japan are themselves unhappy with the process, as some feel the mirror-imaging of their art skews their original intentions.

We are proud to bring you Yusei Matsui's **Assasssination Classroom** in the original unflopped format.
For now, though, turn to the other side of the book and let the adventure begin...!

—Editor